BRITISH CAMPAIGNS IN FLANDERS

BRITISH CAMPAIGNS IN FLANDERS

1690-1794

BEING EXTRACTS FROM
"A HISTORY OF THE BRITISH ARMY"

BY

The Hon. J. W. FORTESCUE

The Naval & Military Press Ltd

in association with

The National Army Museum, London

Published jointly by

The Naval & Military Press Ltd
Unit 10 Ridgewood Industrial Park,
Uckfield, East Sussex,
TN22 5QE England

Tel: +44 (0) 1825 749494
Fax: +44 (0) 1825 765701

www.naval-military-press.com
www.military-genealogy.com
www.militarymaproom.com

and

The National Army Museum, London
www.national-army-museum.ac.uk

PREFACE

THIS volume consists simply of extracts reprinted from my *History of the British Army*. It is published in order that the troops at the front may, if they wish it, study the experiences of their forerunners in the Low Countries in a book which is fairly portable and fairly inexpensive, though neither so cheap nor so compendious as *The British Soldiers' Guide to Northern France and Flanders.*

J. W. F.

CONTENTS

MAPS AND PLANS

VOL. I. BOOK V. CHAPTER II

I PASS now to Flanders, which is about to become for
the second time the training ground of the British Army.
The judicious help sent by Lewis the Fourteenth to
Ireland had practically diverted the entire strength of
William to that quarter for two whole campaigns ; and
though, as has been seen, there were English in Flanders
in 1689 and 1690, the contingents which they furnished
were too small and the operations too trifling to warrant
description in detail.   After the battle of the Boyne the
case was somewhat altered, for, though a large force was
still required in Ireland for Ginkell's final pacification of
1691, William was none the less at liberty to take the
field in Flanders in person.   Moreover, Parliament with 1690.
great good-will had voted seventy thousand men for the October.
ensuing year, of which fully fifty thousand were British,[1]
so that England was about to put forth her strength in
Europe on a scale unknown since the loss of Calais.

But first a short space must be devoted to the
theatre of war, where England was to meet and break
down the overweening power of France.   Few studies
are more difficult, even to the professed student, than
that of the old campaigns in Flanders, and still fewer
more hopeless of simplification to the ordinary reader.
Nevertheless, however desperate the task, an effort

---

[1] Four troops of life guards, ten regiments of horse, five of
dragoons, forty-seven battalions of foot.

1690. must be made once for all to give a broad idea of the scene of innumerable great actions.

Taking his stand on the northern frontier of France and looking northward, the reader will note three great rivers running through the country before him in, roughly speaking, three parallel semicircles, from south-east to north-west. These are, from east to west, the Moselle, which is merged in the Rhine at Coblentz, the Meuse, and the Scheldt, all three of which discharge themselves into the great delta whereof the southern key is Antwerp. But for the present let the reader narrow the field from the Meuse in the east to the sea in the west, and let him devote his attention first to the Meuse. He will see that, a little to the north of the French frontier, it picks up a large tributary from the south-west, the Sambre, which runs past Maubeuge and Charleroi and joins the Meuse at Namur. Thence the united rivers flow on past the fortified towns of Huy, Liège, and Maestricht to the sea. But let the reader's northern boundary on the Meuse for the present be Maestricht, and let him note another river which rises a little to the west of Maestricht and runs almost due west past Arschot and Mechlin to the sea at Antwerp. Let this river, the Demer, be his northern, and the Meuse from Maestricht to Namur his eastern, boundary.

Returning to the south, let him note a river rising immediately to the west of Charleroi, the Haine, which joins the Scheldt at Tournay, and let him draw a line from Tournay westward through Lille and Ypres to the sea at Dunkirk. Let this line from Dunkirk to Charleroi be carried eastward to Namur ; and there is his southern boundary. His western boundary is, of course, the sea. Within this quadrilateral, Antwerp (or more strictly speaking the mouth of the Scheldt),

Dunkirk, Namur, and Maestricht, lies the most famous 1690.
fighting-ground of Europe.

Glancing at it on the map, the reader will see that
this quadrilateral is cut by a number of rivers running
parallel to each other from south to north, and flowing
into the main streams of the Demer and the Scheldt.
The first of these, beginning from the east, are the
Great and Little Geete, which become one before they
join the main stream. It is worth while to pause for a
moment over this little slip of land between the Geete
and the Meuse. We shall see much of Namur, Huy,
Liège, and Maestricht, which command the navigation
of the greater river, but we shall see still more of the
Geete, and of two smaller streams, the Jaar and the
Mehaigne, which rise almost in the same table-land with
it. On the Lower Jaar, close to Maestricht, stands the
village of Lauffeld, which shall be better known to
us fifty years hence. On the Little Geete, just above
its junction with its greater namesake, are the villages
of Neerwinden and Landen. In the small space
between the heads of the Geete and the Mehaigne lies
the village of Ramillies. For this network of streams
is the protection against an enemy that would threaten
the navigation of the Meuse from the north and west,
and the barrier of Spanish Flanders against invasion
from the east ; and the ground is rich with the corpses
and fat with the blood of men.

The next stream to westward is the Dyle, which
flows past Louvain to the Demer, and gives its name,
after the junction, to that river. The next in order is
the Senne, which flows past Park and Hal and Brussels
to the same main stream. At the head of the Senne
stands the village of Steenkirk ; midway between the
Dyle and Senne are the forest of Soignies and the field
of Waterloo.

1690.   Here the tributaries of the Demer come to an end, but the row of parallel streams is continued by the tributaries of another system, that of the Scheldt. Easternmost of these, and next in order to the Senne, is the Dender, which rises near Leüse and flows past Ath and Alost to the Scheldt at Dendermond. Next comes the Scheldt itself, with the Scarpe and the Haine, its tributaries, which it carries past Tournay and Oudenarde to Ghent, and to the sea at Antwerp. Westernmost of all, the Lys runs past St. Venant, where in Cromwell's time we saw Sir Thomas Morgan and his immortal six thousand, past Menin and Courtrai, and is merged in the Scheldt at Ghent.

The whole extent of the quadrilateral is about one hundred miles long by fifty broad, with a great waterway to the west, a second to the east, and a third, whereof the key is Ghent, roughly speaking midway between them. The earth, fruitful by nature and enriched by art, bears food for man and beast ; the waterways provide transport for stores and ammunition. It was a country where men could kill each other without being starved, and hence for centuries the cockpit of Europe.

A glance at any old map of Flanders shows how thickly studded was this country with walled towns of less or greater strength, and explains why a war in Flanders should generally have been a war of sieges. Every one of these little towns, of course, had its garrison ; and the manœuvres of contending forces were governed very greatly by the effort, on one side, to release these garrisons for active service in the field, and, on the other, to keep them confined within their walls for as long as possible. Hence it is obvious that an invading army necessarily enjoyed a great advantage, since it menaced the fortresses of the enemy while its own were unthreatened.   Thus ten thousand 1690. men on the Upper Lys could paralyse thrice their number in Ghent and Bruges and the adjacent towns. On the other hand, if an invading general contemplated the siege of an important town, he manœuvred to entice the garrison into the field before he laid siege in form.   Still, once set down to a great siege, an army was stationary, and the bare fact was sufficient to liberate hostile garrisons all over the country ; and hence arose the necessity of a second army to cover the besieging force.   The skill and subtlety manifested by great generals to compass these different ends is unfortunately only to be apprehended by closer study than can be expected of any but the military student.

A second cause contributed not a little to increase the taste for a war of sieges, namely, the example of France, then the first military nation in Europe.[1]   The Court of Versailles was particularly fond of a siege, since it could attend the ceremony in state and take nominal charge of the operations with much glory and little discomfort or danger.   The French passion for rule and formula also found a happy outlet in the conduct of a siege, for, while there is no nation more brilliant or more original, particularly in military affairs, there is also none that is more conceited or pedantic.   The craving for sieges among the French was so great that the King took pains, by the grant of extra pay and rations, to render this species of warfare popular with his soldiers.[2]

Again, it must be remembered that the object of a campaign in those days was not necessarily to seek out

---

[1] I had almost written that France was then, as always, the first military nation ; and though Prussia wrested the position from her under Frederick the Great and again in 1870, the lesson of history seems to teach that she is as truly the first military, as England is the first naval, nation.   [2] Belhomme, p. 153.

1690. an enemy and beat him. There were two alternatives prescribed by the best authorities, namely, to fight at an advantage or to subsist comfortably.[1] Comfortable subsistence meant at its best subsistence at an enemy's expense. A campaign wherein an army lived on the enemy's country and destroyed all that it could not consume was eminently successful, even though not a shot was fired. To force an enemy to consume his own supplies was much, to compel him to supply his opponent was more, to take up winter-quarters in his territory was very much more. Thus to enter an enemy's borders and keep him marching backwards and forwards for weeks without giving him a chance of striking a blow, was in itself no small success, and success of a kind which galled inferior generals, such as William of Orange, to desperation and so to disaster. The tendency to these negative campaigns was heightened once more by French example. The French ministry of war interfered with its generals to an extent that was always dangerous, and eventually proved calamitous. Nominally the marshal commanding-in-chief in the field was supreme ; but the intendant or head of the administrative service, though he received his orders from the marshal, was instructed by the King to forward those orders at once by special messenger to Louvois, and not to execute them without the royal authority. Great commanders such as Luxemburg had the strength from time to time to kick themselves free from this bondage, but the rest, embarrassed by the surveillance of an inferior officer, preferred to live as long as possible in an enemy's country without risking a general action. It was left to Marlborough to advance triumphant in one magnificent campaign from the Meuse to the sea.

[1] Feuquières.

Next, a glance must be thrown at the contending 1690.
parties. The defenders of the Spanish Netherlands,
for they cannot be called the assailants of France, were
confederate allies from a number of independent states
—England, Holland, Spain, the Empire, sundry states
of Germany, and Denmark, all somewhat selfish, few
very efficient, and none, except the first, very punctual.
From such a heterogeneous collection swift, secret, and
united action was not to be expected. King William
held the command-in-chief, and, from his position as
the soul of the alliance, was undoubtedly the fittest
for the post. But though he had carefully studied the
art of war, and though his phlegmatic temperament
found its only genuine pleasure in the excitement of
the battlefield, he was not a great general. He could
form good plans, and up to a certain point could
execute them, but up to a certain point only. It
should seem that his physical weakness debarred him
from steady and sustained effort. He was strangely
incapable of conducting a campaign with equal ability
throughout ; he would manœuvre admirably for weeks,
and forfeit all the advantage that he had gained by the
carelessness of a single day. In a general action, of
which he was fonder than most commanders of his
time, he never shone except in virtue of conspicuous
personal bravery. He lacked tactical instinct, and
above all he lacked patience ; in a word, to use a
modern phrase, he was a very clever amateur.

France, on the other hand, possessed the finest
and strongest army in Europe,—well equipped, well
trained, well organised, and inured to work by countless campaigns. She had a single man in supreme
control of affairs, King Lewis the Fourteenth ; a great
war - minister, Louvois ; one really great general,
Luxemburg ; and one with flashes of genius, Boufflers.

1690. Moreover, she possessed a line of posts in Spanish Flanders extending from Dunkirk to the Meuse. On the Lys she had Aire and Menin ; on the Scarpe, Douay ; on the Upper Scheldt, Cambray, Bouchain, Valenciennes, and Condé ; on the Sambre, Maubeuge ; between Sambre and Meuse, Philippeville and Marienburg ; and on the Meuse, Dinant. Further, in the one space where the frontier was not covered by a friendly river, between the sea and the Scheldt, the French had constructed fortified lines from the sea to Menin and from thence to the Scheldt at Espierre. Thus with their frontier covered, with a place of arms on every river, with secrecy and with unity of purpose, the French enjoyed the approximate certainty of being able to take the field in every campaign before the Allies could be collected to oppose them.

1691. The campaign of 1691 happily typifies the relative positions of the combatants in almost every respect. The French concentrated ten thousand men on the Lys. This was sufficient to paralyse all the garrisons of the Allies on and about the river. They posted another corps on the Moselle, which threatened the territory of Cleves. Now Cleves was the property of the Elector of Brandenburg, and it was not to be expected that he should allow his contingent of troops to join King William at the general rendezvous at Brussels, and suffer the French to play havoc among his possessions. Thus the Prussian contingent likewise was paralysed. So while William was still ordering his troops to concentrate at Brussels, Boufflers, who had been making preparations all the winter, suddenly marched up from Maubeuge and, before William was aware that he was in motion, had besieged Mons. The fortress presently surrendered after a feeble resistance, and the line of the Allies' frontier

between the Scheldt and Sambre was broken. William
moved down from Brussels across the Sambre in the
hope of recovering the lost town, outmanœuvred
Luxemburg, who was opposed to him, and for three
days held the recapture of Mons in the hollow of his
hand. He wasted those three days in an aimless halt ;
Luxemburg recovered himself by an extraordinary
march ; and William, finding that there was no alternative before him but to retire to Brussels and remain
inactive, handed over the command to an incompetent
officer and returned to England. Luxemburg then
closed the campaign by a brilliant action of cavalry,
which scattered the horse of the Allies to the four
winds. As no British troops except the Life Guards
were present, and as they at any rate did not disgrace
themselves, it is unnecessary to say more of the combat
of Leuse. It had, however, one remarkable effect : it
increased William's dread of the French cavalry, already
morbidly strong, to such a pitch as to lead him subse-
quently to a disastrous military blunder.

The campaign of 1691 was therefore decidedly
unfavourable to the Allies, but there was ground for
hope that all might be set right in 1692. The Treasurer,
Godolphin, was nervously apprehensive that Parliament
might be unwilling to vote money for an English army
in Flanders ; but the Commons cheerfully granted a
total of sixty-six thousand men, British and foreign ;
which, after deduction of garrisons for the safety of
the British Isles, left forty thousand free to cross the
German Ocean.

Of these, twenty-three thousand were British, the
most important force that England had sent to the
Continent since the days of King Henry the Eighth.
The organisation was remarkably like that of the New
Model. William was, of course, Commander-in-Chief,

1692. and under him were a general of horse and a general of
foot, with a due allowance of lieutenant-generals,
major-generals, and brigadiers.   There is, however, no
sign of an officer in command of artillery or engineers,
nor any of a commissary in charge of the transport.[1]
The one strangely conspicuous functionary is the
Secretary-at-War, who in this and the following
campaigns for the last time accompanied the Commander-in-Chief on active service.   But the most
significant feature in the list of the staff is the omission
of the name of Marlborough.   Originally included
among the generals for Flanders, he had been struck
off the roll, and dismissed from all public employment, in disgrace, before the opening of the campaign.   Though this dismissal did not want justifica-
tion, it was perhaps of all William's blunders the
greatest.

As usual, the French were beforehand with the
Allies in opening the campaign.   They had already
broken the line of the defending fortresses by the
capture of Mons ; they now designed to make the
breach still wider.   All through the winter a vast
siege-train was collecting on the Scheldt and Meuse,
with Vauban, first of living engineers, in charge of it.
May. In May all was ready.   Marshal Joyeuse, with one
corps, was on the Moselle, as in the previous year, to
hold the Brandenburgers in check.   Boufflers, with
eighteen thousand men, lay on the right bank of the
Meuse, near Dinant ; Luxemburg, with one hundred
May $\frac{10}{20}$. and fifteen thousand more, stood in rear of the river
Haine.   On the 20th of May, King Lewis in person
May $\frac{13}{23}$. reviewed the grand army ; on the 23rd it marched for

[1] That is to say, of land-transport.   After the sad experience
of the Irish war the marine transport was entrusted to an officer
specially established for the purpose.—*Commons Journals.*

Namur ; and on the 26th it had wound itself round
two sides of the town, while Boufflers, moving up from
Dinant, completed the circuit on the third side.   Thus
Namur was completely invested ; unless William could
save it, the line of the Sambre and one of the most
important fortresses on the Meuse were lost to the
Allies.

William, to do him justice, had strained every nerve
to spur his indolent allies to be first in the field.   The
contingents, awaked by the sudden stroke at Namur,
came in fast to Brussels ; but it was too late.   The
French had destroyed all forage and supplies on the
direct route to Namur, and William's only way to the
city lay across the Mehaigne.   Behind the Mehaigne
lay Luxemburg, the ablest of the French generals.
The best of luck was essential to William's success, and
instead of the best came the worst.   Heavy rain
swelled the narrow stream into a broad flood, and the
building of bridges became impossible.   There was
beautiful fencing, skilful feint, and more skilful parry,
between the two generals, but William could not get
under Luxemburg's guard.   On the 5th of June, after
a discreditably short defence, Namur fell, almost before
William's eyes, into the hands of the French.

Then Luxemburg thought it time to draw the
enemy away from the vicinity of the captured city ; so
recrossing the Sambre, and keeping Boufflers always
between himself and that river, he marched for the
Senne as if to threaten Brussels.   William followed, as
in duty bound ; and French and Allies pursued a
parallel course to the Senne, William on the north and
Luxemburg on the south.   The 2nd of August found
both armies across the Senne, William at Hal, facing
west with the river in his rear, and Luxemburg some
five miles south of him with his right at Steenkirk, and

1692. his centre between Hoves and Enghien, while Boufflers lay at Manny St. Jean, seven miles in his rear.

The terrible state of the roads owing to heavy rain had induced Luxemburg to leave most of his artillery at Mons ; and, as he had designed merely to tempt the Allies away from Namur, the principal object left to him was to take up a strong position wherein his worn and harassed army could watch the enemy without fear of attack.   Such a position he thought that he had found at Steenkirk.[1]   The country at this point is more broken and rugged than is usual in Belgium.   The camp lay on high ground, with its right resting on the river Sennette and its right front covered by a ravine, which gradually fades away northward into a high plateau of about a mile in extent.   Beyond the ravine was a network of wooded defiles, through which Luxemburg seems to have hoped that no enemy could fall upon him in force unawares.   It so happened, however, that one of his most useful spies was detected, in his true character, in William's camp at Hal ; and this was an opportunity not to be lost.   A pistol was held to the spy's head, and he was ordered to write a letter to Luxemburg, announcing that large bodies of the enemy would be in motion next morning, but that nothing more serious was contemplated than a foraging expedition.   This done, William laid his plans to surprise his enemy on the morrow.

July 23.   An hour before daybreak the advanced guard of
Aug. 3.   William's army fell silently into its ranks, together with a strong force of pioneers to clear the way for a march through the woods.   This force consisted of the First Guards, the Royal Scots, the Twenty-first,

[1] I spell the village according to the popular fashion in England, and according to the Flemish pronunciation.   So many names in Flanders seem to halt between the Flemish and the French that it is difficult to know how to set them down.

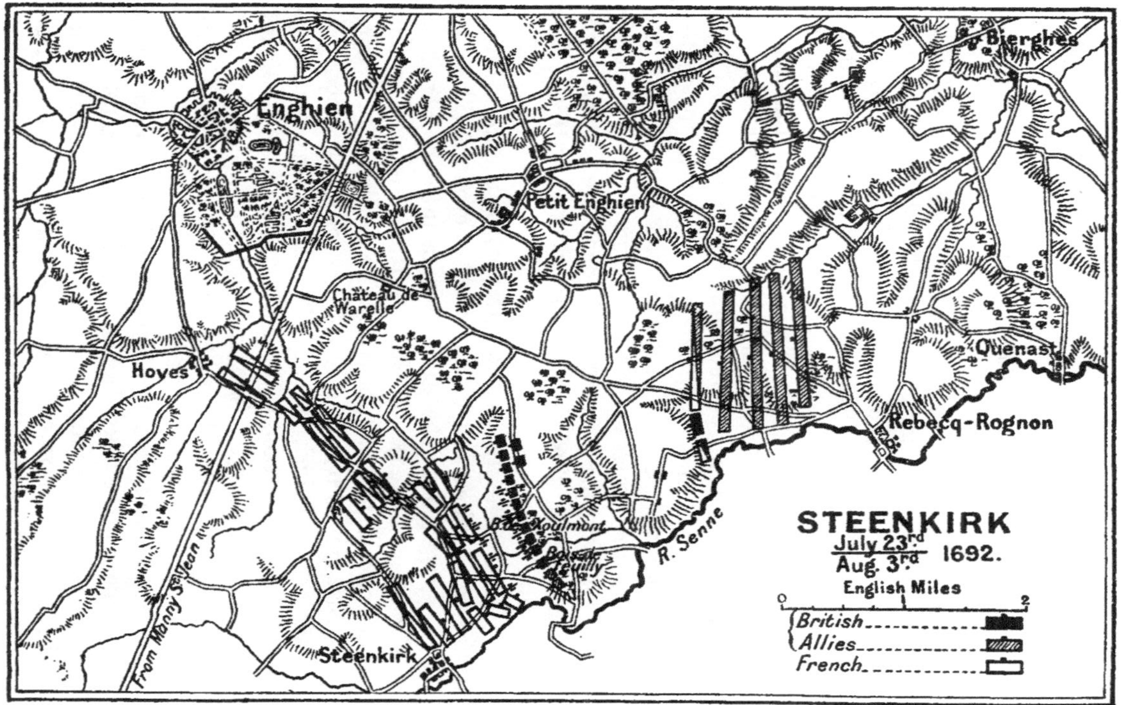

STEENKIRK
July 23rd / Aug. 3rd 1692.

English Miles

British
Allies
French

Stanford's Geog. Estab.

Berghes

Quenast

Rebecq-Rognon

R. Senne

R. Sennette

Petit Enghien

Enghien

Château de Vargelle

Hoves

Steenkirk

from Mauny Saveon R.

Fitzpatrick's regiment of Fusiliers, and two Danish regiments of great reputation, the whole under the command of the Duke of Würtemberg. Presently they moved away, and, as the sun rose, the whole army followed them in two columns, without sound of drum or trumpet, towards Steenkirk. French patrols scouring the country in the direction of Tubise saw the two long lines of scarlet and white and blue wind away into the woods, and reported what they had witnessed at headquarters; but Luxemburg, sickly of constitution, and, in spite of his occasional energy, indolent of temperament, rejoiced to think that, as his spy had told him, it was no more than a foraging party. Another patrol presently sent in another message that a large force of cavalry was advancing towards the Sennette. Once more Luxemburg lulled himself into security with the same comfort.

Meanwhile the allied army was trailing through narrow defiles and cramped close ground, till at last it emerged from the stifling woods into an open space. Here it halted, as the straitness of the ground demanded, in dense, heavy masses. But the advanced guard moved on steadily till it reached the woods over against Steenkirk, where Würtemberg disposed it for the coming attack. On his left the Bois de Feuilly covered a spur of the same plateau as that occupied by the French right, and there he stationed the English Guards and the two battalions of Danes. To the right of these, but separated from them by a ravine, he placed the three remaining British battalions in the Bois de Zoulmont. His guns he posted, some between the two woods, and the remainder on the right of his division. These dispositions complete, the advanced party awaited orders to open the attack.

It was now eleven o'clock. Luxemburg had left
his bed and had ridden out to a commanding height
on his extreme right, when a third letter was brought
to him that the Allies were certainly advancing in force.
He read it, and looking to his front, saw the red coats
of the Guards moving through the wood before him,
while beyond them he caught a glimpse of the dense
masses of the main body.   Instantly he saw the danger,
and divined that William's attack was designed
against his right.   His own camp was formed, according to rule, with the cavalry on the wings ; and there
was nothing in position to check the Allies but a
single brigade of infantry, famous under the name of
Bourbonnois, which was quartered in advance of the
cavalry's camp on his extreme right.   Moreover,
nothing was ready, not a horse was bridled, not a
man standing to his arms.   He despatched a messenger
to summon Boufflers to his aid, and in a few minutes
was flying through the camp with his staff, energetic
but perfectly self-possessed, to set his force in order
of battle.   The two battalions of Bourbonnois fell in
hastily before their camp, with a battery of six guns
before them.   The dragoons of the right wing dismounted and hastened to seal up the space between
Bourbonnois and the Sennette.   The horse of the
right was collected, and some of it sent off in hot
speed to the left to bring the infantry up behind them
on their horses' croups.   All along the line the alarm
was given, drums were beating, men snatching hastily
at their arms and falling into their ranks ready to file
away to the right.   Such was the haste, that there was
no time to think of regimental precedence, a very
serious matter in the French army, and each successive
brigade hurried into the place where it was most
needed, as it happened to come up.

Meanwhile Würtemberg's batteries had opened fire, and a cunning officer of the Royal Scots was laying his guns with admirable precision. French batteries hastened into position to reply to them with as deadly an aim, and for an hour and a half the rival guns thundered against each other unceasingly. All this time the French battalions kept massing themselves thicker and thicker on Luxemburg's right, and the front line was working with desperate haste, felling trees, making breastworks, and lining the hedges and copses while yet they might. But still Würtemberg's division remained unsupported, and the precious minutes flew fast. William, or his staff for him, had made a serious blunder. Intent though he was on fighting a battle with his infantry only, he had put all the cavalry of one wing of his army before them on the march, so that there was no room for the infantry to pass. Fortunately six battalions had been intermixed with the squadrons of this wing, and these were now with some difficulty disentangled and sent forward. Cutts's, Mackay's, Lauder's, and the Twenty-sixth formed up on Würtemberg's right, with the Sixth and Twenty-fifth in support ; and at last, at half-past twelve, Würtemberg gave the order to attack.

His little force shook itself up and pressed forward with eagerness. The Guards and Danes on the extreme left, being on the same ridge with the enemy, were the first that came into action. Pushing on under a terrible fire at point-blank range from the French batteries, they fell upon Bourbonnois and the dragoons, beat them back, captured their guns, and turned them against the enemy. On their right the Royal Scots, Twenty-first, and Fitzpatrick's plunged down into the ravine into closer and more difficult ground, past

copses and hedges and thickets, until a single thick 1692.
fence alone divided them from the enemy.   Through July 23.
this they fired at each other furiously for a time, till Aug. 3.
the Scots burst through the fence with their Colonel
at their head, and swept the French before them.
Still further to the right, the remaining regiments came
also into action ; muzzle met muzzle among the
branches, and the slaughter was terrible.   Young
Angus, still not yet of age, dropped dead at the head of
the Cameronians, and the veteran Mackay found the
death which he had missed at Killiecrankie.   He had
before the attack sent word to General Count Solmes,
that the contemplated assault could lead only to
waste of life ; and he had been answered with the
order to advance.   " God's will be done," he said
calmly, and he was among the first that fell.

Still the British, in spite of all losses, pressed
furiously on ; and famous French regiments, spoiled
children of victory, wavered and gave way before them.
Bourbonnois, unable to face the Guards and Danes,
doubled its left battalion in rear of its right ; Chartres,
which stood next to them, also gave way and doubled
itself in rear of its neighbour Orléans.   A wide gap
was thus torn in the first French line, but not a
regiment of the second line would step into it.   The
colonel of the brigade in rear of it ordered, entreated,
implored his men to come forward, but they would
not follow him into that terrible fire.   Suddenly the
wild voice ceased, and the gesticulating figure fell in
a heap to the ground : the colonel had been shot dead,
and the gap was still unfilled.

The first French line was broken ; the second and
third were dismayed and paralysed : a little more and
the British would carry the French camp.   Luxemburg
perceived that this was a moment when only his best

1692.
July 23.
Aug. 3.

troops could save him.   In the fourth line stood the flower of his infantry, the seven battalions of French and Swiss Guards.   These were now ordered forward to the gap ; the princes of the blood placed themselves at their head, and without firing a shot they charged down the slope upon the British and Danes.   The English Guards, thinned to half their numbers, faced the huge columns of the Swiss and stood up to them undaunted, till by sheer weight they were slowly rolled back.   On their right the Royal Scots also were forced back, fighting desperately from hedge to hedge and contesting every inch of ground.   Once, the French made a dash through a fence and carried off one of their colours.   The Colonel, Sir Robert Douglas, instantly turned back alone through the fence, re-captured the colour, and was returning with it when he was struck by a bullet.   He flung the flag over to his men and fell to the ground dead.

Slowly the twelve battalions retired, still fighting furiously at every step.   So fierce had been their onslaught that five lines of infantry backed by two more of cavalry [1] had hardly sufficed to stop them, and with but a little support they might have won the day.   But that support was not forthcoming.   Message after message had been sent to the Dutch general, Count Solmes, for reinforcements, but there came not a man.   The main body, as has been told, was all clubbed together a mile and a half from the scene of action, with the infantry in the rear ; and Solmes, with almost criminal folly, instead of endeavouring to extricate the foot, had ordered forward the horse.   William rectified the error as soon as he could ; but the correction led to further delay and to the increased confusion

[1] Fifty-three battalions of infantry and seven regiments of dragoons.—*Beaurain.*

which is the inevitable result of contradictory orders.
The English infantry in rear, mad with impatience to
rescue their comrades, ran forward in disorder, probably
with loud curses on the Dutchman who had kept them
back so long ; and some time was lost before they
could be re-formed. Discipline was evidently a little
at fault. Solmes lost both his head and his temper.
" Damn the English," he growled ; " if they are so
fond of fighting, let them have a bellyful " ; and he
sent forward not a man. Fortunately junior officers
took matters into their own hands ; and it was time,
for Boufflers had now arrived on the field to throw
additional weight into the French scale. The English
Horse-grenadiers, the Fourth Dragoons, and a regiment of Dutch dragoons rode forward and, dismounting,
covered the retreat of the Guards and Danes by a
brilliant counter-attack. The Buffs and Tenth advanced farther to the right, and holding their fire
till within point-blank range, poured in a volley which
gave time for the rest of Würtemberg's division to
withdraw. A demonstration against the French left
made a further diversion, and the shattered fragments
of the attacking force, grimed with sweat and smoke,
fell back to the open ground in rear of the woods,
repulsed but unbeaten, and furious with rage.

William, it is said, could not repress a cry of anguish
when he saw them ; but there was no time for emotion.
Some Dutch and Danish infantry was sent forward to
check further advance of the enemy, and preparations
were made for immediate retreat. Once again the
hardest of the work was entrusted to the British ; and
when the columns were formed, the grenadiers of the
British regiments brought up the rear, halting and
turning about continually, until failing light put an
end to what was at worst but a half-hearted pursuit.

1692. The retreat was conducted with admirable order ;
July 23. but it was not until the chill, dead hour that precedes
Aug. 3. the dawn that the Allies regained their camp, worn
out with the fatigue of the past four-and-twenty hours.

The action was set down at the time as the severest
ever fought by infantry, and the losses on both sides
were very heavy. The Allies lost about three thousand
killed and the same number wounded, besides thirteen
hundred prisoners, nearly all of whom were wounded.
Ten guns were abandoned, the horses being too weary
to draw them ; the English battalions lost two colours,
and the foreign three or four more. The British,
having borne the brunt of the action, suffered most
heavily of all, the Guards, Cutts's, and the Sixth being
terribly punished. The total French loss was about
equal to that of the Allies, but the list of the officers
that fell tells a more significant tale. On the side of
the Allies four hundred and fifty officers were killed
and wounded, no fewer than seventy lieutenants in
the ten battalions of Churchill's British brigade being
killed outright. The French on their side lost no fewer
than six hundred and twenty officers killed and
wounded, a noble testimony to their self-sacrifice,
but sad evidence of their difficulty in making their
men stand. In truth, with proper management
William must have won a brilliant victory ; but he
was a general by book and not by instinct. Würtemberg's advanced guard could almost have done the
work by itself but for the mistake of a long preliminary
cannonade ; his attack could have been supported
earlier but for the pedantry that gave the horse precedence of the foot in the march to the field ; the foot
could have pierced the French position in a dozen
different columns but for the pedantry which caused
it to be first deployed. Finally, William's knowledge

of the ground was imperfect, and Solmes, his general 1692.
of foot, was incompetent. The plan was admirably July 23.
designed and abominably executed. Nevertheless, Aug. 3.
British troops have never fought a finer action than
Steenkirk. Luxemburg thought himself lucky to
have escaped destruction ; his troops were much
shaken ; and he crossed the Scheldt and marched
away to his winter-quarters as quietly as possible.
So ended the campaign of 1692.

VOL. I. BOOK V. CHAPTER III

1692. IN November the English Parliament met, heartened
Nov. indeed by the naval victory of La Hogue, but not a
little grieved over the failure of Steenkirk. Again,
the financial aspect was extremely discouraging ; and
Sir Stephen Fox announced that there was not another
day's subsistence for the Army in the treasury. The
prevailing discontent found vent in furious denunciations of Count Solmes, and a cry that English soldiers
ought to be commanded by English officers. The
debate waxed hot. The hardest of hard words were
used about the Dutch generals, and a vast deal of
nonsense was talked about military matters. There
were, however, a great number of officers in the House
of Commons, many of whom had been present at the
action. With much modesty and good sense they
refused to join in the outcry against the Dutch, and
contrived so to compose matters that the House
committed itself to no very foolish resolution. The
votes for the Army were passed ; and no difficulty
was made over the preparations for the next campaign.
Finally, two new regiments of cavalry were raised—
Lord Macclesfield's Horse, which was disbanded
twenty years later ; and Conyngham's Irish Dragoons,
which still abides with us as the Eighth, King's Royal
Irish, Hussars.

Meanwhile the French military system had suffered 1693.
an irreparable loss in Louvois's death, the source of
woes unnumbered to France in the years that were
soon to come.   Nevertheless, the traditions of his rule
were strong, and the French once more were first in
the field, with, as usual, a vast siege-train massed on
the Meuse and on the Scheldt.   But a late spring and
incessant rain delayed the opening of the campaign
till the beginning of May, when Luxemburg assembled
seventy thousand men in rear of the Haine by Mons,
and Boufflers forty-eight thousand more on the Scheldt
at Tournay.   The French king was with the troops in
person ; and the original design was, as usual, to carry
on a war of sieges on the Meuse, Boufflers reducing
the fortresses while Luxemburg shielded him with a
covering army.   Lewis, however, finding that the
towns which he had intended to invest were likely to
make an inconveniently stubborn defence, presently
returned home, and after detaching thirty thousand
men to the war in Germany, left Luxemburg to do
as he would.   It had been better for William if the
Grand Monarch had remained in Flanders.

The English king, on his side, assembled sixty
thousand men at Brussels as soon as the French began
to move, and led them with desperate haste to the
Senne, where he took up an impregnable position at
Park.   Luxemburg marched up to a position over
against him, and then came one of those deadlocks
which were so common in the old campaigns.   The
two armies stood looking at each other for a whole
month, neither venturing to move, neither daring to
attack, both ill-supplied, both discontented, and as a
natural consequence both losing scores, hundreds, and
even thousands of men through desertion.

At last the position became insupportable, and on

1693.
June 26.
July 6.

the 6th of July Luxemburg moved eastward as if to resume the original plan of operations on the Meuse. William thereupon resolved to create a diversion by detaching a force to attack the French lines of the Scheldt and Lys, a project which was brilliantly executed by Würtemberg, thanks not a little to three British regiments—the Tenth, Argyll's, and Castleton's —which formed part of his division. But meanwhile Luxemburg, quite ignorant of the diversion, advanced to the Meuse and laid siege to Huy, in the hope of forcing William to come to its relief. He judged rightly. William left his impregnable camp at Park and hurried to the rescue. But he came too late, and Huy fell after a trifling resistance. Luxemburg then made great seeming preparations for the siege of Liège, and William, trembling for the safety of that city and of Maestricht, detached eight thousand men to reinforce those garrisons, and then withdrew to the line of the Geete. Luxemburg watched the whole proceeding with grim delight. Würtemberg's success was no doubt annoying, but William had weakened his army by detaching this force to the Lys, and had been beguiled into weakening it still further by reinforcing the garrison on the Meuse. This was exactly what Luxemburg wanted. If he could bring the Allies to action forthwith, he could reasonably hope for success.

The ground occupied by William was a triangular space enclosed between the Little Geete and a stream called the Landen Beck, which joins it at Leuw. The position was not without features of strength. The camp, which faced almost due south, was pitched on a gentle ridge rising out of a vast plain.[1] This ridge

[1] No battlefield can be taken in more readily at a glance than that of Landen. On the path alongside the railway from Landen Station is a mound formed of earth thrown out of a cutting, from the top of which the whole position can be seen.

runs parallel to the Little Geete and has that river in 1693.
its rear. The left flank was protected by marshy July.
ground and by the Landen Beck itself, while the villages
of Neerlanden and Rumsdorp, one on either side of the
Beck and the latter well forward on the plain, offered
the further security of advanced posts. The right
rested on a little stream which runs at right angles to
the Geete and joins it at Elixheim, and on the villages
of Laer and Neerwinden which stand on its banks.
From Neerlanden on the left to Neerwinden on the
right the position measured close on four miles ; and
to guard this extent, besides supplying strong garrisons
for the villages, William had little more than fifty
thousand men. Here then was one signal defect : the
front was too long to permit troops to be readily moved
from flank to flank, or to be withdrawn without serious
risk from the centre. But this was not all. The depth
of the position was less than half of its frontage, and
thus allowed no space for the action of cavalry. This
William ignored : he was afraid of the French horse,
and was anxious that the action should be fought by
infantry only. Finally, retreat was barred by the
Geete, which was unfordable and insufficiently bridged ;
and therefore the forcing of the allied right must inevitably drive the whole army into a pinfold, as Leslie's
had been driven at the battle of Dunbar.

Luxemburg, who knew every inch of the ground,
was now anxious only lest William should retire before
he could catch him. On the 28th of July, by a great July $\frac{18}{28}$.
effort and a magnificent march, he brought the whole
of his army, eighty thousand strong, before William's
position. He was now sure of his game, but he need
not have been anxious, for William, charmed with the
notion of excluding the French cavalry from all share
in the action, was resolved to stand his ground   Many

1693. officers urged him to cross the Geete while yet he might ;
but he would not listen.   Fifteen hundred men were
told off to entrench the open ground between Neerwinden and Neerlanden.   The hedges, mud-walls, and
natural defences of Neerwinden and Laer were improved
to the uttermost, and the ditches surrounding them were
enlarged.   Till late into the night the King rode backward and forward, ordering matters under his own eyes,
and after a few hours' rest began very early in the
morning to make his dispositions.

The key of the position was the village of Neerwinden with the adjoining hamlet of Laer, and here
accordingly he stationed the best of his troops.   The
defence of Laer was entrusted to Brigadier Ramsey
with the Scots Brigade, namely, the Twenty-first,
Twenty-fifth, Twenty-sixth, Mackay's and Lauder's
regiments, reinforced by the Buffs and the Fourth Foot.
Between Laer and Neerwinden stood six battalions of
Brandenburgers, troops already of great and deserved
reputation, of whom we shall see more in the years
before us.   Neerwinden itself was committed to the
Hanoverians, the Dutch Guards, a battalion of the
First and a battalion of the Scots Guards.   Immediately to the north or left of the village the entrenchment
was lined by the two remaining battalions of the First
and Scots Guards, the Coldstream Guards, a battalion
of the Royal Scots, and the Seventh Fusiliers.   On the
extreme left of the position Neerlanden was held by the
other battalion of the Royal Scots, the Second Queen's,
and two Danish regiments, while Rumsdorp was
occupied by the Fourteenth, Sixteenth, Nineteenth,
and Collingwood's regiments.   In a word, every important post was committed to the British.   The
remainder of the infantry, with one hundred guns, was
ranged along the entrenchment, and in rear of them

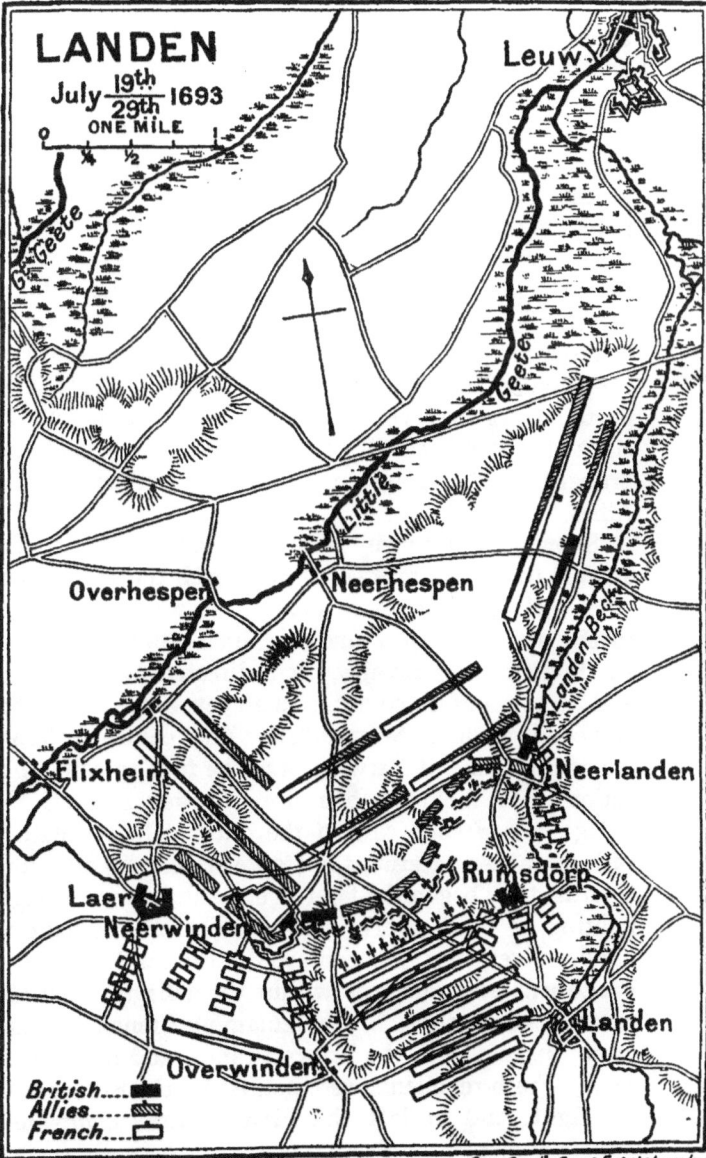

LANDEN

July 19th/29th 1693

ONE MILE

Gr. Geete

Leuw

Geete

Little

Overhesper

Neerhespen

Landen-Beek

Elixheim

Neerlanden

Rumsdorp

Laer

Neerwinden

Landen

Overwinden

British

Allies

French

Stanford's Geog. Estab. London

1693. stood the cavalry, powerless to act outside the trench, and too much cramped for space to manœuvre within it.

Luxemburg also was early astir, and was amazed to find how far the front of the position had been strengthened during the night. His centre he formed in eight lines over against the Allies' entrenchments between Oberwinden and Landen, every line except the second and fourth being composed of cavalry. For the attack on Neerlanden and Rumsdorp he detailed fifteen thousand foot and two thousand five hundred dismounted dragoons. For the principal assault on Neerwinden he told off eighteen thousand foot, supported by a reserve of two thousand more and by eight thousand cavalry; while seventy guns were brought into position to answer the artillery of the Allies.

July $\frac{19}{29}$. Shortly after sunrise William's cannon opened fire against the heavy masses of the French centre; and at eight o'clock Luxemburg moved the whole of his left to the attack of Neerwinden. Six battalions, backed by dragoons and cavalry, were directed against Laer, and three columns, counting in all seven brigades, were launched against Neerwinden. The centre column, under the Duke of Berwick, was the first to come into action. Withholding their fire till they reached the village, the French carried the outer defences with a rush, and then meeting the Hanoverians and the First Guards, they began the fight in earnest. It was hedge-fighting, as at Steenkirk, muzzle to muzzle and hand to hand. Every step was contested; the combat swayed backwards and forwards within the village; and the carnage was frightful. The remaining French columns came up, met with the like resistance, and made little way. Fresh regiments were poured by the French into the fight, and at last the First Guards, completely

broken by its losses, gave way.   But it was only for
a moment.   They rallied on the Scots Guards; the
Dutch and Hanoverians rallied behind them, and,
though the enemy had been again reinforced, they
resumed the unequal fight, nine battalions against
twenty-six, with unshaken tenacity.   At Laer, on the
extreme right, the fight was equally sharp.   Ramsey
for a time was driven out of the village, and the French
cavalry actually forced its way into the Allies' position.
There, however, it was charged in flank by the Elector
of Bavaria, and driven out with great slaughter.
Ramsey seized the moment to rally his brigade.   The
French columns, despite their success, still remained
isolated and detached, and presented no united front.
The King placed himself at the head of the Guards and
Hanoverians, and with one charge British, Dutch, and
Germans fell upon the Frenchmen and swept them out
of both villages.

The first attack on Neerwinden had failed, and a
similar attack on the allied left had been little more
successful.   At Neerlanden the First and Second Foot
had successfully held their own against four French
battalions until reinforcements enabled them to drive
them back.   At Rumsdorp the British, being but three
thousand against thirteen thousand, were pushed out of
the village, but being reinforced, recovered a part of it
and stood successfully at bay.   Luxemburg, however,
was not easily discouraged.   The broken troops in the
left were rallied, fresh regiments were brought forward,
and a second effort was made to carry Neerwinden.
Again French impetuosity bore all before it, and again
the British and Germans, weakened and weary though
they were, rallied when all seemed lost, and hurled the
enemy back, not merely repulsed, but in confused and
disorderly retreat.

1693.

July $\frac{19}{29}$.

1693.   On the failure of the second attack the majority of
July 19/29 the French officers urged Luxemburg to retire ; but
the marshal was not to be turned from his purpose.
The fourteen thousand men of the Allies in Laer and
Neerwinden had lost more than a third of their numbers,
while he himself had still a considerable force of infantry
interlined with the cavalry in the centre. Twelve
thousand of them, including the French and Swiss
Guards, were now drawn off to the left for a third
attack. When they were clear of the cavalry, the
whole six lines of horse, which had stood heroically for
hours motionless under a heavy fire, moved forward at
a trot to the edge of the entrenchments ; [1] but the
demonstration, for such it seems to have been, cost
them dear, for they were very roughly handled and
compelled to retire. But now the French reinforcements, supported by the defeated battalions, drew
near, and a third attack was delivered on Neerwinden.
British and Dutch still made a gallant fight, but the
odds against their weakened battalions were too great,
and ammunition began to fail. They fought on in-
domitably till the last cartridge was expended before
they gave way, but they were forced back, and Neerwinden was lost. Five French brigades then assailed
the central entrenchment at its junction with Neerwinden, where stood the Coldstream Guards and the
Seventh Fusiliers. Wholly unmoved by the overwhelming numbers in their front and the fire from
Neerwinden on their flank, the two regiments stood
firm and drove their assailants back over the breastwork. Even when the French Household Cavalry
came spurring through Neerwinden and fell upon their

---

[1] St. Simon. With the exception of one hollow, which might
hold three or four squadrons in double rank in line, there is not the
slightest shelter in the plain wherein the French horse could find
protection.

flank, they fought on undismayed, and the Cold-
streamers not only repelled the charge but captured
a colour.

Such fighting, however, could not continue for long.
William, on observing Luxemburg's preparations for
the final assault, had ordered nine battalions from his
left to reinforce his right. These never reached their
destination. The Marquis of Feuquières, an officer
even more celebrated for his acuteness as a military
critic than for his skill in the field, watched them as they
moved, and suddenly led his cavalry forward to the
weakest point of the entrenchment. The battalions
hesitated, halted, and then turned about to meet this
new danger, but too late to save the forcing of the
entrenchment. The battle was now virtually over.
Neerwinden was carried, Ramsey after a superb defence
had been driven out of Laer, the Brandenburgers had
perforce retreated with him, the infantry that lined
the centre of the entrenchment had forsaken it, and the
French cavalry was pouring in and cutting down the
fugitives by scores. William, who had galloped away
in desperation to the left, now returned at headlong
speed with six regiments of English cavalry,[1] which
delivered charge after charge with splendid gallantry,
to cover the retreat of the foot. On the left Tolmach
and Bellasys by great exertion brought off their infantry
in good order, but on the right the confusion was
terrible. The rout was complete, the few bridges were
choked by a heaving mass of guns, waggons, pack-
animals, and men, and thousands of fugitives were cut
down, drowned, or trampled to death. William did all
that a gallant man could do to save the day, but in
vain. His troops had done heroic things to redeem his

[1] Life Guards, 1st, 3rd, 4th, 6th Dragoon Guards, Galway's
Horse.

1693. bad generalship; and against any living man but
July $\frac{19}{29}$. Marlborough or Luxemburg they would probably have
held their own. It was the general, not the soldiers
that failed.

The losses on both sides were very severe. That
of the French was about eight thousand men ; that
of the Allies about twelve thousand, killed, wounded,
and prisoners, and among the dead was Count Solmes,
the hated Solmes of Steenkirk. The nineteen British
battalions present lost one hundred and thirty-five
officers killed, wounded, and taken. The French
captured eighty guns and a vast quantity of colours,
but the Allies, although beaten, could also show fifty-six
French flags. And, indeed, though Luxemburg won,
and deserved to win a great victory, yet the action was
not such as to make the allied troops afraid to meet
the French. They had stood up, fifty thousand against
eighty thousand, and if they were beaten they had at
any rate dismayed every Frenchman on the field but
Luxemburg. In another ten years their turn was to
come, and they were to take a part of their revenge
on the very ground over which many of them had fled.

The campaign closed with the surrender of Charleroi,
and the gain by the French of the whole line of the
Sambre. William came home to meet the House of
Commons and recommend an augmentation of the Army
by eight regiments of horse, four of dragoons, and
twenty-five of foot. The House reduced this list by the
whole of the regiments of horse and fifteen of foot, but
even so it brought the total establishment up to eighty-
three thousand men. There is, however, but one new
regiment of which note need be taken in the campaign
of 1694, namely, the Seventh Dragoons, now known
as the Seventh Hussars, which, raised in 1689–90 in
Scotland, now for the first time took its place on the

English establishment and its turn of service in the 1693.
war of Flanders.

I shall not dwell on the campaign of 1694, which 1694.
is memorable only for a marvellous march by which
Luxemburg upset William's entire plan of campaign.
Nor shall I speak at length of the abortive descent on
Brest, which is remembered mainly for the indelible
stain which it has left on the memory of Marlborough.
It is only necessary to say that the French, by Marlborough's information, though not on Marlborough's
information only, had full warning of an expedition
which had been planned as a surprise, and that Tolmach,[1]
who was in command, unfortunately, though most
pardonably, lacked the moral courage to abandon an
attack which, unless executed as a surprise, had no
chance of success.   He was repulsed with heavy loss,
and died of wounds received in the action—a hard fate
for a good soldier and a gallant man.   But it is unjust
to lay his death at Marlborough's door.   For the
failure of the expedition Marlborough was undoubtedly
responsible, and that is quite bad enough ; but Tolmach alone was to blame for attempting an enterprise
which he knew to be hopeless.   Marlborough cannot
have calculated that he would deliberately essay to
do impossibilities and perish in the effort, so cannot
be held guilty of poor Tolmach's blunders.

Before the new campaign could be opened there had 1695.
come changes of vital importance to France.   The vast
expense of the war had told heavily on the country,
and the King's ministers were at their wit's end to
raise money.   Moreover, the War Department had
deteriorated rapidly since the death of Louvois ; and

---

[1] This is, of course, the Talmash of *Tristram Shandy* and of
Macaulay's History.   He signed his name, however, as I spell it
here, and I use his own spelling the more readily since it is more
easily identified with the Tollemache of to-day.

D

1695.
January.
to this misfortune was now added the death of Luxemburg, a loss which was absolutely irreparable.   Lastly,
with the object of maintaining the position which they
had won on the Sambre, the French had extended their
system of fortified lines from Namur to the sea.   Works
so important could not be left unguarded, so that a
considerable force was locked up behind these entrenchments, and was for all offensive purposes useless.   We
shall see before long how a really great commander
could laugh at these lines, and how, in consequence, it
became an open question whether they were not rather
an encumbrance than an advantage.   The subject is
one which is still of interest ; and it is remarkable that
the French still seem to cling to their old principles, if
they may be judged by the works which they have
constructed for defence against a German invasion.

His enemy being practically restricted to the
defensive, William did not neglect the opportunity of
initiating aggressive operations.   Masking his design
by a series of feints, he marched swiftly to the Meuse
and invested Namur.   This fortress, more famous
through its connection with the immortal Uncle Toby
even than as the masterpiece of Cohorn, carried to yet
higher perfection by Vauban, stands at the junction of
the Sambre and the Meuse, the citadel lying in the
angle between the two rivers, and the town with its
defences on the left bank of the Meuse.   To the northward of the town outworks had been thrown up on
the heights of Bouge by both of these famous engineers ;
and it was against these outworks that William directed
his first attack.

June 23.
July 3.
June 26.
July 6.
Ground was broken on the 3rd of July, and three
days later an assault was delivered on the lines of
Bouge.   As usual, the hardest of the work was given
to the British, and the post of greatest danger was

made over, as their high reputation demanded, to 1695.
the Brigade of Guards. On this occasion the Guards June 26.
surpassed themselves alike by the coolness of their July 6.
valour and by the ardour of their attack. They marched
under a heavy fire up to the French palisades, thrust
their muskets between them, poured in one terrible
volley, the first shot that they had yet fired, and
charged forthwith. In spite of a stout resistance they
swept the French out of the first work, pursued them
to the second, swept them out of that, and gathering
impetus with success, drove them from stronghold to
stronghold, far beyond the original design of the
engineers, and actually to the gates of the town. In
another quarter the Royal Scots and the Seventh
Fusiliers gained not less brilliant success ; and in fact
it was the most creditable action that William had
fought during the whole war. It cost the Allies two
thousand men killed and wounded, the three battalions
of Guards alone losing thirty-two officers. The British
were to fight many such bloody combats during the
next twenty years—combats forgotten since they were
merely incidents in the history of a siege, and so frequent
that they were hardly chronicled, and are not to be
restored to memory now. I mention this, the first
of such actions, only as a type of many more to come.

The outworks captured, the trenches were opened
against the town itself, and the next assault was directed
against the counterguard of St. Nicholas gate. This
again was carried by the British, with a loss of eight
hundred men. Then came the famous attack on the
counterscarp before the gate itself, where Captain
Tobias Shandy received his memorable wound. This
gave William the possession of the town. Then came
the siege of the citadel, wherein the British had the
honour of marching to the assault over half a mile of

1695. open ground, a trial which proved too much even for
them.   Nevertheless, it was they who eventually
stormed a breach from which another of the assaulting
columns had been repulsed, and ensured the surrender
of the citadel a few days later.   For their service on
this occasion the Eighteenth Foot were made the Royal
Irish ; and a Latin inscription on their colours still
records that this was the reward of their valour at
Namur.

Thus William on his return to England could for
the first time show his Parliament a solid success due
to the British red-coats ; and the House of Commons
gladly voted once more a total force of eighty-seven
thousand men.   But the war need be followed no
further.   The campaign of 1696 was interrupted by a
futile attempt of the French to invade England, and
in 1697 France, reduced to utter exhaustion, gladly
concluded the Peace of Ryswick.   So ended, not without honour, the first stage of the great conflict with
King Lewis the Fourteenth.   The position of the two
protagonists, England and France, was not wholly
unlike that which they occupied a century later at
the Peace of Amiens.   The British, though they had
not reaped great victories, had made their presence
felt, and terribly felt, on the battlefield ; and, as the
French in the Peninsula remembered that the British
had fought them with a tenacity which they had not
found in other nations, not only in Egypt, but even
earlier at Tournay and Linselles, so, too, after Blenheim
and Ramillies they looked back to the furious attack
at Steenkirk and the indomitable defence of Neerwinden.   " Without the concurrence of the valour and
power of England," said William to the Parliament at
the close of 1695, " it were impossible to put a stop
to the ambition and greatness of France."   So it was

then, and so it was a century later, for though none 1695. know better the superlative qualities of the French as a fighting people, yet the English are the one nation that has never been afraid to meet them. With the Peace of Ryswick the 'prentice years of the standing Army are ended, and within five years the old spirit, which has carried it through the bitter schooling under King William, will break forth with overwhelming power under the guiding genius of Marlborough.

AUTHORITIES.—The leading authority for William's campaigns on the English side is D'Auvergne, and on the French side the compilation, with its superb series of maps, by Beaurain. Supplementary on one side are Tindal's History, Carleton's Memoirs, and Sterne's *Tristram Shandy* ; and on the other the *Mémoires* of Berwick and St. Simon, Quincy's *Histoire Militaire de Louis XIV*, and in particular the *Mémoires* of Feuquières. Many details as to Steenkirk, in particular, respecting the casualties, are drawn from *Present State of Europe, or Monthly Mercury*, August 1692, and as to Landen from the official relation of the battle, published by authority, 1693. Beautiful plans of both actions are in Beaurain, rougher plans in Quincy and Feuquières. All details as to the establishment voted are from the Journals of the House of Commons. Very elaborate details of the operations are given in Colonel Clifford Walton's *History of the British Standing Army*.

VOL. I. BOOK VI. CHAPTER I

A EUROPEAN quarrel over the succession to the Spanish throne,[1] on the death of the imbecile King Charles the Second, had long been foreseen by William, and had been provided against, as he hoped, by a Partition Treaty in the year 1698. The arrangement then made had been upset by the death of the Electoral Prince of Bavaria, and had been superseded by a second Partition Treaty in March 1700. In November of the same year King Charles the Second died, leaving a will wherein Philip, Duke of Anjou, and second son of the Dauphin, was named heir to the whole Empire of Spain. Hereupon the second Partition Treaty went for naught. Lewis the Fourteenth, after a becoming interval of hesitation, accepted the Spanish crown for the Duke of Anjou under the title of King Philip the Fifth.

The Emperor at once entered a protest against the

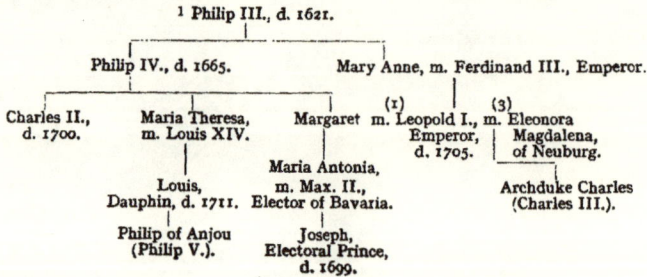

[1] Philip III., d. 1621.

Philip IV., d. 1665.　　　　Mary Anne, m. Ferdinand III., Emperor.

Charles II., d. 1700.　Maria Theresa, m. Louis XIV.　Margaret m. Leopold I., m. Eleonora (1) Emperor, d. 1705. (3) Magdalena, of Neuburg.

Louis, Dauphin, d. 1711.　Maria Antonia, m. Max. II., Elector of Bavaria.　Archduke Charles (Charles III.).

Philip of Anjou (Philip V.).　Joseph, Electoral Prince, d. 1699.

38

will, and Lewis prepared without delay for a campaign 1701.
in Italy. William, however, for the present merely
postponed his recognition of Philip the Fifth ; and his
example was followed by the United Provinces. Lewis,
ever ready and prompt, at once took measures to
quicken the States to a decision. Several towns [1] in
Spanish Flanders were garrisoned, under previous
treaties, by Dutch troops. Lewis by a swift movement
surrounded the whole of them, and, having thus secured
fifteen thousand of the best men in the Dutch army,
could dictate what terms he pleased. William expected
that the House of Commons would be roused to indignation by this aggressive step, but the House was far
too busy with its own factious quarrels. When,
however, the States appealed to England for the six
thousand four hundred men, which under the treaty of
1668 [2] she was bound to furnish, both Houses prepared
faithfully to fulfil the obligation.

Then, as invariably happens in England, the work
which Parliament had undone required to be done
again. Twelve battalions were ordered to the Low
Countries from Ireland, and directions were issued for
the levying of ten thousand recruits in England to take
their place. But, immediately after, came bad news
from the West Indies, and it was thought necessary to
despatch thither four more battalions from Ireland.
Three regiments [3] were hastily brought up to a joint

[1] Namur, Luxemburg, Mons, Charleroi, Ath, Oudenarde, Nieuport, Ostend.
[2] By the defensive alliance concluded between England and
Holland early in 1668, it was laid down that either party, on being
attacked, had the right to require from the other the aid of a fixed
proportion of forces both naval and military. This treaty was
arranged by Sir William Temple shortly after the Treaty of Breda
had brought to a close the Dutch War of 1665-1667 ; it was known
as the Triple Alliance, Sweden being the third signatory.
[3] 12th, 22nd, 27th.

1701. strength of two thousand men, and shipped off. Thus, within fifteen months of the disbandment of 1699, the garrison of Ireland had been depleted by fifteen battalions out of twenty-one ; and four new battalions required to be raised immediately. Of these, two, namely Brudenell's and Mountjoy's, were afterwards disbanded, but two more, Lord Charlemont's and Lord Donegal's, are still with us as the Thirty-fifth and Thirty-sixth of the Line.

In June the twelve battalions [1] were shipped off to Holland, under the command of John, Earl of Marlborough. Since 1698 he had been restored to the King's favour and was to fill his place as head of the European coalition and General of the confederate armies in a fashion that no man had yet dreamed of. He was full fifty years of age ; so long had the ablest man in Europe waited for work that was worthy of his powers ; and now his time was come at last. His first duties, however, were diplomatic ; and during the summer and autumn of 1701 he was engaged in negotiations with Sweden, Prussia, and the Empire for the formation of a Grand Alliance against France and Spain. Needless to say he brought all to a successful issue by his inexhaustible charm, patience, and tact.

Sept.   Still the attitude of the English people towards the contest remained doubtful, until, on the death of King James the Second, Lewis made the fatal mistake of recognising and proclaiming his son as King of England. Then the smouldering animosity against France leaped instantly into flame. William seized the opportunity to dissolve Parliament, and was rewarded by the election of a House of Commons more nearly resembling

[1] 1st batt. First Guards, 1st Royals (2 batts.), 8th, 9th, 10th, 13th, 15th, 16th, 17th, 18th, 23rd, 24th. The Guards had been substituted (after careful explanation to Parliament) by William's own direction for the 9th Foot.

that which had carried him through the first war to 1701. the Peace of Ryswick. He did not fail to rouse its patriotism and self-respect by a stirring speech from the throne, and obtained the ratification of his agreement with the Allies, that England should furnish a contingent of forty thousand men, eighteen thousand of them to be British and the remainder foreigners. So the country was committed to the War of the Spanish Succession.

It was soon decided that all regiments in pay must be increased at once to war-strength, and that six more battalions, together with five regiments of horse and three of dragoons, should be sent to join the troops already in Holland. Then, as usual, there was a rush to do in a hurry what should have been done at leisure ; and it is significant of the results of the late ill-treatment of the Army that, though the country was full of unemployed soldiers, it was necessary to offer three pounds, or thrice the usual amount of levy-money, to obtain recruits. The next step was to raise fifteen new regiments—Meredith's, Coote's, Huntingdon's, Farrington's, Gibson's, Lucas's, Mohun's, Temple's, and Stringer's of foot ; Fox's, Saunderson's, Villiers', Shannon's, Mordaunt's and Holt's of marines. Of the foot, Gibson's and Farrington's had been raised in 1694, but the officers of Farrington's, if not of both regiments, had been retained on half-pay, and, returning in a body, continued the life of the regiment without interruption. Both are still with us as the Twenty-eighth and Twenty-ninth of the Line. Huntingdon's and Lucas's also survive as the Thirty-third and Thirty-fourth, and Meredith's and Coote's, which were raised in Ireland, as the Thirty-seventh and Thirty-ninth, while the remainder were disbanded at the close of the war. Of the marines, Saunderson's had origin-

1701. ally been raised in 1694, and eventually passed into the
Line as the Thirtieth Foot, followed by Fox's and
Villiers' as the Thirty-first and Thirty-second. Nothing
now remained but to pass the Mutiny Act, which was
speedily done ; and on the 5th of May, just two months
after the death of King William, the great work of his
life was continued by a formal declaration of war.

The field of operations, which will chiefly concern us,
is mainly the same as that wherein we followed the
campaigns of King William. The eastern boundary of
the cock-pit must for a time be extended from the
Meuse to the Rhine, the northern from the Demer to
the Waal, and the southern limit must be carried from
Dunkirk beyond Namur to Bonn. But the reader
should bear in mind that, in consequence of the Spanish
alliance, Spanish Flanders was no longer hostile, but
friendly, to France, so that the French frontier, for all
practical purposes, extended to the boundary of Dutch
Brabant. Moreover, the French, besides the seizure,
already related, of the barrier-towns, had contrived
to occupy every stronghold on the Meuse except
Maestricht, from Namur to Venloo, so that practically
they were masters so far of the whole line of the river.

A few leagues below Venloo stands the fortified
town of Grave, and beyond Grave, on the parallel
branch of the Waal, stands the fortified city of Nimeguen. A little to the east of Nimeguen, at a point
where the Rhine formerly forked into two streams,
stood Fort Schenck, a stronghold famous in the wars of
Morgan and of Vere. These three fortresses were the
three eastern gates of the Dutch Netherlands, commanding the two great waterways, doubly important
in those days of bad roads, which lead into the heart
of the United Provinces.

It is here that we must watch the opening of the

campaign of 1702. There were detachments of the 1702. French and of the Allies opposed to each other on the Upper Rhine, on the Lower Rhine, and on the Lower Scheldt ; but the French grand army of sixty thousand men was designed to operate on the Meuse, and the presence of a Prince of the blood, the Duke of Burgundy, with old Marshal Boufflers to instruct him, sufficiently showed that this was the quarter in which France designed to strike her grand blow. Marlborough being still kept from the field by other business, the command of the Allied army on the Meuse was entrusted to Lord Athlone, better known as that Ginkell who had completed the pacification of Ireland in 1691. His force consisted of twenty-five thousand men, with which he lay near Cleve, in the centre of the crescent formed by Grave, Nimeguen, and Fort Schenck, watching under shelter of these three fortresses the army of Boufflers, which was encamped some twenty miles to south-east of him at Uden and Xanten. On May 30. the 10th of June Boufflers made a sudden dash to cut June 10. off Athlone from Nimeguen and Grave, a catastrophe which Athlone barely averted by an almost discreditably precipitate retreat. Having reached Nimeguen Athlone withdrew to the north of the Waal, while all Holland trembled over the danger which had thus been so narrowly escaped.

Such was the position when Marlborough at last took the field, after long grappling at the Hague with the difficulties which were fated to dog him throughout the war. In England his position was comparatively easy, for though Prince George of Denmark, the consort of Queen Anne, was nominally generalissimo of all forces by sea and land, yet Marlborough was Captain-General of all the English forces at home and in Holland, and in addition Master-General of the

1702. Ordnance. But it was only after considerable dispute that he was appointed Commander-in-Chief of the Allied forces, and then not without provoking much dissatisfaction among the Dutch generals, and much jealousy in the Prince of Nassau-Saarbrück and in Athlone, both of whom aspired to the office. These obstacles overcome, there came the question of the plan of campaign. Here again endless obstruction was raised. The Dutch, after their recent fright, were nervously apprehensive for the safety of Nimeguen, the King of Prussia was much disturbed over his territory of Cleve, and all parties who had not interests of their own to put forward made it their business to thwart the Commander-in-Chief. With infinite patience Marlborough soothed them, and at last, on the 2nd of July, he left the Hague for Nimeguen, accompanied by two Dutch deputies, civilians, whose duty it was to see that he did nothing imprudent. Arrived there he concentrated sixty thousand men, of which twelve thousand were British,[1] recrossed the Waal and encamped at Ober-Hasselt over against Grave, within two leagues of the French. Then once more the obstruction of his colleagues caused delay, and it was not until the 26th of July that he could cross to the left bank of the Meuse. " Now," he said to the Dutch deputies, as he pointed to the French camp, " I shall soon rid you of these troublesome neighbours."

June 21.
July 2.

July $\frac{15}{26}$.

Five swift marches due south brought his army over the Spanish frontier by Hamont. Boufflers thereupon in alarm broke up his camp, summoned Marshal Tallard from the Rhine to his assistance, crossed the Meuse with all haste at Venloo, and pushed

[1] Seven regiments of horse and dragoons, fourteen battalions of foot, fifty-six guns.

on at nervous speed for the Demer. On the 2nd of 1702.
August he lay between Peer and Bray, his camping- July 22.
ground ill-chosen, and his army worn out by a week Aug. 2.
of desperate marching. Within easy striking distance,
a mile or two to the northward, lay Marlborough, his
army fresh, ready, and confident. He held the game
in his hand; for an immediate attack would have
dealt the French as rude a buffet as they were to
receive later at Ramillies. But the Dutch deputies
interposed; these Dogberries were content to thank
God that they were rid of a rogue. So Boufflers was
allowed to cross the Demer safely at Diest, and a first
great opportunity was lost.

Marlborough, having drawn the French away from
the Meuse, was now at liberty to add the garrison of
Maestricht to his field-force, and to besiege the fortresses
on the river. Boufflers, however, emboldened by his
escape, again advanced north in the hope of cutting
off a convoy of stores that was on its way to join the
Allies. Marlborough therefore perforce moved back
to Hamont and picked up his convoy. Then, before
Boufflers could divine his purpose, he had moved
swiftly south, and thrown himself across the line of
the French retreat to the Demer. The French marshal Aug. $\frac{11}{22}$.
hurried southward with all possible haste, and came
blundering through the defiles before Hochtel on the
road to Hasselt, only to find Marlborough waiting
ready for him at Helchteren. Once again the game
was in the Englishman's hand. The French were in
great disorder, their left in particular being hopelessly
entangled in marshy and difficult ground. Marlborough instantly gave the order to advance, and by
three o'clock the artillery of the two armies was
exchanging fire. At five Marlborough directed the
whole of his right to fall on the French left; but to

1702. his surprise and dismay, the right did not move. A surly Dutchman, General Opdam, was in command of the troops in question and, for no greater object than to annoy the Commander-in-Chief, refused to execute his orders. So a second great opportunity was lost.

Aug. 12/23. Still much might yet be won by a general attack on the next day; and for this accordingly Marlborough at once made his preparations. But, when the time came, the Dutch deputies interposed, entreating him to defer the attack till the morrow morning. "By to-morrow morning they will be gone," answered Marlborough; but all remonstrance was unavailing. The attack was perforce deferred; the French slipped away in the night; and, though it was still possible to cut up their rearguard with cavalry, a third great opportunity was lost.

Marlborough was deeply chagrined; but although with unconquerable patience and tact he excused Opdam's conduct in his public despatches, he could not deceive the troops, who were loud in their indignation against both deputies and generals. There was now nothing left but to reduce the fortresses on the Meuse, a part of the army being detached for the siege while the remainder covered the operations under the command of Marlborough. Even over their favourite pastime of a siege, however, the Dutch were dilatory beyond measure. "England is famous for negligence," wrote Marlborough, "but if Englishmen were half as negligent as the people here, they would be torn to pieces by Parliament."[1] Venloo

Aug. 18/29. was at length invested on the 29th of August,[2] and

[1] Coxe, vol. i. p. 182.

[2] So Quincy. Coxe gives August 25–September 5 as the date, but the difference depends merely on the interpretation of the word investment.

after a siege of eighteen days compelled to capitulate. 1702.
The English distinguished themselves after their own
peculiar fashion. In the assault on the principal
defence General Cutts, who from his love of a hot fire
was known as the Salamander, gave orders that the
attacking force, if it carried the covered way, should
not stop there but rush forward and carry as much
more as it could. It was a mad design, criminally so
in the opinion of officers who took part in it,[1] but it
was madly executed, with the result that the whole
fort was captured out of hand.

The reduction of Stevenswaert, Maseyk, and Ruremond quickly followed ; and the French now became Sept. 26.
alarmed lest Marlborough should transfer operations Oct. 7.
to the Rhine. Tallard was therefore sent back with a
large force to Cologne and Bonn, while Boufflers, much
weakened by this and by other detachments, lay
helpless at Tongres. But the season was now far
advanced, and Marlborough had no intention of
leaving Boufflers for the winter in a position from
which he might at any moment move out and bombard
Maestricht. No sooner, therefore, were his troops
released by the capture of Ruremond than he prepared
to oust Boufflers. The French, according to their
usual practice, had barred the eastern entrance to
Brabant by fortified lines, which followed the line of
the Geete to its head-waters, and were thence carried
across to that of the Mehaigne. In his position at
Tongres Boufflers lay midway between these lines and
Liège, in the hope of covering both ; but after the
fall of so many fortresses on the Meuse he became
specially anxious for Liège, and resolved to post
himself under its walls. He accordingly examined
the defences, selected his camping-ground, and on

---

[1] See the description in Kane.

1702. the 12th of October marched up with his army to
Oct. $\frac{1}{12}$. occupy it. Quite unconscious of any danger he
arrived within cannon-shot of his chosen position ;
and there stood Marlborough, calmly awaiting him
with a superior force. For the fourth time Marlborough
held his enemy within his grasp, but the Dutch deputies,
as usual, interposed to forbid an attack ; and Boufflers,
a fourth time delivered, hurried away in the night to
his lines at Landen. Had he thrown himself into
Liège Marlborough would have made him equally un-
comfortable by marching on the lines ; as things were,
the French marshal perforce left the city to its fate.

The town of Liège, which was unfortified, at once
opened its gates to the Allies ; and within a week
Marlborough's batteries were playing on the citadel.
Oct. $\frac{12}{23}$. On the 23rd of October the citadel was stormed, the
English being first in the breach, and a few days later
Liège, with the whole line of the Meuse, had passed
into the hands of the Allies. Thus brilliantly, in
spite of four great opportunities marred by the Dutch,
ended Marlborough's first campaign. Athlone, like
an honest man, confessed that as second in command
he had opposed every one of Marlborough's projects,
and that the success was due entirely to his incomparable chief. He at any rate had an inkling that in
Turenne's handsome Englishman there had arisen one
of the great captains of all time.

Nevertheless the French had not been without
their consolations in other quarters. Towards the
end of the campaign the Elector of Bavaria had
declared himself for France against the Empire, and,
surprising the all-important position of Ulm on the
Danube, had opened communication with the French
force on the Upper Rhine. Villars, who commanded
in that quarter, had seconded him by defeating his

opponent, Prince Lewis of Baden, at Friedlingen, and 1702. had cleared the passages of the Black Forest ; while Tallard had, almost without an effort, possessed himself of Trèves and Trarbach on the Moselle. The rival competitors for the crown of Spain were France and the Empire, and the centre of the struggle, as no one saw more clearly than Marlborough, was for the present moving steadily towards the territory of the Empire.

While Marlborough was engaged in his operations on the Meuse, ten thousand English and Dutch, under the Duke of Ormonde and Admiral Sir George Rooke, had been despatched to make a descent upon Cadiz. The expedition was so complete a failure that there is no object in dwelling on it. Rooke would not support Ormonde, and Ormonde was not strong enough to master Rooke ; landsmen quarrelled with seamen, and English with Dutch. No discipline was maintained, and after some weeks of feeble operations and shameful scenes of indiscipline and pillage, the commanders found that they could do no more than return to England. They were fortunate enough, however, on their way, to fall in with the plate-fleet at Vigo, of which they captured twenty-five galleons containing treasure worth a million sterling. Comforted by this good fortune Rooke and Ormonde sailed homeward, and dropped anchor safely in Portsmouth harbour.

Meanwhile a mishap, which Marlborough called an accident, had gone near to neutralise all the success of the past campaign. At the close of operations the Earl, together with the Dutch deputies, had taken ship down the Meuse, with a guard of twenty-five men on board and an escort of fifty horse on the bank. In the night the horse lost their way, and the boat was surprised and overpowered by a French partisan with a following of marauders. The Dutch deputies

E

1702. produced French passes, but Marlborough had none and was therefore a prisoner.   Fortunately his servant slipped into his hand an old pass that had been made out for his brother Charles Churchill.   With perfect serenity Marlborough presented it as genuine, and was allowed to go on his way, the French contenting themselves with the capture of the guard and the plunder of the vessel, and never dreaming of the prize that they had let slip.   The news of his escape reached the Hague, where on his arrival rich and poor came out to welcome him, men and women weeping for joy over his safety.   So deep was the fascination exerted on all of his kind by this extraordinary man.

A few days later he returned to England, where a new Parliament had already congratulated Queen Anne on the retrieving of England's honour by the success of his arms.   The word retrieving was warmly resented, but though doubtless suggested by unworthy and factious animosity against the memory of William, it was strictly true.   The nation felt that it was not in the fitness of things that Englishmen should be beaten by Frenchmen, and they rejoiced to see the wrong set right.   Nevertheless party spirit found a still meaner level when Parliament extended to Rooke and Ormonde the same vote of thanks that they tendered to Marlborough.   This precious pair owed even this honour to the wisdom and good sense of their far greater comrade, for they would have carried their quarrel over the expedition within the walls of Parliament, had not Marlborough told them gently that the whole of their operations were indefensible and that the less they called attention to themselves the better.   The Queen, with more discernment, created Marlborough a Duke and settled on him a pension of £5000 a year.

MEANWHILE Parliament had met on the 29th of the previous October, full of congratulations to the Queen on the triumphs of the past campaign. There were not wanting, of course, men who, in the madness of faction, doubted whether Blenheim were really a victory, for the very remarkable reason that Marlborough had won it, but they were soon silenced by the retort that the King of France at any rate had no doubts on the point.[1] The plans for the next campaign were designed on a large scale, and were likely to strain the resources of the Army to the uttermost. The West Indies demanded six battalions and Gibraltar three battalions for garrison ; Portugal claimed ten thousand men, Flanders from twenty to twenty-five thousand ; while besides this a design was on foot, as shall presently be seen, for the further relief of Portugal by a diversion in Catalonia. Five millions were cheerfully voted for the support of the war, and six new battalions were raised, namely, Wynne's, Bretton's, Lepell's, Saomes's, Sir Charles Hotham's, and Lillingston's, the last of which alone has survived to our day with the rank of the Thirty-eighth of the Line.[2]

1704.

1705.

[1] St. Simon gives a curious account of Lewis's difficulty in arriving at the truth, owing to the general unwillingness to tell him bad news.

[2] It is stated in *Records and Badges of the Army* that Lillingston's was formed in 1702. But Narcissus Luttrell, Millar, and the Military Entry Books all give the date as 25th March (New Year's Day) 1705.

1705.   Marlborough's plan of campaign had been suffi-
ciently foreshadowed at the close of the previous year,
namely, to advance on the line of the Moselle and
carry the war into Lorraine.   The Emperor and all the
German Princes promised to be in the field early, the
Dutch were with infinite difficulty persuaded to give
their consent, and after much vexatious delay Marl-
May $\frac{15}{26}$. borough joined his army at Trèves on the 26th of May.
Here he waited until the 17th of June for the arrival of
June $\frac{6}{17}$. the German and Imperial troops.   Not a man nor a
horse appeared.   In deep chagrin he broke up his
camp and returned to the Meuse, having lost, as he
said, one of the fairest opportunities in the world,
through the faithlessness of his allies.[1]

His presence was sorely needed on the Meuse.
Villeroy, who commanded the French in Flanders,
finding no occasion for his presence on the Moselle,
May 21. had moved out of his lines, captured Huy, and then
marching on to Liège had invested the citadel.   The
States-General in a panic of fright urged Marlborough
to return without delay, and Overkirk, who commanded
the Dutch on the Meuse, added his entreaties to theirs.
Marlborough, when once he had made up his mind to
June $\frac{14}{25}$. move, never moved slowly, and by the 25th of June he
was at Düren, to the eastward of Aix-la-Chapelle.
Here he was still the best part of forty miles from the
Meuse, but that distance was too near for Villeroy, who
at once abandoned Liège and fell back on Tongres.
June 21. Marlborough, continuing his advance, crossed the
July 2. Meuse at Visé on the 2nd of July, and on the same day
united his army with Overkirk's at Haneff on the
Upper Jaar.   Villeroy thereupon retired ignominiously
within his fortified lines.

[1] Quincy's account of this portion of the campaign is, so far as
concerns Marlborough, full of falsehoods.

These lines, which had been making during the past 1705. three years, were now complete. They started from the Meuse a little to the east of Namur, passed from thence to the Mehaigne and the Little Geete, followed the Little Geete along its left bank to Leuw, the Great Geete from Leuw to the Demer, and the Demer itself as far as Arschot, from which point a new line of entrenchments carried the barrier through Lierre to Antwerp. Near Antwerp Marlborough had already had to do with these lines in 1703, but hitherto he had made no attempt to force them. Villeroy and the Elector of Bavaria now lay before him with seventy thousand men, a force superior to his own, but necessarily spread over a wide front for the protection of the entrenchments. The marshal's headquarters were at Meerdorp, in the space between the Geete and the Mehaigne, which he probably regarded as a weak point. Marlborough posted himself over against him at Lens-les-Beguines, detaching a small force to recapture Huy, while Overkirk with the Dutch army covered the siege from Vignamont. Thus, as if daring the French to take advantage of the dispersion of his troops, he quietly laid his plans for forcing the lines.

The point that he selected was on the Little Geete between Elixheim and Neerhespen, exactly in rear of the battlefield of Landen. The abrupt and slippery banks of the river, which the English knew but too well, together with the entrenchments beyond it, presented extraordinary difficulties ; but the lines were on that account the less likely to be well guarded at that particular point. Marlborough had already obtained the leave of the States-General for the project, but he had now the far more difficult task of gaining the consent of the Dutch generals at a Council of War. Slangenberg and others opposed the scheme vehe-

1705. mently, but were overruled ; and the Duke was at
length at liberty to fall to work.

June 30.   Huy fell on the 11th of July, but to the general
July 11. surprise the besieging force was not recalled.   Six days
later Overkirk and the covering army crossed the
July. Mehaigne from Vignamont, and pushed forward detachments to the very edge of the lines between
Meffle and Namur.   Villeroy fell into the trap, withdrew troops from all parts of the lines and concentrated
forty thousand men at Meerdorp.   Marlborough then
recalled the troops from Huy, and made them up to a
total of about eight thousand men, both cavalry and
infantry,[1] the whole being under the command of the
Count of Noyelles.   The utmost secrecy was observed
in every particular.   The corps composing the detachment knew nothing of each other, and nothing of the
work before them ; and, lest the sight of fascines should
suggest an attack on entrenchments, these were dis-
pensed with, the troopers only at the last moment
receiving orders to carry each a truss of forage on the
saddle before them.

July $\frac{6}{17}$.   At tattoo the detachment fell in silently before the
camp of the right wing, and at nine o'clock moved off
without a sound in two columns, the one upon Neerhespen, the other upon the Castle of Wanghe before
Elixheim.   An hour later the rest of the army followed,
while at the same time Overkirk, under cover of the
darkness, crossed the Mehaigne at Tourines and joined
his van to the rear of Marlborough's army.   The
distance to be traversed was from ten to fifteen miles ;
the night though dry was dark ; and the guides,
frequently at fault, were fain to direct themselves by
the trusses dropped on the way by the advanced

---

[1] Four British regiments were of this detachment.   Two battalions of the 1st Royals, the 3rd Buffs, and the 10th Foot.

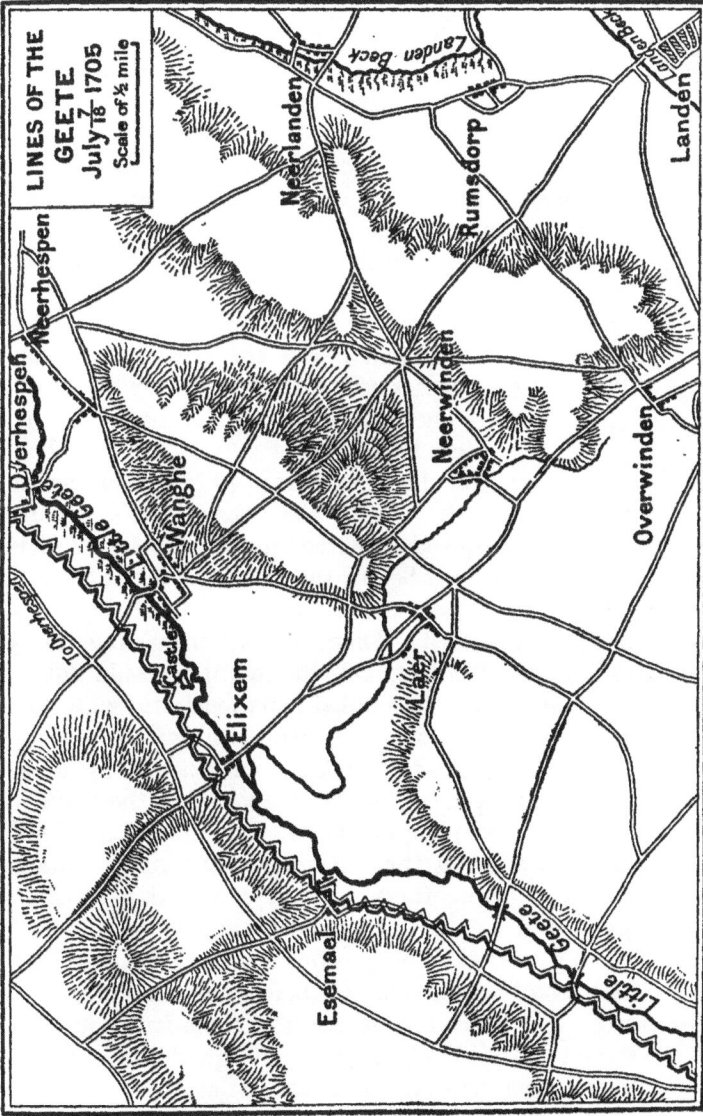

LINES OF THE
GEETE
July 18 1705
Scale of ½ mile

Neerhespen

Overhespen

Wanghe

Eastern

Elixem

To Tirlemont

Esemael

Neerlanden

Landen Beck

Rumsdorp

Landen

Neerwinden

Overwinden

Little GEETE

Stanford's Geog. Estab. London

1705.
July $\frac{6-7}{17-18}$.
detachment.   Twelve years before to the very day, a French army had toiled along the same route, wearied out and stifled by the sun, and only kept to its task by an ugly little hunch-backed man whom it had reverenced as Marshal Luxemburg.   Now English and Dutch were blundering on to take revenge for Luxemburg's victory at the close of that march.   The hours fled on, the light began to break, and the army found itself on the field of Landen, William's entrenchment grass-grown before it, Neerwinden and Laer lying silent to the left, and before the villages the mound that hid the corpses of the dead.   Then some at least of the soldiers knew the work that lay before them.

July $\frac{7}{18}$.
At four o'clock the heads of the columns halted within a mile of the Geete, wrapped in a thick mist and hidden from the eye of the enemy.   The advanced detachment quickly cleared the villages by the river, seized the bridge before the Castle of Wanghe, which had not been broken down, and drove out the garrison of the Castle itself.   Then the pontoniers came forward to lay their bridges ; but the infantry would not wait for them.   They scrambled impatiently through hedges and over bogs, down one steep bank of the river and up the other, into the ditch beyond, and finally, breathless and dripping, over the rampart into the lines.   So numerous were the hot-heads who thus went forward that they forced three regiments of French dragoons to retire before them without attempting resistance.   Then the cavalry of the detachment began to file rapidly over the pontoon-bridges ; but meanwhile the alarm had been given, and, before the main army could cross, the French came down in force from the north, some twenty battalions and forty squadrons, in all close upon fifteen thousand men, with a battery of eight guns.   The enemy advanced rapidly, their cavalry leading,

until checked by a hollow way which lay between them 1705.
and the Allies, when they halted to deploy. Marl- July $\frac{7}{18}$.
borough took in the whole situation at a glance.
Forming his thirty-eight squadrons into two lines,
with the first line composed entirely of British, he led
them across the hollow way and charged the French
sword in hand. They answered by a feeble fire from the
saddle and broke in confusion, but, presently rallying,
fell in counter-attack upon the British and broke them
in their turn. Marlborough, who was riding on the
flank, was cut off and left isolated with his trumpeter
and groom. A Frenchman galloped up and aimed at
him so furious a blow that, striking the air, he fell
from his horse and was captured by the trumpeter.
Then the allied squadrons rallied, and charging the
French once more broke them past all reforming, and
captured the guns. The French infantry now retired
very steadily in square, and the Duke sent urgent
messages for his own foot. But by some mistake the
battalions had been halted after crossing the Geete, so
that the French were able to make good their retreat.

By this time Villeroy, who had spent the night in
anxious expectation of an attack at Meerdorp, had
hurried up with his cavalry, only to find that the Duke
was master of the lines. Hastily giving orders for his
scattered troops to pass the Geete at Judoigne, he began
his retreat upon Louvain. Presently up came Marlborough's infantry at an extraordinary pace, the men
as fresh and lively after fifteen hours of fatigue as if
they had just left camp. The Duke was anxious to
follow up his success forthwith, a movement which
the French had good reason to dread, but the Dutch
generals opposed him, and Marlborough was reluctantly
constrained to yield. The loss of the French seems to
have been about two thousand men, most of them

1705.
July $\frac{7}{18}$.

prisoners, a score of standards and colours, of which
the Fifth Dragoon Guards claimed four as their own,
and eighteen guns, eight of which were triple-barrelled
and were sent across the Channel to be copied in
England.[1]

July $\frac{8}{19}$.

The Allies halted for the night at Tirlemont, and
advancing next day upon Louvain struck against the
rear of the French columns and captured fifteen hundred
prisoners. That night they encamped a mile to the
east of Louvain, while the French, once again distri-
buting their force along a wider front, lined the left
bank of the Dyle from the Demer to the Yssche, with
their centre at Louvain. Marlborough had hoped to
push on at once, but was stopped by heavy rains that
rendered the Dyle impassable ; and it was not until
ten days later that, after infinite trouble with the
Dutch, he was able to pursue his design.

July $\frac{18}{29}$.

The operations for the passage of the Dyle were
conducted in much the same way as in the forcing of
the lines. An advanced detachment was sent forward
from each wing of the army, that from the right or
English[2] flank being appointed to cross the river under
the Duke of Würtemberg at Corbeek Dyle, that
from the left under General Heukelom to pass it at
Neeryssche. The detachments fell in at five in the
evening, reached their appointed destination at ten,
and effected their passage with perfect success. The
main bodies started at midnight, and went somewhat
astray in the darkness, though by three o'clock the
Dutch army was within supporting distance of its
detachment and the British rapidly approaching it.
The river had been in fact forced, when suddenly the

[1] Narcissus Luttrell.
[2] It is worth noting that this was the first campaign in which
Marlborough and the British took the post of honour at the extreme
right of the Allied order of battle.

Dutch generals halted their main body. Marlborough 1705.
rode up to inquire the cause, and was at once taken
aside by Slangenberg.   " For God's sake, my Lord—"
began the Dutchman vehemently, and continued to
protest with violent gesticulations. No sooner was
Marlborough's back turned than the Dutch generals,
like a parcel of naughty schoolboys, recalled Heukelom's detachment. Thus the passage won with so
much skill was for no cause whatever abandoned,
without loss indeed, but also not without mischievous encouragement to the French, who boasted
loudly that they had repulsed their redoubtable
adversary.

Deeply hurt and annoyed though he was, the
Duke, with miraculous patience, excused in his public
despatches the treachery and imbecility which had
thwarted him, and prepared to effect his purpose in
another way. His movements were hastened by news
that French reinforcements, set free by the culpable
inaction of Prince Lewis of Baden, were on their way
from Alsace. Unable to pass the Dyle he turned its Aug.$\frac{5}{16}$.
head-waters at Genappe, and wheeling north towards
the forest of Soignies encamped between La Hulpe and
Braine l'Alleud.[1] The French promptly took the
alarm and posted themselves behind the river Yssche,
with their left at Neeryssche, and their right at Overyssche resting on the forest of Soignies. Marlborough
at once resolved to force the passage of the river. On
the evening of the 17th of August he detached his Aug.$\frac{6}{17}$.
brother Charles Churchill with ten thousand foot and
two thousand horse to advance through the forest and
turn the French right ; while he himself marched away

---

[1] His camp thus lay across the whole of Wellington's position
at Waterloo, from east to west and considerably beyond it to westward, but fronted in the reverse direction.

1705. at daybreak with the rest of the army and emerged
Aug. $\frac{7}{19}$. into the plain between the Yssche and the Lasne.   The
Duke quickly found two assailable points, and choosing
that of Overyssche, halted the army pending the
arrival of the artillery.   The guns were long in arriving,
Slangenberg having insisted, despite the Duke's express
instructions, on forcing his own baggage into the
column for the express purpose of causing delay.   At
last about noon the artillery appeared, and Marlborough asked formal permission of the Dutch deputies
to attack.   To his surprise, although Overkirk had
already consented, they claimed to consult their generals.
Slangenberg with every mark of insolence condemned
the project as murder and massacre, the rest solemnly
debated the matter for another two hours, the auspicious
moment passed away exactly as they had intended, and
another great opportunity was lost.   The French reinforcements arrived, and having been the weaker became
the stronger force.   Nothing more could be done for
the rest of the campaign, but to level the French lines
from the Demer to the Mehaigne.

    Thus for the third time a brilliant campaign was
spoilt by the Dutch generals and deputies.   Fortunately
the public indignation both in England and in Holland
was too strong for them, and Slangenberg, though
not indeed hanged as he deserved, was deprived of
all further command.   Jealousy, timidity, ignorance,
treachery, and flat imbecility seem to have been the
motives that inspired these men, whose conduct has
never been reprobated according to its demerit.   It
was they who were responsible for the prolongation of
the war, for the burden that it laid on England, and
for the untold misery that it wrought in France.   Left
to himself Marlborough would have forced the French
to peace in three campaigns, and the war would not

have been ended in shame and disgrace by the Treaty 1705. of Utrecht.[1]

[1] ORDER OF BATTLE.   CAMPAIGN OF 1705.

Left.
1st Line.

RIGHT WING ONLY.

Right.

Foreign Troops

15th
24th
,, ,,
Evans's Foot.
Macartney's Foot.
37th Foot.
21st Royal Scots Fusiliers.
3rd Buffs,

16th Foot.
26th Cameronians.
Stringer's Foot.
28th Foot.
23rd Royal Welsh.
18th Royal Irish.
,, ,, Royal Scots.
1 Batt. 1st Guards.

3rd
6th
7th
5th
1st Dragoon Guards, 3 squadrons.
,, ,, ,, 2
,, ,, ,, 2
,, ,, ,, 2
. ,, ,, ,,

Scots Greys, 3 squadrons.
5th Dragoons, 3 ,,

2nd Line.
Extreme Right of Centre.

8th
29th Foot.
Temple's Foot.
10th Foot.
2nd Batt. Royal Scots.
,,

Foreign troops

Newspaper.

VOL. I. BOOK VI. CHAPTER V

1706. It is now time to revert to England and to the preparations for the campaign of 1706. Marlborough, as usual, directly that the military operations were concluded, had been deputed to visit the courts of Vienna and of sundry German states in order to keep the Allies up to the necessary pitch of unity and energy. These duties detained him in Germany and at the Hague until January 1706, when he was at last able to return to England. There he encountered far less obstruction than in former years, but found, nevertheless, an increasing burden of work. The vast extension of operations in the Peninsula, and the general sickliness of the troops in that quarter, demanded the enlistment of an unusually large number of recruits. One new regiment of dragoons and eleven new battalions of foot were formed in the course of the spring, to which it was necessary to add yet another battalion before the close of the year.[1] Again the epidemic sickness among the horses in Flanders had caused an extraordinary demand for them. The Dutch, after their wonted manner, had actually taken pains to prevent the supply of these animals to the British,[2] though, even if they had not, the Duke had

[1] Peterborough's Dragoons ; Mark Kerr's, Stanwix's, Lovelace's, Townsend's, Tunbridge's, Bradshaw's, Sybourg's, Price's Foot. Sybourg's was made up of Huguenots.
[2] Marlborough's *Despatches*, vol. ii. p. 262.

a prejudice in favour of English horses, as of English 1706.
men, as superior to any other. Finally, the stores of
the Ordnance were unequal to the constant drain of
small arms, and it was necessary to make good the
deficiency by purchases from abroad. All these
difficulties and a thousand more were of course referred
for solution to Marlborough.

When in April he crossed once more to the Hague April $\frac{14}{25}$
he found a most discouraging state of affairs. The
Dutch were backward in their preparations ; Prussia
and Hanover were recalcitrant over the furnishing of
their contingents ; Prince Lewis of Baden was sulking
within his lines, refusing to communicate a word of
his intentions to any one ; and everybody was ready
with a separate plan of campaign. The Emperor of
course desired further operations on the Moselle for
his own relief ; but, after the experience of the last
campaign, the Duke had wisely resolved never again
to move eastward to co-operate with the forces of the
Empire. The Dutch for their part wished to keep
Marlborough in Flanders, where he should be under
the control of their deputies ; but the imbecile caprice
of these worthies was little more to his taste than
the sullen jealousy of Baden. Marlborough himself
was anxious to lead a force to the help of Eugene in
Italy, a scheme which, if executed, would have carried
the British to a great fighting ground with which they
are unfamiliar, the plains of Lombardy. He had
almost persuaded the States-General to approve of
this plan, when all was changed by Marshal Villars,
who surprised Prince Lewis of Baden in his lines on
the Motter, and captured two important magazines.
The Dutch at once took fright and, in their anxiety
to keep Marlborough for their own defence, agreed to
appoint deputies who should receive rather than issue

1706. orders. So to the Duke's great disappointment it was settled that the main theatre of war should once again be Flanders.

Villeroy meanwhile lay safely entrenched in his position of the preceding year behind the Dyle, from which Marlborough saw little hope of enticing him. It is said that an agent was employed to rouse Villeroy by telling him that the Duke, knowing that the French were afraid to leave their entrenchments, would take advantage of their inaction to capture Namur.[1] Be that as it may, Villeroy resolved to quit the Dyle. He knew that the Prussian and Hanoverian contingents had not yet joined Marlborough, and that the Danish cavalry had refused to march to him until their wages were paid ; so that interest as well as injured pride prompted the hazard of a general action. On the 19th of May, therefore, he left his lines for Tirlemont on the Great Geete. Marlborough, who was at Maestricht, saw with delight that the end, for which he had not dared to hope, was accomplished. Hastily making arrangements for the payment of the Danish troops, he concentrated the Dutch and British at Bilsen on the Upper Demer, and moved southward to Borchloen. Here the arrival of the Danes raised his total force to sixty thousand men, a number but little inferior to that of the enemy. On the very same day came the intelligence that Villeroy had crossed the Great Geete and was moving on Judoigne. The Duke resolved to advance forthwith and attack him there.

May $\frac{8}{19}$.

May $\frac{9}{20}$.

May $\frac{11}{22}$.

May $\frac{12}{23}$.
At one o'clock in the morning of Whitsunday the 23rd of May, Quartermaster-general Cadogan rode forward from the headquarters at Corswarem with six hundred horse and the camp-colours towards the head of the Great Geete, to mark out a camp by the village

[1] This is the story told in Lamberti.

of Ramillies. The morning was wet and foggy, and
it was not until eight o'clock that, on ascending the
heights of Merdorp, the party dimly descried troops in
motion on the rolling ground before them. The Allied
army had not marched until two hours later than
Cadogan, but Marlborough, who had ridden on in
advance of it, presently came up and pushed the
cavalry forward through the mist. Then at ten
o'clock the clouds rolled away, revealing the whole of
the French army in full march towards them.

Villeroy's eyes were rudely opened, for he had not
expected Marlborough before the following day; but
he knew the ground well, for he had been over it
before with Luxemburg, and he proceeded to take up
a position which he had seen Luxemburg deliberately
reject. The table-land whereon he stood is the highest
point in the plains of Brabant. To his right flowed
the Mehaigne; in his rear ran the Great Geete; across
his centre and left the Little Geete rose and crept
away sluggishly in marsh and swamp.[1] In his front
lay four villages: Taviers on the Mehaigne to his
right, Ramillies, less advanced than Taviers, on the
source of the Little Geete to his right centre, Offus,
parallel to Ramillies but lower down the stream, to
his left centre, Autréglise or Anderkirch, between
two branches of the Little Geete and parallel to Taviers,
to his left. Along the concave line formed by these
villages Villeroy drew up his army in two lines facing
due east.

The Mehaigne, on which his right rested, is at
ordinary times a rapid stream little more than twelve
feet wide, with a muddy bottom, but is bordered by
swampy meadows on both sides, which are flooded
after heavy rain. From this stream the ground rises

---

[1] The ground, though now drained, is still very wet.

F

northward in a steady wave for about half a mile,
sinks gradually and rises into a higher wave at
Ramillies, sinks once more to northward of that village
and rolls downward in a gentler undulation to Autréglise. Between the Mehaigne and Ramillies, a distance
of about a mile and a half, the ground east and west
is broken by sundry hollows of sufficient inclination
to offer decided advantage or disadvantage in a combat
of cavalry. A single high knoll rises in the midst of
these hollows, offering a place of vantage from which
Marlborough must almost certainly have reconnoitred
the disposition of the French right. The access to
Ramillies itself is steep and broken both to north and
south ; but on the eastern front the ground rises to it
for half a mile in a gentle, unbroken slope, which
modern rifles would make impassable by the bravest
troops.   In rear, or to westward of the French position,
the table-land is clear and unbroken, and to the right
rear or south-west stands a mound or barrow called
the tomb of Ottomond, still conspicuous and still
valuable as a key to the actions of the day.[1] The
full extent of the French front from Taviers to Autréglise covered something over four miles.

Having chosen his position, Villeroy lost no time
in setting his troops in order. His left, consisting of
infantry backed by cavalry,[2] extended from Autréglise
to Offus, both of which villages were strongly occupied.
His centre from Offus to Ramillies was likewise composed of infantry. On his right, in the expanse of
sound ground which stretches for a mile and a half

[1] I have described the field at some length, since the map given
by Coxe is most misleading.
[2] Coxe, by a singular error, makes the left consist exclusively of
infantry, in face of Quincy, Feuquières, the *London Gazette* and
other authorities, thereby missing almost unaccountably an important feature in the action.

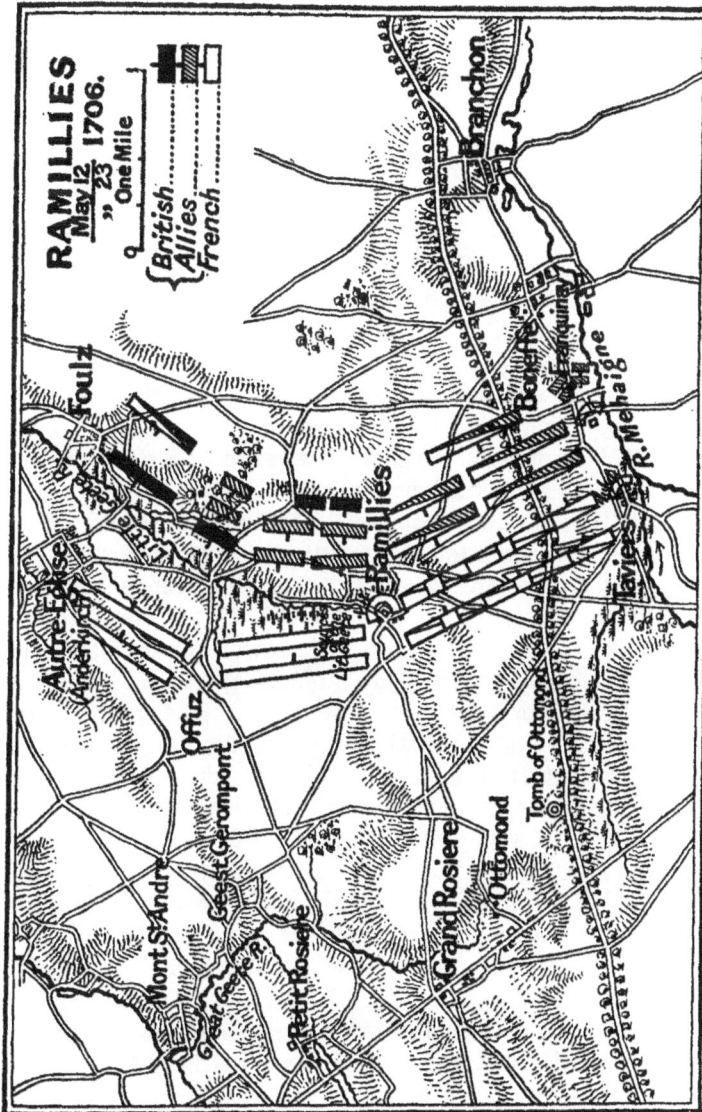

RAMILLIES
May 12 1706.
" 23
One Mile

British ....
Allies ....
French ....

Branchon

Foulz

Autre Eglise
Anderlucht

Offuz

Boss F.

R. Mehaigne

Ramillies

St. Ramillies

Franquiné

Taviers

Geest Geromport

Mont St. Andre

Geest Gerom?

Petit Rossiere

Grand Rosiere

Ottomond

Tomb of Ottomond

Stanford's Geog.l Estab.t London.

from the marshes of the Geete at Ramillies to those
of the Mehaigne, were massed more than one hundred
and twenty squadrons of cavalry with some battalions
of infantry interlined with them, the famous French
Household Cavalry (Maison du Roi) being in the first
line. The left flank of this expanse was covered by
the village of Ramillies, which was surrounded by a
ditch and defended by twenty battalions and twenty-
four guns. On the right flank not only Taviers but
Franquinay, a village still further in advance, were
occupied by detachments of infantry, while Taviers
was further defended by cannon.

Marlborough quickly perceived the defects of
Villeroy's dispositions, which were not unlike those
of Tallard at Blenheim. Taviers was too remote
from Ramillies for the maintenance of a cross-fire of
artillery. Again, the cavalry of the French left was
doubtless secure against attack behind the marshes
of the Geete, but for this very reason it was incapable
of aggressive action. The French right could therefore
be turned, provided that it were not further reinforced ;
and accordingly the Duke opened his manœuvres by
a demonstration against the French left.

Presently the infantry of the Allied right moved
forward in two lines towards Offus and Autréglise,
marching in all the pomp and circumstance of war,
Dutch, Germans, and British, with the red-coats conspicuous on the extreme right flank. Striding forward
to the river they halted and seemed to be very busy
in laying their pontoons. Villeroy marked the mass
of scarlet, and remembering its usual place in the
battlefield, instantly began to withdraw several
battalions from his right and centre to his left. Marlborough watched the white coats streaming away to
their new positions, and after a time ordered the

infantry of his right to fall back to some heights in their rear. The two lines faced about and retired accordingly over the height until the first line was out of sight. Then the second line halted and faced about once more, crowning the ascent with the well-known scarlet, while the first marched away with all speed, under cover of the hill and unseen by the French, to the opposite flank. Many British battalions [1] stood on that height all day without moving a step or firing a shot, but none the less paralysing the French left wing.

About half-past one the guns of both armies opened fire, and shortly afterwards four Dutch battalions were ordered forward to carry Franquinay and Taviers, and twelve more to attack Ramillies, while Overkirk advanced slowly on the left with the cavalry. Franquinay was soon cleared; Taviers resisted stoutly for a time, but was carried; and a strong reinforcement on its way to the village was intercepted and cut to pieces. Then Overkirk, his left flank being now cleared, pushed forward his horse and charged. The Dutch routed the first French line, but were driven back in confusion by the second; and the victorious French were only checked by the advance of fresh squadrons under Marlborough himself. Even so the Allies were at a decided disadvantage; and Marlborough, after despatching messengers to bring up every squadron, except the British, to the left, plunged into the thick of the mêlée to rally the broken horse. He was recognised by some French dragoons, who left their ranks to surround him, and in the general confusion he was borne to the ground and in imminent

1706.

May $\frac{12}{23}$.

---

[1] Apparently the whole of Meredith's brigade, viz.: 1st, 18th, 29th, 37th, 24th, and 10th regiments. The place is still easily identifiable.

danger of capture. His aide-de-camp, Captain Molesworth, dismounted at once, and giving him his own
horse enabled him to escape. The cavalry, however,
encouraged by the Duke's example, recovered themselves, and Marlborough took the opportunity to
shift from Molesworth's horse to his own. Colonel
Bringfield, his equerry, held the stirrup while he
mounted, but Marlborough was hardly in the saddle
before the hand that held the stirrup relaxed its grasp,
and the equerry fell to the ground, his head carried
away by a round shot.[1]

Meanwhile the attack of the infantry on Ramillies
was fully developed, and relieved the horse from the
fire of the village. Twenty fresh squadrons came
galloping up at the top of their speed and ranged themselves in rear of the re-forming lines. But before they
could come into action the Duke of Würtemberg
pushed his Danish horse along the Mehaigne upon the
right flank of the French, while the Dutch guards
advanced still further so as to fall upon their rear.
These last now emerged upon the table-land by the
tomb of Ottomond, and the rest of the Allied horse
dashed themselves once against the French front.
The famous Maison du Roi after a hard fight was cut
to pieces, and the whole of the French horse, despite
Villeroy's efforts to stay them, were driven in headlong
flight across the rear of their line of battle, leaving the
battalions of infantry helpless and alone, to be ridden
over and trampled out of existence.

Villeroy made frantic efforts to bring forward
the cavalry of his left to cover their retreat, but the
ground was encumbered by his baggage, which he had
carelessly posted too close in his rear. The French

[1] Molesworth escaped and was rewarded four years later, at the
age of twenty-two, with a regiment of foot.

troops in Ramillies now gave way, and Marlborough 1706.
ordered the whole of the infantry that was massed May $\frac{12}{23}$
before the village to advance across the morass upon
Offus, with the Third and Sixth Dragoon Guards in
support. The French broke and fled at their approach ;
and meanwhile the Buffs and Twenty-first, which had
so far remained inactive on the right, forced their way
through the swamps before them, and taking Autréglise
in rear swept away the last vestige of the French line
on the left. Five British squadrons followed them
up and captured the entire King's Regiment (Régiment
du Roi). The Third and Sixth Dragoon Guards also
pressed on, and coming upon the Spanish and Bavarian
horse-guards, who were striving to cover the retreat
of the French artillery, charged them and swept
them away, only narrowly missing the capture of the
Elector himself, who was at their head.[1] On this the

[1] ORDER OF BATTLE. RAMILLIES, 12TH-23RD MAY 1706.

Left.
1st Line.

Foreign Infantry.

RIGHT WING ONLY.

15th Foot. Stringer's Foot. Macartney's Foot. Evans's Foot. 21st Royal Scots Fusiliers. 3rd Buffs.

8th Foot. 23rd Royal Welsh. 28th Foot. 26th Cameronians. 16th Foot. 1 Royal Scots. 1 Batt. 1st Guards.

Eighteen Dutch Squadrons. 3rd : : : : 6th 7th 5th

1st Dragoon Guards. : : : :

5th Royal Irish Dragoons. Scots Greys.

Right.

2nd Line.

Foreign Infantry.

10th 24th 37th 29th Foot. 18th Royal Irish. 2nd Batt. Royal Scots. : : :

Foreign Cavalry.

From Kane's *Campaigns.*

1706.
May $\frac{12}{23}$.

whole French army, which so far had struggled to effect an orderly retreat, broke up in panic and fled in all directions.

The mass of the fugitives made for Judoigne ; but the ways were blocked by broken-down baggage-waggons and abandoned guns, and the crush and confusion was appalling. The British cavalry, being quite fresh, quickly took up the pursuit over the table-land. The guns and baggage fell an easy prey, but these were left to others, while the red-coated troopers, not without memories of Landen, pressed on, like hounds running for blood, after the beaten enemy. The chase lay northwards to Judoigne and beyond it towards the refuge of Louvain. Not until two o'clock in the morning did the cavalry pause, having by that time reached Meldert, fifteen miles from the battlefield ; nay, even then Lord Orkney with some few squadrons spurred on to Louvain itself, rekindled the panic and set the unhappy French once more in flight across the Dyle.

May $\frac{13}{24}$.

Nor was the main army far behind the horse. Marching far into the night, the men slept under arms for two or three hours, started again at three o'clock, and before the next noon had also reached Meldert and were preparing to force the passage of the Dyle. Marlborough, who had been in the saddle with little intermission for nearly twenty-eight hours, here wrote to the Queen that he intended to march again that same night ; but, through the desertion of the lines of the Dyle by the French, the army gained some respite.

May $\frac{14}{25}$.

The next day he crossed the Dyle at Louvain and

May $\frac{15}{26}$.

encamped at Betlehem, the next he advanced to Dieghem, a few miles north of Brussels, the next he

May $\frac{16}{27}$.

passed the Senne at Vilvorde and encamped at Grimberghen, and here at last, after six days of incessant

marching, the Duke granted his weary troops a halt, 1706.
while the French, hopelessly beaten and demoralised,
retired with all haste to Ghent.

So ended the fight and pursuit of Ramillies, which
effectually disposed of the taunt levelled at Marlborough
after Blenheim, that he did not know how to improve
a victory. The loss of the French in killed, wounded,
and prisoners was thirteen thousand men, swelled by
desertion during the pursuit to full two thousand more.
The trophies of the victors were eighty standards and
colours, fifty guns, and a vast quantity of baggage.
The loss of the Allies was from four to five thousand
killed and wounded, which fell almost entirely on the
Dutch and Danes, the British, owing to their position
on the extreme right, being but little engaged until
the close of the day. The chief service of the British,
therefore, was rendered in the pursuit, which they
carried forward with relentless thoroughness and
vigour. The Dutch were delighted that their troops
should have done the heaviest of the work in such an
action, and the British could console themselves with
the performance of their cavalry, and above all, with
the reflection that the whole of the success was due
to their incomparable chief.

The effect of the victory and of the rapid advance May-June
that followed it was instantaneous. Louvain and the
whole line of Dyle fell into Marlborough's hands on
the day after the battle ; Brussels, Malines, and Lierre
surrendered before the first halt, and gave him the line
of the Senne and the key of the French entrenchments
about Antwerp ; and one day later, the surrender of
Alost delivered to him one of the strongholds on the
Dender. Never pausing for a moment, he sent forward
a party to lay bridges on the Scheldt below Oudenarde
in order to cut off the French retreat into France, a

1706. movement which obliged Villeroy forthwith to abandon the lines about Ghent and to retire up the Lys to Courtrai. Ghent, Bruges, and Damme thereupon surrendered on the spot ; Oudenarde followed them, and after a few days Antwerp itself. Thus within a fortnight after the victory the whole of Flanders and Brabant, with the exception of Dendermond and one or two places of minor importance, had succumbed to the Allies, and the French had fallen back to their own frontier.

June.   Nor was even this all. A contribution of two million livres levied in French Flanders brought home to the Grand Monarch that the war was now knocking at his own gates. Villars, with the greater part of his army, was recalled from the Rhine to the Lys, and a number of French troops were withdrawn to the same quarter from Italy. Baden had thus the game in his own hand on the Rhine, and though he was too sulky and incapable to turn the advantage to account, yet his inaction was no fault of Marlborough's. We are hardly surprised to find that in the middle of this fortnight the Duke made urgent request for fresh stores of champagne ; he may well have needed the stimulant amid such pressure of work and fatigue.[1]

He now detached Overkirk to besiege Ostend and another party to blockade Dendermond, at the same time sending off five British battalions, which we shall presently meet again, for a descent on the Charente which was then contemplated in England. This done he took post with the rest of the Army at Roulers, to westward of the Lys, whence he could at once cover the siege of Ostend and menace Menin and Ypres. The operations at Ostend were delayed for some time

[1] *Despatches*, vol. ii. p. 554.

through want of artillery and the necessity of waiting 1706.
for the co-operation of the Fleet ; but the trenches
were finally opened on the 17th of June, and a few June $\frac{6}{17}$.
weeks later the town surrendered.

Three days after this the army was reassembled for June 27.
the siege of Menin. This fortress was of peculiar July 8.
strength, being esteemed one of Vauban's masterpieces,
and was garrisoned by five thousand men. Moreover,
the French, being in command of the upper sluices of
the Lys, were able greatly to impede the operations
by cutting off the water from the lower stream, and
thus rendering it less useful for purposes of transport,
But all this availed it little ; for three weeks after
the opening of the trenches Menin surrendered. The Aug. $\frac{11}{22}$.
British battalions [1] which had been kept inactive at
Ramillies took a leading share in the work, and some
of them suffered very heavily ; but they had the
satisfaction of recapturing four of the British guns
that had been taken at Landen.

A few days later Dendermond was attacked in Aug. 25.
earnest and was likewise taken, after which Marl- Sept. 5.
borough fell back across the Scheldt to secure the Sept. $\frac{12}{23}$.
whole line of the Dender by the capture of Ath. Ten
days sufficed for the work, after which Ath also fell Sept. 21.
into the hands of the Allies. The apathy of the Oct. 2.
French throughout these operations sufficiently show
their discouragement. Owing to the supineness of
Prince Lewis of Baden, Villars had been able to bring
up thirty-five thousand men to the assistance of
Marshal Vendôme, who had now superseded Villeroy ;

---

[1] The British regiments regularly employed in the besieging
army were the 8th, 10th, and 18th, and Evans's Foot; the Scots
Greys, 3rd and 6th Dragoon Guards. The total loss of the Allies
was 32 officers and 551 men killed, 83 officers and 1941 men wounded.
The 18th Royal Irish alone lost 15 officers, and in one attack over
100 men in half an hour.

1706. but even with this reinforcement the two commanders only looked on helplessly while Marlborough reduced fortress after fortress before their eyes. They were, indeed, more anxious to strengthen the defences of Mons and Charleroi, lest the Duke should break into France by that line, than to approach him in the field. Nor were they not wholly unreasonable in their anxiety, for Marlborough's next move was upon the Sambre ; but incessant rain and tempestuous weather forbade any further operations, so that Ath proved to be the last conquest of the year. Thus ended the campaign of Ramillies, one of the most brilliant in the annals of war, wherein Marlborough in a single month carried his arms triumphant from the Meuse to the sea.

ALMANZA was a bad opening for the new year, but 1707. worse was to follow. Throughout the winter Marlborough had, as usual, been employed in diplomatic negotiations, which nothing but his skill and fascination could have carried to a successful issue. But on one most important point the Duke was foiled by the treachery of the Emperor, who, to further his own selfish designs on Naples, secretly concluded a treaty with France for the neutrality of Italy, and thus enabled the whole of the French garrisons in Italy to be withdrawn unmolested. The forces thus liberated were at once brought up to the scene of action on the Rhine and in Flanders, and the French were enabled to lead a superior force in the field against Marlborough. Again, the Duke had hoped to save Spain by an invasion of France from the side of Savoy, but this project had been deferred until too late, owing to the Emperor's cupidity for the possession of Naples. Finally, though Prince Lewis of Baden had died during the winter, he had been replaced on the Rhine by a still more incompetent prince, the Margrave of Baireuth, who, far from making any diversion in the Duke's favour, never ceased pestering him to come to his assistance. So flagrant was this deplorable person's incapacity that he too was superseded before the close of the campaign, though too late for any effective purpose. His successor, however, deserves particular notice, being none other than the Elector of Hanover, afterwards our own King George

1707. the First, no genius in the field, but, as shall be seen in due time, an extremely sensible and clear-headed soldier.

The result of these complications was that Marlborough spent the greater part of the summer encamped, in the face of a superior French force, at Meldert, on a branch of the Great Geete, to cover his conquests in Flanders and Brabant. At last the Emperor, having accomplished his desires in Naples, made a diversion towards Provence, which drew away a part of the French force to that quarter and enabled the Duke to move. But then bad weather intervened to prevent any successful operations. Twice Marlborough was within an ace of surprising Vendôme, who had superseded Villeroy in Flanders, and twice the marshal decamped in haste and confusion only just in time to save his army. Even so the Duke would have struck one heavy blow but for the intervention of the Dutch deputies. But fortune favoured the French ; the rain came down in torrents, and the country was poached into such a quagmire by the cavalry that many of the infantry were fairly swallowed up and lost.[1] Thus tamely ended the campaign which should have continued the work of Ramillies.[2]

[1] Parker.

[2] ORDER OF BATTLE. CAMPAIGN OF 1707.

Left.
1st Line.

RIGHT WING ONLY.

Right.

Lord North and Grey's Brigade.	Temple's Brigade.	Meredith's Brigade.		Palmer's Brigade.	Stair's Brigade.
3rd Buffs.	2nd Batt. Royal Scots.	1 Batt. 1st Guards.	Orrery's Foot.	1st Dragoon Guards.	Scots Greys.
21st Royal Scots Fusiliers.	18th Royal Irish.	1 ,, Royal Scots.	Evans's ,,	5th ,,	5th Royal Irish Dragoons.
37th Foot.	Temple's Foot.	16th Foot.		7th ,,	
26th Cameronians.	24th Foot.	23rd Royal Welsh.	3rd ,,	6th ,,	
15th Foot.	10th ,,	8th Foot.		3rd ,,	
Gore's ,,		Foreign horse.			

No British in the Second Line.

Postboy 26th June 1707.

Returning home in November Marlborough found 1707. difficulties almost as great as he had left behind him in Flanders. There were quarrels in the Cabinet, already foreboding the time when the Queen and the people should turn against him. The Court of France was reverting to its old methods and endeavouring to divide England by providing the Pretender with a force for invasion. Again the hardships of the campaign in Flanders and the defeat of Almanza had not only created discontent, but had enormously increased the demand for recruits. The evil work of the Dutch deputies and the incorrigible selfishness and jealousy of the Empire had already prolonged the war beyond the limit assigned by the short patience of the English people.

Happily Parliament was for the present still loyal to the war, and voted not only the usual supplies but money for an additional ten thousand men. Five new battalions [1] were raised, and three more of the old establishment were detailed for service in Flanders.[2] But far more satisfactory was the fact that in 1708 all regiments took the field with new colours, bearing the cross of St. Andrew blended with that of St. George, pursuant to the first article of the Treaty of Union, passed in the previous year, between England and Scotland.

The early spring of 1708 was wasted by the French 1708. in a futile endeavour to set the Pretender afoot in Scotland with a French force at his back ; nor was it until the 9th of April that Marlborough sailed for Mar. 29. the Hague, where Eugene was already awaiting him. April 9. There the two agreed that the Duke should as usual

---

[1] Slane's, Brazier's, Delaune's, Jones's, Carles's, all raised in September.
[2] Mixed battalion of Guards, 19th Foot, Prendergast's (late Orrery's).

1708. command in Flanders, while Eugene should take charge of an army on the Moselle, nominally for operations on that river, but in reality to unite with Marlborough by a rapid march and give battle to the French before they could call in their remoter detachments. There was a considerable difficulty with the Elector of Hanover, who was to command on the Rhine, owing to his jealousy of Eugene ; but this trouble was satisfactorily settled, as were all troubles of the time, by the intervention of Marlborough. Thereupon the Electoral Prince, true to the quarrelsome traditions of his family, at · once insisted on taking service with Eugene, simply for the sake of annoying his father ; thus adding one more to the many causes of friction which, but for Marlborough, would soon have brought the Grand Alliance to a standstill. This Electoral Prince will become better known to us as King George the Second.

The French on their part had made extraordinary exertions in the hope of a successful campaign. Since Ramillies they had drawn troops from all quarters to Flanders ; and from thenceforth the tendency in every succeeding year grew stronger for all operations to centre in that familiar battle-ground. On the Rhine the Elector of Bavaria held command, with Berwick, much exalted since Almanza, to help him. The French main army in Flanders numbered little less than a hundred thousand men, and was under the orders of Vendôme, with the Duke of Burgundy in supreme command. The presence of the heir to the throne, of his brother the Duke of Berry, and of the Chevalier de St. George, as the Pretender called himself, all portended an unusual effort.

May.   Marching up at the end of May from their rendezvous on the south of the Haine, the French army moved

north to the forest of Soignies. Marlborough thereupon 1708.
at once concentrated at Hal and summoned Eugene
to him with all haste. His own army numbered but
eighty thousand men, and, though as usual he showed
a bold front, he knew that such disparity of numbers
was serious. The French then manœuvred towards
Waterloo as if to threaten Louvain, a movement which
the Duke met by a forced march to Park on the Dyle.
Here he remained perforce inactive for a whole month, May 24.
waiting for Eugene, who was delayed by some petty June 4.
                                                      to
formalities which were judged by the Imperial Court June 24.
to be far more important than military operations. July 5.
Suddenly, on the night of the 4th of July, the French June 23.
                                                       July 4.
broke up their camp, marched westward to cross the
Senne at Hal and detached small corps against Bruges
and Ghent. Unable to meet the Allies with the sword,
the French had substituted gold for steel and had for
some time been tampering with the new authorities
in these towns. The gold had done its work. Within
twenty-four hours Ghent and Bruges had opened their
gates, and the keys to the navigation of the Scheldt
and Lys were lost.

Marlborough, who was quite ready for a march, was June 24.
                                                     July 5.
up and after the French army immediately. At two
o'clock in the morning his army was in motion, streaming off to pass the Senne at Anderlecht. The march
was long and severe, the roads being in so bad a state
that the right wing did not reach its halting-ground
until six o'clock in the evening, nor the left wing till
two o'clock on the following morning ; but this great
effort brought the Allies almost within reach of the
French army. In the night, intelligence was brought June 25.
to Marlborough that the enemy was turning back to July 6.
fight him. He was in the saddle at once, to form his
line of battle ; but the news was false. The French in

G

1708. reality were making off as fast as they could ; and, before the truth could reach Marlborough, they were across the Dender. Marlborough's cavalry was instantly on their track, but could do no more than capture a few hundred prisoners, together with most of the French baggage. That same day came definite information of the loss of Ghent and Bruges, and of the investment of the citadel of Ghent. Brussels took the alarm at once. The French, as they feared, had for once got the better of the Duke. The French army was encamped at Alost, where, like a king between two pieces at draughts, it threatened both the citadel of Ghent and Brussels ; and all was panic in the capital. The Duke was fain to move on to Assche, midway between Alost and Brussels, to restore the confidence of the fearful city.

Here Eugene joined him. Finding it hopeless to arrive in time with his army, the Prince had pushed on alone ; nor could he have arrived more opportunely, for Marlborough was so much weakened by an attack of fever that he was hardly fit for duty. It was indeed a trying moment. The next design of the French was evidently aimed at Oudenarde for the recovery of the line of the Scheldt. They were already across the Dender and ahead of Marlborough on the road to it, and moreover had broken down the bridges behind them ; yet the Duke dared not move lest he should expose Brussels. He sent orders to the Governor of Ath to collect as many troops as possible, and to throw himself into Oudenarde, which that officer punctually did ; and then there was nothing to be done but to wait. Two days sufficed to place the citadel of Ghent in the hands of the French, and to set their army free for further operations. Accordingly on the 9th of July Vendôme sent forward detachments to invest

Oudenarde, and moved with the main army up the 1708. Dender to Lessines, from which point he intended to cover the siege. Great was his astonishment on approaching the town on the following day to find that Marlborough had arrived there before him, and was not only within reach of Oudenarde, but interposed between him and his own frontier.

For at two o'clock on the morning of the 9th of July the Allied army had marched off in beautiful order in five columns, and by noon had covered fifteen miles to Herfelingen on the road to the Dender. Four hours later Cadogan was sent forward with eight battalions and as many squadrons to occupy Lessines and throw bridges over the Dender ; and, when tattoo beat that night, the army silently entered on a march of thirteen further miles to the same point. Before dawn came June 29. the welcome intelligence that Cadogan had reached his July 10. destination at midnight, laid his bridges, and made his dispositions to cover the passage of the troops. The army tramped on, always in perfect order, crossed the river and was taking up its camping-ground, when the heads of the enemy's columns appeared on the distant heights and were seen first to halt and then to retire. Marlborough on the curve of the arc had outmarched Vendôme on the chord.

The French, finding the whole of their plans disconcerted, now wheeled about north-westward towards Gavre on the Scheldt, to shelter themselves behind the river and bar the advance of the Allies on Bruges. But the Duke had no intention to let them off so easily. Burgundy and Vendôme were not on good terms ; their differences had already caused considerable confusion in the army ; and Marlborough was fully aware of the fact. At dawn on the morning of the 11th the June 30. unwearied Cadogan started off with some eleven July 11.

thousand men [1] and twenty-four guns, to prepare the
roads, construct bridges, and make dispositions to
cover the passage of the Scheldt below Oudenarde.
By half-past ten he had reached the river, just above
the village of Eyne, and on ascending the low heights
above the stream and looking westward he saw before
him a kind of shallow basin or amphitheatre, seamed
by little ditches and rivulets, and broken by hedges
and enclosures. To the south the rising ground on
which he stood swept round almost to the glacis of
Oudenarde, thence curved westward from the village
of Bevere into another broad hill, called the Boser
Couter, to the village of Oycke and beyond, turned
from thence northward across the valley of the river
Norken to Huysse, from which point trending still to
northward it died away in the marshes of the Scheldt.
Near Oycke two small streams rise which, after pursuing for some way a parallel course, unite to run down
into the Scheldt at Eyne ; beyond them the Norken
flows beneath the heights of Huysse in a line parallel
to the Scheldt.

Presently parties of French horse appeared on the
ground to the north. Vendôme's advanced-guard,
under the Marquis of Biron, had crossed the Scheldt
leisurely at Gavre, six miles farther down the river, and
was now moving across his front with foragers out, in
happy unconsciousness of the presence of an enemy.
A dash of Cadogan's squadrons upon the foragers
quickly brought Biron to Eyne and beyond it, where
he caught sight of Cadogan's detachment of scarlet and
blue battalions guarding the bridge, and presently of a
body of cavalry in the act of crossing ; for Marlborough,

---

[1] 16 battalions and 30 squadrons. In these were included the
brigades of Sabine, viz., 8th, 18th, 23rd, 37th ; of Evans, viz.,
Orrery's, Evans's, and two foreign battalions ; and of Plattenberg,
which included the Scottish regiments in the Dutch service.

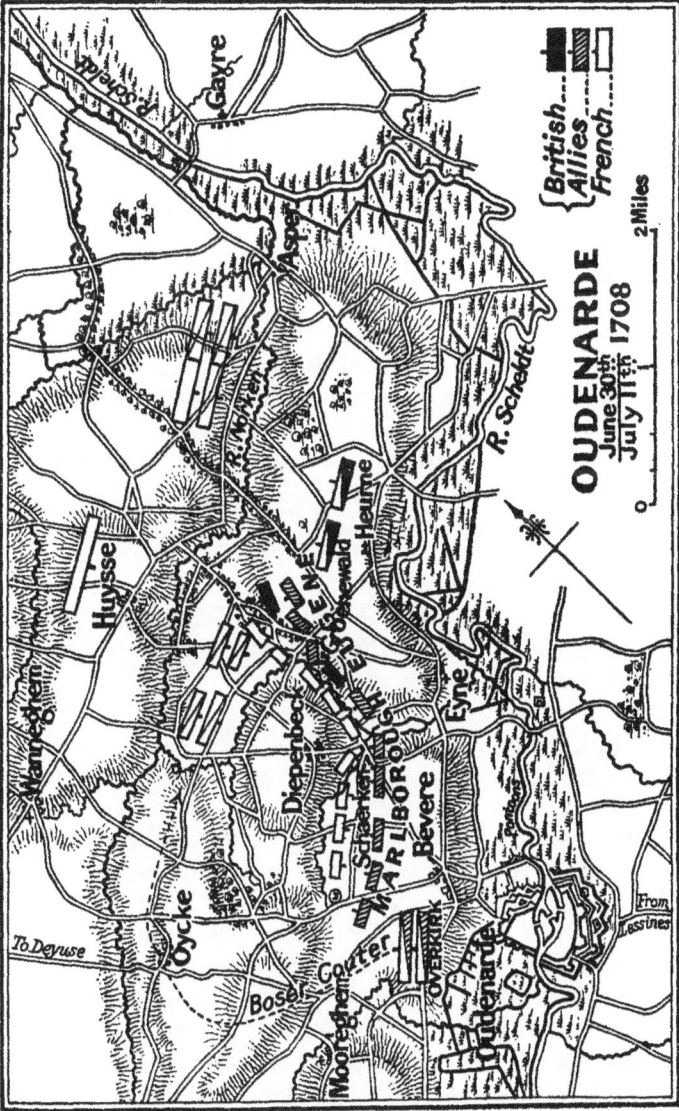

OUDENARDE
June 30th
July 11th 1708

British
Allies
French

2 Miles

Stanford's Geog.¹ Estab.¹ London.

R. Scheldt

Gavre

Marca d

Asper

Ringheim

Heurne

Boisenwald

E I N E

Diepenbeck

Huysse

Wannegham

Schaerken

MARLBOROUGH

Bevere

Eyne

Dycke

Mooreghem

OVERKIRK

Bosel Couter

Oudenarde

To Deyuse

From
Lessines

1708.
June 30.
July 11.

uneasy while his advanced-guard was still in the air, had caught up a column of Prussian horse and galloped forward with it in all haste.   Biron at once reported what he had seen to Vendôme, who, perceiving that the mass of the Allied army was still on the wrong side of the Scheldt, gave orders to take up a position parallel to the river ; the line to rest its left on the village of Heurne and extend by Eyne and Beveren to Mooregem on the right.   In pursuance of his design he directed seven battalions to occupy Heurne forthwith ; but at this point the Duke of Burgundy interposed.   The heights of Huysse in rear of the Norken from Asper to Wannegem formed in his judgment a preferable position ; and there, two miles from the Scheldt, he should form his line of battle, facing south-east.   So the army was guided to the left bank of the Norken, while the seven battalions, obeying what they conceived to be their orders, marched down to the village not of Heurne but of Eyne, and backed by a few squadrons, took up the position assigned to them by Vendôme.

Meanwhile, responding to urgent messages from Marlborough, the main body of the Allies was hurrying forward, and by two o'clock the head of the infantry had reached the Scheldt.   Part of the cavalry passed through Oudenarde to take advantage of the town bridge ; the foot began to cross by the pontoons, and Cadogan, who had marked the march of the French into Eyne, at once summoned the whole of his advanced-guard across to the left bank.   Sabine's brigade, supported by the other two, crossed the rivulet against Eyne, while the Hanoverian cavalry moved up to the rear of the village and cut off all hope of retreat. Presently Sabine's British were hotly engaged ; but the French made only a poor resistance.   It is the

weakness of the French soldier that he apprehends too
quickly when his officers have not given him a fair
chance. Three battalions out of the seven were captured
entire, the remaining four were killed or taken piecemeal in their flight. The cavalry, flushed by their
success, then advanced under Prince George against
the few French squadrons in rear of the village, charged
them, routed them, and drove them across the Norken.
The Prince had his horse shot under him in this
encounter, for his family has never wanted for courage,
and he remembered the day of Oudenarde to the end
of his life.

The Duke of Burgundy now determined upon a
general action, and made every preparation for defence
of the position behind the Norken. But when four
o'clock came and the Allied army was not yet in order
of battle, he changed his plan, pushed a body of cavalry
from his right across the stream, and set the whole of
his centre and right in motion to advance likewise.
Marlborough, perceiving the movement, judged that
the attack would be directed against his left, in the
hope that Cadogan's battalions about Eyne would be
left isolated and open to be crushed by an advance of
the French left. Two of Cadogan's regiments, Prussians,
which had been pushed forward half a mile beyond
Eyne to Groenewald, were at once reinforced by twelve
more of the advanced-guard ; the British cavalry was
formed up on the heights at Bevere, and the Prussian
horse further to the Allied right near Heurne. No
more could be done until the rest of the army should
gradually cross the river which divided it from the
battlefield.

At length about five o'clock thirty French battalions
debouched upon Groenewald, which was as yet held
only by Cadogan's two advanced regiments, and began

the attack.   The Prussians stuck to their post gallantly
and held their own among the hedges, until presently
Cadogan's reinforcement, and later on twenty more
battalions under the Duke of Argyll,[1] came up to their
assistance.   Forming in succession on the left of the
Prussians as they reached the fighting line, these regiments extended the field of action as far south as
Schaerken ; and the combat was carried on with great
spirit.   The ground was so strongly enclosed that the
fight resolved itself into duels of battalions, the cream
of the infantry on both sides being engaged.   At one
moment the French outflanked the left of the Allies
and drove them back, but fresh battalions of Marlborough's army kept constantly streaming into action,
which recovered the lost ground and prolonged the line
of fire always further to the south.

Marlborough and Eugene, who had hitherto remained together, now parted, and the Duke handing
over eighteen battalions to the Prince entrusted him
with the command of the right.   This accession of
strength enabled Eugene to relieve Cadogan's corps,
which had yielded ground somewhat before Groenewald, and even to pierce through the first line of the
enemy's infantry.   General Natzmar thereupon seized
the moment to throw the Prussian cavalry against the
second line.   His squadrons were received with a biting
fire from the hedges as they advanced ; and the French
Household Cavalry, watching the favourable moment
for a charge, drove back the Prussians with very heavy
loss.

Meanwhile Marlborough with the Hanoverian and
Dutch infantry was pressing forward slowly on his left,
the French fighting with great stubbornness and
gallantry, and contesting every inch of ground from

---

[1] Among them the Royal Scots and Buffs.

hedge to hedge.   At last the enemy, being forced back 1708.
to Diepenbeck, a few hundred yards in rear of Schaerken, June 30.
stood fast, and refused, despite all the Duke's efforts, July 11.
to give way another foot.   But Marlborough had still
twenty battalions of Dutch and Danes with almost
the entire cavalry of the left at his disposal, and he had
noticed that the French right flank rested on the air.
He now directed Marshal Overkirk to lead these troops
under cover of the Boser Couter round the French
right and to fall with them upon the enemy's rear.
The gallant old Dutchman, though infirm and sick unto
death, joyfully obeyed.   Two brigades were thrown
at once on the flank of the troops that were so stoutly
opposing Marlborough ;   while the cavalry advanced
quickly on the reverse slope of the Boser Couter,[1] and
then wheeling to the right, fell on the rear of the unsuspecting French.   A part of the Household Cavalry
and some squadrons of dragoons tried bravely to stand
their ground, but they were borne back and swept
away.   Overkirk's troops pressed rapidly on ;   and the
French right was fairly surrounded on all sides.

Now at last an effort was made to bring forward the
French left, which, through Burgundy's perversity or
for some inscrutable reason, had been left motionless
on the other side of the Norken ;   but it was too late.
The infantry, though led by Vendôme himself, failed to
make the slightest impression, and the cavalry dared
not advance.   The ground before them was intricate
and swampy, and the whole of the British cavalry, withdrawn from their first position by Eugene, stood waiting
to plunge down upon them directly they should move.
The daylight faded and the night came on, but the
musketry flashed out incessantly in an ever-narrowing

[1] That is to say, on the western side of the road from Oudenarde
to Deynze.

girdle of fire, as the Allies wound themselves closer and
closer round the enveloped French right.   At length
at nine o'clock Marlborough and Eugene, fearful lest
their own troops should engage each other in the darkness, with some difficulty enforced the order to halt and
cease firing.   Vast numbers of the French seized the
moment to escape, but presently all the drums of the
Allies began with one accord to beat the French retreat,
while the Huguenot officers shouted " À moi, Picardie !
À moi, Roussillon ! " to gather the relics of the scattered
regiments of the enemy around them.   In this way
some thousands of prisoners were gleaned, though the
harvest which would have been reaped in another hour
of daylight was lost.   In the French army all was
confusion.   Vendôme tried in vain to keep the troops
together till the morning, but Burgundy gave the word
for retreat ; and the whole mass ran off in disorder
towards Ghent.

So ended the battle of Oudenarde, presenting on
one side a feature rare in these days, namely, a general
engagement without an order of battle.[1]   It was undoubtedly the most hazardous action that Marlborough
ever fought.   His troops were much harassed by forced
marches.   They had started at two o'clock on Monday
morning and had covered fifty miles, including the
passage of two rivers, when they came into action at
two o'clock on Wednesday afternoon.   It would be
reckoned no small feat in these days to move eighty
thousand men over fifty miles in sixty hours, but in
those days of bad roads and heavy packs the effort
must have been enormous.   Finally, the army had to
pass the Scheldt in the face of the enemy, and ran no
small risk of being destroyed in detail.   Yet the hazard

[1] The ground, though drained and built over about Bevere, seems
to have lost little of its original character, and is worth a visit.

was probably less than it now seems to us, and generals in our own day have not hesitated to risk similar peril with success. The French commanders were at variance ; the less competent of them, being heir-apparent, was likely to be toadied by officers and supported by them against their better judgment ; and, finally, the entire French army was very much afraid of Marlborough. Notwithstanding their slight success in Ghent and Bruges, their elation had evaporated speedily when they found the Duke before them at Lessines. All this Marlborough knew well ; and he knew also that, if an impromptu action (if one may use the term) must be fought, there was not a man on the French side who had an eye for a battlefield comparable to Eugene's or his own. The event justified his calculations ; for the victory was one of men who knew their own minds over men who did not. Another hour of daylight, so Marlborough declared, would have enabled him to finish the war. The total loss of the Allies in the battle was about three thousand killed and wounded, the British infantry, though early engaged, suffering but little, while the British cavalry, being employed to watch the inactive French left, hardly suffered at all.[1] The French lost six thousand killed and wounded and nine thousand prisoners only, but they were thoroughly shaken and demoralised for the remainder of the campaign. The wearied army of the Allies lay on its arms on the battlefield, while Marlborough and Eugene waited impatiently for the dawn. As soon as it was light, forty squadrons, for the most part British, were sent forward in pursuit, while Eugene returned to his own army to hasten its march and to collect material for a siege. The main army halted to rest for two days

[1] British losses : 4 officers and 49 men killed, 17 officers and 160 men wounded.

1708. where it lay, during which time the intelligence came
July $\frac{1}{12}$. that Berwick had been summoned with his army from
the Moselle, and was marching with all haste to occupy
certain lines constructed by the French to cover their
July $\frac{2\text{-}3}{13\text{-}14}$. frontier from Ypres to the Lys. At midnight fifty
squadrons and thirty battalions under Count Lottum,
a distinguished Prussian officer, started for these lines ;
the whole army followed at daybreak, and, while on the
march, the Duke received the satisfactory news that
Lottum had captured the lines without difficulty.
Next day the whole of Marlborough's army was camped
along the Lys between Menin and Commines, within
the actual territory of France.

Detached columns were at once sent out to forage
and levy contributions. The suburbs of Arras were
burnt, and no effort was spared to bring home to the
French that war was hammering at their own gates.
But the Allies were still doubtful as to the operations
that they should next undertake. So long as the
French held Bruges and Ghent they held also the
navigation of the Scheldt and Lys, so that it was of
vital importance to tempt Vendôme, if possible, to
evacuate those towns. The British Government was
preparing a force [1] under General Erle for a descent
upon Normandy by sea, and Marlborough was for
co-operating with this expedition, masking the fortress
of Lille, and penetrating straight into France—a plan
which the reader should, if possible, bear in mind.
But the proposal was too adventurous to meet with
the approval of the Dutch, and was judged impractic-
able even by Eugene unless Lille were first captured
as a place of arms. Ultimately it was decided, not-

[1] The force consisted of detachments of the 3rd and 4th
Dragoons (now Hussars), 12th, 29th, Hamilton's, Dormer's,
Johnson's, Moore's, Caulfield's, Townsend's, Wynne's Foot.

withstanding the closing of the Scheldt and Lys, to 1708. undertake the siege of Lille ; and all the energies of July. the Allies were turned to the collection of sixteen thousand horses to haul the siege-train overland from Brussels.

During the enforced inaction of the army for the next few weeks, the monotony was broken only by the arrival of a distinguished visitor, Augustus the Strong, Elector of Saxony and King of Poland, together with one of his three hundred and sixty-four bastards, a little boy of twelve named Maurice, who had run away from school to join the army. We shall meet with this boy again as a man of fifty, under the name of Marshal Saxe, at a village some twenty miles distant called Fontenoy. '

At length the preparations for the siege were complete, and the huge convoy set out from Brussels for its long march. Now, if ever, was the time for the French to strike a blow. Vendôme in the north at Ghent and Berwick in the south at Douay had, between them, one hundred and ten thousand men : the distance to be traversed by the convoy was seventy-five miles, and the way was barred by the Dender and the Scheldt. Such, however, was the skill with which the march was conducted that the French never succeeded even in threatening the vast, unwieldy columns, which duly reached their destination without the loss even of a Aug. $\frac{1}{12}$. single waggon. Of all the achievements of Marlborough and Eugene, this seems to have been judged by contemporary military men to be the greatest.[1]

Lille, the capital of French Flanders, was one of the early conquests of Lewis the Fourteenth, and, if the expression may be allowed, the darling town of the Court of Versailles. Situated in a swampy plain and

[1] See, for instance, the commendations of Feuquières.

1708. watered by two rivers, the Deule and Marque, its natural position presented difficulties of no ordinary kind to a besieging force ; and, in addition, it had been fortified by Vauban with his utmost skill. The garrison, which had been strengthened by Berwick, amounted to fifteen thousand men, under the command of brave old Marshal Boufflers, who had solicited the honour of defending the fortress. To the north, as we have seen, lay Vendôme, and to the south Berwick, with a joint force now amounting to about ninety-four thousand men.[1] It was for Marlborough and Eugene with an inferior strength of eighty-four thousand men [2] to hold them at bay and to take one of the strongest fortresses in the world before their eyes.

A detailed account even of so famous a siege would be wearisome, the more so since the proportion of British troops detailed for regular work in the trenches was but five battalions,[3] but there are a few salient features which cannot be omitted. The point selected for attack was the north side, the first advance to which was opened by a single English soldier, Sergeant Littler of the First Guards,[4] who swam across the Marquette to a French post, which commanded the passage of the stream, and let down the drawbridge. Aug. $\frac{2}{13}$. Two days later the town was fully invested, and Marlborough took post with the covering army at Helchin on the Scheldt.

[1] 135 battalions, 260 squadrons.

[2] 122 battalions, 230 squadrons.

[3] These were, according to a contemporary plan (Fricx), the 16th, 18th, 21st, 23rd, 24th Foot.

[4] He is claimed as a Guardsman by General Hamilton (*Hist. Grenadier Guards*), though Millner assigns him to the 16th Foot. This is the only name of a man below the rank of a commissioned officer that I have encountered in any of the books on the wars of Marlborough, not excluding the works of Sergeants Deane and Millner. Littler was deservedly rewarded with a commission.

The investment had not been accomplished for 1708. more than a fortnight, when the Duke was informed that Berwick and Vendôme were advancing towards the Dender to unite their forces at Lessines. After manœuvring at first to hinder the junction Marlborough finally decided to let it come to pass, being satisfied that, if the French designed to relieve Lille, they could not penetrate to it in the face of his army on the east side, but must go round and approach the city from the south. In this case, as both armies would move in concentric circles around Lille as a centre, Marlborough, being nearer to that centre, could be certain of reaching any given point on the way to it before the French. Moreover, the removal of the enemy from the east to the south would free the convoys from Brussels from all annoyance on their march to the siege.

As he had expected, the French moved south to Aug. 22. Tournay, and then wheeling northward entered the Sept. 2. plain of Lille, where they found Marlborough and Eugene drawn up ready to receive them.[1] Vendôme and Berwick had positive orders to risk a battle ; and there had been much big talk of annihilating the Allies. Yet face to face with their redoubtable enemies they hesitated. Finally, after a week's delay, which enabled Marlborough greatly to strengthen his position by entrenchment, they advanced as if to attack in earnest, but withdrew ignominiously after a useless cannonade, without accepting battle. Had not Marlborough and Eugene been restrained by the Dutch deputies, the marshals would have had a battle forced

[1] The Allied order of battle was peculiar. The artillery was all drawn up in front, in rear of it came a first line of 100 squadrons, then a second line of 80 squadrons, then a third line of 104 battalions, with wings of 14 squadrons more thrown out to the right and left rear. *Daily Courant*, 6th September 1708.

1708. on them whether they liked it or not, but, as things were, they were permitted to retire. To such depth of humiliation had Marlborough reduced the proud and gallant French army.

Aug. 27-28.
Sept. 7-8.

The retreat left Eugene free to press the siege with vigour ; but a great assault, which cost him three thousand men,[1] failed to give him the advantage for which he had hoped ; and a week later Marlborough was called in from the covering army to give assistance.

Sept. 19-20.
30-31.

For the next attack, on the counterscarp, the Duke lent the Prince five thousand English, and it is said that English and French never fought more worthily of their reputation than on that day ; but the assault was thrice repelled, and it was only through the exertions of Eugene himself that a portion of the works was at last captured, after a desperate effort and at frightful expense of life. Altogether the siege was not going well. The engineers had made blunders ; a vast number of men had been thrown away to no purpose ; and ammunition and stores were beginning to run short. Lastly, Boufflers maintained always a very grand and extremely able defence.

Vendôme and Berwick could now think of no better expedient than to throw themselves into strong positions along the Scarpe and Scheldt, from Douay to Ghent, in order to cut off all convoys from Brussels. But Marlborough was prepared for this, and had not captured Ostend after Ramillies for nothing. England held command of the sea ; and Erle's expedition, which had effected little or nothing on the coast of Normandy, was at hand to help in the transport of supplies from the new base. Erle, who had consider-

---

[1] The five English regiments lost about 350 killed and wounded in this assault. This would mean probably from a fifth to a sixth of their numbers. *Daily Courant*, 6th September 1708.

able talent for organisation, soon set Ostend in order, 1708.
seized two passages over the Nieuport Canal at Leffinghe
and Oudenburg, and prepared to send off his first
convoy. As its arrival was of vital importance to the
maintenance of the siege, the French were as anxious
to intercept as the English to forward it. Vendôme Sept.$\frac{16}{27}$.
accordingly sent off Count de la Mothe with twenty-
two thousand men to attack it on its way, while
Marlborough despatched twelve battalions and
fifteen hundred horse to Ostend itself, twelve battalions more under General Webb to Thourout,
and eighteen squadrons under Cadogan to Roulers,
at two different points on the road, to help it to its
destination.

The convoy started at night; and in the morning Sept. $\frac{17}{28}$.
Cadogan sent forward Count Lottum with a hundred
and fifty horse to meet it. At noon Lottum returned
to Thourout with the intelligence that he had struck
against the advanced guard of a French force at
Ichtegem, two miles beyond Wynendale and some
four miles from Thourout, on the road to Ostend.
Webb at once collected every battalion within his
reach, twenty-two in all, and marched with all
speed for Ichtegem, with Lottum's squadron in
advance. The horse, however, on emerging from
the defile of Wynendale, found the enemy advancing towards them into the plains that lay beyond
it. Lottum retired slowly, skirmishing, while Webb
pushed on and posted his men in two lines at the
entrance to the defile. The strait was bounded on
either hand by a wood, and in each of these woods
Webb stationed a battalion of Germans to take the
French in flank. The dispositions were hardly complete when the enemy came up and opened fire from
nineteen pieces of artillery. Lottum and his handful

H

of horse then retired, while just in the nick of time three more battalions reached Webb from the rear and formed his third line.

The French cannonade was prolohged for nearly two hours, but with little effect, for Webb had ordered his men to lie down. At length at five o'clock the French advanced in four lines of infantry, backed by as many of horse and dragoons. They came on with great steadiness and entered the space between the two woods, with their flanks almost brushing the covert as they passed, serenely unconscious of the peril that awaited them. Then from right and left a staggering volley crashed into them from the battalions concealed among the trees. Both flanks shrank back from the fire, and huddled themselves in confusion upon their centre. De la Mothe sent forward some dragoons in support ; and the foot, recovering themselves, pressed on against the lines before them. So vigorous was their attack that they broke through two battalions of the first line ; but, the gap being instantly filled from the second, they were forced back. Again they struggled forward, trusting by the sheer weight of eight lines against two to sweep their enemy away. But the eternal fire on front and flank became unendurable, and, notwithstanding the blows and entreaties of their officers, the eight lines broke up in confusion, while Webb's battalions, coolly advancing by platoons " as if they were at exercise," poured volley after volley into them as they retired. Cadogan, who had hastened up with a few squadrons to the sound of the firing, was anxious to charge the broken troops, but his force was considered too weak ; and thus after two hours of hot conflict ended the combat of Wynendale. The French engaged therein numbered almost double of the Allies, and lost close on three thousand men, while the Allies lost rather less than a thousand of all ranks. The 1708. signal incapacity displayed by the French commander did not lessen the credit of Webb, and Wynendale was reckoned one of the most brilliant little affairs of the whole war.[1]

The safe arrival of the convoy before Lille raised the hope of the besiegers ; and Vendôme, now fully alive to the importance of cutting off communication with Ostend, marched towards that side with a considerable force, and opening the dykes laid the whole country under water. Marlborough went quickly after him, but the marshal would not await his coming ; and the Duke, by means of high-wheeled vehicles and punts, contrived to overcome the difficulties caused by the inundation. At last, after a siege of sixty days the Oct. $\frac{11}{22}$. town capitulated ; and the garrison retired into the citadel, where Eugene proceeded to beleaguer it anew.

While the new siege was going forward, the Elector of Bavaria arrived on the scene from the Rhine, from whence the apathy of the Elector of Hanover had most unpardonably allowed him to withdraw, and laid siege Nov. $\frac{13}{24}$. to Brussels with fifteen thousand men. This was an entirely new complication ; and, since the French held the line of the Scheldt in force, it was difficult to see

---

[1] I have failed, in spite of much search, to identify the British regiments present, excepting one battalion of the 1st Royals. Marlborough, as Thackeray has reminded us by a famous scene in *Esmond*, attributed the credit of the action in his first despatch to Cadogan. Another letter, however, which appeared in the *Gazette* three days later (23rd September), does full justice to Webb, as does also a letter from the Duke to Lord Sunderland of 18th-29th September (*Despatches*, vol. iv. p. 243). Webb's own version of the affair appeared in the *Gazette* of 9th October, but does not mention the regiments engaged. Webb became a celebrated bore with his stories of Wynendale, but the story of his grievance against Marlborough would have been forgotten but for Thackeray, who either ignored or was unaware of the second despatch.

1708. how Marlborough could parry the blow. Fortunately the garrison defended itself with great spirit, the English regiments [1] setting a fine example ; and the Duke, in no wise dismayed, laid his plans with his usual secrecy and decision. Spreading reports, which he confirmed by feint movements, that he was about to place his troops in cantonments, he marched suddenly and silently east-

Nov. $\frac{15}{26}$. ward on the night of the 26th of November, crossed the Scheldt at two different points before the enemy knew that he was near them, took a thousand prisoners, and then remitting the bulk of his force to the siege of Lille, pushed on with a detachment of cavalry and two

Nov. $\frac{17}{28}$. battalions of English Guards to Alost. On his arrival he learned that the Elector had raised the siege of Brussels and marched off with precipitation. The bare name of Marlborough had been sufficient to scare him away.

Meanwhile Eugene's preparations before the citadel of Lille were in rapid progress, and Marlborough was already maturing plans for a further design before the close of the campaign. It had been the earnest desire of both commanders to reduce Boufflers to uncondi-

Nov. 28. tional surrender ; but time was an object, so on the
Dec. 9. 9th of December the gallant old marshal and his heroic garrison marched out with the honours of war. So ended the memorable siege of Lille. It had cost the garrison eight thousand men, or more than half of its numbers, and the Allies no fewer than fourteen thousand men. The honours of the struggle rested decidedly with Boufflers, and were paid to him by none more ungrudgingly than Marlborough and Eugene. Yet as an operation of war, conducted under extraordinary difficulties in respect of transport, under the eyes of a superior force and subject to diversions, such

[1] Notably Prendergast's. *Gazette*, 25th November.

as that of the Elector of Bavaria, this siege remains 1708. one of the highest examples of consummate military skill.

The fall of Lille was a heavy blow for France, but it was not the last of the campaign. Within eight days Marlborough and Eugene had invested Ghent, which after a brief resistance surrendered with the honours of war. The capitulation of Bruges quickly followed, and the navigation of the Scheldt and Lys having been regained, the two commanders at last sent their troops into winter quarters.

But even this did not close the sum of English successes for 1708. From the Mediterranean had come news of another conquest, due to the far-seeing eye and far-reaching hand of Marlborough. Early in the year Galway had withdrawn from Catalonia to Lisbon, and the command in Catalonia had been given at Marlborough's instance to Field-Marshal von Staremberg, an Imperial officer of much experience and deservedly high reputation. Staremberg, however, could do little with but ten thousand men against the Bourbon's army of twice his strength ; so by Marlborough's advice the troops were used to second the operations of the Mediterranean squadron. Sardinia, the first point aimed at, was captured almost without resistance ; and the fleet then sailed for Minorca. Here somewhat more opposition was encountered ; but after less than a fortnight's work, creditably managed by Major-general Stanhope, the Island was taken at a trifling cost of life.[1] Thus the English gained their Sept. $\frac{13}{24}$. first port in the Mediterranean ; and the news of the capture of Minorca reached London on the same day as that of the fall of Lille.

---

[1] The British troops employed were the 6th Foot, 600 marines, and a battalion of seamen.

1708.   NOTE.—I have been unable to discover any Order of Battle for the campaign of 1708.   The regiments that bear the name of Oudenarde on their appointments are the 1st, 3rd, 5th, 6th, and 7th Dragoon Guards, the 2nd Dragoons, 5th Lancers, Grenadier Guards, Coldstream Guards, 1st, 3rd, 8th, 10th, 15th, 16th, 18th, 21st, 23rd, 24th, 26th, 37th Foot.

VOL. I. BOOK VI. CHAPTER VIII

THE successes of the past campaign were sufficient to 1708. put the British Parliament in good humour, and to prompt it to vote a further increase of ten thousand German mercenaries for the following year. Nevertheless political troubles were increasing, and there were already signs that the rule of Godolphin and Marlborough was in danger. The death of the Prince Consort had been a heavy blow to the Duke. Prince George may have deserved Lord Macaulay's character for impenetrable stupidity, but there can be little doubt that his heavy phlegmatic character was of infinite service to steady the weak and unstable Queen Anne.

In the spring of 1709, however, it seemed reasonable to hope that peace, which would have set all matters right, was well-nigh assured. France, already at the last gasp through the exhaustion caused by the war, was weakened still further by a severe winter which had added famine to all her other troubles ; and Lewis sought anxiously, even at the price of humiliation, for peace. He approached Marlborough, reputed the most 1709. avaricious and corruptible of men, with a gigantic bribe to obtain good terms, but was unhesitatingly rebuffed. The Duke stated the conditions which might be acceptable to England ; and, had the negotiations been trusted to him, there can be little doubt but that he would have

1709. obtained the honourable peace which he above all men most earnestly desired. He was, however, overruled by instructions from home, imposing terms which Lewis could not be expected to grant ; the war was continued ; and Marlborough, who had striven his hardest to bring it to an end, was of course accused of prolonging it deliberately for his own selfish ends.

The French, now menaced by an invasion and a march of the Allies to Paris, had strengthened their army enormously by withdrawing troops from all quarters to Flanders, and had set in command their only fortunate general, that very able soldier and incomparable liar, Marshal Villars. To cover Arras, the north-eastern gate of France, Villars had thrown up a strong line of entrenchments from the Scarpe at Douay to the Lys, which were generally known, after the name of his headquarters, as the lines of La Bassée. There he lay, entrenched to the teeth, while Marlborough and Eugene, after long delay owing to the lateness of the spring, encamped with one hundred and ten thousand men to the south-east of Lille,

June. between two villages, with which the reader will in due time make closer acquaintance, called Linselles and Fontenoy. Thence they moved south straight upon Villars's lines, with every apparent preparation for a direct attack upon them and for forcing their way into France at that point. The heavy artillery was sent to Menin on the Lys ; report was everywhere rife of the coming assault, and Villars lost no time in summoning the garrison of Tournay to his assistance.

June $\frac{15}{26}$. On the 26th of June, at seven in the evening, Marlborough issued his orders to strike tents and march ; and the whole army made up its mind for a bloody action before the lines at dawn. To the general surprise, after advancing some time in the direction

of the French, the columns received orders to change 1709.
direction to the left. After some hours' march eastward they crossed a river, but the men did not know
that the bridge lay over the Marque and that it led
them towards the battlefield of Bouvines ; nor was it
until dawn that they saw the gray walls and the four
spires of Tournay before them, and discovered that
they had invested the city.

Tournay had been fortified by Vauban and was one
of the strongest fortresses in France,[1] but its garrison
had been weakened by the unsuspecting Villars, and
there was little hope for it. The heavy artillery of
the Allies, which had been sent to Menin, went down
the Lys to Ghent and up the Scheldt to the besieged
city, the trenches were opened on the 7th of July, June 26.
and after three weeks, despite of the demonstrations July 7.
of Villars and incessant heavy rain, Tournay was
reduced to surrender.[2] Then followed the siege of July $\frac{19}{23}$.
the citadel, the most desperate enterprise yet under-
taken by the Allied troops, inasmuch as the sub-
terraneous works were more numerous and formidable
than those above ground. The operations were,
therefore, conducted by mine and countermine, with
destructive explosions and confused combats in the
darkness, which tried the nerves of the soldiers almost
beyond endurance. The men did not object to be shot,
but they dreaded to be buried alive by the hundred
together through the springing of a single mine.[3] Four

---

[1] There are still some remains of the old walls of Tournay on
the south side of the town, and the ruins of Vauban's citadel close
by, from which the extent of the works may be judged.

[2] The British regiments employed in the siege were the 1st
Royals (2 battalions), 3rd Buffs, 37th, Temple's, Evans's and
Prendergast's Foot.

[3] The following description written from the trenches gives some
idea of the work : " Now as to our fighting underground, blowing
up like kites in the air, not being sure of a foot of ground we stand

1709. English regiments[1] bore their share in this work and suffered heavily in the course of it, until on the 3rd of September the citadel capitulated.

Aug. 23.
Sept. 3.

Before the close of the siege Marlborough and Eugene, leaving a sufficient force before Tournay, had moved back with the main army before the lines at Douay. They had long decided that the lines were far too formidable to be forced, but they saw no reason for communicating this opinion to Villars.

Aug. $\frac{20}{31}$.

On the 31st of August Lord Orkney, with twenty squadrons and the whole of the grenadiers of the army, marched away silently and swiftly eastward towards

Aug. 23.
Sept. 3.

St. Ghislain on the Haine. Three days later, immediately after the capitulation of the citadel of Tournay, the Prince of Hessen-Cassel started at four o'clock in the afternoon in the same direction ; at nine o'clock Cadogan followed him with forty squadrons more, and at midnight the whole army broke up its camp and marched after them. Twenty-six battalions alone were left before Tournay to superintend the evacuation and to level the siege-works, with orders to watch Villars carefully and not to move until he did.

The Prince of Hessen-Cassel soon overtook Orkney, from whom he learned that St. Ghislain was too strongly held to be carried by his small force. The

---

on while in the trenches. Our miners and the enemy very often meet each other, when they have sharp combats till one side gives way. We have got into three or four of the enemy's great galleries, which are thirty or forty feet underground and lead to several of their chambers ; and in these we fight in armour by lanthorn and candle, they disputing every inch of the gallery with us to hinder our finding out their great mines. Yesternight we found one which was placed just under our bomb batteries, in which were eighteen hundredweight of powder besides many bombs : and if we had not been so lucky as to find it, in a very few hours our batteries and some hundreds of men had taken a flight into the air."—*Daily Courant*, 20th August.   [1] 8th, 10th, 15th, 16th.

Prince therefore at once pushed on.   Rain was falling 1709.
in torrents, and the roads were like rivers, but he
continued his advance eastward, behind the woods
that line the Haine, almost without a halt, till at
length at two o'clock on the morning of the 6th of Aug. 26.
September he wheeled to the right and crossed the Sept. 6.
river at Obourg three miles to the north-east of Mons.
Before him lay the river Trouille curving round to
the south by Mons, and in rear of it a line of entrenchments, thrown up during the last war, from Mons
to the Sambre, to cover the province of Hainault. A
short survey showed him that the lines were weakly
guarded ; and before noon he had passed them without
opposition.   His force, notwithstanding the weather
and the state of the roads, had traversed the fifty miles
to Obourg in fifty-six hours.

Too late Villars discovered that for the second time
he had been duped, and that Marlborough had no
intention of forcing his way into France through the
lines of La Bassée and the wet swampy country beyond
them, when he could pass the lines of the Trouille
without loss of a man.   He was in a difficult position,
for Mons was slenderly garrisoned and difficult of
access, though, if captured, it would be a valuable
acquisition to the Allies.   The approach to it from the
westward was practically shut off by a kind of natural
barrier of forest, running, roughly speaking, from St.
Ghislain on the Haine to the north to Maubeuge on
the Sambre to the south.   In this barrier there were
but two openings, the Trouée de Boussut between the
village of that name and the Haine, and the Trouées
d'Aulnois and de Louvière, which are practically the
same, some miles further to the south.   These will be
more readily remembered, the northern entrance by
the name of Jemappes, the southern by the name of

1709. Malplaquet. Villars no sooner knew what was going forward than he pushed forward a detachment with

Aug. 27. all speed upon the northern entrance, which was the
Sept. 7. nearer to him. The detachment came too late. The Prince of Hessen-Cassel was already astride of the opening, his right at Jemappes, his left at Ciply. The French thereupon fell back to await the approach of the main army of the Allies.

Aug. 26. Meanwhile that army had toiled through a sea of
Sept. 6. mud on the northern bank of the Haine, and crossing the river had by evening invested Mons on the eastern

Aug. 27. side. On the following day Villars and his whole army
Sept. 7. also arrived on the scene and encamped a couple of miles to westward of the forest-barrier, from Montreuil to Athis. Here he was joined by old Marshal Boufflers, who had volunteered his services at a time of such peril to France. The arrival of the gallant veteran caused such a tumult of rejoicing in the French camp that Marlborough and Eugene, not knowing what the clamour might portend, withdrew all but a fraction of the investing force from the town, and, advancing westward into the plain of Mons, caused the army to bivouac between Ciply and Quévy in order of battle.

Aug. 28. Villars meanwhile had not moved, being adroit
Sept. 8. enough to threaten both passages and keep the Allies in doubt as to which he should select. While, therefore, the mass of the Allied army was moved towards the Trouée d'Aulnois, a strong detachment was sent up to watch the Trouée de Boussut. That night Villars sent detachments forward to occupy the

Aug. 29. southern passage, and by mid-day of the morrow his
Sept. 9. whole army was taking up its position across the opening. Marlborough at once moved his army forward, approaching so close that his left wing ex-

changed cannon-shot with Villars's right. Everything 1709. pointed to an immediate attack on the French before they should have time to entrench themselves. Whether the Dutch deputies intervened to stay further movements is uncertain. All that is known is that a council of war was held by the commanders of the Allies, and that, after much debate, it was resolved to await the arrival of the detachment from the Trouée de Boussut and of the troops that had been left behind at Tournay, to turn the siege of Mons into a blockade, and in the meanwhile to send eighteen battalions north to capture St. Ghislain. Evidently in some quarter there was reluctance to hazard a general action.

Villars now set himself with immense energy to strengthen his position ; and, when Marlborough and Eugene surveyed the defences at daybreak of the following morning, they were astonished at the formid- Aug. 30. ─────── Sept. 10. able appearance of the entrenchments. Marlborough was once more for attacking without further delay, but he was opposed by the Dutch deputies and even by Eugene. The attack was therefore fixed for the morrow ; and another day was lost which Villars did not fail to turn to excellent account.

The entrance from the westward to the Trouée d'Aulnois or southern entrance to the plain of Mons was marked by the two villages of Campe du Hamlet on the north and Malplaquet on the south. About a mile in advance of these villages the ground rose to its highest elevation, the opening being about three thousand paces wide, and the ground broken and hollowed to right and left by small rivulets. This was the point selected by Villars for his position. It was bounded on his right by the forest of Laignières, the greatest length of which ran parallel to the Trouée,

1709. and on the left by a forest, known at different points by the names of Taisnières, Sart and Blangies, the greatest length of which ran at right angles to the Trouée. Villars occupied the forest of Laignières with his extreme right, his battalions strengthening the natural obstacles of a thick and tangled covert by means of abatis. From the edge of the wood he constructed a triple line of entrenchments, which ran across the opening for full a third of its width, when they gave way to a line of nine redans. These redans in turn yielded place to a swamp backed by more entrenchments, which carried the defences across to the wood of Taisnières. Several cannon were mounted on the entrenchments, and a battery of twenty guns before the redans. On Villars's left the forests of Taisnières and Sart projected before the general front, forming a salient and re-entering angle. Entrenchments and abatis were constructed in accordance with this configuration, and two more batteries were erected on this side, in addition to several guns at various points along the line, to enfilade an advancing enemy. Feeling even thus insecure, Villars threw up more entrenchments at the villages of Malplaquet and Chaussée du Bois in rear of the wood of Sart, and was still hard at work on them to the last possible moment before the action. Finally in rear of all stood his cavalry, drawn up in several lines. The whole of his force amounted to ninety-five thousand men.

The position was most formidable, but it had its defects. In the first place the open space before the entrenchments was broken at about half a mile's distance by a small coppice, called the wood of Tiry, which could serve to mask the movements of the Allied centre. In the second place the forest of Sart ran out beyond the fortified angle in a long tongue,

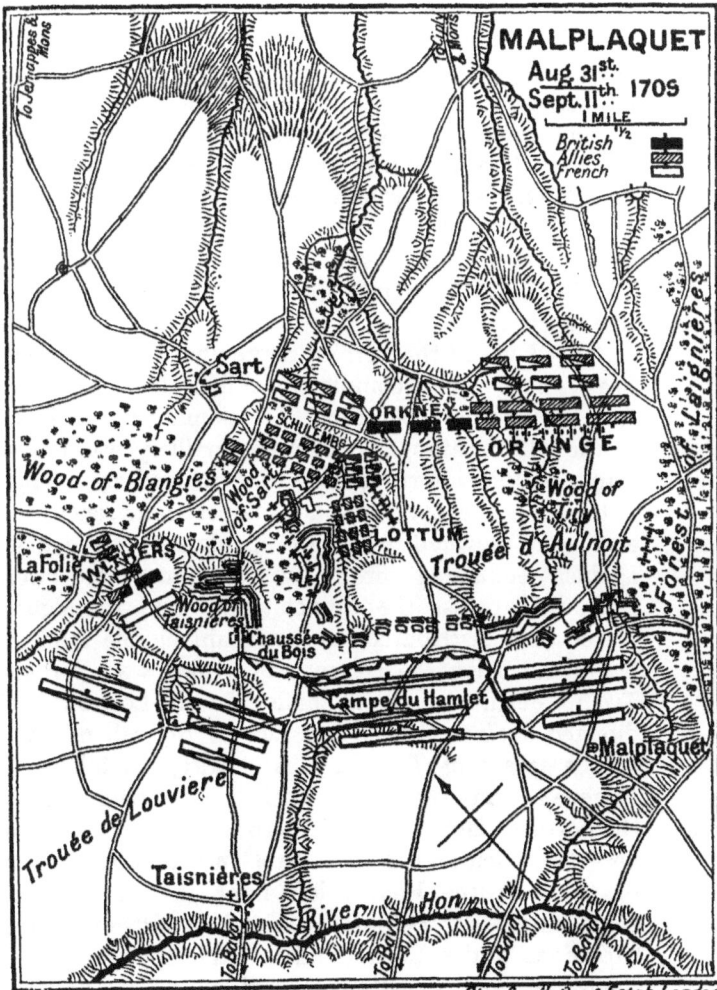

MALPLAQUET
Aug 31ˢᵗ.
Sept. 11ᵗʰ. 1709
1 MILE
British
Allies
French

To Jenappes &
Mons

To Mons

Sart

Forest of Laignières

ORKNEY
ORANGE
SCHULEMBERG
Wood of Sars
Wood-of-Blangies
Wood of
Tiry
La Folie
WITTERS
LOTTUM
Trouée d'Aulnoit
Wood of
Taisnière
Chaussée
du Bois
Campe du Hamlet
Malplaquet
Trouée de Louvière
Taisnières
River Hon

To Bavai
To Bavai
To Bavai
To Bavai

Stanford's Geog. Estab. London.

1709. which would effectually conceal any troops that might be directed against the extreme left flank. Finally the French cavalry, being massed in rear of the entrenchments, could take no part in the action until the defences were forced, and was therefore incapable of delivering any counterstroke. Marlborough and Eugene accordingly decided to make a feint attack on the French right and a true attack on their left front and flank. Villars would then be obliged to reinforce his left from his centre, which would enable the defences across the open to be carried, and the whole of the allied cavalry to charge forward and cut the French line in twain.

Aug. 31.
Sept. 11.
The dawn of the 11th of September broke in dense heavy mist which completely veiled the combatants from each other. At three o'clock prayers were said in the Allied camp, and then the artillery was moved into position. Forty pieces were massed in a single battery on the open ground against the French left, and were covered with an epaulment for defence against enfilading fire; twenty-eight more were stationed against the French right, and the lighter pieces were distributed, as usual, among the different brigades. Then the columns of attack were formed. Twenty - eight battalions under Count Lottum were directed against the eastern face of the salient angle of the forest of Taisnières, and forty battalions of Eugene's army under General Schulemberg against the northern face, while a little to the right of Schulemberg two thousand men under General Gauvain were to press on the French left flank in rear of their entrenchments. Behind Schulemberg fifteen British battalions under Lord Orkney were drawn up in a single line on the open ground, ready to advance against the centre as soon as Schulemberg and Lottum

should have done their work. Far away beyond
Gauvain, General Withers with five British and fourteen
foreign battalions and six squadrons was to turn the
extreme French left at the village of La Folie.

For the feint against the French right, thirty-one
battalions, chiefly Dutch, were massed together under
the Prince of Orange. The cavalry was detailed in
different divisions to support the infantry. The
Prince of Orange was backed by twenty-one Dutch
squadrons under the Prince of Hesse, Orkney by thirty
more under Auvergne, Lottum by the British and
Hanoverian cavalry, and Schulemberg by Eugene's
horse. The orders given to the cavalry were to sustain
the foot as closely as possible without advancing into
range of grape-shot, and, as soon as the central entrenchments were forced, to press forward, form
before the entrenchments and drive the French army
from the field. The whole force of the Allies was, as
near as may be, equal to that of the French.

At half-past seven the fog lifted, and the guns of
both armies opened fire. Eugene and Marlborough
thereupon parted, the former taking charge of the
right, the latter of the left of the army. Then the
divisions of Orange and of Lottum advanced in two
dense columns up the glade. Presently the Dutch
halted, just beyond range of grape-shot, while Lottum's
column pushed on under a terrific fire to the rear of
the forty-gun battery and deployed to the right in
three lines. Then the fire of the cannon slackened
for a time, till about nine o'clock a salvo of the forty
guns gave the signal for attack. Lottum's and
Schulemberg's divisions thereupon advanced per-
pendicularly to each other, each in three lines, Gauvain's
men crept into the wood unperceived, and Orkney
extended his scarlet battalions across the glade.

I

Entering the wood, Schulemberg's Austrians made the best of their way through marshes and streams and fallen trees, nearer and nearer to the French entrenchments. The enemy suffered them to approach within pistol-shot, only to deliver a volley which sent them staggering back; and, though the Austrians extended their line till it joined Gauvain's detachment, yet they could make little way against the French fire. Lottum's attack was hardly more successful. Heedless of the tempest of shot in their front and flank the Germans pressed steadily on, passed a swamp and a stream under a galling fire, and fell fiercely upon the breastwork beyond; but, being disordered by the ground and thinned by heavy losses, they were forced to fall back. Schulemberg then resumed the attack with his second line, but with all his exertions could not carry the face of the angle opposed to him. Picardie, the senior regiment of the French Line, held this post and would not yield it to the fiercest assault. The utmost that Schulemberg could accomplish was to sweep away the regiments in the wood, and so to uncover its flank.

Lottum, too, extended his front and attacked once more, Orkney detaching three British battalions, the Buffs, Sixteenth, and Temple's, to his assistance, while Marlborough took personal command of Auvergne's cavalry in support. The Buffs on Lottum's extreme left found a swamp between them and the entrenchments, so deep as to be almost impassable. In they plunged, notwithstanding, and were struggling through it when a French officer drew out twelve battalions and moved them down straight upon their left flank. The British brigade would have been in a sorry plight had not Villars caught sight of Marlborough at the head of Auvergne's horse and instantly recalled his

troops. So the red-coats scrambled on, and, turning
the flank of the entrenchment while Lottum's men
attacked the front, at length with desperate fighting
and heavy loss forced the French back into the wood.
·Thus exposed to the double attack of Lottum and
Schulemberg, Picardie at last fell back, but joined
itself to Champagne, the next regiment in seniority ;
and the two gallant corps, finding a rallying-point
behind an abatis, turned and stood once more. Their
comrades gave way in disorder, but the wood was so
dense that the troops on both sides became disjointed,
and the opposing lines broke up into a succession of
small parties, fighting desperately from tree to tree
with no further guidance than their own fury.

The entrenchments on the French left had been
forced ; and Villars sent urgent messages to his right
for reinforcements. But Boufflers could spare him
none. After Schulemberg and Lottum had been
engaged for half an hour, the Prince of Orange lost
patience and, without waiting for orders, opened not a
false but a real attack against the French right. On
the extreme left of Orange's division were two Highland regiments of the Dutch service, Tullibardine's and
Hepburn's, and next to them King William's favourite
Blue Guards. These were to attack the defences in the
forest of Laignières, while the rest fell upon the entrenchments in the open ; and it was at the head of the
Highlanders and of the Blue Guards that Orange took
his place. A tremendous fire of grape and musketry
saluted them as they advanced, and within the first few
yards most of the Prince's staff were struck dead by his
side. His own horse was killed beneath him, but he
disentangled himself and continued to lead the advance
on foot. A few minutes more brought his battalions
under the fire of a French battery on their left flank.

Whole ranks were swept away, but still the Prince was to be seen waving his hat in front of his troops ; and Highlanders and Dutchmen pressing steadily on carried the first entrenchment with a rush. They then halted to deploy, but, before they could advance further, Boufflers had rallied his men, and charging down upon his assailants drove them back headlong. On Orange's right, success as short-lived was bought at as dear a price. The Prince still exerted himself with the utmost gallantry, but his attack was beaten back at all points. The loss of the Dutch amounted to six thousand killed and wounded ; the Blue Guards had been annihilated, and the Hanoverian battalions, which had supported them, had suffered little less severely. In fact, the Prince's precipitation had brought about little less than a disaster.

The confusion in this part of the field called both Marlborough and Eugene to the Allied left to restore order. Further useless sacrifice of life was checked, for enough and more than enough had been done to prevent Boufflers from detaching troops to Villars. But soon came an urgent message requiring the presence of the Duke and the Prince once more on the right. Schulemberg and Lottum had continued to push their attack as best they could ; and red-coated English, blue-coated Prussians, and white-coated Austrians were struggling forward from tree to tree, tripping over felled trunks, bursting through tangled foliage, panting through quagmires, loading and firing and cursing, guided only by the flashes before them in the cloud of foul blinding smoke. But now on the extreme right Withers was steadily advancing ; and his turning movement, though the Duke and Eugene knew it not, was gradually forcing the French out of the wood. Villars, seeing the danger, called the Irish Brigade and other regiments

from the centre, and launched them full upon the 1709.
British and Prussians. Such was the impetuosity of Aug. 31.
the Irish that they forced their opponents back some Sept. 11.
way, until their own formation was broken by the
density of the forest. Eugene hastened to the spot to
rally the retreating battalions and, though struck by a
musket ball in the head, refused to leave the field.
Then up came Withers, just when he was wanted.
The Eighteenth Royal Irish met the French Royal
Regiment of Ireland, crushed it with two volleys by
sheer superiority of fire, drove it back in disorder, and
pressed on.[1] Eugene also advanced and was met by
Villars, who at this critical moment was bringing
forward his reinforcements in person. A musket shot
struck the Marshal above the knee. Totally unmoved,
the gallant man called for a chair from which to continue to direct his troops, but presently fainting from
pain was carried insensible from the field. The French,
notwithstanding his fall, still barred the advance of the
Allies, but they had been driven from their entrenchments and from the wood on the left, and only held
their own by the help of the troops that had been withdrawn from the centre. The moment for which Marlborough had waited was now come.

The forty-gun battery was moved forward, and
Orkney leading his British battalions against the redans
captured them, though not without considerable loss, at
the first rush. Two Hanoverian battalions on their
left turned the flank of the adjoining entrenchments ;
and Orange, renewing his attack, cleared the whole of
the defences in the glade. The Allied cavalry followed
close behind him. Auvergne's Dutch were the first to
pass the entrenchments, and, though charged by the
French while in the act of deploying, succeeded in

[1] Parker.

repelling the first attack.   But now Boufflers came up
at the head of the French Gendarmerie, and drove
Auvergne's men back irresistibly to the edge of the
entrenchments.   Here, however, the French were
checked, for Orkney had lined the parapet with his
British ; and, though the Gendarmerie thrice strove
gallantly to make an end of the Dutch, they were every
time driven back by the fire of the infantry.   Meanwhile the central battery, which had been parted right
and left into two divisions, advanced and supported
the infantry by a cross-fire, and Marlborough, coming
up with the British and Prussian horse, charged the
Gendarmerie in their turn.   Boufflers, however, was
again ready with fresh troops, and falling upon Marlborough with the French Household Cavalry crashed
through his two leading lines and threw even the third
into disorder.   Then Eugene advancing at the head of
the Imperial horse threw the last reserves into the
mêlée and drove the French back.   Simultaneously
the Prince of Hesse hurled his squadrons against the
infantry of the French right, and, with the help of the
Dutch foot, isolated it still further from the centre.
Boufflers now saw that the day was lost and ordered a
general retreat to Bavay, while he could yet keep his
troops together.   The movement was conducted in
admirable order, for the French, though beaten, were
not routed, while the Allies were too much exhausted
to pursue.   So Boufflers retired unmolested, though
it was not yet three o'clock, honoured alike by friend
and foe for his bravery and his skill.

Thus ended the battle of Malplaquet, one of the
bloodiest ever fought by mortal men.   Little is known
of the details of the fighting, these being swallowed up
in the shade of the forest of Taisnières, where no man
could see what was going forward.   All that is certain

is that neither side gave quarter, and that the combat 1709 was not only fierce but savage. The loss of the French was about twelve thousand men, and the trophies taken from them, against which they could show trophies of their own, were five hundred prisoners, fifty standards and colours and sixteen guns. The loss of the Allies was not less than twenty thousand men killed and wounded, due chiefly to the mad onset of the Prince of Orange. The Dutch infantry out of thirty battalions lost eight thousand men, or more than half of their number; the British out of twenty battalions lost nineteen hundred men,[1] the heaviest sufferers being the Coldstream Guards, Buffs, Orrery's and Temple's.[2]

The more closely the battle is studied, the more the conviction grows that no action of Marlborough's was fought less in accordance with his own plans. We have seen that he would have preferred to fight it on either of the two preceding days, and that he yielded

---

[1] A nominal list in the *Postboy* of 1st October gives 36 officers killed and 46 wounded. An earlier list of 17th September gives 40 officers and 511 men killed, 66 officers and 1020 men wounded; but this is admittedly imperfect.

[2]

ORDER OF BATTLE. CAMPAIGN OF 1709.

Left.
1st Line.   RIGHT WING ONLY.   Right.

                                        Two   Orrery's Kelburn's Sybourg's
                                     Foreign   Brigade. Brigade.   Brigade.
                                  Brigadiers.

18th Royal Irish.
21st Royal Scots Fusiliers.
24th Foot.
8th Foot.
3rd Buffs.
Temple's Foot.
Evans's Foot.
16th Foot.
Orrery's Foot.
23rd Royal Welsh.
2nd Batt. Royal Scots.
10th Foot.
37th Foot.
1 " Royal Scots.
1 " Coldstream Guards.
1 Batt. 1st Guards.

Twenty-seven squadrons of foreign dragoons.

26th Cameronians.
Two foreign battalions.
Prendergast's Foot.

3rd
6th
7th
5th

1st Dragoon Guards, 2 squadrons.
5th Royal Irish Dragoons, 2 squadrons.
Scots Greys, 3 squadrons.

No British troops in the second line; but the 15th and 19th Foot were also present at the action of Malplaquet.

1709. to Eugene against his own judgment in suffering it to be postponed. Then again there was the almost criminal folly of the Prince of Orange, which upset all preconcerted arrangements, threw away thousands of lives to no purpose, and not only permitted the French to retreat unharmed at the close of the day, but seriously imperilled the success of the action at its beginning. Nevertheless there are still not wanting men to believe the slanders of the contemptible faction then rising to power in England, that Marlborough fought the battle from pure lust of slaughter.

Notwithstanding all blunders, which were none of Marlborough's making, Malplaquet was a very grand action. The French were equal in number to the Allies, and occupied a position which was described at the time as a fortified citadel. They were commanded by an able general, whom they liked and trusted, they were in good heart, and they looked forward confidently to victory. Yet they were driven back and obliged to leave Mons to its fate; and though Villars with his usual bluster described the victory as more disastrous than defeat, yet French officers could not help asking themselves whether resistance to Marlborough and Eugene were not hopeless. Luxemburg with seventy-five thousand men against fifty thousand had only with difficulty succeeded in forcing the faulty position of Landen; yet the French had failed to hold the far more formidable lines of Malplaquet against an army no stronger than their own. Say Villars what he might, and beyond all doubt he fought a fine fight, the inference could not be encouraging to France.

It was not until the third day after the fight that the Allies returned to the investment of Mons. Eugene was wounded, and Marlborough not only worn out by fatigue but deeply distressed over the enormous

sacrifice of life. The siege was retarded by the marshy 1709.
nature of the ground and by heavy rain ; but on the
9th of October the garrison capitulated, and therewith Sept. 28.
the campaign came to an end. Tournay had given the Oct. 9.
Allies firm foothold on the Upper Scheldt, and Mons
was of great value to cover the captured towns in
Flanders and Brabant. The season's operations had
not been without good fruit, despite the heavy losses
at Malplaquet.

1711. THE French, fully aware of the political changes in England, had during the winter made extraordinary exertions to prolong the war for yet one more campaign, and to that end had covered the northern frontier with a fortified barrier on a gigantic scale. Starting from the coast of Picardy the lines followed the course of the river Canche almost to its source. From thence across to the Gy, or southern fork of the Upper Scarpe, ran a line of earthworks, extending from Oppy to Montenancourt. From the latter point the Gy and the Scarpe were dammed so as to form inundations as far as Biache, at which place a canal led the line of defence from the Scarpe to the Sensée. Here more inundations between the two rivers carried the barrier to Bouchain, whence it followed the Scheldt to Valenciennes. From thence more earthworks prolonged the lines to the Sambre, which carried them at last to their end at Namur.

This was a formidable obstacle to the advance of the Allies, but no lines had sufficed to stop Marlborough yet ; and with Eugene by his side the Duke did not despair. Before he could start for the campaign, however, the news came that the Emperor Joseph was dead of smallpox, an event which signified the almost certain accession of the Archduke Charles to the Imperial crown and the consequent withdrawal of his candidature for the throne of Spain. Eugene was consequently

detained at home ; and, worse than this, a fine oppor- 1711.
tunity was afforded for making a breach in the Grand
Alliance.   To render the Duke's difficulties still greater,
though his force was already weakened by the necessity
of finding garrisons for the towns captured in the
previous year, the English Government had withdrawn
from him five battalions [1] for an useless expedition to
Newfoundland under the command of Mrs. Masham's
brother, General Hill ; an expedition which may be
dismissed for the present without further mention than
that it was dogged by misfortune from first to last,
suffered heavy loss through shipwreck, and accomplished literally nothing.

Nevertheless the Imperial army was present, though
without Eugene.   The whole of the forces were
assembled a little to the south of Lille at Orchies ; and April 20.
on the 1st of May Marlborough moved forward to a May 1.
position parallel to that of Villars, who lay in rear of
the river Sensée with his left at Oisy and his right at
Bouchain.   There both armies remained stationary
and inactive for six weeks.   Eugene came, but presently received orders to return and to bring his troops
with him.   On the 14th of June Marlborough moved June 3.
away one march westward to the plain of Lens in order   14
to conceal this enforced diminution of his strength.
The position invited a battle, but Villars only moved
down within his lines, parallel to the Duke ; and once
more both armies remained inactive for five weeks.
After the departure of Eugene the French commander
detached a portion of his troops to the Rhine, but even
so he had one hundred and thirty-one battalions
against ninety-four, and one hundred and eighty-seven

---

[1] 11th, 37th, Kane's, Clayton's, and one foreign battalion of
foot. The losses of the expedition were 29 officers and 676 men
drowned.

1711. squadrons against one hundred and forty-five of the Allies.

We now approach what is perhaps the most remarkable and certainly the most entertaining feat of the Duke during the whole war. Villars, bound by his instructions, would not come out and fight ; his lines could not be forced by an army of inferior strength, and they could therefore be passed only by stratagem. The inundation on the Sensée between Arras and Bouchain could be traversed only by two causeways, the larger of which was defended by a strong fort at Arleux, while the other was covered by a redoubt at Aubigny, half a mile below it. Marlborough knew that he could take the fort at Arleux at any time and demolish it, but he knew also that Villars would certainly retake it and rebuild as soon as his back was turned. He therefore set himself to induce Villars to demolish it himself. With this view he detached a strong force under General Rantzau to capture the fort, which was done without difficulty. The Duke then gave orders that the captured works should be greatly strengthened, and, for their further protection, posted a large force under the Prussian General Hompesch on the glacis of Douay, some six miles distant from the fort.

June 25.<hr>July 6.

As fate ordained it, Hompesch, thinking himself secure under the guns of Douay, neglected his outposts and even his sentries, and was surprised two days later by a sudden attack from Villars, which was only repulsed with considerable difficulty and not a little shame. Villars was in ecstasies over his success, and Marlborough displayed considerable annoyance. However, the Duke reinforced Hompesch, as if to show the value which he attached to Arleux, and pushed forward the new works with the greatest vigour. Finally, when all was completed, he threw a weak garrison into the

June 28.<hr>July 9.

THE CAMPAIGN
OF
1711.

English Miles
5   0   5   10   15

Stanford's Geog¹ Estab¹, London.

1711. fort and led the rest of the army away two marches westward, encamping opposite the lines between the Canche and the Scarpe. Villars likewise moved westward parallel to him, and took up a position between Oppy and Montenancourt ; but, before he started, he detached a force to attack Arleux. The commander of the fort sent a message to Marlborough that he could not possibly hold it, and the Duke at once despatched Cadogan with a strong force to relieve it. It was noticed, however, that Cadogan made no such haste as the urgency of the occasion would have seemed to require ; and indeed, before he had gone half-way, he returned with the intelligence that Arleux had surrendered.

July $\frac{10}{21}$.

Villars was elated beyond measure ; and Marlborough for the first time in his life seemed to be greatly distressed and cast down. Throwing off his usual serenity, he proclaimed in public with much passion that he would be even with Villars yet, and would attack him, come what might of it, where he lay. Then came the news that Villars had razed the entire works of Arleux, over which Marlborough had spent such pains, entirely to the ground. This increased the Duke's ill-temper. He declared that he would avenge this insult to his army, and renewed his menace of a direct attack on the entrenchments. Villars now detached a force to make a diversion in Brabant ; and this step seemed to drive Marlborough distracted. Vowing that he would check the march of this detachment, he sent off ten thousand men under Lord Albemarle to Béthune, and the whole of his baggage and heavy artillery to Douay. Having thus weakened an army already inferior to that of the French, he repaired the roads that led towards the enemy's entrenchments, and on the 1st of August, with much display of vindictiveness,

July $\frac{15}{26}$.

July $\frac{17}{28}$.

sulkiness, and general vexation, advanced one march
nearer to the lines, encamping between Houdain and
St. Pol. His army watched his proceedings with
amazement, for it had never expected such behaviour
from Corporal John.

Villars meanwhile was in a transport of delight.
He drew every man, not only from all parts of the lines
but also from the neighbouring garrisons, towards the
threatened point, and asked nothing better than that
Marlborough should attack. In the height of exultation he actually wrote to Versailles that he had brought
the Duke to his *ne plus ultra*. Marlborough's strange
manner still remained the same. On the 2nd of August
he advanced to within a league of the lines, his left
being opposite to Aubigny on the Upper Scarpe ; and
during that day and the next set the whole of his
cavalry to work to collect fascines. At nightfall of the
3rd he sent away all his light artillery, together with
every wheeled vehicle, under escort of a strong detachment, and next morning rode forward with most of his
generals to reconnoitre the eastern end of the lines.
Captain Parker of the Eighteenth Royal Irish, who had
obtained permission to ride with the Staff, was amazed
at the Duke's demeanour. Marlborough had now
thrown off all his ill-temper and was calm and cool as
usual, indicating this point and that to his officers.
" Your brigade, General, will attack here, such and such
brigades will be on your right and left, such another in
support, and you will be careful of this, that, and
other." The generals listened and stared ; they understood the instructions clearly enough, but they could not
help regarding them as madness. So the reconnaissance
proceeded, drearily enough, and was just concluding
when General Cadogan turned his horse, unnoticed,
out of the crowd, struck in his spurs and galloped

1711.
July 21.
Aug. 1.

July 22.
August 2

July 23.
August 3.

July 24
August 4.

back to camp at the top of his speed. Presently the Duke also turned, and, riding back very slowly, issued orders to prepare for a general attack on the morrow.

At this all ranks of the army, from the general to the drummer, fell into the deepest depression. Not a man could fail to see that direct assault of the lines was a hopeless enterprise at the best of times, and doubly hopeless now that half of the army and the whole of the artillery had been detached for other service. Again the violent and unprecedented outburst of surliness and ill-temper was difficult to explain ; and the only possible explanation was that the Duke, rendered desperate by failure and misfortunes, had thrown prudence to the winds and cared not what he did. A few only clung faintly to the hope that the chief, who had led them so often to victory, might still have some surprise in store for them ; but the most part gave themselves up for lost, and lamented loudly that they should ever have lived to see such a change come over the Old Corporal.

So passed the afternoon among the tents of the Allies ; but meanwhile Cadogan with forty hussars at his heels had long started from the camp and was galloping hard across the plain of Lens to Douay, five leagues away. There he found Hompesch ready with his garrison, now strengthened by detachments from Béthune and elsewhere to twelve thousand foot and two thousand horse, and told him that the time was come. Hompesch thereupon issued his orders for the troops to be ready to march that night. Still the main army under Marlborough knew nothing of this, and passed the day in dismal apprehension till the sun went down, and the drummers came forward to beat tattoo. Then a column of cavalry trotted out westward, attracting every French eye and stirring every French brain with curiosity as to the purport of the movement.

The drums began to roll; and the order ran quietly 1711. down the line to strike tents and prepare to march immediately.

Never was command more welcome. Within an hour all was ready and the army was formed into four columns. The cavalry, having done their work of distracting French vigilance to the wrong quarter, returned unseen by the enemy; and at nine o'clock the whole army faced to its left and marched off eastward in utter silence, with Marlborough himself at the head of the vanguard.

The night was fine, and under the radiant moonlight July 24-25. the men swung forward bravely hour after hour over August 4-5. the plain of Lens. The moon paled; the dawn crept up into the east throwing its ghastly light on the host of weary, sleepless faces; and presently the columns reached the Scarpe at Vitry. So far the march had lasted eight hours, and fifteen miles had been passed. Pontoon-bridges were already laid across the river, and on the further bank, punctual to appointment, stood Brigadier Sutton with the field-artillery. The river was passed, and presently a messenger came spurring from the east with a despatch for the Duke of Marlborough. He read it; and words were passed down the columns of march which filled them with July 25. new life. "Generals Cadogan and Hompesch" (such August 5. was their purport) "crossed the causeway at Arleux unopposed at three o'clock this morning, and are in possession of the enemy's lines. The Duke desires that the infantry will step out." The right wing of horse halted to form the rearguard and bring up stragglers, while a cloud of dust in the van told that the Duke and fifty squadrons with him were pushing forward at the trot. Then the infantry shook themselves up and stepped out with a will.

K

Villars had received intelligence of Marlborough's march only two hours after he had started, but he was so thoroughly bewildered by the Duke's intricate manœuvres that he did not awake to the true position until three hours later. Then, quite distracted, he put himself at the head of the Household Cavalry and galloped off at full speed. So furiously rode he that he wore down all but a hundred of his troopers and pushed on with these alone. But even so Marlborough was before him. At eight o'clock he crossed the lower causeway at Aubanchœuil-au-bac and passing his cavalry over the Sensée barred the road from the west by the village of Oisy. Presently Villars, advancing reckless of all precautions, blundered into the middle of the outposts. Before he could retire, his whole escort was captured, and he himself only by miracle escaped the same fate.

The Marshal now looked anxiously for the arrival of his main body of horse ; but the Allied infantry had caught sight of the French on the other side of the Sensée, and, weary though they were, had braced themselves to race them for the goal. Nevertheless the severity of the march and the burden of their packs began to tell heavily on the foot. Hundreds dropped down unconscious, and many died there and then, but they were left where they lay to await the arrival of the rearguard ; for no halt was called, and each regiment pushed on as cheerfully as possible with such men as still survived. Thus they were still ahead of the French when they turned off to the causeway at Arleux, and, Marlborough having thrown additional bridges over the Sensée, they came quickly into their positions. The right wing of infantry crossed the river about four o'clock in the afternoon, having covered close upon forty miles in eighteen hours ; and by five o'clock the

whole force was drawn up between Oisy and the Scheldt
within striking distance of Arras, Cambrai, and Bouchain. So vanished the *ne plus ultra* of Villars, a
warning to all generals who put their sole trust in
fortified lines.

Marlborough halted for the next day to give his
troops rest and to allow the stragglers to come in.
Fully half the men of the infantry had fallen out, and
there were many who did not rejoin the army until the
third day. Villars on his side moved forward and
offered Marlborough battle under the walls of Cambrai ;
but the Duke would not accept it, though the Dutch
deputies, perverse and treacherous to the last, tried
hard to persuade him. Had the deputies marched in
the ranks of the infantry with muskets on their shoulders
and a kit of fifty pounds' weight on their backs, they
would have been less eager for the fray. Marlborough's
own design, long matured in his own mind, was the
capture of Bouchain, and his only fear was lest Villars
should cross the Scheldt before him and prevent it.
The deputies, however, who had been so anxious to
hurry the army into an engagement under every possible
disadvantage, shrank from the peril of a siege carried
on by an inferior under the eyes of a superior force.
But Marlborough, even if he had not been able to
adduce Lille as a precedent, was determined to have
his own way, and carried his point. At noon on the
7th of August he marched down almost within cannon-
shot of Cambrai, ready to fall on Villars should he
attempt to pass the Scheldt, halted until his pontoon-
bridges had been laid a few miles further down the
stream, and then gradually withdrawing his troops
threw the whole of them across the river unmolested.

It is hardly credible that a vast number of foolish
civilians, Dutch, Austrian, and even English, blamed

1711. Marlborough for declining battle before Cambrai, and that he was actually obliged to explain why he refused to sacrifice the fruit of his manœuvres by attacking a superior force in a strong position with an army not only smaller in numbers at its best, but much thinned by a forced march and exhausted by fatigue. " I despair of being ever able to please all men," he wrote. " Those who are capable of judging will be satisfied with my endeavours : others I leave to their own reflections, and go on with the discharge of my duty."

It is possible that Villars only refrained from hindering Marlborough's passage of the Scheldt in deference to orders from Versailles, of which the Duke was as well aware as himself ; but it is more than doubtful whether he ever intended the British to capture Bouchain. Though inferior in numbers, however, Marlborough covered himself so skilfully with entrenchments that Villars could not hinder him, while all attempts at diversion were met so readily that not one

Sept. $\frac{2}{13}$. of them succeeded. Finally, the garrison surrendered as prisoners of war under the very eyes of Villars. The Duke would have followed up his success by the siege of Quesnoi, the town before which English troops first came under the fire of cannon in the year of Crecy ; but by this time Lewis, with the help of the contemptible Harley, had succeeded in detaching England from the Grand Alliance. Though, therefore, the English ministers continued to encourage Marlborough in his operations, in order to conceal their own infamous conduct from the Allies, yet they took good care that those operations should proceed no further. So with the capture of Bouchain the last and not the least remarkable of Marlborough's campaigns came, always victoriously, to an end.

CAMPAIGNS OF 1744–1748

VOL. II. BOOK VII. CHAPTER V

HOWEVER fortunate might be the issue of Dettingen, it served at least its purpose in preventing the despatch of French reinforcements to the Danube and to Bohemia ; and the campaign of 1743 closed with the utter collapse of Belleisle's great schemes and with the expulsion of the French from Germany. It was now clear that the war would be carried on in the familiar cockpit of the Austrian Netherlands. Such a theatre was convenient for France, since it lay close to her own borders, and convenient for the Allies, because the Dutch had at last been persuaded to join them, and because the British would be brought nearer to their base at Ostend. Marshal Saxe, whose fine talent had hitherto been wasted under incompetent French Generals in Bohemia, was appointed to the chief command of the French in Flanders ; and every effort was made to give him a numerous and well-equipped army, and to enable him to open his campaign in good time.

In England the preparations by no means corre- ^{1744.} sponded with the necessities of the position. The estimates indeed provided for a force of twenty-one thousand British in Flanders in 1744 as against sixteen thousand in the previous year, but only at the cost of

1744. depleting the weak garrison left in England ; for the actual number of men voted for the two years was the same. All British officers of experience strongly urged upon the Government the importance of being first in the field,[1] but, when an army was to be made up in different proportions of English, Dutch, Germans and Austrians, it needed a Marlborough to bring the discordant Courts into harmony as well as to make ready the troops for an early campaign. By the beginning of April eighty thousand French soldiers had marched from their winter quarters, and were concentrated on the frontier between the Scheldt and the Sambre, while the Allies were still scattered about in cantonments, not exceeding even then a total strength of fifty-five thousand men. Wade, the English commander, delayed first by confusion at home and next by contrary winds, was still in England while the French were concentrating, and not a single English recruit, to repair the losses of the past campaign, had arrived in Flanders. Then arose disputes as to the disposition of the Allied forces, both Austrians and Dutch being nervously apprehensive of leaving their towns on the frontier without garrisons. When in the second week in May the Allied Army was at last collected close to Brussels, it was still weaker by twenty thousand men than it should have been, and found itself confronted with the task of holding Flanders, Brabant, Hainault, and the Sambre against a superior force of French.[2] May passed away and June came, but the Allies remained helpless and

[1] Honeywood to Carteret, Jan. $\frac{7}{18}$; Ligonier to Carteret, $\frac{\text{March } 21}{\text{April } 1}$, 1744.

[2] Ligonier to Carteret, $\frac{\text{April } 29}{\text{May } 10}$.

motionless in their camp, while Saxe, after a short 1744. march westward, turned north and advanced steadily between the Scheldt and the Lys. His principal object was not very difficult to divine. By the middle of June his detachments had seized Ypres and Fort Knock, which commanded the canal from Nieuport to Ypres, thus cutting off the British from one of their bases on the coast. It remained to be seen whether he would aim next at Ostend, where the whole of the British stores of ordnance were accumulated, or whether he would attempt Bruges and Ghent in order to secure the navigation of the Bruges Canal as well as of the Scheldt and Lys. Again, it was always open to him, if he pleased, to besiege Tournay, a fortress which the Allies would not willingly lose. Thus the problem set to the Allies was not easy of solution ; but of all solutions they chose the worst. The Dutch and Austrians could not bear the notion of forsaking any one of their darling strongholds, and insisted that the strength of the army should be frittered away in providing weak garrisons for the defence of all.[1] Wade, to do him justice, was for keeping all the troops together, crossing the Scheldt, and taking up a strong position to cover Ghent ; but the Austrians would not consent, lest they should expose Brussels.[2] Wade was certainly not a strong man, but he must not be too hardly judged. Marlborough had spent the most anxious days of all his campaigns in distraction between the safety of Ghent and of Brussels, and had only extricated himself by the march that preceded the battle of Oudenarde.

[1] Wade to Carteret, $\frac{\text{May 30}}{\text{June 10}}$, $\frac{\text{June 25}}{\text{July 6}}$.

[2] Carteret to Wade, $\frac{\text{May 25}}{\text{June 5}}$.

1744.   Meanwhile King George had been exerting himself
with great energy, though two months too late, to
provide Wade with additional troops, both British
and Dutch, and had begged that Prince Charles of
Lorraine might cross the Rhine with his whole army,
and direct the operations in Flanders as Commander-
in-Chief of all the Allies.   It was a wise step in every
way, since the Prince's relationship to Queen Maria
Theresa assured to him the seniority in rank which
was needed to hold so heterogeneous a host in coher-
ence.   Prince Charles did his share of the work
July. admirably, forcing his passage across the Rhine with
great skill in the face of the French, and taking up
a strong position on the frontier of Alsace.   A few
days later the British reinforcements reached Wade,
and King George issued positive orders to him to take
the offensive and " commence hostilities of all kinds." [1]

It seemed, indeed, as if the time were come for
pressing home upon the French ; but just at this
critical moment Frederick of Prussia intervened in
favour of France, and, by a threat to invade Bohemia,
brought Prince Charles back quickly over the Rhine.
None the less Wade and his fellows held a council of
war and resolved to bring Saxe to action if possible.
July $\frac{20}{31}$. King George gave his gracious approval to their plan,
and on the 31st of July the Allies turned westward
and crossed the Scheldt.   It still remained to be seen,
however, whether Saxe would allow an action to be
forced on him ; for he lay now, entrenched to the
teeth, on the Lys between Menin and Courtrai, which
was a pretty clear indication that he would not.   At
this moment Lord Stair, who had followed the course
of operations carefully from England, came forward,

[1] Carteret to Wade, July $\frac{13}{24}$, $\frac{17}{28}$.

like a true pupil of Marlborough, with a new plan of 1744. campaign. His advice was that the Allies should turn Saxe's tactics against himself. They should march south to Orchies, between Lille and Tournay, and there encamp, where they would be within reach of half-a-dozen French fortified towns. The French would not dare to leave the fortresses defenceless; and the garrisons necessary to render them secure would absorb the whole of their force in the field. Then the Allies could send detachments into France and lay Picardy under contribution, or possibly carry out the plan, rejected two years before, of a march to the Seine. The King of Prussia's action only made some bold stroke of the kind the more imperative.[1]

Stair had gained over the Austrian general D'Arenberg to this project in 1742; but it was hardly likely to be accepted by him now. Carteret, in forwarding Stair's memorandum to Wade, gave him no positive orders except at least to do something; but poor Wade found it impossible to make the Austrians do anything. The Allies having crossed the Scheldt halted inactive for weeks, and no persuasion could induce D'Arenberg to move. At last the army did march down to the plains of Lille, but without its artillery, so that it could not be said seriously to threaten the French fortresses. The Dutch and Austrians had undertaken to furnish a siege-train, but had taken no step to procure one of the ten thousand horses that were required to transport it. After a short sojourn in the south the Allies marched helplessly northward once more. August passed away and September came, but even in the fourth month of the campaign the Dutch and Austrians were still without

[1] Carteret to Wade, $\frac{\text{July 31}}{\text{Aug. 11}}$, Aug. $\frac{14}{25}$, $\frac{17}{28}$.

1744. their artillery.[1] Wade boldly proposed to force
Saxe's lines on the Lys : the Austrians refused.   He
proposed to pounce on a detachment of fourteen
thousand men, which Saxe had imprudently isolated
from his main army : D'Arenberg carefully sent a
weak body of cavalry to reveal to the detachment the
danger of its position.   Finally, in the first week of
October the Allies retired into winter-quarters, which
was precisely the object for which D'Arenberg had
been working from the first.   Despite of the English
subsidies, he had no money with which to pay his
troops, and he wished to spare the Austrian Netherlands
the burden of furnishing forage and contributions.
Wade, sick in body and distressed in mind, at once
resigned his command.   He had had enough of the
Austrian alliance, and King George before long was
to have enough of it also.[2]

Once again, despite the endless length to which
the war was dragging on, the establishment of the
British forces remained virtually unaugmented for
the year 1745.   The troops allotted for service in
Flanders were indeed raised to a strength of twenty-
five thousand men, but this was effected only by
1745. reducing the garrison of Great Britain to fifteen
thousand, which, as events were to prove before the
year's end, created a situation of perilous weakness.
Moreover, the past campaign had revealed a failing
in one of the confederate powers which was hardly
less serious than the impecuniosity and selfishness of
Austria.   The Dutch army, which under Marlborough
had done such brilliant service, was become hopelessly

---

[1] Wade to Carteret, $\frac{\text{Aug. 26}}{\text{Sept. 6}}$.

[2] *Ibid.*, Aug. $\frac{19}{30}$, $\frac{\text{Aug. 25}}{\text{Sept. 5}}$, Sept. $\frac{16}{27}$, $\frac{\text{Sept. 22}}{\text{Oct. 3}}$, Oct. $\frac{1}{12}$, $\frac{10}{12}$.

inefficient. The competition of rival demagogues 1745. for popular favour had reduced it to such weakness in numbers, that it hardly sufficed to find efficient garrisons for the fortified towns. Concurrently its discipline had suffered; and General Ligonier had already complained that the Dutch troops which served with the Allies in 1744 were intolerably insubordinate and disorderly, setting a bad example to the whole army.[1] In February 1745 Ligonier again brought the matter to the notice of the English Government. The Dutch, he said, would probably keep all their men in garrison, and, if the Allies were so weak that they could only find garrisons for the fortresses on the frontier, the French would be free to go where they pleased. It would be far better, therefore, to make a great effort, collect a hundred thousand men, take the offensive, and end the war in a single campaign. Ten thousand men would be required to guard the line of the Bruges Canal, and the remainder should besiege Maubeuge and Landrecies and enter France by the line of the Sambre, making the Meuse the main line of communication, as open alike to the passage of reinforcements from England, from Holland, and from Germany.[2] Such counsel was not likely to find acceptance with the men who had mismanaged the war so far. One important change, however, was made by the appointment of the Duke of Cumberland to be Commander-in-Chief in Flanders, and also in Great Britain.[3] The Duke at the time of this promotion still wanted a month

[1] Ligonier to Carteret, $\dfrac{\text{July 31}}{\text{Aug. 11}}$, 1744.

[2] Ligonier to Harrington, $\dfrac{\text{Jan. 29}}{\text{Feb. 9}}$, Feb. $\dfrac{6}{17}$, 1745.

[3] *Gazette*, $\dfrac{\text{Feb. 23}}{\text{March 6}}$, March $\dfrac{1}{12}$, 1745.

1745. to complete his twenty-fifth year, but he had from his boyhood been an enthusiastic soldier, he had studied his profession, he had shown bravery at Dettingen, and, young though he might be, he was older than Condé had been when he first gained military fame. Finally, it was an immense advantage that a Prince of a reigning family should preside over so motley an army as that of the Allies, since there would be the less disposition to cavil at his authority.

Cumberland entered upon his work energetically enough, crossed over to Flanders early in April, made all his arrangements for concentration at Brussels on the 2nd of May, and actually began his march south-

April 22.
May 3.
ward on the following day.[1] Even so, however, Marshal Saxe had taken the field before him, assembling his troops in Hainault, as in the previous year, so that it was impossible to divine which of the fortresses of the barrier he might intend to attack. After a feint which pointed to the siege of Mons, he marched

Apr. $\frac{19}{30}$.
rapidly upon Tournay and invested it on the 30th of April, screening his movements so skilfully with his cavalry that not a word as to his operations reached Cumberland until nearly a week later. Cumberland, after leaving Soignies on the 3rd of May, moved slowly south-westward by Cambron, Maulbay, and Leuse,

April 28.
May 9.
and arrived on the evening of the 9th at Brissoel, within sight of Saxe's army. The ground immediately in front of the Allies was broken by little copses, woods, and enclosures, all of them crammed with mercenary irregular troops—Pandours, Grassins, and the like—which, imitated first from the Austrians, had by this time become a necessary part of the French as of every army. Beyond this broken ground a

---

[1] Cumberland to Harrington, April $\frac{1}{12}$, $\frac{12}{23}$.

wide plain swept in a gentle, almost unbroken slope 1745. to the village of Fontenoy, which formed the centre of Saxe's position. The advanced parties of irregulars, together with twelve squadrons drawn up on the slope before Fontenoy, forbade Cumberland's further advance for that day, and the Allies encamped for the night. Headquarters were fixed at Maubray, a village in full sight of Fontenoy, and a bare mile and a half to the south-eastward of the French camp.

On the next day the French advanced posts were April 29. pushed out of the copses, and Cumberland, together May 10. with the Prince of Waldeck and the Count of Königseck, who commanded the Dutch and the Austrians respectively, went forward to reconnoitre the position. Saxe's army occupied the crest of the slope, lying astride of the two roads that lead from Condé and from Leuse to Tournay. His right rested on the village of Anthoin and on the Scheldt, the tower of Anthoin Castle marking the western boundary of his position with clearness enough. From thence his line extended due east along the crest of the height for about a mile to the village of Fontenoy. A few hundred yards before Fontenoy stands the hamlet of Bourgeon, but this was now veiled in smoke and flame, having been fired by the Pandours as they re-tired. From Anthoin to Fontenoy Saxe's front faced due south, but eastward from Fontenoy it turned back almost at right angles to the forest of Barry and the village of Ramecroix, fronting considerably to east-ward of south. The village of Vezon, however, which lies in the same straight line with Fontenoy, due east of Anthoin, was also occupied by the French as an advanced post. This was quickly cleared by Cum-berland's troops, and the Allied Generals completed their reconnaissance. Saxe's position was undoubtedly strong by nature and had been strengthened still further by art. Beyond Anthoin the French right flank was secured by a battery erected on the western bank of the Scheldt, while the village itself was entrenched, and held by two brigades. Between Anthoin and Fontenoy three redoubts had been constructed, and the space was defended by three brigades of infantry backed by eight squadrons of horse. Fontenoy itself had been fortified with works and cannon, and made as strong as possible ; and from Fontenoy to the forest of Barry ran a double line of entrenchments, the first line held by nine and the second by eleven battalions of infantry. At the edge of the forest of Barry were two more redoubts, the foremost of them called the Redoubt d'Eu, both armed with cannon to sweep the open space between the forest and Fontenoy ; in rear of the forest were posted nine more battalions, and in rear of all two strong lines of cavalry. The flower of the French army, both horse and foot, was stationed in this space on Saxe's left, for the English had the right of the line in the Allied Army, and Saxe knew the reputation of the red-coats.

The Allied Generals decided to attack on the following day. Königseck, it is said, was for harassing Saxe's communications and compelling him to raise the siege of Tournay ; but, finding himself overruled by Cumberland and by Waldeck, he gave way. Cumberland's force was decidedly inferior in numbers, being less than fifty thousand against fifty-six thousand men, but he was young and impetuous, and had been strongly impressed by the disastrous inaction of the preceding campaign. It was agreed that the Dutch and Austrians should assail the French centre and right, the Dutch in particular being responsible

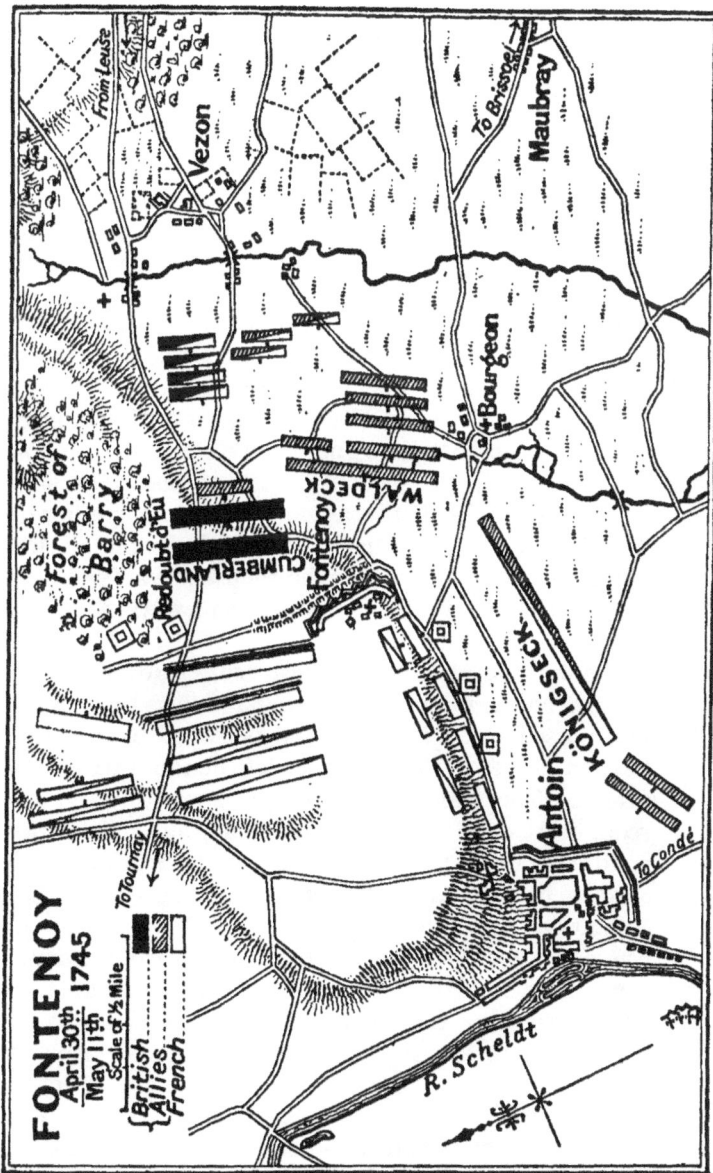

FONTENOY
April 30th 1745
May 11th
Scale of ½ Mile

British
Allies
French

Stanford's Geog.l Estabt, London.

From Leuse

Vezon

To Brisoel

Maubray

+ Bourgeon

Forest of
Barry

WALDECK

Redoubt d'Eu

CUMBERLAND

Fontenoy

KÖNIGSECK

Antoin

To Condé

To Tournai

R. Scheldt

1745. for Fontenoy, while the British attacked the French left between that village and the forest of Barry.

April 30.
May 11.
At two o'clock on the following morning the British began to move out of their camp upon Vezon, the cavalry leading. The advance took much time, for there were many narrow lanes to be traversed before the force could debouch upon the slope, and, when the slope was passed, it was still necessary to defile through the village of Vezon. Cumberland's order of attack was simple. Brigadier Ingoldsby, with the Twelfth and Thirteenth Foot, the Forty-second Highlanders, a Hanoverian battalion, and three six-pounder cannon, was to assault the Redoubt d'Eu on the right flank of the line of the British advance, and to carry it with the bayonet. The remainder of the infantry was simply to march up across the thousand yards of open ground between it and Fontenoy and sweep the enemy out of their entrenchments.

Before five o'clock the advanced squadrons of the British horse, fifteen in all, under General Campbell, had passed through Vezon and deployed in the plain beyond, to cover the formation of the infantry for the attack. The French batteries in Fontenoy and the redoubt at once opened fire on them, but the cavalry endured the fire for an hour unmoved, until at length a shot carried away General Campbell's leg. The gallant veteran, who had fought at Malplaquet and was now seventy-eight years of age, was carried dying from the field, full of lamentation that he could take no further part in the action. No one but himself seems to have known for what purpose his squadrons had been brought forward, and accordingly after his fall they were withdrawn. The infantry then moved up to the front, where General Ligonier proceeded to form them in two lines, without further interruption,

to use his own simple words, than a lively and murderous cannonade from the French. Cumberland
meanwhile ordered up seven six-pounders to the right
of the British front, which quickly came into action.
Conspicuous before the French front rode an officer
on a white horse, and the English gunners at once
began to lay wagers who should kill him. The second
or third shot brought the white charger to the ground,
and his rider was carried, shattered and dying, to the
rear. He was Count Grammont, the gallant but
thoughtless officer who had spoiled the combinations
of Noailles at Dettingen. Then, turning to their
more legitimate work, the gunners quickly made
their presence felt among the French field-batteries;
but the round shot never ceased to plough into the
scarlet ranks of the British from Fontenoy and from
the Redoubt d'Eu. Ligonier's two lines of infantry
were soon formed, with the cavalry in two more lines
in their rear; and the General presently sent word
to Cumberland that he was ready to advance as soon
as Waldeck should lead his Dutch against Fontenoy.
The name of the aide-de-camp who carried this message
should not be omitted, for he was Captain Jeffery
Amherst of the First Guards.

Thereupon the Dutch and Austrians, in the centre
and left, advanced against Fontenoy and Anthoin, but
flinching from the fire in front, and above all from that
in their flank from the battery on the other side of the
Scheldt, soon shrank back under cover and could not
be induced to move forward again.[1] Worst of all,
the Dutch cavalry was smitten with panic, galloped
back on to the top of some of the British squadrons,

[1] The ground immediately before Fontenoy presents for fully
eight hundred yards a gentle and unbroken slope. An officer, who
went over the ground with me, assured me that St. Privat itself does
not offer a more perfect natural glacis for modern rifle-fire.

L

and fled away wildly to Hal crying out that all was lost. Things therefore went ill on the Allied left ; and meanwhile on the right there was enacted a blunder still more fatal. For Ingoldsby, misconceiving his instructions, hesitated to make his attack on the Redoubt d'Eu, and despite repeated orders from Cumberland never delivered it at all. Cumberland, however, was impatient. Without further delay he placed himself at the head of the British, who were standing as Ligonier had arrayed them, in most beautiful order. In the first line, counting from right to left, stood a battalion of the First Guards, another of the Scots Guards, and another of the Coldstream, the First, Twenty-first, Thirty-first, Eighth, Twenty-fifth, Thirty-third, and Nineteenth ; in the second line the Buffs occupied the post of honour on the right, and next to them came in succession the Twenty-third, Thirty-second, Eleventh, Twenty-eighth, Thirty-fourth, and Twentieth. Certain Hanoverian battalions joined them on the extreme left. The drums beat, the men shouldered arms, and the detachments harnessed themselves to the two light field-guns that accompanied each battalion. Ingoldsby saw what was going forward and aligned his battalions with them on the right. Then the word was given to advance, and the two lines moved off with the slow and measured step for which they were famous in Europe.

Forward tramped the ranks of scarlet, silent and stately as if on parade. Full half a mile of ground was to be traversed before they could close with the invisible enemy that awaited them in the entrenchments over the crest of the slope, and the way was marked clearly by the red flashes and puffs of white smoke that leaped from Fontenoy and the Redoubt d'Eu on either

flank. The shot plunged fiercely and more fiercely
into the serried lines as they advanced into that
murderous cross-fire, but the gaping ranks were quietly
closed, the perfect order was never lost, the stately
step was never hurried. Only the Hanoverians in
the second line, finding that they were cramped for
space, dropped back quietly and decorously, and
marched on in third line behind the British. Silent
and inexorable the scarlet lines strode on. They came
abreast of village and redoubt, and the shot which had
hitherto swept away files now swept away ranks.
Then the first line passed beyond redoubt and village,
and the French cannon took it in reverse. The gaps
grew wider and more frequent, the front grew narrower
as the men closed up, but still the proud battalions
advanced, strewing the sward behind them with
scarlet, like some mass of red blossom that floats
down a lazy stream and sheds its petals as it goes.

At last the crest of the ridge was gained and the
ranks of the French battalions came suddenly into view
little more than a hundred yards distant, their coats
alone visible behind the breastwork. Next to the
forest of Barry, and exposed to the extreme right of
the British, a line of red showed the presence of the
Swiss Guards ; next to them stood a line of blue, the
four battalions of the French Guards, and next to the
Guards a line of white, the regiments of Courtin,
Aubeterre, and of the King, the choicest battalions
of the French Army. Closer and closer came the
British, still with arms shouldered, always silent,
always with the same slow, measured tread, till they
had advanced to within fifty yards of the French.
Then at length Lord Charles Hay of the First Guards
stepped forward with flask in hand, and doffing his
hat drank politely to his enemies. " I hope, gentle-

men," he shouted, " that you are going to wait for
us to-day and not swim the Scheldt as you swam the
Main at Dettingen. Men of the King's company,"
he continued, turning round to his own people, " these
are the French Guards, and I hope you are going to
beat them to-day " ; and the English Guards answered
with a cheer. The French officers hurried to the front,
for the appearance of the British was a surprise to
them, and called for a cheer in reply. But only a half-
hearted murmur came from the French ranks, which
quickly died away and gave place to a few sharp
words of command ; for the British were now within
thirty yards. " For what we are about to receive may
the Lord make us truly thankful," murmured an
English Guardsman as he looked down the barrels of
the French muskets, but before his comrades round
him had done laughing the French Guards had fired ;
and the turn of the British had come at last.[1]

For despite of that deadly march through the cross-
fire of the French batteries to the muzzles of the French
muskets, the scarlet ranks still glared unbroken through
the smoke ; and now the British muskets, so long
shouldered, were levelled, and with crash upon crash
the volleys rang out from end to end of the line, first
the First Guards, then the Coldstreams, then the Scots,
and so through brigade after brigade, two battalions
loading while the third fired, a ceaseless, rolling, infernal
fire. Down dropped the whole of the French front
rank, blue coats, red coats and white, before the storm.
Nineteen officers and six hundred men of the French

---

[1] Every one knows the legend of "Messieurs les Gardes
Françaises, tirez les premiers." "Non, messieurs, nous ne tirons
jamais les premiers." But every English account agrees that the
French fired first, long before the question had been raised, and I
take the authority of Ligonier (who drew up the official account) as
final. He says distinctly, " We received their fire."

and Swiss Guards fell at the first discharge ; regiment
Courtin was crushed out of existence ; regiment
Aubeterre, striving hard to stem the tide, was swept
aside by a single imperious volley which laid half of its
men on the ground. The British infantry were perfectly in hand ; their officers could be seen coolly
tapping the muskets of the men with their canes so
that every discharge might be low and deadly ; while
the battalion-guns also poured in round after round
of grape with terrible effect. The first French line
was utterly shattered and broken. Even while the
British were advancing, Saxe had brought up additional troops to meet them and had posted regiments
Couronne and Soissonois in rear of the King's regiment,
and the Brigade Royal in rear of the French Guards ;
but all alike went down before the irresistible volleys.
The red-coats continued their triumphant advance for
full three hundred yards into the heart of the French
camp, and old Ligonier's heart leaped within him, for
he thought that the battle was won.

Saxe for his part thought little differently from
Ligonier ; but though half dead with dropsy, reduced
to suck a bullet to assuage his intolerable thirst, so
weak that he could not ride but was carried about the
field in a wicker litter, the gallant German never for a
moment lost his head. Sending a message to the
French King, who with the Dauphin was watching the
action from a windmill in the rear, to retire across the
Scheldt without delay, he strove to gain time to rally
his infantry. On the first repulse of the French Guards
Cumberland had detached two battalions to help the
Dutch by a flanking attack on Fontenoy. Seeing that
this movement must be checked at all hazards, Saxe
headed these troops back by a charge of cavalry ;
whereupon one of the battalions extended itself along

the left flank of the British.   Partly in this way, partly owing to the incessant play of the French artillery on both flanks, the two British lines assumed the form of two huge oblong columns which gradually became welded into one.   The change was not untimely, for now the first line of the French cavalry, which had been posted in rear of the forest of Barry, came down upon the British at full gallop, only to reel back shivered to fragments by the same terrible fire.   Then the second line tried its fortune, but met with no better fate.   Finally, the Household Cavalry, the famous Maison du Roi, burning with all the ardour of Dettingen unavenged, was launched against the scarlet columns, and like its predecessors, came flying back, a mob of riderless horses and uncontrollable men, decimated, shattered and repulsed by the never-ending fire.   " It was like charging two flaming fortresses rather than two columns of infantry." [1]

Nevertheless some time was hereby gained for the broken French infantry to re-form.   The British, once arrived within the French camp, came to a halt, and looked at last to see how the Dutch were faring on their left.   As has already been told, Waldeck's attack had been a total failure, and the British, unsupported and always under a cross-fire of artillery, fell back to the crest of the ridge and were re-formed for a second attack.   Waldeck undertook to make another attempt on Fontenoy, and Cumberland, in reliance upon his help, again advanced at the head of the British.   But meanwhile Saxe had brought forward his reserves from Ramecroix, and among them the Irish brigade, to meet him, while artillery had also been brought up from the French right to play upon the British front.   The French Guards and the rest of the troops of the French

[1] *Campagnes des Pays Bas.*

first line had also been rallied, and the task of the
British was well-nigh desperate. The Irish brigade,
which consisted of six battalions, was made up not of
Irish only but of Scots and English also, desperate
characters who went into action with a rope round
their necks, and would fight like devils. Yet, even
in this second attack the British carried their advance
as far as in the first, the perfection of their fire-discipline
enabling them to beat back even the Irish brigade for
a time. But their losses had been frightfully heavy;
the Dutch would not move one foot to the attack of
Fontenoy, and the cannonade in front added to that
in the flanks became unendurable. The French
infantry likewise closed round on them in superior
numbers on both flanks, and it became apparent that
there was nothing for it but a retreat.

Ligonier sent back two battalions to secure the
roads leading through Vezon, and the retreat then
began in perfectly good order. The French Household
Cavalry made a furious charge upon the rear of the
column as it faced about, but found to its cost that
the infernal fire was not yet quenched. The three
battalions of Guards and a battalion of Hanoverians
turned sternly about to meet them, and gave them a
few parting volleys, which wholly extinguished one
regiment and brought down every officer of another.
A few British squadrons, the Blues conspicuous among
them, pushed forward, in spite of heavy losses, through
the cross-fire to lend what help they could, and the
remnant of the heroic battalions retired, facing about
in succession at every hundred yards, as steadily and
proudly as they had advanced.

Their losses in the action were terribly severe. Of
the fifteen thousand infantry, English and Hanoverian,
for the Hanoverians bore themselves not less nobly

than their Allies, nearly six thousand were killed or wounded, the casualties of the twenty English battalions just exceeding four thousand men. The heaviest sufferers were the Twelfth and Twenty-third regiments, both of which lost over three hundred men, the Twenty-first and Thirty-first, which lost rather fewer than three hundred men apiece, and the three battalions of Guards, which lost each of them about two hundred and fifty. Of the Generals of Foot, Cumberland, Ligonier, and Brigadier Skelton, though in the hottest of the fire, alone came off unhurt ; all of the rest were either killed or wounded. Many regiments of cavalry also suffered not a little, in particular the Blues and Royal Dragoons ; and the total loss of the British cavalry exceeded three hundred men and six hundred horses. The loss of the French was never made public, but was certainly at least equal to that of the Allies. Contemporary accounts set it down, with no great improbability, at fully ten thousand men. As an example of the prowess of British infantry, Fontenoy stands almost without a parallel in its history. The battalions formed under a cross-fire of artillery, remained halted under the same fire, advanced slowly for half a mile in perfect order under the same fire, and marched up to within pistol-shot of the French infantry to receive their volley before they discharged a shot. They shattered the French battalions to pieces, repulsed three separate attacks of cavalry, halted under a heavy cannonade, retired for some distance and re-formed under a cross-fire, advanced again with both artillery and musketry playing on front and flanks, made the bravest brigade in the French service recoil, repelled another desperate attack of cavalry, and retired slowly and orderly under a cross-fire almost to the end. By consent of all the

British commanders it was Ingoldsby's misunder-
standing of his orders and his failure to capture the
Redoubt d'Eu that lost the battle ; and Ingoldsby was
duly tried by court-martial for his behaviour. He
was, however, acquitted of all but an error in judgment ;
and indeed there was no question of cowardice, for he
accompanied the remainder of the infantry in its
advance with his own detachment and was severely
wounded. It is customary to blame Cumberland for
dashing his head against a wall in attempting such an
attack ; and no doubt he was guilty of a tactical
blunder in assaulting a re-entrant angle before the
salient had been carried. But he could hardly have
been expected to count on such bad luck as the failure
of Ingoldsby on one flank and of the Dutch on the
other. The sheer audacity of his advance went near
to give him the victory. Saxe owned that he never
dreamed that any General would attempt such a stroke,
or that any troops would execute it. Cumberland is
blamed also for not attacking either the Redoubt d'Eu
or Fontenoy after he had penetrated into the French
camp. This charge is less easy to rebut, for the French
always know when they are beaten, and seeing their
left rolled up and troops advancing on Fontenoy in
flank and rear would probably have given up the game
for lost, and that the more readily since their ammunition in Fontenoy was for the moment nearly exhausted.
Even so, however, Saxe's reserves were always at hand
at Ramecroix, and would have required to be held in
check. Another puzzling question, namely, why Cumberland did not make greater use of his artillery in the
action, is answered by the fact that the contractors for
the horsing of the guns ran off with the horses early in
the day. Such an occurrence was by no means unusual, and yet it never happened to Marlborough, not

1745. even at Malplaquet.   Altogether, the conclusion seems
to be that Cumberland stumbled on to a brilliant feat
of arms by mistake, and, though seconded by his
troops with bravery equal to his own, was not a
General of sufficient capacity to turn his success to
account.

At the close of the action Cumberland retreated to
Ath and encamped under the guns of that fortress,
leaving his wounded to the mercy of the French, who,
by a strange perversion of their usual chivalry, treated
them with shameful barbarity.   Among the wounded,
strangely enough, were a few of the new sect of
Methodists founded by John Wesley, who faced death
and wounds with the stern exultation that had once
inspired the troopers of Cromwell.   One of them wrote
to Wesley that, even after a bullet in each arm had
forced him to retire from the field, he hardly knew
whether he was on earth or in heaven, such was the
sweetness of the day.   This man and a few more of
his kind probably helped their fellow-sufferers through
the misery of the days following the battle, until
Cumberland's furious remonstrances with Saxe pro-
cured for them better treatment.

From Ath Cumberland fell back to Lessines and
drew out such British corps as were in garrison in
Flanders, to replace those which had suffered most
heavily in the action.   Meanwhile Tournay, very
shortly after the battle, fell by treachery into the
hands of the French ;   and Saxe's field-army being
thus raised to a force nearly double that of the Allies,
Cumberland was reduced to utter helplessness.   The
mischief of Fontenoy lay not in the repulse and the
loss of men, for the British did not consider themselves
to have been beaten, but in the destruction of all
confidence in the Dutch troops.   The troubles which

had harassed Wade to despair now reappeared. Cum- 1745.
berland, notwithstanding his inferiority in strength,
was expected somehow to defend Flanders, Brabant,
and above all Brussels, and yet simultaneously to
keep an active army in the field. Worse than this, he
attempted to fulfil the expectation. Against his better
judgment he weakened his force still further by detaching a force for the garrison of Mons,[1] after which,
instead of taking up a strong position on the Scheldt
to cover Ghent at all hazards, he yielded to the pressure
of the Austrians and crossed the Dender to protect
Brussels.[2] Halting too long between two opinions he
at last sent off a detachment for the defence of Ghent,
half of which was cut off and driven back with heavy
loss, while the other half, after enduring much rough
usage on the march, entered Ghent only to see the town
surprised by the French on the following day. Four June 30.
British regiments took part in this unlucky enterprise July 11.
and suffered severely, while the Royal Scots and the
Twenty-third, which had been despatched to Ghent
after Fontenoy, of course became prisoners.[3] Moreover, a vast quantity of British military stores were
captured in Ghent, although Cumberland had a week
before ordered that they should be removed.[4] After
this blow Cumberland retired to Vilvorde, a little to
the north of Brussels, still hoping to cover both that
city and Antwerp, and so to preserve his communica-

[1] Ligonier to Harrington, May $\frac{5}{16}$. Cumberland to Harrington, May $\frac{11}{22}$.

[2] Fawkener to Harrington, July $\frac{19}{30}$.

[3] General Bligh to Cumberland, $\frac{\text{June 28}}{\text{July 9}}$.

[4] Cumberland to Harrington, July $\frac{2}{13}$.

1745. tions both with Germany and with the sea. Here again he sacrificed his better judgment to the clamour of the Austrians, for he would much have preferred to secure Antwerp only. His position was in fact most critical, and he was keenly alive to it.[1] Just when his anxiety was greatest there came a letter from the Secretary of State, announcing that invasion of England was imminent, and hoping that troops could be spared from Flanders without prejudice to his operations. " What ! " answered Ligonier indignantly ; " are you aware that the enemy has seventy thousand men against our thirty thousand, and that they can place a superior force on the canal before us and send another army round between us and Antwerp, to cut off our supplies August. and force us to fight at a disadvantage ? This is our position, and this is the result of providing His Royal Highness with insufficient troops ; and yet you speak of our having a corps to spare to defend England ! " [2]

Saxe's plan for reducing the Allies was in fact uniformly the same throughout the whole of the war, namely to cut off their communications with the sea on one side and with Germany on the other. Even before he began to press Cumberland northward toward Antwerp, he had detached a force to lay siege to Ostend, which was the English base. Cumberland, on his side, had advised that the dykes should be broken down and the country inundated in order to preserve it, and both Dutch and Austrians had promised that this should be done ; but as usual it was not done, Aug. $\frac{13}{24}$. and before the end of August Ostend had surrendered to the French. The English base was then perforce

---

[1] Cumberland to Harrington, July $\frac{14}{25}$.

[2] Ligonier to Harrington, July $\frac{14}{25}$.

shifted to Antwerp. But by this time the requests 1745. for the return of troops to England had become urgent and imperative orders. First ten battalions were Sept.-Oct. recalled, then the rest of the foot, and at last practically the whole of the army, including Cumberland himself.[1] The cause was the Jacobite rebellion which was stamped out by the victory of Culloden in April 1746.

[AUTHORITIES.—The official account of Fontenoy was drawn up by Ligonier in French and translated into English, with some omissions, for publication. The French version is far the better and will be found in the State Papers. The account in the *Life of the Duke of Cumberland* is poor, though valuable as having been drawn up from the reports of the English Generals. Of the French accounts Voltaire's is the best known, and, as might be expected from such a hand, admirably spirited. More valuable are the accounts in the *Conquête des Pays Bas*, in the *Mémoires du Maréchal de Saxe*, where Saxe's own report may be read, in the *Campagnes des Pays Bas*, and in Espagnac. The newspapers furnish a few picturesque incidents of some value.

---

[1] Harrington to Cumberland, Sept. $\frac{4}{15}$; Oct. $\frac{1}{12}$, $\frac{19}{30}$.

1746. THE virtual evacuation of the Low Countries by the British, in consequence of the Jacobite Rebellion, was an advantage too obvious to be overlooked by the French. At the end of January, though winter-quarters were not yet broken up, they severed the communication between Antwerp and Brussels, and a week later took the town of Brussels itself by escalade. The citadel, after defending itself for a fortnight, went the way of the town, and the capital of the Spanish Netherlands was turned into a French place of arms.[1] The consternation in Holland was great, and was increased when the French presently besieged May $\frac{20}{31}$. and captured Antwerp. Meanwhile the British Commander, Lord Dunmore, who had been left in the Netherlands with a few squadrons of cavalry, could only look on in absolute helplessness. It was not until June that the Hessian troops in British pay and a few British battalions could be embarked, together with General Ligonier to command them, from England; and it was not until July, owing to foul winds, that they were finally landed at Williamstadt. The change of base was significant in itself, for, since the capture of Ostend and Antwerp, there was no haven for British ships except in the United Provinces. Even after

---

[1] Dunmore to Harrington, Jan. $\frac{20}{31}$, $\frac{\text{Jan. 27}}{\text{Feb. 7}}$, Feb. $\frac{12}{23}$.

the disembarkation these forces were found to be still 1746.
unready to take the field.   The Hessians had not a
grain of powder among them, and there were neither
horses for the artillery nor waggons for the baggage.
Again, to add small difficulties to great, the Austrian
General, Batthyany, having no British officer as his
peer in command, denied to the British troops the place
of honour at the right of the line.   It was a trifling
matter, but yet sufficient to embarrass counsel, destroy
harmony, and delay operations.[1]

While the Allies were thus painfully drawing their
forces together, the activity of the French never ceased.
The Prince of Conti was detached with a considerable June 30.
force to the Haine, where he quickly reduced Mons July 11.
and St. Ghislain, thus throwing down almost the last July $\frac{13}{24}$
relics of the Austrian barrier in the south.   Thence
moving to the Sambre, Conti laid siege to Charleroi.
It was now sufficiently clear that the plan of the French
campaign was to operate on the line of the Meuse for
the invasion of Holland.   Maestricht once taken, the
rest would be easy, for most of the Dutch army were
prisoners in the hands of the French ; and, with the
possession of the line of the Meuse, communication
between the Allied forces of England and of Austria
would be cut off.   But before Maestricht could be
touched, Namur must first be captured ; and the
campaign of 1746 accordingly centred about Namur.

For the first fortnight of July the Allies remained
at Terheyden, a little to the north of Breda, Saxe's
army lying some thirty miles south-westward of them
about Antwerp.   On the 17th of July the Allies at July $\frac{6}{17}$.
last got on the march, still with some faint hopes of
saving Charleroi, and proceeded south-eastward, a

---

[1] Ligonier to Harrington, July $\frac{1}{12}$, 1746.

1746. movement which Saxe at once parried by marching parallel with them to the Dyle between Arschot and Louvain. Pushing forward, despite endless difficulties of transport and forage, through a wretched barren country, the Allies, now under command of Prince Charles of Lorraine, reached Peer, turned southward across the Demer at Hasselt, and by the 27th of July were at Borchloen. They were thus actually on the eastern side of the French main army, within reach of the Mehaigne and not without good hope of saving Namur if not Charleroi. On the 1st of August they crossed the Mehaigne, only to learn to their bitter disappointment that Charleroi had surrendered that very morning. Saxe meanwhile, with the principal part of his army, still lay entrenched at Louvain, with detachments pushed forward to Tirlemont and Gembloux. The Allies continued their march before the eyes of these detachments to Masy on the Orneau, and there took up a position between that river and the head-waters of the Mehaigne, fronting to the north-east. This was the line approved through many generations of war as the best for the protection of Namur.[1]

July $\frac{16}{27}$.

July 21. Aug. 1.

Saxe now drew nearer to them, and the two armies lay opposite to each other, in many places not more than a musket-shot apart, both entrenched to the teeth. The Allies so far had decidedly gained a success, but they were outnumbered by the French by three to two, and they were confined within a narrow space wherein subsistence was extremely difficult ; while, if they moved, Namur was lost. Ligonier, who was most uneasy over the situation, longed for five thousand cavalry with which to make a dash at

[1] Ligonier to Harrington, July $\frac{9}{20}$, $\frac{13}{24}$, $\frac{16}{27}$.

Malines and so to call the enemy back in haste to 1746.
defend Brussels and Antwerp.[1] Prince Charles, however, was averse from operations of such a nature.
His hope was that Saxe would offer him battle on the
historic plain of Ramillies, where, notwithstanding
the disparity of numbers, he trusted that the quality
of his troops and the traditions of victory would
enable him to prevail. But Saxe had no intention of
doing anything of the kind. He did indeed shift his
position farther to the north and east, with the field
of Ramillies in his rear, but it was not to offer battle.
Pushing out detachments to eastward he captured
Huy, and cutting off the Allies' communications with Aug. $\frac{18}{29}$.
Liège and Maestricht forced them to cross the Meuse
and to fall back on Maestricht from the other side of
the river. Cross the Meuse the Allies accordingly
did, unmolested, to Ligonier's great relief, by twenty
thousand French who were stationed on the eastern
bank of the stream. They then opened communication
with Maestricht, five leagues away, while Saxe extended
his army comfortably with its face to the eastward
along the line of the Jaar from Warem to Tongres,
waiting till want of forage should compel the Allies Sept. $\frac{2}{13}$.
to recross the Meuse. Back they came over the river
within a fortnight, as he had expected, and the Marshal,
without attempting to dispute the passage, retreated
quietly for a few miles, knowing full well that his
enemy could not follow him from lack of bread.
Ligonier never in his life longed so intensely for the
end of a campaign.[2]

On the 17th of September the Allies advanced upon

---

[1] *Ibid.*, $\frac{\text{July } 23}{\text{Aug. } 3}$, Aug. $\frac{2}{13}$.

[2] Ligonier to Harrington, Aug. $\frac{9}{20}$, $\frac{19}{30}$, $\frac{\text{Aug. } 26}{\text{Sept. } 6}$, Sept. $\frac{4}{15}$.

M

1746. the French and offered battle. Saxe answered by

Sept. $\frac{6}{17}$. retiring to an impregnable position between Tongres and the Demer. There was no occasion for him to fight, when his enemies were short of provisions and their cavalry was going to ruin from want of forage. So there the two armies remained once more, within sight of each other but unwilling to fight, because an attack on the entrenchments of either host would have led to the certain destruction of the attacking force. But meanwhile the trenches had been opened

Aug. 30. before Namur by a French corps under the Prince of
Sept. 10. Clermont, and within nine days the town had fallen. Ligonier again urged his design, for which he had prepared the necessary magazines, to upset Saxe's plans by a dash upon Antwerp, but he could find no support in the council of war ; so there was nothing for the Allies to do but to wait until some further French success should compel them to move. Such a success was not long in coming. The castle of Namur sur- rendered after a miserable defence of but eleven days ; Clermont's corps was released for operations in the field, and the Allies were forced to fall back for the

Sept. 27. protection of Liège. Accordingly, on the 7th of
Oct. 7. October they crossed the Jaar, not without annoyance from the enemy, and took up a new position, which gave them indeed possession of Liège, but placed them between the Meuse in their rear, and an army of nearly twice their strength on the Jaar before their front.[1]

Sept. 29. Now at last Saxe resolved to strike a blow. On
Oct. 10. the 10th of October he crossed the Jaar with evident intention of an attack, and the Allied army received orders to þe ready for action before the following dawn.

[1] Ligonier to Harrington, $\frac{\text{Sept. 24}}{\text{Oct. 5}}$, $\frac{\text{Sept. 28}}{\text{Oct. 9}}$.

The Allies' position faced very nearly due west, the 1746. army being drawn up astride of the two paved roads leading into Liège from Tongres and St. Trond. Their extreme right rested on the Jaar and was covered by the villages of Slins, Fexhe, and Enick, all of which were strongly entrenched and occupied by the Austrians. South of Enick extended an open plain from that village to the village of Liers, and in this plain was

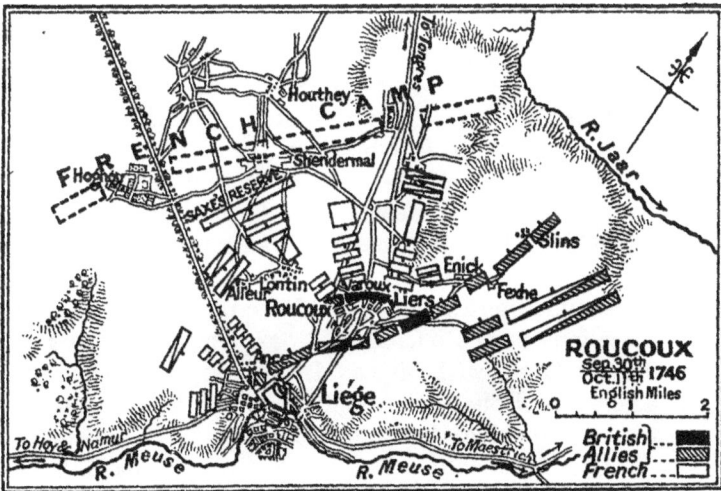

posted the Hanoverian infantry and four British battalions, the Eighth, Nineteenth, Thirty-third, and Forty-third Foot, with the Hessian infantry on their left, in rear of Liers. The Hanoverian cavalry prolonged the line southward to the village of Varoux, and the Sixth and Seventh Dragoons and Scots Greys continued it to the village of Roucoux, from which point Dutch troops carried it on to the village of Ance, which formed the extreme left of the position. Ligonier did not like the situation, for he did not see how the

1746. turning of the left flank could be prevented if, as would certainly be the case, the French should seriously attempt it. Prince Charles, knowing that, if his right were turned, his retreat to Maestricht would be cut off, had taken care to hold the right flank in real strength and dared not weaken it ; but the position, with the Meuse in its rear, was perilously shallow, while the convergence of two ravines from the Jaar and Mehaigne into its centre allowed of but one narrow way of communication between the right and the left of the army. The defects of the Allies' dispositions were in fact not unlike those which had proved fatal to King William at Landen ; and Ligonier's anxiety was proved to rest on all too good foundation.

Sept. 30.
Oct. 11.
The morning of the 11th of October opened with bad news for the Allies. The French had been admitted into Liège by the inhabitants behind the backs of the Dutch, so that the Prince of Waldeck, who commanded on the left, was obliged to withdraw eight battalions from Roucoux and post them *en potence* on his left flank, with his cavalry in support. Thus the defence of Roucoux, as well as of Liers and Varoux, was left to eight battalions of British, Hanoverians, and Hessians only. This made the outlook for the Allied left the worse, since it was evident that the brunt of the French attack would fall upon it. Saxe gave Prince Charles little time for reflection. He had one hundred and twenty thousand men against eighty thousand, and he knew that of the eighty thousand at least one-third were tied to the Austrian entrenchments about the Jaar. He opened the action by a furious assault upon the Dutch on the left wing, his infantry being formed in dense columns, so that the attack could be renewed continually by fresh troops. Simultaneously fifty-five battalions in three similar

columns were launched upon Liers, Varoux, and 1746.
Roucoux. Outmatched though they were, Dutch,
Germans, and British all fought splendidly and repelled
more than one attack. But, to use Ligonier's words,
as soon as two French brigades had been repulsed in
each village, a third brigade ran in ; and the eight
battalions, though they still held Liers, were forced to
withdraw both from Roucoux and Varoux. Being
rallied, however, by Ligonier, they advanced again
and recaptured both villages ; and the Nineteenth
and Forty-third took up a position in a hollow road
which they held to the last. The Dutch now began
to retire across the rear of the position from the left,
in good order despite of heavy losses, while Ligonier
checked the enemy in the plain with the British
cavalry. When the Dutch had passed, he ordered his
own men to retreat in the same direction, still covering
the movement with the cavalry and with the Thirteenth
and Twenty-sixth Foot, which had been sent to the
field from the garrison of Maestricht. The Austrians
formed a rear-guard in turn when the British and their
German comrades had passed ; and thus the whole
army filed off, unpursued and in perfect order, and
crossed the Meuse in safety on the following morning.

The action may be looked upon as a fortunate
escape for the Allies, since it was impossible, humanly
speaking, that it could have issued favourably for them.
Prince Charles, in seeking to cover both Liège and
Maestricht, had attempted too much. His army thus
occupied too wide a front, the villages in the centre
were too weakly held, there was hardly anywhere a
second line of infantry, and the left flank could not be
sustained against so superior an enemy. The total
loss of the Allies was about five thousand men, which
was sufficiently severe considering that but a third

1746. of the army was engaged.   The casualties of the British were three hundred and fifty killed and wounded, of whom no fewer than two hundred belonged to the Forty-third.   The French lost as many men as the Allies, or more, and gained little by the action except eight guns captured from the British, Hanoverians, and Hessians.   Had not the Allied troops been far better in quality and discipline than the French, they must have been lost during their retreat with superior numbers both in flank and rear.   Both armies presently retired into winter-quarters, and the campaign ended far less disastrously than might have been feared for the Allies.[1]

Unfortunately, however, it was not in Flanders only that discredit fell upon the British arms.   At the end of September a force of six battalions [2] was sent, under command of General St. Clair, to the coast of Brittany to attack Port L'Orient and destroy the stores of the French East India Company there.   The

Sept. 20. enterprise was conducted with amazing feebleness.
Oct. 1. The troops landed at Quimperle Bay practically unopposed, but, being fired at on their march on the following day, were turned loose to the plunder of a small town as a punishment to the inhabitants for their resistance.   On the following day they reached L'Orient, which the Deputy Governor of the East India Company offered to surrender on good terms.   His overtures, however, were rejected and a siege was begun in form ; but, after a few days of firing and the loss of about a hundred men killed and wounded, St. Clair thought it prudent to retreat ; and on the

Oct. $\frac{1}{12}$. 12th of October the troops re-embarked and returned

---

[1] Ligonier to Harrington, $\frac{\text{Sept. 28}}{\text{Oct. 9}}$, Oct. $\frac{20}{31}$.

[2] 1st, 15th, 28th, 30th, 39th, and 42nd Foot.

to England.   Anything more pointless than the design 1746.
or more contemptible than the execution of this project
can hardly be conceived, for it simply employed
regiments which were badly needed in Flanders and
America, in useless operations which did not amount
to a diversion.

If the cause of Queen Maria Theresa was to be 1747.
saved, it was evident that great efforts were imperative
in the coming campaign of 1747. To meet the vast
numbers brought into the field by the French the
Austrians promised to have sixty thousand men at
Maseyck on the Meuse by April ; the British contributed four regiments of cavalry and fourteen
battalions of infantry ; and it was hoped that the
Allies would take the field with a total strength of one
hundred and ten battalions, one hundred and sixty
squadrons, and two hundred and twenty guns, besides
irregular troops, the whole to be under command of
the Duke of Cumberland.[1]   Unfortunately the weather
was adverse to an early opening of the campaign ; and
the French, by the seizure of Cadsand and Sluys,
which were shamefully surrendered by the Dutch,
closed the southern mouth of the Scheldt below Antwerp.   This was a sad blow to the arrangements for
the transport of the Allies, since it brought about
the necessity of hauling all the forage for the British
overland from Breda.   Had Cumberland been in a
position to open the campaign before the French, he
meant to have laid siege to Antwerp ; as things were,
he was compelled, thanks chiefly to the apathy of the
Dutch, to attempt to bring Saxe to a general action.
His last letter before beginning operations has, however,
an interest of another kind.   It contained a recom-

[1] Cumberland to Harrington, Feb. $\frac{6}{17}$, March $\frac{20}{31}$, $\frac{\text{March } 24}{\text{April } 4}$.

1747.   mendation that Major James Wolfe might be permitted to purchase a vacant lieutenant-colonelcy in the Eighth Foot, that officer having served constantly and well during the past two years as a major of brigade, and proved himself capable and desirous to do his duty.[1]

The French being encamped between Malines and Louvain, Cumberland collected his troops at Tilburg and advanced straight upon them, encamping on the 26th of May on the Great Neth, a little to the east of Antwerp, between Lierre and Herenthout. Saxe, entrenched as usual to the teeth, remained immovable for three weeks, and Cumberland despaired of bringing him to action. At length the news that a detached corps of thirty thousand French, under the Prince of Clermont, was on the old ground about Tongres, moved Cumberland to march to the Demer, in the hope of overwhelming Clermont before Saxe could join him. Saxe, however, was on his guard, and on the 29th of June prepared to concentrate the whole of his army at Tongres. Cumberland thereupon decided to take up Saxe's camp of the previous year, from Bilsen, on the head-waters of the Demer, to Tongres. So sending forward Count Daun, afterwards well known as an antagonist of Frederick the Great, with a corps of Austrians to occupy Bilsen, he ordered the rest of the army to follow as quickly as possible on the next day. Riding forward at daybreak of the morrow, Cumberland was dismayed to see the French advancing in two columns from Tongres, as if to fall upon the head of his own army. This was a surprise. Cumberland knew that Saxe was in motion but had not expected him so soon ; and indeed Saxe had made a notable march, for his army had not left Louvain until the 29th of June

May $\frac{15}{26}$.

June $\frac{15}{26}$.

June $\frac{18}{29}$.

June $\frac{19}{30}$.

June 20.
July 1.

----

[1] Cumberland to Chesterfield, May $\frac{1}{12}$, $\frac{9}{20}$

and had traversed little less than fifty miles in two days. 1747.
The Duke lost no time in setting such troops as were
on the spot in order of battle, and hurried away to see
if those on the march could be brought up in time to
force back the French, and to secure the position of his
choice. But the French cavalry was too quick for him,
and, before Ligonier could bring up the English horse,
had occupied the centre of the ground which Cumberland had intended for himself. Ligonier drew up his
squadrons before them to bar their farther advance,
and the Allied infantry, as it came up, was formed in
order of battle, fronting, however, not to eastward, as
had been originally designed, but almost due south.
In fact, owing to Saxe's unexpected arrival and to
deficient arrangements by the staff of the Allies, there
seems to have been considerable delay in putting the
Allied army into any formation at all, or the French
might certainly have been forced back to Tongres.
Saxe's rear had not yet come up and the men were
fatigued by a long and harassing march ; but Cumberland was not the man to fight an action of the type of
Oudenarde, and the opportunity was lost.[1]

The position now occupied by the Allies extended
from some rising ground known as the Commanderie,
a little to the south-east of Bilsen, along a chain of
villages and low heights to the Jaar, a little to the south
of Maestricht. The Commanderie being the right of
the line was held by the Austrians, with a strong corps
thrown back *en potence* to Bilsen to protect the right
flank ; for it was as important on this field as on that
of Roucoux that the retreat into Holland should not

---

[1] Cumberland blamed the Austrian General, Baroney, and his
irregulars for supine negligence on the march. Cumberland to
Chesterfield, July $\frac{6}{17}$, 1747.

1747. be cut off. The ground possessed natural features of strength which were turned to good account, so good account indeed that the Allied right, like the French left at Ramillies, could neither attack nor be attacked. Eastward from the Commanderie the Austrians occupied the heights of Spaeven, together with the villages of Gross and Klein Spaeven ; next to them the Dutch formed the centre of the line, while the Hanoverians and British held the villages of Val, or Vlytingen, and Lauffeld, and prolonged the line to its extreme left at the village of Kesselt.

There the Allies lay on their arms until nightfall, while Saxe's weary battalions tramped on till far into the night up to their bivouacs. At daybreak the French were seen to be in motion, marching and countermarching in a way that Cumberland did not quite understand ; the fact being that Saxe, as at Roucoux, was doubling the left wing of his army in rear of the right, for the formation of those dense columns of attack which he could handle with such consummate skill. After observing them until nine o'clock, Cumberland came to the conclusion that the Marshal meditated no immediate movement, and retired to the Commanderie for breakfast. He had hardly sat down when an urgent message arrived from Ligonier that the enemy was on the point of attacking. Cumberland at once returned and moved the left of his line somewhat forward, setting fire to the village of Vlytingen and occupying Lauffeld with three British and two Hessian battalions. Lauffeld was a straggling village a quarter of a mile long, covered by a multitude of small enclosures with mud walls about six feet high, which were topped by growing hedges. It was thus easily turned into a strong post for infantry ; and cannon were posted both in its front and flanks. The remainder

June 21.
July 2.

of the British were drawn up for the most part in rear 1747.
of Lauffeld in order to feed and relieve its garrison, the June 21.
brigade of Guards being posted in the hedges before July 2.
Vlytingen.   The British cavalry stood on the right of
the infantry and joined their line to that of the Dutch.

Meanwhile Saxe, sending forward a cloud of irregular troops to mask his movements, had despatched
Count d'Estrées and the Count of Ségur with a strong

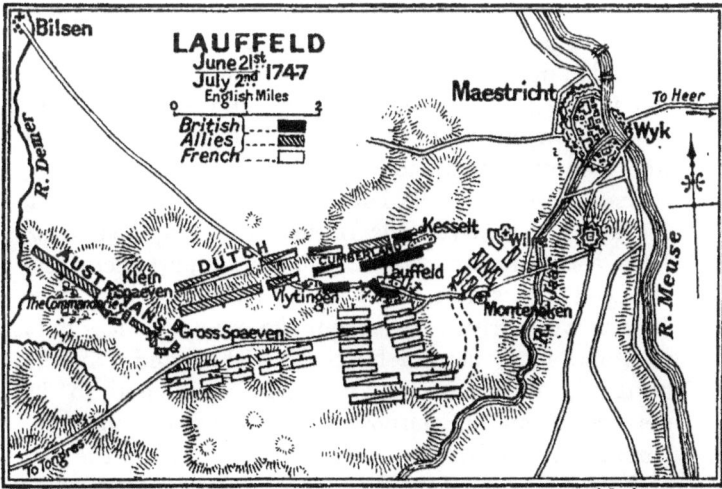

Stanfords Geog.¹ Estab.ᵗ London

force of infantry and cavalry to seize the villages of
Montenaken and Wilre on the left flank of the Allies.
This service was performed with little loss.   At the
same time he directed the Marquis of Salières, with six
brigades of foot and twenty guns, to attack Vlytingen,
and launched five brigades, with as many guns, backed
by a large force of cavalry, against Lauffeld.   The
assault of the French infantry upon Lauffeld was met by
a furious resistance.   It was just such another struggle
as that of Neerwinden, from hedge to hedge and from

wall to wall ; and the French, for all their superiority of numbers, were driven back headlong from the village with terrible loss. Salières met with little better success against the brigade of Guards in the hedges of Vlytingen ; but with great readiness he turned half of his guns to his right against Lauffeld and the remainder against a ravine on his left, with most destructive effect. Cumberland, observing the fury with which Saxe had concentrated his attack against these two villages, asked the Austrians to relieve him by a diversion upon his right ; but the Austrian troops could not face the fire of Salières's guns, and it became clear that Vlytingen and Lauffeld must be held by the British and Hanoverians alone.

Saxe's first attack had been brilliantly repulsed. He at once replaced the beaten troops by two fresh brigades of infantry, with cavalry to support them, and renewed the assault, but with no better success. The British were driven back from the outer defences only to stand more fiercely by those within, and Lauffeld remained unconquered. But Saxe was not to be deterred from his purpose. Two more brigades, including the six Irish battalions that had saved the day at Fontenoy, were added to those already on the spot, and the whole of them launched for a third attack against Lauffeld. They were met by the same stubborn resistance and the same deadly fire ; and the Irish brigade lost no fewer than sixty officers in the struggle. Nevertheless Irish impetuosity carried the rest of the troops forward ; the British were borne back to the rearmost edge of the village, and the French began to swarm up the slope beyond it. Cumberland promptly ordered the whole of his line of infantry to advance ; and the French at once gave way before them. The French cavalry was obliged to drive the foot forward

at the sword's point, but Cumberland continued steadily
to gain ground despite their efforts. Then at an unlucky moment, some Dutch squadrons in the centre
were seized with panic and came galloping straight
into the British line, carried away the Hessians and
one squadron of the Greys and fell pell-mell upon the
Twenty-first and Twenty-third Fusiliers. The Twenty-
first, anticipating the treatment of the Belgians at
Waterloo, gave the Dutchmen a volley and partly
saved themselves, but the Twenty - third suffered
terribly, and the whole line was thrown into confusion.
Before order could be restored, Salières had thrown
three more brigades upon Lauffeld, which closed in
round it, blocking up a hollow road which formed the
entrance into it from the rear, and barring the way for
all further reinforcements of the Allies. The few troops
that were left in the village were speedily overpowered,
and Lauffeld was lost.

Some of Daun's Austrians now advanced to Cumberland's help from the right ; but three French brigades
of cavalry, which were waiting before Vlytingen, at
once moved forward to check them, and charging boldly
into them succeeded in turning them back, though
themselves roughly handled when retiring from the
charge. Meanwhile Saxe had brought up ten guns
to right and left of Lauffeld, and reinforcing the cavalry
of D'Estrées and Ségur extended it in one long line
from Lauffeld to Wilre, for a final crushing attack on
the Allied left. Order had been restored among the
British infantry, who were now retreating with great
steadiness ; but they were wholly unsupported.
Ligonier, determined to save them at any cost, caught
up the Greys, Inniskillings, and Cumberland's dragoons,
and led them straight against the masses of the French
cavalry. The gallant brigade charged home, crashed

headlong through the horse, and fell upon the infantry beyond, but being galled by their fire and attacked in all quarters by other French squadrons, was broken past all rallying and very heavily punished. Ligonier himself was overthrown and taken prisoner. Cumberland, who had plunged into the broken ranks to try to rally the British troopers, was cut off by the French dragoons, and only with difficulty contrived to join the remainder of his cavalry on the left. With these he covered the retreat of the army, which was successfully effected in good order and with little further loss.

So ended the battle of Lauffeld, in which the British bore the brunt with a firmness that extorted the praise even of Frenchmen, but of which few Englishmen have ever heard. The troops, in Cumberland's words, behaved one and all so well that he could not commend any one regiment without doing injustice to the rest. The total loss of the five regiments of horse and fourteen battalions of foot was close upon two thousand men.[1] The three devoted regiments which charged with Ligonier were the worst sufferers, the Greys losing one hundred and sixty men, the Inniskillings one hundred and twenty, and Cumberland's dragoons nearly one hundred. The loss of the whole of the Allies was about six thousand men, that of the French decidedly greater, amounting indeed, according to Saxe's account, to not less than ten thousand men. The British, moreover, had nine French colours and five French standards as trophies for their consolation. Finally, the French failed to accomplish the object of the action, which was to cut off the Allies from Maestricht.

---

[1] The regiments present at Lauffeld were the Greys, 4th Hussars, Inniskillings, 7th Hussars, and Cumberland's dragoons, one battalion each of the 1st and 3rd Guards, 3rd, 4th, 13th, 19th, 21st, 23rd, 25th, 32nd, 33rd, 36th, 37th, 48th Foot. The two last had no casualties.

After the battle the Allies crossed the Meuse and 1747. encamped at Heer, a little to the east of Maestricht, while Saxe returned to his quarters at Tongres. The French then detached a corps for the capture of Bergen-op-Zoom ; but the most important transactions of the war still went forward on the Meuse, where constant negotiations were carried on between Saxe and Cumberland. The campaign closed with the fall of Bergen-op-Zoom and with the capture of most of the strong places in Dutch Brabant.

By this time King George and his people in England were thoroughly sick of the war. The British had suffered severely in every action, but had reaped no success except in the fortunate victory of Dettingen. The Dutch had proved themselves useless and contemptible as Allies, their Government feeble and corrupt in council, their troops unstable if not dangerous in action. The Austrians, in spite of lavish subsidies, had never furnished the troops that they had promised, and had invariably obstructed operations through the obstinacy of their Generals and the selfishness of their ends. The opening of the campaign of 1748 was even 1748. more unpromising for the Allies. Saxe, strong in the possession of a superior force, kept Cumberland in suspense between apprehensions for Breda and for Maestricht, and, when finally he laid siege to Maestricht, could match one hundred and fifteen thousand men against Cumberland's five-and-thirty thousand. War on such terms against such a master as Saxe was ridiculous. Moreover, the Dutch, despite of a recent revolution, were more supine than ever ; the Prince of Orange, who was the new ruler, actually keeping two thousand of his troops from the field that they might adorn the baptism of one of his babies. In the face of such facts Cumberland pressed earnestly for

1748.
Apr. $\frac{19}{30}$.
October.

peace ;[1] and on the 30th of April preliminaries were signed, which six months later were expanded into the definite treaty of Aix-la-Chapelle.

The peace left matters practically as they had stood before the war, with the significant exception that Frederick the Great retained Silesia. Not a word was said as to the regulation of trade between England and Spain, which had been the original ground of quarrel ; and, as between England and France, it was agreed that there should be mutual restitution of all captures. Yet this could not set the two countries in the same position as before the war. The French were utterly exhausted ; but the British, though not a little harassed by the cost of maintaining armies and producing subsidies, had received a military training which was to stand them in good stead for the great struggle that lay before them.

AUTHORITIES.—The official correspondence in the Record Office. *F.O. Military Auxiliary Expeditions. Campagnes de Louis XV. Espagnac. Life of the Duke of Cumberland.* Some useful details as to Lauffeld are to be found in the *Gentleman's Magazine.*

---

[1] Cumberland to Newcastle, March $\frac{18}{29}$, $\frac{\text{March 22}}{\text{April 2}}$, $\frac{\text{March 26}}{\text{April 6}}$.

THE CAMPAIGN OF 1793-1794

VOL. IV. BOOK XII. CHAPTER III

WAR was declared by the French Convention on the 1st of February 1793, and Dumouriez was ordered to invade Holland forthwith. The Convention, thirsting for the wealth of the Bank of Amsterdam, was anxious to make sure of it before the Allies could put their strength into the field. Two months earlier, when his troops were heartened by the victory of Jemappe, no order could have been more welcome to Dumouriez than this ; and even now, though he had few men upon whom he could depend, he resolved if possible to make good the defects of his army by swift and sudden action. The French troops on the northern frontier were very widely scattered, their cantonments extending north and south on the lower Meuse from Roermond to Maastricht, and east and west from the upper Rhine through Aachen to Liège and Namur. His original plan had been to turn all the waterways and fortresses that bar the entrance into Holland from the south, and to invade it by way of Nimeguen ; but time was so precious that he resolved to collect a small force of but seventeen thousand men at Antwerp, and to march from thence with all secrecy direct upon Amsterdam. At the same time he directed thirty

1793. thousand men from the east under General Miranda to take the Dutch fortresses of Maastricht and Venloo, and then to make for Nimeguen. Speed, in his view, was everything, for the Austrians had already forty thousand men cantoned to the east of the Rhine, and were shortly to be reinforced.

Meanwhile the Allies were still making up their plans for the next campaign. Brunswick and Prince Frederick Josias of Coburg-Saalfeld, who had been appointed Commander-in-Chief of the Austrian army, met at Frankfurt, and, after many conferences between the 6th and the 14th of February, decided upon a scheme of operations, which by their own showing required forty thousand more men than they had any expectation of collecting. They saved themselves, however, by laying it down as a cardinal principle that, until Mainz were recovered from the French, the Allied forces must not attempt to pass from the east to the west bank of the Meuse. Belgium (so argued the Austrians) had been eaten up, and so long as the navigation of the Rhine was blocked at Mainz, the subsistence of the Imperial troops on the west of the Meuse must be difficult. Moreover, if the French should retire before an Austrian advance, and mass all their forces on the Rhine, then they might beat Brunswick, who, unless his retreat were assured by the possession of Mainz, would be in danger of utter destruction. The reader should take note of this decision, for not only is it the key to much that appears puzzling in the coming campaign, but it is an excellent example of the principle on which Coburg and Brunswick conducted war, namely, to look at risks first and at objects afterwards. The immediate problem of the defence of the Dutch provinces was left without so much as an attempt at solution. Both Grenville

in England and Auckland at the Hague had long 1793.
foreseen the certainty of a French attack upon them,
and had strained every nerve to stir the authorities to
action. But the Stadtholder was a man of almost
inhuman dulness, apathy and stupidity; and all
popular energy was paralysed by the spirit of faction,
which, never inactive in Holland, had under the influence of French agents become almost a spirit of revolution. The Dutch army was so defective in training,
equipment and discipline that it had ceased to exist
as an efficient force; and its few foreign corps, which
alone deserved the name of regiments, had been driven
to mutiny by a reduction of their pay below the rate
fixed by their contract. Even in January and
February, Auckland wrote that the Stadtholder looked
for British ships and British troops to save him,[1] and
that the French party was derisively insinuating that
England, nominally the faithful ally of the Dutch Republic, was content to desert her in the hour of danger.
Finally, on the 15th of February he begged that the
Duke of York might be sent over with a few officers of
experience, even if without troops, to take command
of the Dutch. " Men, commanders, ships and money,"
he wrote, " we could not ask for more if this country
were a part of Yorkshire, but I incline to think that it
should be considered so for the present; and if it is
brought to a question whether we are to conquer it
and keep it, or whether Dumouriez is to do it, I have
no doubt as to the decision."

Still the British Government hesitated, for, thanks
to its neglect of the Army, it possessed but a handful
of troops, and was unwilling to move them to the Con-

---

[1] *Dropmore Papers*, Auckland to Grenville, 21st and 25th
January; 14th and 15th February. *F.O. Holland*, 16th February
1793. And see *Auckland Correspondence* and *Dropmore Papers*
generally, November 1792 to February 1793.

1793. tinent. Then suddenly, on the 16th of February,
Feb. 16. Dumouriez dashed out from Antwerp with his tiny
force in four columns. One small body instantly
pushed northward towards Moerdyk, to collect boats
for the passage of the arm of the sea called the
Hollandsdiep ; another marched upon Klundert and
Willemstadt, a third north-eastward to attack Breda,
and a fourth to the north-west to blockade Bergen-op-
Zoom and Steenbergen. Everywhere his coming was
welcomed by the Dutch. Breda, with large stores
of munitions of war, was disgracefully surrendered
Feb. 26. on the 26th of February ; Klundert and Gertruyden-
berg fell in quick succession ; Willemstadt was then
besieged with the captured cannon, and by the 9th of
March 9. March Dumouriez was prepared to essay the passage
of the Hollandsdiep. But here his course was stayed,
for his activity had stirred his enemies on every side.
Feb. 20.   On the 20th of February the seven battalions of
British Guards were suddenly paraded before the Horse
Guards ; and the Duke of York, announcing that the
first battalions of the three regiments were ordered to
proceed on active service, called for volunteers from
the others to bring them up to strength. The whole
brigade thereupon stepped forward as one man ; and
five days later three battalions, numbering under two
thousand men of all ranks and denominations, marched
to Greenwich amid the cheers, and something more
than the cheers, of an enormous and enthusiastic
crowd.[1] By nightfall the whole were embarked upon
vessels too small to carry more than two-thirds of
their number in safety, without medicines or medical
appliances, without the slightest reserve of ammuni-

[1] The head of the column was able to keep sober ; the rear, under
the endearments of the populace, subsided dead drunk on the
road and was brought on in carts. *Narrative of an Officer of the
Guards.*

tion, and of course without transport of any descrip- 1793.
tion. Their commander was Colonel Gerard Lake
of the First Guards, and he was ordered on no account
to move his men above twenty-four hours' distance
from Helvoetsluis, so as to be able to return on the
shortest notice. By the mercy of Heaven these March 1.
troops safely reached that port, narrowly escaping a
gale which would probably have condemned them either
to drowning or asphyxiation ; and four days later they
proceeded to Dort to oppose Dumouriez's passage of March 5.
the Hollandsdiep. About the same time a flotilla of
Dutch gunboats arrived in the Meuse, many of them
manned by British sailors and flying British colours.
Auckland, by threatening to take command in Holland
himself, had at last compelled the miserable Stadtholder
to issue orders for the defence of his country.[1]

But the obstacles which were multiplying in
Dumouriez's front were as nothing to the storm that
suddenly broke upon his flank. Miranda had duly Feb. 20.
moved up to the siege of Maastricht with a force
inadequate to the task and, moreover, dangerously
dispersed ; but the Austrians, declaring themselves
too weak to move, still remained torpid in their cantonments, perhaps the more stubbornly because the
Prussian Agent at the Austrian headquarters was
perpetually urging them to action. At last, however,
Coburg on the 26th began to concentrate his forty Feb. 26.
thousand men and to pass them in five columns across
the river ; and on the 1st of March, to the great sur- March 1.
prise of the French, he burst upon their cantonments
on the Meuse, and for four days drove them in utter
rout before him. Coburg himself and the left wing

---

[1] Lake to Dundas, 2nd March 1793. Lake's Instructions, 23rd
February. Grenville to Auckland, 20th February 1793. *F.O.
Holland*, Auckland to Grenville, 4th March 1793.

1793. halted before Liège, but on the right the Archduke Charles, with the impetuosity of twenty-one years and the instinct of a born soldier, followed up the disorderly rabble from Maastricht southward upon Tongres, boldly attacking wherever he met the enemy. Such of the French as had been in action fled in all directions, abandoning everything ; ten thousand deserters hurried across the frontier into France ; and a small remnant took refuge behind the canal at Louvain, where it was joined by such French divisions as had not been engaged. Had Coburg pursued his advantage and advanced instantly with all his forces, he could have ended the campaign at once, for the people, furious at the exactions of the Jacobins, and, above all, at the theft of the plate from their churches, had turned savagely upon the retreating French.

March 5. Instead of this he halted on the 5th, and wasted ten whole days in cantonments between Maastricht and Tongres. The Convention now ordered Dumouriez at once to proceed to Louvain and assume command,

March 9. which he did with a very bad grace, leaving General Flers to take his place in Holland. His presence did much to restore confidence in the French army, and he was not a little helped by Coburg's inaction. Nevertheless the news that reached him was singularly disquieting. Fresh regiments were embarking from England for Helvoetsluis ; two reinforcing columns of Austrians were advancing from the Rhine upon Namur ; and eight thousand Prussians, under the Duke of Brunswick-Oels, had arrived at Bois-le-Duc

March 11. on the 11th, and were moving with five thousand British and Dutch upon Breda, to cut off the troops on the Hollandsdiep from France and Dumouriez's own soldiers from Antwerp. In so desperate a situation there was no choice but to take the offensive.

On the 15th Coburg at last resumed his advance 1793.
with forty-two thousand men; and on the 16th March 15.
Dumouriez marched with forty-eight thousand to
meet him. On the 18th the decisive action was March 18.
fought at Neerwinden, when the French were totally
defeated, with a loss of five thousand men and three
guns. The volunteers and the National Guards were
the troops that failed in the battle; and after it the
men broke up and fled by whole battalions. Ten
thousand deserted in the ten days following the
action, and Dumouriez was fain to form a rearguard
out of his artillery and his few battalions of the Line,
and to fall back on Louvain. Coburg, who had lost
about three thousand men, made little attempt at
pursuit, keeping his main body halted at Tirlemont
until the 22nd, but exhorting the Duke of Brunswick-
Oels to hasten from Bois-le-Duc to Malines to cut
off Dumouriez's retreat to Antwerp. The Duke,
who had already permitted Flers to withdraw with
impunity the bulk of his forces to Antwerp, was evidently not disposed to second Austrian operations
with Prussian troops, for he refused to move. However, the advance of the Austrians compelled
Dumouriez to evacuate first Louvain and then Mar. 23-24.
Brussels; and on the 25th, finding himself obliged March 25.
to abandon Namur also, he opened negotiations with
Coburg. He had quarrelled with the Convention
beyond hope of reconciliation over the iniquity of
its rule in Belgium; and he now proposed that the
French should retreat from the whole country, and
that he should march to Paris to re-establish the
monarchy, the Allies meanwhile halting on the frontier
and receiving the fortress of Condé as a guarantee.
An agreement to this effect was duly made with the
Chief of the Austrian Staff on the 27th, and a circular March 27.

1793. was issued from the Austrian headquarters, suggesting a conference of the representatives of the powers to decide as to the measures to be next taken.

There is no need to tell at length the story of Dumouriez's adventures during the following days. It must suffice that he was driven from the midst of April 5. his army, and on the 5th of April was fain to take refuge with the Austrians. Fragments of several corps and one complete regiment of Hussars followed him, unwilling to part with their beloved General ; but several thousand French troops in Belgium and Holland, which might have been cut off to a man, were allowed to retire in peace to the frontier. None the less the fact remained that even a dilatory commander at the head of a force of discordant Allies had sufficed to drive the armies of the Revolution in shameful disorder from the Austrian Netherlands.

VOL. IV. BOOK XII. CHAPTER IV

ON the 5th of March it was resolved to send the 1793.
Fourteenth, Thirty - seventh, and Fifty - third Foot, March 5.
completed by drafts from the new independent companies, to join the Duke as a brigade under Major-
general Ralph Abercromby. These regiments, however, were subject to the same instructions as the
Guards, namely, to remain within immediate reach of
their transports in case their services should be required
elsewhere. Their quality was such that the Adjutant-
general felt constrained to apologise for them both
to Abercromby and to the Duke of York. " I am
afraid," he wrote to the Duke, " that you will not reap
the advantage that you might have expected from
the brigade of the Line just sent over to you, as so
considerable a part of it is composed of nothing but
undisciplined and raw recruits ; and how they are to
be disposed of until they can be taught their business I
am at a loss to imagine. . . . I was not consulted upon
the subject until it was too late to remedy the evil, but
I hope that my remonstrances will be of some use in
the modelling of troops for the Continent in future." It
need hardly be added that, on their arrival in Holland, April 1
two out of the three battalions were found utterly unfit
for service, the new recruits being old men and weakly
boys, worse than the worst that had been accepted
even at the period of greatest exhaustion during the

1793. American War. To send them on active service was, therefore, simply waste of money.[1]

But this was only one of the evils which ensued because an extremely ignorant civilian was too vain to consult his military advisers before giving military orders. Any soldier at the War Office could have told him that the method of raising independent companies to recruit existing regiments had been found wasteful and unsatisfactory in the past ; and, indeed, at this very time the Chief Secretary Cooke wrote to him from Ireland a strong protest against the whole system. It was expensive, because it meant the provision of half-pay for their officers as soon as the men had been drafted out ; it was unfair to old subalterns, because they were passed over by boys who by good fortune had raised recruits cheaply.   It produced a bad class of recruit, because these young officers were poor judges of men ; and finally it encouraged desertion, for the crimps, so long as they poured a certain number of recruits into the depots by a certain time, cared not the least whether they deserted afterwards.   Nor was Cooke content only to criticise, for he produced an alternative plan for allowing each of the fourteen battalions in Ireland to raise two additional companies of one hundred men apiece, and for granting to the commanding officers the privilege of recommending officers for them.   The scheme was approved and was found to be most successful ; but it was not introduced into England, where, on the contrary, the number of independent companies was still further increased.[2]

[1] *Dropmore Papers*, Auckland to Grenville, 5th and 13th March 1793.   *S.C.L.B.* 5th March ; Abercromby's instructions, 9th March ; Dundas to York, 15th March 1793 ; *C.C.L.B.* 2nd March ; Adj.-gen. to York, 27th March, 12th April 1793. Calvert, pp. 53, 67.

[2] *S.P. Ireland*, Cooke to Hobart, 23rd April ; Westmoreland to Hobart, 27th April ; Dundas to Westmoreland, 16th May, 31st July 1793 ; *S.C.L.B.* 18th May 1793.

Again, the Adjutant - general, if consulted, could 1793.
have warned Dundas to be chary of his battalions,
since some of them would certainly be required for
the Fleet. The King's Navy was labouring under
the grievances which in four years were to drive the
seamen to mutiny; and as a natural consequence
men were hardly to be obtained by any means. On
the very day when the declaration of war was received, Feb. 7.
the Fleet swallowed up two battalions; and by the
end of March it had absorbed so many men that only
three regiments of the Line were to be found south
of the Tweed. In fact the Horse Guards did not know
where to turn for another battalion. This, however,
did not prevent Dundas from presently sending another
emissary to Jamaica, to commit England still more
deeply to operations in the most leeward sphere of the
West Indies. Yet he had no reserve of any description
to rely upon, except fourteen thousand Hanoverians
and eight thousand Hessians, which, pursuant to the
time-honoured practice, were taken into British pay;
and of these the latter only, being mercenaries pure
and simple, could be counted upon for service beyond
sea.[1]

Since the kingdom was thus stripped of regular
troops, it was necessary to raise other forces for its
security; but this also was done as foolishly as possible.
Early in February it was rightly and wisely decided to
call out nineteen thousand additional Militia; but in
the execution precisely the same mistake was made as
in France. Personal service was not insisted upon;
there arose a great demand for substitutes; and the
Militia, instead of gaining a substantial increase, simply
cut off from the Army the sources of its supply of

[1] *S.C.L.B.* 7th February. *C.C.L.B.* Adj.-gen. to Duke of York,
2nd and 12th April 1793. Dundas to Williamson, 4th April 1793.

188 BRITISH CAMPAIGNS IN FLANDERS

1793. recruits. In Scotland, which as yet had no Militia, recourse was made to the raising of Fencible regiments, that is to say, of regular troops enlisted for home-service and for the duration of the war only. This system had so far been applied only on a small scale, the regiments of Fencibles during the Seven Years' War and the American War of Independence having been but few;[1] but it now received great and sudden expansion. On the 2nd of March authority was issued for the raising of seven regiments of Fencible Infantry in Scotland at a stroke ; besides one already authorised Feb. 20. for the Isle of Man, and another, added in April, for the Orkney Islands.[2] With the leading magnates of Scotland at their head, these new corps were speedily completed ; but there was one Scottish nobleman who went further than his peers, and raised a regiment in the Highlands for general service. This was Thomas Humberstone Mackenzie, afterwards the last Earl of Seaforth ; and his regiment remains with us, still known by his name, but yet more famous under its number of the Seventy-eighth. The reader should take note of the Fencible regiments, for in the years before us we shall see them increased and multiplied in all three kingdoms. Meanwhile, he should remark that within a month of the declaration of war there were already three distinct forces, the Army, the Fencibles, and the Militia, all bidding against each other for the recruits which only the Regular Army could turn to efficient account.

[1] Duke of Argyll's and Earl of Sutherland's, 1759 ; Lord Fred. Campbell's, 1778 ; Earl of Sutherland's, Fauconberg's (Yorkshire), North's (Cinque Ports), 1779.

[2] Athol's or the Manx, Sir J. Grant's, Gower's (or Wemyss's), Eglinton's (or Montgomery's), Breadalbane's, Argyll's, Duke of Gordon's, Hopetoun's, Balfour's (Orkney). Their strength was 650 of all ranks, except the Manx, which were 323 strong.

It is not difficult to perceive the lurking possibilities 1793. of disaster in Dundas's military policy; but until April it showed at any rate a certain consistency. The despatch of troops to the Continent was treated as a temporary measure, designed for the protection of Holland only; and, though the Prince of Coburg had called upon the Duke of York to co-operate in his great sweeping movement from north-east to south-west, the Duke had complied only so far as his instructions and, it may be added, his lack of transport permitted.[1] But much, besides the expulsion of the French from Holland and Belgium, had occurred in March, all tending to embarrass England in the principal object of her Continental policy, the securing of a strong barrier between France and Holland. The fatal question of indemnity, first brought forward by the King of Prussia, had aroused the cupidity of his brother potentate in Austria, who valued the recovery of Belgium chiefly in order that he might exchange it for Bavaria. Pitt had for a moment been willing to consent to the Bavarian exchange (as it was called) for the sake of peace; but upon the outbreak of war he reverted to absolute rejection of it; and, in an evil hour, the British Ambassador at Vienna, Sir Morton March 2. Eden, put forward a suggestion that Austria should be bribed to retain Belgium by the promise of an extension of her frontiers on the side of France. Realising that Austria refused to act disinterestedly, Grenville April 3. reluctantly accepted the proposal; and at the same time the British Government seems to have taken it for granted that it must give the Emperor some assistance towards the conquest of the new barrier.[2]

Accordingly, since no more infantry was to be

[1] Murray to Dundas, 26th March 1793.
[2] Sybel, ii. 230; Grenville to Auckland, 3rd April 1793.

spared from England, eleven regiments of cavalry were ordered to prepare for service on the Continent, though their numbers were so weak that they could not between them muster more than twenty-three squadrons, or about two thousand five hundred of all ranks, fit for service. But, at the same time, the British Ministers shrank from supplying British troops for the advantage of other nations without gaining some equivalent to satisfy the electors of England; wherefore they decided, apparently at the instance of Grenville's elder brother, Lord Buckingham, to claim Dunkirk as Great Britain's indemnity for the war. The choice, viewed from the standpoint of the party-politician, was a good one. Dunkirk, having been taken by Cromwell, sold by Charles the Second, and dismantled under the conditions imposed by the sword of Marlborough, possessed sentimental attractions to the public at large and to the Whigs in particular; while, as a nest of privateers, its extirpation could not but be welcome not only to every merchant in England, but especially to the Chancellor of the Exchequer. No scheme of operations had yet been concerted with Austria, for, indeed, Coburg had advanced from the Roer before nearly all his forces had been collected; but Pitt seems to have thought that, while the Austrian reinforcements were on their way to the front, the mixed force of British, Hanoverians, Hessians, and Dutch might very well master Dunkirk in the course of April, afterwards leaving the Austrians in sufficient strength to pursue their operations in Flanders alone, while the British struck at some other part of France. Thus Pitt was not true even to his own plan of ruining his enemy by the destruction of her colonial trade. Moreover, it is difficult to define what he meant by some other part of France. The old Marquis of

Bouillé, knowing that the heart of the Revolution 1793. could be pierced at Paris, had suggested a descent upon Havre with thirty thousand men; and there was by this time another vulnerable point—namely, La Vendée—in the west of France. But why it should have been necessary to seek out a new point of attack, when troops were already massed or massing on the French frontier within twelve days' march of the capital, and with only a demoralised enemy before them, was a question which seems never to have occurred either to Pitt or to Dundas. There can be no doubt that they fell into a common pitfall of the British politician. They gave so much thought to the treaty which they should lay before Parliament at the close of the war, that they omitted to consider the means of bringing the war itself to a close.[1]

It was in such inauspicious circumstances that the representatives of the various powers met in conference at Antwerp. Coburg, who loathed the war and had hoped to end it by an agreement with Dumouriez, had issued a proclamation declaring himself to be the April 5. ally of all friends of order, and abjuring all projects of conquest in the Emperor's name. Instantly Austrians, Prussians, and English with one voice required him to withdraw it, and to publish a new declaration that he would prosecute the war vigorously. He did so, but with great reluctance; indeed, so bitter was his opposition to the new policy that he tried to open further negotiations with the Convention, and even furnished it with information which he ought to have kept to himself.[2] Meanwhile Lord Auckland

[1] *S.C.L.B.* 21st March, 2nd April; *C.C.L.B.* 25th March 1793. *Dropmore Papers*, ii. 360, 387-89. Buckingham to Grenville, 20th January; the King of Grenville, 29th March; Pitt to Grenville, 1st April 1793. Auckland to Grenville, 31st May 1793.
[2] Sybel, ii. 142.

1793. announced that England, as well as the other powers, would expect an indemnity for her share in the war ; whereupon the Dutch representative announced that, as every one else was taking compensation, he hoped that Holland's claims would not be forgotten.[1] The sharing of the lion's skin having thus been determined, the next thing was to decide upon a plan of operations for slaying the lion. A vague project was drawn out for the attack of the frontier-fortresses, in which Coburg reckoned upon the co-operation of over twenty thousand men, that is to say, of thirteen thousand Hanoverians and seven thousand five hundred British, in British pay, besides fifteen thousand Dutch. Dundas was staggered ; for he had not yet the slightest idea what were the ultimate designs of either of the German powers, who, as he justly complained, were very backward to give an explicit account of their views either as to the conduct of the war or the termination of it. " We cannot advise the King," he wrote, " to give a blind co-operation to measures not distinctly explained." But he hinted that if the Austrians would spare a detachment to help the British to capture Dunkirk at once, England might make fewer difficulties about lending her troops for subsequent operations. The English, he explained, were prejudiced against Continental enterprises ; wherefore it was important to convince the nation early that its troops in Holland were employed for an object intimately connected with the interests of Great Britain and the security of her commerce. " The early capture of Dunkirk by a Prince of the blood," he added, " would give much éclat to the commencement of the war."

---

[1] The insisting upon an indemnity must have been the work of Pitt, probably under the influence of Dundas. Grenville trembled at the word indemnity. *Dropmore Papers*, ii. 392.

In other words, Dundas was ready to employ British 1793. troops in the Low Countries only for a political campaign, and not for the military purposes of the war— to use them, in fact, primarily to win votes rather than battles. The attitude is but too characteristic of British Ministers for War.[1]

Meanwhile the Allies on the frontiers of France remained inactive ; the Austrians, indeed, blockading Condé, where the French kept them engaged with incessant affairs of outposts, but the British contingent still awaiting the orders which Dundas hesitated to give. In the third week of April the chief of the British staff reported that a considerable force of French was entrenched about Dunkirk, too strong to be attacked by the Duke of York's troops, and that there was no operation on which the latter could be employed except in support of the Austrians.[2] We shall presently recognise the unseen hand which had been working at Dunkirk. Ten days more of uncertainty passed away, and at last, on the 1st of May, Coburg produced May 1. a plan of operations. By the middle of May he hoped to have about ninety-two thousand men,[3] to which by the beginning of June would be added thirteen thousand more. He proposed, therefore, to hasten the fall of Condé by a bombardment, and then to advance with fifty-two thousand men to the siege of

[1] Protocol of conference of 7th April. Dundas to Auckland and to Murray, 16th April; Auckland to Grenville, 19th April 1793.

[2] Murray to Dundas, 22nd April 1793.

[3] Prussians, 8000, of which 1800 cavalry ; Austrians, 55,000, of which 10,000 cavalry ; Dutch, 15,000, of which 2500 cavalry ; Hanoverians, 12,000, of which 3000 cavalry ; Hessians, 8000, of which 1500 cavalry ; British, 7200, of which 3000 cavalry. Total, 105,200, of which 27,200 in the pay of England. About 5000 of the Austrians and the 8000 Hessians were not expected till June. Witzleben, ii. 117, 181-186. Coburg to York, 1st and 3rd May ; Murray to Dundas, 5th May ; Dundas to Murray, 10th May 1793.

O

1793. Valenciennes, leaving a cordon of some forty thousand
to cover every imaginable point along a front of some
fifty miles from Maubeuge on the Sambre to Ostend
on the sea. Valenciennes might be expected to fall
at the end of July, and then ten thousand men could
be left to mask Lille, while fifty thousand marched
to the siege of Dunkirk. If this plan were accepted,
Coburg pledged himself to the Duke of York to lend
his best good-will to the attack on Dunkirk. On this
assurance the Duke recommended the plan to which
at last Dundas gave his consent, on the understanding
that the other powers in general and Austria in particular should give an immediate explanation of their
ulterior views. England, he repeated, could not
allow so large a force in her pay to be employed
on operations whose object was undefined ; and he
emphasised the statement by an inquiry as to the
security of Ostend, which so far had been the British
port of disembarkation, evidently as a hint that
England reserved her right to withdraw her troops
at any moment.

This is a good instance of the manner in which
British Ministers evade their responsibility. The
British General had, nearly three weeks before, laid
before Dundas the following issue. " There is no use
for British troops in the Netherlands except to act
in support of the Austrians. Their commander has
submitted a plan based on the active co-operation of
all our troops, present and expected. We think the
plan a good one. Are we to act with him, or are we
not ? " Upon this it was for the Ministry to say at
once to Austria, " Our Generals favour your plan of
campaign, but until we know your ultimate intentions
we cannot take part in it. Unless you come to a
definite understanding with us by a certain day, we

shall order our troops on the spot to re-embark, and 1793. meanwhile we have suspended the march of our reinforcements." Instead of this they said in effect, " We approve the plan of campaign, and thereby commit our troops to it ; but we reserve to ourselves the right to withdraw them, or, in other words, to wreck the operations, whenever we think proper." If, therefore, the enemy should in the meantime take the offensive and press the Austrians hard, which, as shall be seen, was what actually happened, the responsibility for granting or withholding British assistance was thrown entirely upon the General.

It remains to say a word of the plan itself, and of the troops and commanders who were appointed to carry it out. The enormous front along which Coburg proposed to disperse his force is an example of the system known as the cordon-system, which was in particular favour with the Austrians at this time. It consisted in covering every possible access to a theatre of war with some small body of troops, and had been formulated by Marshal Lacy upon the experience of the war of the Bavarian Succession in 1778, when he had held a front of fifty miles in the labyrinthine country of the Upper Elbe, and reduced the campaign to a mere scuffle of foraging parties. Well calculated to exclude the plague or contraband goods from a country, it was, of course, ridiculous against the invasion of an enemy ; for it meant weakness at all points and strength at none, and in fact simply invited the destruction of the army in detail by a force of inferior strength. Nevertheless it was in high favour with all armies of Europe, excepting the British, at that time ; and it was a matter of rule that, wherever the enemy stationed a battalion or a company, a countervailing battalion or company must be posted over against it. The Austrians had suffered much from this system in their recent war with the Turks ; but their commanders, of whom Coburg had been one, had learned little from the experience. Apart from his adherence to this new and utterly false fashion, which precluded the concentration of troops for a vigorous offensive, Coburg was a sound, slow, cautious commander of the old Austrian type, more intent upon preserving his own army than destroying the enemy's, and, perhaps, happiest when firmly set down to conduct a siege in form according to the most scientific principles. Withal he was a sensible and honourable gentleman, and extremely popular with his troops. The chief of his staff, and, by common report, the virtual Commander-in-Chief, was the unfortunate Mack, then a colonel forty years of age, who enjoyed the reputation of being the most scientific officer in Europe. The theory of war, as then understood in many quarters, assigned as the first object not the annihilation of the enemy's force in the field, but the possession of certain geographical points, which were called Strategic Objects. At this game of maps and coloured labels Mack excelled ; and, when called upon to fight an action, he so elaborated his plans for the overwhelming of his enemies by the simultaneous onslaught of a number of converging columns that, if everything went right and every column reached exactly the appointed place at exactly the appointed time, he assured to himself not only victory but conquest. But, since he made no allowance for the possible failure of any one of his combinations through unforeseen contingencies or accidents of any description, Mack's actions were rarely successful and always unduly hazardous. He seems to have been an honest man, of real though misdirected ability ; while his character gained for him a confidence and respect 1793. which the British in the field accorded to no other foreign officer. But though, as shall be seen, his methods by no means commended themselves to all British commanders, they nevertheless made a fatally favourable impression upon the British Ministry.

To judge with the wisdom that comes after the event, it may be said that the Allied Army was tactically deficient in two principal respects, namely, in the numerical weakness of its light infantry and in the faulty organisation of its artillery. Light infantry and light cavalry at this time were still treated mainly as accessories, useful for the "little war" (to use the French expression) of outposts and reconnaissance, but as something apart from the "great war," which was reserved for the more solid squadrons and battalions that enjoyed the dignity of a place in the formal Order of Battle. In fact, the work of outposts was supposed to fall wholly upon the light corps, while the regular troops husbanded their strength in security behind them. Hostilities with any nation which is driven back on primitive methods of self-defence, and which neither knows nor respects the contemporary usage of civilised warfare, invariably upset any such arrangement ; and the British, after the experience of America, should have been awake to this truth. Indeed, in justice to the officers, many of them were alive to it ; but Pitt, since 1783, had been more solicitous for the reduction than the training of the Army. In the matter of artillery the practice of all the nations was the same. Each battalion possessed its two guns, three-pounders or six-pounders, and the remainder of the ordnance was massed into a park, with or without an inner distribution into brigades or batteries. The handling of the artillery

1793. by the Count of Bückeburg at Minden had not yet found sufficient appreciation to be made the foundation of a system.[1]

The Austrian troops, in spite of the exhaustion of the long Turkish war, were for the most part worthy of their high reputation, and aroused at first the greatest admiration among British officers. They included, however, a certain number of irregular corps, both horse and foot, chiefly Slavs, which were simply savage banditti of the most dangerous type. They would murder or plunder any one, friend or foe, even to the vedettes of their own army ; and no Austrian general would trust himself among them without an escort. The quality of the higher officers was, however, unworthy that of the men, many of them being old, supine, and narrow-minded ; and the corps of officers at large was sharply divided between two factions, which espoused the two opposite schools of Loudon and Lacy. The organisation also was imperfect, for, though the army was indeed distributed into brigades and divisions, these were not kept together, but all detachments were formed of squadrons and battalions arbitrarily collected and entrusted to a general as arbitrarily chosen, who knew no more of the men than they knew of him. In the matter of tactics the Austrians had made no progress since the Seven Years' War. Cavalry and infantry alike were still formed in three ranks, and the art of handling large bodies of cavalry had been nearly, though not wholly, forgotten.

The Prussians still enjoyed the fame which they had won under Frederick the Great, but they had not been improved by the false training observed by Cornwallis

[1] The authorities for this and the next paragraph are Ditfurth, i. 29, 35, 36 ; Witzleben, ii. 59 ; Calvert, p. 83 ; Sybel, ii. 154.

at their manœuvres ; while their commander, von 1793.
Knobelsdorf, though full of zeal, was also full of years,
having passed his seventieth birthday. Superior to
them were the Hessians, the majority of whom had
served in America, where they had learned to manœuvre
rapidly and to fight in dispersed order, though the
lesson had never been practised since their return to
their own land.[1] The Hessian Jäger were particularly
good light troops, and were armed with rifles. The
whole corps, moreover, was the more effective since it
was equipped with regimental transport upon a lavish
scale, and was therefore mobile and self-dependent.[2]
On the whole, the Hessians seem to have been the
most valuable fighting men in the army, though they
were not exempt from the love of plunder, a failing
which mercenary veterans are apt to judge more
leniently, at certain times, than other troops. The
Hanoverians were then, as always, fine soldiers, but
without the advantage of the Hessians in experience
and training. The Dutch, being hastily raised, were
ill organised, disciplined, trained, and equipped.

The British, with the exception of the Guards,
were, in the opinion of foreign critics, very deficient in
training and discipline, for precisely the same reason
as the Dutch, namely, persistent neglect. The cavalry
was of better material than the infantry, and was
very well mounted ; but both officers and men were
so ignorant of their work that, at first, they could not
even throw out vedettes and outposts without instruction from foreigners. The field-guns were inferior to
those of the rest of the Allies ; the ammunition-waggons

[1] Ditfurth, i. 48.
[2] 231 horses, draught and pack, and 116 drivers, etc., per battalion of 1100 men, of which 82 horses and 34 men were for the
officers. Each company had one four-horse waggon, and each
battalion one pair-horse hospital-waggon.

1793. were heavy and unwieldy; and the horses were harnessed one before the other instead of abreast, which made them difficult to drive, and took up much room on the road. The models of both harness and waggons were, in fact, of Marlborough's time; while the medical arrangements, or what passed for such, were those of a still remoter age. Discipline for the most part was bad, especially among the officers, who were subject rather to political than military authority, and, though there were still among their infantry good men who had learned their business in America, far too many were absolutely ignorant as well as neglectful of their duty. Hard drinking in all ranks accounted for much both of the indiscipline and the neglect. To the men, of course, drunkenness brought a flogging at the halberts, but to the officers, unfortunately, it did not necessarily mean punishment; nor was it possible that it should, when respectful consideration was shown to both Prime Minister and Secretary of State for War if they appeared incapably drunk at the House of Commons, because the leaders of the Opposition drank even harder than they. This vice of drunkenness was the most formidable with which good officers had to contend throughout the twenty years of the war, simply because it was a fashion set in high places.[1]

It was no easy task to command such a force as the British, Hanoverians and Hessians, under the orders of such a man as Dundas, and the immediate direction of such generals as Coburg and Mack. Frederick, Duke of York, second son of King George the Third, was in 1793 thirty years old. At the age of sixteen he had been sent to Berlin to study the profession

[1] Ditfurth, i. 33; Witzleben, ii. 66. York to Dundas, 25th January 1794. Vol. iii. of this *History*, pp. 524, 525.

of arms under the eye of Frederick the Great himself, 1793.
and had returned with a practical knowledge which
made him later an admirable Commander-in-Chief
at the Horse Guards, but also with an undue preference
for the weaker points of the stiff and formal Prussian
system. In 1791 he had become Colonel of the Coldstream Guards, in which post he had at first shown
himself enough of a martinet to excite discontent;[1]
and, though he had wisely changed his ways after a
year's experience, he was not at this time popular
with his men, while his officers, who had been taught
to look for preferment from politicians, resented his
authority whether for good or ill. In this respect he
was hampered by the same disadvantages as had beset
Lord Stair in 1743; and, unfortunately, he did not
possess the qualifications to gain the confidence of
his troops in the field. He had the cool personal
bravery which belongs to his race, but not the higher
moral courage which gives constancy and patience in
difficulty or misfortune; and hence he was at once
sanguine and easily discouraged. He had learned his
work, so far as it could be acquired by the industry of
a mediocre intellect, but he was slow of apprehension,
without sagacity, penetration or width of view, and
with so little imagination or resource that an unforeseen
emergency confounded him. On the other hand, his
dutiful loyalty and submission, in most trying circumstances, towards Coburg on the one hand, and the
Cabinet on the other, were beyond all praise. The
Ministry had some just doubts as to his fitness to
command, but the King had set his heart upon the
appointment; and indeed, where so many Serene High-
nesses were gathered together, the superior rank of
the Duke was a decided advantage. It was hoped,

[1] *Dropmore Papers*, ii. 349.

1793. therefore, to make good his deficiencies by joining to him Sir James Murray, better known by the name which he afterwards assumed as Sir James Pulteney, nominally as Adjutant-general, but really as Chief of the Staff and something more ; for it was to his correspondence that the Government looked for information and advice.

Murray was a singular character. He had served in the Seven Years' War ; he had distinguished himself in the West Indies during the American War of Independence ; and he had trained an intellect, which was of no common order, not only by shrewd observation of the world but by solid and extensive study. His knowledge was great, his grasp and outlook wide, his judgment cool and accurate, his indifference to danger and hardship absolute ; but he was shy, awkward and diffident, with a dreamy indolence which led him too readily to surrender his own correct opinion, and to amuse himself with speculation upon the incorrect opinions of others.[1] When roused he could sum up a situation with an insight, terseness and vigour which showed how close was his hold upon facts ; but he was not the helpmate who could make good the defects of the Duke of York. The situation, indeed, demanded a Marlborough, with the insight to see the one thing that was needed, and the tact and ascendency to bring cautious commanders, intriguing Ministers, narrow-minded potentates and irresolute Cabinets into line, for the one true object,—an immediate march on Paris.

Such a march could undoubtedly not have been made without risk, owing to the dearth of food in France ; yet the opportunity was favourable, and the hazard was slight compared with the certain danger of delay. Feb. 19. Already in February the Republic had wantonly made

[1] Bunbury, *Great War with France*, p. 46.

a fresh enemy by declaring war upon Spain ; and the 1793. campaign in Belgium had produced results for which the most sanguine of her enemies could hardly have hoped. On the first news of the Austrian successes, March 8. the Convention instantly formed a special tribunal for the trial of traitors and conspirators against France, and summoned two of the defeated generals to appear before it. This done, it proceeded to take measures for hastening the levy of the three hundred thousand men, decreed a fortnight before. The scenes of ridiculous enthusiasm, which had become usual in Paris, followed as a matter of course ; but the multitude of men who, for various reasons, claimed exemption, was astonishing, and the rascality of many who were enrolled was flagrant. A great many of these rogues made a trade of fraudulent enlistment, receiving a bounty from several corps and selling the arms and clothing received from each of them ; while the number of women, who claimed allowances for the removal of their husbands to the army, sufficed to warrant the belief that ' every recruit was a polygamist. In the provinces, both north and south, there was violent resistance to the levy ; and on the 10th of March, at March 10. Saint Florent le Vieil on the Loire, the peasants turned upon the troops which had been brought up to enforce the ballot, and, though armed only with cudgels, dispersed them and drove them from the town. That evening the alarm-bell rang in every church of the surrounding parishes ; and five days later bands of peasants drove the National Guards from Chollet, some twenty miles south of Saint Florent, and took that town also. This was the first manifestation of a great counter-revolutionary movement, famous in history as the revolt of La Vendée.

The Convention, however, did not at first realise the

1793. importance of this outbreak, in the critical state of things in the north. An attempt to reinforce Dumouriez at Louvain, by calling out ten thousand of the National Guards of the northern provinces, provided only a few worn-out men and boys,[1] whom the General contemptuously dismissed to their homes. Then came the defection of Dumouriez himself, which was well-nigh fatal to all military improvement. The General had disparaged the election of officers by their men ; he had urged that the volunteers should be incorporated in the Line ; he had tried to enforce discipline upon all ; and, finally, he had turned traitor and taken some of his regular troops with him. It was therefore plain that discipline was an abomination, that all his recommendations were vicious, that the regular troops were not to be trusted, and that volunteers only were to be accounted faithful. Never was the regular army of France so near to total dissolution at the hands of its countrymen as at this moment of supreme military peril. Beurnonville, having tried to abolish abuses, was driven from the War Office ; a good Jacobin, Bouchotte, with a

April 6. still better Jacobin, Vincent, at his elbow, was installed in Beurnonville's place, and the whole of Pache's vile following returned with them to office.[2] A camp was ordered to be formed at Peronne, and in it were assembled, not with disgrace but with honour, all the soldiers who had been imprisoned by Dumouriez for misconduct, all the deserters, the cowards and the skulkers, who had fled from the army of Belgium. Further, it was resolved that representatives of the people, with absolute powers, should be sent to rally and reorganise the northern forces, and to set the fortresses in order. If ever a nation seemed bent upon

---

[1] Poisson, ii. 239, 240.   [2] Rousset, p. 183.

compassing its own destruction by piling madness upon 1793.
madness, it was the French at this moment.

Yet, amid all the confusion, there appeared the first
sign of the powers which by terrible means were to
reduce France and, through France, the whole Continent
of Europe to discipline and order. On the 6th of April
the Convention chose nine of its members, renewable
by monthly election, to wield the Dictatorship of
France, with the title of the Committee of Public Safety.
On the 10th of April a rough Alsatian officer, Kellerman April 10.
by name, whose gallantry had raised him from the
ranks to a commission during the Seven Years' War,
came forward with a scheme which preserved the famous
regiments of the French Line. Finally, among the
six representatives despatched to save the wreck of
Dumouriez's army was Captain Lazare Carnot of the
Engineers ; by birth a younger son in a respectable
family of Burgundy, by repute well known in Europe
as an original thinker upon military matters in general,
and upon the defence of fortresses in particular.
Though now forty years of age and of twenty years'
standing in the army, he was still a captain, for his
military opinions had given offence in high quarters
under the Monarchy ; and it was as a simple captain
that he was to appoint generals, and to organise victory
under the Republic. Deeply read in theology and
history, a passionate devotee of mathematics and of
science, he had framed for himself high ideals, which,
as he thought, the Revolution was appointed to fulfil ;
and he upheld its principles through good report and
evil report, not with the Gallic effervescence that is
bred of self-consciousness, but with the austere fanati-
cism of a Scot who takes his stand upon the Covenant.
He believed ; and in his faith he had buried all thought
of self. Rank, wealth, fame alike were indifferent

1793. to this spare, stern, ascetic soldier. To give all that lay in him for the cause, to render faithful account of every trust reposed in him for the cause, to forward all that would further it, to combat all that could impede it—such were the principles that governed his conduct. With these motives to inspire him, with great natural gifts, and with every faculty of mind and body trained to the highest point, it is not surprising that his intellectual grasp was wide, his insight clear, his energy infectious, his industry indefatigable. Such was the man who in the early days of April hurried to the north, his brain teeming with thoughts, long since conceived, as to the training best suited to the French soldier, with his natural aptitude for attack. Five years before, while advocating a scheme of short service, he had written that it is war and not a lifetime in the barrack-yard that makes the old soldier.[1] To General Dampierre, who had been appointed on his recommendation to succeed Dumouriez, Carnot left it to apply this precept, while he himself, with ominous directness, hastened northward to repair the half-ruined fortress of Dunkirk.

[1] *Vie de Carnot*, i. 138.

THE effect of Carnot's arrival at Dunkirk in over- 1793. throwing Pitt's original plan has already been told. There can be no doubt that the French had full information of the Minister's designs, for it became a proverb that the most. secret projects of the British War Office were always well known to the enemy and to everybody in England.[1] Nevertheless, if the British Cabinet had thereupon frankly abandoned any attempt upon Dunkirk, Carnot's labours might have been turned to naught. The French army was only slowly assembled during April, and even at the end of the month was of inferior force and scattered over a wide front ; for the French were not free from the vices of the cordon-system, nor were likely to be, so long as civilians interfered with their military dispositions. Apart from the garrisons of Quesnoy, Valenciennes, Condé, Lille and Dunkirk, Dampierre kept ten thousand men on

[1] " The squadron of men of war and transports was collected, the commodore's flag hoisted, and the expedition sailed with *most secret* orders, which as usual were as well known to the enemy and everybody in England as to those by whom they were given " (Marryat, *The King's Own*, ch. vii. *ad init.*). Marryat attributes this failing to the multitude of counsellors that compose a Cabinet. He may be right, but those who are acquainted with the scandalous carelessness with which Ministers treat confidential military documents, find no difficulty in accounting for it otherwise. This evil still continues, and will continue until Cabinet Ministers are subjected to the same penalties for abuse of trust as other servants of the King.

1793.
April. his right, under General Harville, between Maubeuge and Philippeville : ten thousand more, under General Lamarlière, lay on his left, in an entrenched camp thrown up by Carnot at Cassel and at other points between Lille and Dunkirk : and five thousand at Nomain, Orchies, and Hasnon, covered the interval between Lille and the main army. This last, consisting of thirty thousand men under Dampierre's immediate command, lay in an entrenched camp at Famars, a little to the south of Valenciennes, with a detachment in another fortified position at Anzin, to the north-west of that town. In all, therefore, he had about fifty thousand men at hand for service in the field.

April 23. Meanwhile the Allies, who were still below their full strength, occupied the following positions. On their right, that is to say, to westward, six thousand Dutch and about three thousand Imperial troops, under the Hereditary Prince of Orange, lay at Furnes, Ypres and Menin ; next to them two thousand five hundred British and about the same number of Austrians and Prussians, under the Duke of York, occupied Tournai ; next to the Duke of York, Knobelsdorf, with about eight thousand Prussians, held the line of Maulde, Lecelles and Saint Amand on the Scarpe ; next to Knobelsdorf, Clerfaye, with about twelve thousand men at Vicoigne and Raismes, and at Bruay and Fresnes, on the Scheldt, encompassed Condé on the south, while the Prince of Würtemberg with about five thousand men blockaded it on the north. At Onnaing, due south of Condé, lay the principal army, about fifteen thousand strong, with the advance guard at Saint Saulve ; and to the east of the main army General Latour with about six thousand men occupied Bettignies, in observation of Maubeuge, with a detachment at Bavai to preserve communication between

Bettignies and Onnaing. The total force of the Allies 1793. may thus be taken, roughly, at over sixty thousand men, not including thirty thousand Imperial troops under the Prince of Hohenlohe-Kirschberg, which were uselessly detained at Namur, Trèves and Luxemburg. The English cavalry, the Hanoverians and the Hessians, had not yet arrived, though the first detachments of the two former were drawing near to the front ; but none the less the Allies were actually superior to the French in numbers, and very far superior in quality. The whole of their multitudinous posts were strongly entrenched ; but it will be observed that, besides the essential defect of the enormous extension of their front, their line was cut in two by the river Scheldt, which gave the greater opportunity for a successful attack upon one or other of their wings. The general distribution of the Allies corresponded in the main with their lines of retreat, that of the British lying west to the sea, that of the Dutch north-east upon Antwerp, that of the Austrians east upon Namur ; so that a successful attack upon the British would probably lay bare the Austrian right, and a decided defeat of the Austrians must certainly uncover the British left. With their usual jealousy for supreme control, the Austrians mixed a contingent of their own troops with the Allies in every section of the army, an arrangement which gave rise to infinite confusion, since it made even small detachments dependent on two or three different sources of supply. For each nation made provision for its own troops in its own way, and, owing to diversities of system and of differences in calibre of muskets and cannon, it was impossible to enforce any effort towards uniformity.

Still, the inactivity of Coburg during April was marvellous. It never occurred to him to overwhelm

P

1793. any one of Dampierre's isolated divisions of untrained men by concentrating a superior force upon it. He never reflected that, even if both sides adhered to the cordon-system, the French could bring up the whole manhood of their country to make their cordon stronger than his own at every point. He allowed Dampierre to school his troops with impunity by perpetual affairs of outposts, without remembering that the French could more easily replace two men than he could replace one. Finally (but this may be pardoned to him) he did not guess that, while he was wasting a campaign over formal sieges, the French would evolve from the experience of many skirmishes a new system of tactics —that they would abandon the old formal training, and, turning to account the indiscipline which springs from the principle of equality, would grant independence of action to the born fighting men, and trust to the national impetuosity to carry the rest forward in dense masses to the attack.

It is a shameful reproach to the Allies that, over-matched though he was in every respect, the French General took the initiative and made the first move of May 1. the campaign. On the 1st of May he assailed the whole line of the Allies from Saint Saulve to St. Amand ; but, the attacks being unintelligent and incoherent, he was beaten back at every point with a loss of two thousand men and several guns. Urged by the Con-May 8. vention to save Condé, he on the 8th essayed a second attempt, and on this occasion confined himself to demonstrations only upon the flanks of the Allies, concentrating a larger proportion of his force against Clerfaye's position in the centre. These sounder principles brought him within an ace of success. He himself directed a frontal attack from Anzin against Raismes and Vicoigne, and after four successive

repulses carried the position of Raismes, excepting
the village. Lamarlière meanwhile with little difficulty
made his way towards St. Amand, while one of his
divisions, crossing the Scarpe, pressed on unseen
through the forest of Vicoigne, nearly to the road
which leads from St. Amand to Valenciennes. There
this division began to throw up a redoubt and batteries
to cannonade Clerfaye's defences of Vicoigne, so as to
cut off communication between him and Knobelsdorf,
and to ensure a junction with the garrison of Valenciennes. The situation was critical, for, if the French
succeeded in holding possession of the road, the post
at Vicoigne was lost, and the whole line of the Allies
was broken. Fortunately the Duke of York had
moved three battalions of Guards to Nivelle, a little
to the north of St. Amand, having promised Knobelsdorf help in case of need ; and at five o'clock in the
evening the brigade came upon the scene, just as the
French were gaining the upper hand of the Prussians.
The country to north and west of Valenciennes is a
level plain, broken only by the three forests which
bear the names of Marchiennes, Vicoigne, and Raismes,
so that the Duke could see little or nothing of what
was going forward until his troops were actually on
the scene of action. The Coldstream, being first for
duty, by Knobelsdorf's order entered the wood, and
quickly driving the French back, followed them up
to their entrenchments. There, however, they were
met by musketry in front and a fierce fire of grape
from a masked battery in flank ; when, finding themselves unsupported by the Prussians, they fell back
in good order with a loss of over seventy killed and
wounded. Seeing, however, by the appearance of the
red coats, that Knobelsdorf had been reinforced,
Lamarlière's division made no further effort to advance ;

1793. and Dampierre, while leading a last desperate assault upon Vicoigne from the front, was mortally wounded by a cannon-shot. This decided the fate of the day : his successor stopped the attack, and on the following May 9. morning retreated. On the next day Clerfaye and Knobelsdorf stormed the enemy's newly-built batteries and captured their garrison of six hundred men, but failed to take the guns, which, according to the French custom of the time, had been withdrawn and kept limbered up for the night, in readiness for escape.[1] The loss of Clerfaye's and Knobelsdorf's corps in the two days was little short of eight hundred officers and men ; that of the French was far heavier, and was aggravated by the death of Dampierre. It speaks highly for the man that with troops so raw he should have made so fine a fight against some of the best soldiers in Europe.

The losses suffered by the Coldstream Guards on the 8th were made the subject of much complaint both against Knobelsdorf and the Duke of York, and did not promote good feeling among the Allies in the field. The battalion was, in fact, lucky to escape annihilation. Murray blamed Lieutenant-colonel Pennington, who was in command ; but it seems that Knobelsdorf simply told him to enter the wood, which was full of dense undergrowth, without saying a word of the batteries or entrenchments hidden within it, though both an Austrian and a Prussian battalion had already suffered severely in an attempt to carry them. The Duke of York, who had never contemplated so foolhardy an attack, wisely thought it best to make no complaint. The battalion itself, to judge by a letter from one of the officers to Lord Buckingham, was very indignant with the Duke ; and there is every probability that

[1] Calvert, p. 72.

its complaints reached the ear of Pitt. I mention 1793. this, because, though the matter is in itself a small one, it gives conclusive evidence of the incessant friction which arose from the indiscipline of the British officers and from the mistrust which the Allies felt for each other. It is safe to conjecture that this un-informed criticism of generals by their subordinate officers continued throughout the campaign ; and the preservation of the letter above mentioned among Lord Grenville's papers is proof that such criticism was not disregarded by their powerful patrons at home. Unfortunately there is too much reason to fear that this evil even now is not unknown in our Army.[1]

During the following days the Allies were consider-ably strengthened by the arrival of successive detach-ments of Hanoverians and of one brigade of British cavalry under General Ralph Dundas ;[2] but already Murray, with his American experience, had awoke to his weakness in light troops, and was recommending the acceptance of two offers to raise corps of foreign riflemen and Polish Uhlans.[3] The primitive tactics of the French were beginning to tell. The raw levies understood war to signify the killing of the enemy—even of one man rather than none at all—and the saving of themselves. When therefore a mass of them was set in motion, the bravest men advanced, taking advantage of every shelter afforded by the ground, and did their utmost to shoot their opponents down ; while the rest ran away or remained at a safe distance,

---

[1] *Dropmore MSS.* Lieut.-colonel Freemantle to Buckingham, 13th May 1793. Calvert, p. 79. *Narrative by an Officer of the Guards*, i. 29-31. Murray to Dundas, 10th May (private) 1793. There are some significant omissions from his public letter of the same date as published in the Gazette. *Auckland Correspondence*, iii. 58. [2] 7th, 11th, 15th, 16th Light Dragoons.

[3] Murray to Dundas, 15th and 17th May 1793.

1793. to return in a fierce tumultuous swarm if the enemy showed signs of wavering, but not otherwise. How-

May 21. ever, on the 21st, Coburg, much rejoiced by the rein-forcement of British and Hanoverians, judged himself strong enough to pursue his plan of campaign, and decided to drive the French from their camp at Famars preliminarily to the investment of Valenciennes. Mean-while, to the general regret, Mack resigned his post on Coburg's staff, owing partly to ill-health, partly to his sense of Thugut's antagonism to him;[1] and the Prince of Hohenlohe, a veteran of seventy-one, was called from Luxemburg to take his place. It was, however, enough at that time that the attack should be designed by an Austrian General to ensure that it should be repugnant to all good sense.

The entrenched camp of Famars embraced two broad parallel plateaux, divided by the little river Rhonelle, which lie immediately to the south of Valen-ciennes. The western plateau, that of Famars, has a length of about four miles, and abuts on the village of Artres ; the eastern, which is broader and less clearly defined than the other, has a length of about three and a half miles, and terminates at the village of Préseau. Both are practically flat upon the summit, unenclosed, and were covered with crops. The ascent to them is steepest from the west and south, and the valley dug between them by the Rhonelle, though not deep, plunges down so abruptly as to present sides of sharp though short declivity. The ridge of Famars was protected by a series of detached flêches and re-doubts placed on every commanding point on the northern, western, and southern sides. The passages over the Rhonelle at Artres, and at Maresches, a mile and a half above it, were defended by strong entrench-

---

[1] Witzleben, ii. 194.

ments and batteries, and all the fords on this narrow 1793.
but deep and sluggish stream had been destroyed.
The eastern ridge was fortified by a continuous entrenchment with three redoubts, which was carried
for nearly a mile along the length of the summit. The
force at hand for its defence was about twenty-five
thousand men, besides which five thousand men held
the fortified position of Anzin ; while a small detachment due west of it at Aubry maintained communication with the post of Hasnon, still further to north
and west.

The attack of the main position was assigned to two
principal columns, of which the left or southern was
placed under command of the Duke of York, with
orders to assemble his force on the heights between
Préseau and Maresches, and to assail the right flank
of the position. This column was made up of sixteen
battalions, eighteen squadrons, and thirty-eight reserve-
guns,[1] of which the brigade of Guards [2] and the eight
squadrons of Dundas's brigade were British. The
second principal column consisted of twelve battalions,
of which three were the English of Abercromby's
brigade,[3] twelve squadrons and twenty-three reserve-
guns, with five pontoons, under the Austrian General
Ferraris. His orders were to assemble between Saultain and Curgies, a little to the north-east of Préseau,
to drive the enemy from their positions east of the
Rhonelle, and to cross the river itself, or at least feint

[1] That is to say, guns not allotted to the infantry as battalion-
guns.

[2] The brigade was reckoned at four battalions, the flank companies being massed into a fourth battalion.

[3] The Fourteenth and Fifty-third, with the flank companies of
these two regiments and of the Thirty-seventh, massed into a third
battalion. Witzleben (ii. 199) gives a larger number of British
troops, calling all squadrons and battalions in British pay by the
name English.

1793. to do so. Besides these, a third column under Count Colloredo was to observe Valenciennes from between Estreux and Onnaing, and to protect Ferraris's right flank ; a fourth, further to the right, under Clerfaye, was to attack the entrenched camp of Anzin ; a fifth still further to the right under Knobelsdorf was to march from St. Amand against Hasnon ; and a sixth and seventh under the Crown Prince and Prince Frederick of Orange were to move respectively from Tournai upon Orchies, and from Menin upon Tourcoing. Finally, on the extreme left or western flank, there were an eighth column, under General Otto, to protect the Duke of York's left by an advance by Villerspol upon Quesnoy, and a ninth to disquiet the French on the Sambre from Bavai. The scheme was typically Austrian ; that is to say, too full of science to leave room for sense.

May 23. The morning broke in dense fog, so that the main attack did not begin until near seven o'clock, when the Duke of York's column, after marching most of the night, made its way with little resistance to Artres. There failing to force the passage of the river, which was defended by five batteries, the Duke left his heavy guns with about a third of his force to engage the French artillery, and proceeded with the rest higher up the stream to Maresches, where a ford was found, and the passage was with some trouble and delay accomplished. Meanwhile Ferraris attacked the long entrenchment on the eastern ridge, opening fire from three batteries, while Abercromby on the right and four Austrian battalions on the left advanced to the assault, and carried the works with little difficulty, capturing seven guns and over one hundred prisoners. Two French regiments of cavalry, which tried to turn the scale against the assaulting columns, were most

Attack of the Allies
on the
CAMP OF FAMARS
23 May, 1793.
English Miles

Allies ▬▬ French ☐

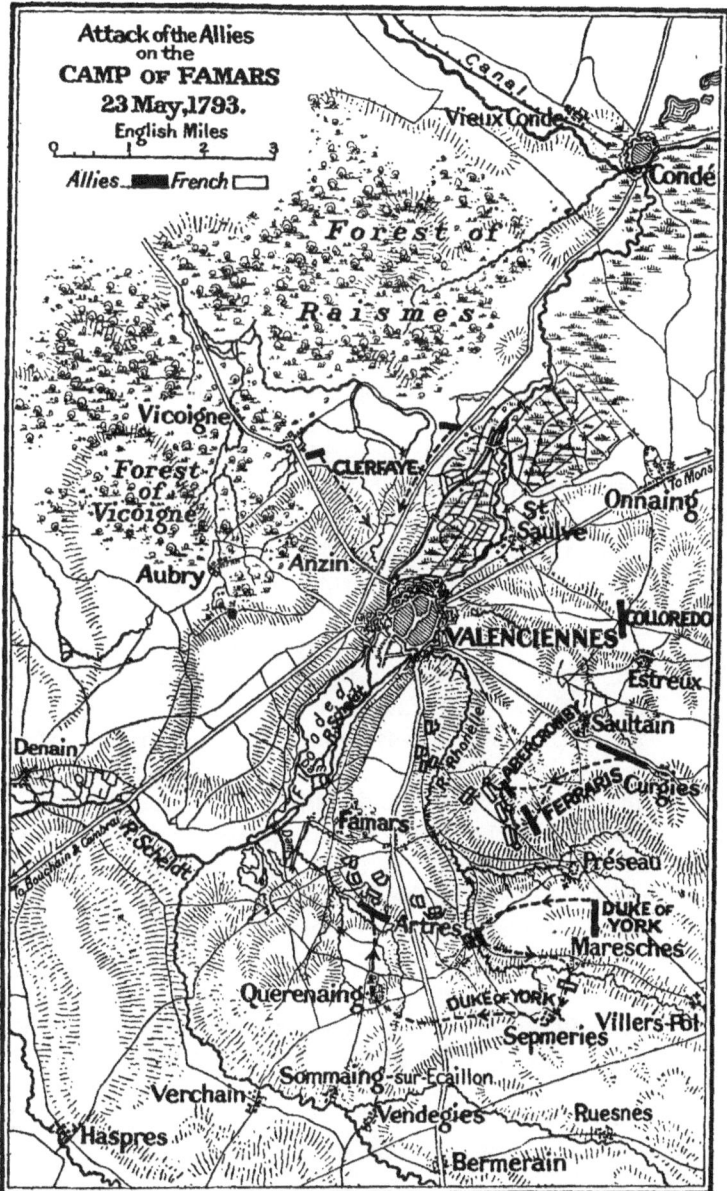

Canal

Vieux Condé

Condé

Forest of

Raismes

Vicoigne

Forest
of
Vicoigne

CLERFAYE

St
Sauve

Onnaing

To Mons

Anzin

Aubry

VALENCIENNES

COLLOREDO

Estreux

Denain

Saultain

PAPENCOURT

FERRARIS

Curgies

Famars

Préseau

To Bouchain & Cambrai

R. Schldt

DUKE OF
YORK

Artres

Maresches

Querenaing

DUKE OF YORK

Sepmeries

Villers Pol

Sommaing-sur-Ecaillon

Verchain

Vendegies

Ruesnès

Haspres

Bermerain

Stanford's Geogl Establt, London.

1793.
May 23. gallantly charged by the Austrian Hussars and the Hanoverian Life Guards, and actually defeated, notwithstanding that the victorious troops had all the disadvantage of a steep ascent against them. Coburg then halted Ferraris's column, until further news should come of the Duke of York's advance. But the Duke, after making a wide turning movement by Querenaing and driving the French from their outlying defences, found himself at sunset at the foot of the most formidable ascent in the whole position, crowned at different points by four redoubts which flanked each other. Thereupon, since his men had been on foot for eighteen hours, he decided to defer the attack till next morning. Elsewhere, the success of the various columns was indifferent. Knobelsdorf could win no more than the outworks of Hasnon ; Clerfaye failed to take the camp of Anzin ; and, though the Prince of Orange drove the French from Orchies, his brother, Prince Frederick of Orange, was foiled before Tourcoing. Coburg gave orders for renewal of the attack on the entrenchments of Famars and Anzin at daybreak of
May 24. the 24th ; but it was found that the French, after reinforcing the garrison of Valenciennes, had evacuated all their positions and retired to Bouchain. The trophies of the Allies were seventeen guns, captured at various points, and three hundred prisoners ; and the further loss of the French was set down, doubtless with exaggeration, at three thousand killed and wounded. Even so the results of the day were unsatisfactory. The Austrians, of course, blamed the Duke of York ; and Murray, without specifying who was in fault, wrote privately that a great deal more might have been done.[1] But, in truth, no one except an Austrian of that period could have looked

[1] Murray to Dundas, 24th May 1793.

for great results from so feeble and faulty a plan of 1793.
attack.

However, the ground was now clear for the siege
of Valenciennes ; and Coburg, as a compliment to the
Duke of York, offered him the command of the besieging force, including fourteen thousand Austrians. There
was much division in the British Cabinet over this
piece of politeness, for Ministers were still in the dark
as to Austria's general intentions ; and some of them
feared that the troops under the Duke of York might
be so much crippled by the siege of Valenciennes as
to be unfit for the subsequent siege of Dunkirk. However, notwithstanding their suspicions of some sinister
design on Austria's part, the Duke received permission
to accept the command ; though Coburg was careful to
attach General Ferraris to his staff with secret orders
to take the entire direction of the operations upon
himself.[1] The chief of the English Engineers, Colonel
Moncrieff, was urgent for storming the town without
further ado, and was confident that, if his plans were
followed, the place could be taken within twelve days ;
but, though Murray was wholly of Moncrieff's opinion,
Ferraris would not hear of it. A fortnight was therefore spent in collecting heavy artillery, after which
ground was duly broken on the 13th of June, before June 13.
a greater and a lesser horn-work on the east side of the
town. About twenty-five thousand men were actually
employed on the siege, while the remainder, about
thirty thousand men, formed the covering army ; and,
practically speaking, active operations upon both sides
ceased except round the walls of the beleaguered
fortress.

[1] Witzleben, ii. 210-211. This author states that the Duke of
York asked for the command of the siege, which I believe to be
absolutely incorrect, and indeed incredible. See Murray to Dundas,
26th and 29th May ; Dundas to Murray, 30th and 31st May 1793.

1793. Yet, far away to westward, there had been a movement disquieting to the British. On the 29th of May forty transports, conveying the second brigade of British cavalry,[1] came into Ostend ; whereupon Captain Carnot, knowing the slackness of the Dutch garrisons at Furnes and Nieuport, which covered that place, determined to surprise them from Dunkirk, and then by a swift march forward to seize and burn the British shipping. Moving out accordingly on the night May 30. of the 30th, he reached Furnes at daybreak, drove the Dutch headlong from the town, and was hoping to follow them up to Nieuport, when the whole of his troops with one accord fell to the plunder of the town, heedless of their officers, and in a short time were reeling or lying in all directions, hopelessly drunk. Far from seizing Ostend, he was thankful that the Dutch did not return and cut his helpless battalions to pieces.[2]

Nevertheless, the movement fulfilled the useful purpose of frightening the British Cabinet. Dundas was possessed by a kind of superstition respecting Ostend, having apparently some idea that it might be held as the gate of the Austrian Netherlands from the sea, even if the rest of the country were evacuated. Though the place itself was part of the Austrian dominions, the guardianship of the whole of the coast, and indeed of the right flank of the Allied army, was entrusted to the Dutch ; and in spite of all protests the Dutch declined to do anything for its defence. Ostend was in fact indefensible, being divided by an unbridged estuary which cut it in two at every flood tide, and was safe from a French attack only for so long as Menin, Ypres, and Nieuport were held by the Allies. The Duke of

[1] Blues, Royals, Greys, Inniskillings.
[2] *Vie de Carnot*, i. 321, *sq.*

York and Murray therefore regarded it as of no military 1793.
value, though of some temporary convenience, looking
upon Antwerp and the Scheldt as their true base and
channel of communication with England. Nothing,
however, would convince Dundas of Ostend's insigni-
ficance. He took the place under his own control, sent
heavy ordnance to be mounted for its defence, appointed
a special officer, General Ainslie, to take command of
it, and plagued Murray so incessantly to fortify it that
the Duke of York, for the sake of peace, consented to
raise a few entrenchments on a small scale. The Duke
had hardly done so, however, before he received a
rebuke from Dundas for spending too much money ;
whereupon he, of course, suspended the work, being, as
Murray said, at a loss to know how to proceed. This
was the beginning of a more minute and persistent
interference of Dundas with the conduct of the operations, with its inevitable consequence of strained
relations between him and the General in the field.[1]

Meanwhile the siege of Valenciennes went forward
slowly and methodically, much more so, indeed, than
seemed necessary either to Murray or to Moncrieff,
though bad weather was accountable in some measure
for the delay. At length, on the 10th of July, Condé July 10.
surrendered after a severe bombardment, and was
occupied in the name of the Emperor Francis. Twelve
days later Mainz opened its gates to the Prussians, July 22.
though the garrison was twenty thousand strong, and
had still bread and wine to last for some days. Finally,
on the 26th, an assault was delivered in three columns July 26.
upon the two horn-works of Valenciennes, one column
being led by a storming party of the Guards, and supported by part of Abercromby's brigade. The attacks

[1] Dundas to Murray, 29th May, 14th June, 12th July ; Murray
to Dundas, 18th June and 16th July 1793.

1793. of all three succeeded with little loss, and Murray, after a strong altercation with the Austrian engineer, insisted, in defiance of Ferraris's orders, upon making a lodgment in the greater horn-work.[1] Thereupon,

July 28. on the 28th of July, the French General, Ferrand, capitulated. The place was taken over, like Condé, in the Emperor's name, amid the loud applause not only of the citizens but of the garrison, who trampled the tricolour under foot and hailed the Duke of York as King of France. All three of the captured garrisons were permitted to return to their own place, on condition that they should not fight against the Allies during the remainder of the war.

Unfortunately, after the fall of Valenciennes the Allies in Flanders, far from pressing their advantage, fell to debating what they should do next. It had been already agreed that the Austrians should give up ten thousand men to the Duke of York for the siege of Dunkirk ; but Coburg, seeing the danger of the plan, made a last effort to avert it by submitting a new scheme for taking the offensive in concert with Prussia ; he himself to move south-east upon Maubeuge from Valenciennes, while the Prussians should advance south-west from Mainz upon Sarrelouis. King Frederick William gladly assented, but the Duke of York protested, as under his instructions he was bound to do ; and he was upheld by a messenger who arrived from Vienna at Coburg's headquarters on the 6th of August. Thugut had been at work on one of his usual subtilties. He had soothed Pitt by renouncing the exchange of Belgium for Bavaria, but had begged that Prussia might not be informed of the renunciation ; for he was still secretly bent on obtaining Bavaria by some means, and had resolved

[1] Murray to Dundas, 25th July.

to purchase it by the cession of Alsace. Hence it 1793.
was his wish that the King of Prussia, and particularly the Austrian troops under General Wurmser
who were serving with him, should move south into
Alsace, and that Coburg should pursue the plan, already
agreed upon, of besieging Quesnoy, while the Duke
of York invested Dunkirk. Coburg thereupon gave
way, though with no very good grace ; and it was
resolved that, before his army was separated from
the Duke's, a general action should be fought, as an
essential preliminary to the subsequent operations.[1]

The position of the French under General Kilmain
was known as that of Caesar's Camp, which lies on
the left bank of the Scheldt about two miles above
Bouchain ; but in reality it formed an irregular quadrilateral, of which a part of Villars's famous lines of
La Bassée formed the northern side. Facing due
east, Kilmain's front was covered by the Scheldt from
Bouchain to Cambrai, his rear by the river Agache,
which runs into the Sensée a little to the south of
Arleux, his right by the Sensée, and his left by the
wood and heights of Bourlon from Cambrai to Mar-
quion. All passages over the Scheldt were closed by
entrenchments, and the valley itself was flooded ; all
passages over the Sensée were equally defended, while
the right from Cambrai to Agache was strengthened
by field-works and abatis. Such a position, held by
sixty thousand men, was formidable, and Coburg
accordingly resolved to turn it by the south. The
turning column, consisting of fourteen thousand men
under the Duke of York, was to assemble about
Villers-en-Cauchies and Saint Aubert, and to cross
the Scheldt at Masnières and Crevecœur, about five
miles south of Cambrai. A second column of about

[1] Sybel, ii. 370-373.

1793. nine thousand men under the Austrian General Colleredo, and a third of about twelve thousand under General Clerfaye, were to force the passage of the Scheldt in the front of the position. The remainder of the army, little less than half of it, was uselessly frittered away in posts of observation.

Murray, foreseeing that the French would retire as soon as they perceived the turning movement, begged persistently that more cavalry should be given to the Duke of York, in order to inflict some punishment on them. His request was refused, and the result was exactly that which he had expected. The

Aug. 7. Duke, after a march of eleven hours on a day of extraordinary heat, found his troops too much exhausted to pass the river at Masnières; and Kilmain, withdrawing quietly in the night, made good his retreat upon Arras with little loss, though the British cavalry made a few prisoners. The Austrians, of course, blamed the Duke of York, though Coburg had sent Hohenlohe with him for the express purpose of superintending his operations; but the arrangements of the day opened Murray's eyes to the essential vices of the Austrian tactics. " We were not in force to attack the enemy," he wrote; " the Duke's column was a long way from support, and between ourselves we were not sorry to see them go off." It was only after long schooling by disaster that the Austrians at last abandoned a system of which the rottenness was clear to the much despised Briton.[1]

After the engagement, Coburg pressed the Duke of York to remain with him for yet another fortnight, in order to renew the attack on the French army or to take Cambrai, the last fortress that blocked

[1] Ditfurth, i. 69. Witzleben, ii. 263-64. Murray to Dundas (private), 9th August 1793.

the way into France. But the Duke could only obey 1793.
his instructions as to Dunkirk, which had lately been Aug. 7
reiterated by Dundas ; [1] and the two armies accordingly parted. Coburg, weakened by the withdrawal
of nine thousand Prussian troops, and not yet com-
pensated by the restoration of fourteen thousand
Austrians from the Rhine, resolved to besiege Quesnoy,
and meanwhile spread his force in several detachments from Denain to Bettignies. The Duke assembled his whole force of about thirty-seven thousand men [2] at Marchiennes on the Scarpe on the 13th Aug. 13.
of August, and on the 15th marched in two columns
north-west by Baisieux and Tourcoing upon Menin.
From Baisieux the route lay across the front of the
great fortress of Lille, and of the French fortified
posts extending from that city to Dunkirk ; and on
the morning of the 18th, soon after the advanced Aug. 18.
guard of the southern column had moved from Tourcoing, heavy firing was heard in the direction of
Linselles, about two miles to the west of that place.
The Prince of Orange, for reasons best known to
himself, had seized the opportunity to sally out from
Menin, and surprise the French posts of Blaton and
Linselles, which being accomplished, he left two
weak battalions to hold them, and retired. About
mid-day the French returned with five thousand
men and drove out the Dutch ; and an hour or two
later an aide-de-camp came galloping into Menin to
ask for help. The Duke of York at once ordered
out the brigade of Guards, which had just arrived at
Menin after a severe march, with a few guns, under

---

[1] Witzleben, ii. 264, 370. Dundas to Murray, 1st August 1793.
[2] Ditfurth, i. 73. 47½ battalions, 58 squadrons. British, 5200
infantry, 1300 cavalry ; Austrians, 10,000 infantry, 1000 cavalry ;
Hanoverians, 9000 infantry, 1600 cavalry ; Hessians, 5500 infantry,
1500 cavalry. Total, 29,700 infantry, 5400 cavalry, 1900 artillery.

Q

1793. General Lake. The three battalions, without their
Aug. 18. flank companies, and therefore little over eleven
hundred strong, at once turned out, and traversed
the six miles to Linselles in little more than an hour,
but, on reaching it, found not a Dutchman there.
They were, however, saluted by a heavy fire of grape
from batteries which they had supposed to be in possession of the Dutch ; and thereupon Lake determined
to attack at once.

The hill, on which the village of Linselles stands,
is fairly steep on its northern face, and was further
strengthened by two redoubts before the village itself
and by a barrier of palisades on the road, while its
flanks were secured by woods and ditches. Lake at
once deployed into line under a heavy fire of grape,
and, after firing three or four volleys, charged with
the bayonet and drove the French from the redoubts
and village. He then halted and re-formed on the
southern side of the hill, not without apprehensions
lest the enemy should rally and make a counter attack
while he was still unsupported. Fortunately, however, the French were not equal to the attempt, being
still of the inferior quality which was inevitable under
the foolish administration of the Jacobins, and so
puny in stature that the Guards cuffed and jostled
them like a London mob, without condescending to
kill them.[1] Lake was therefore left unmolested on
his ground, until at nightfall six battalions of Hessians
arrived, in reply to his urgent messages for reinforcement, to relieve him. His trophies were twelve
guns, seventy prisoners, and a colour, but his losses
amounted to one hundred and eighty-seven officers
and men killed and wounded ; and no real object
whatever was gained. The action was undoubtedly

[1] Hamilton, *History of the Grenadier Guards*, ii. 285.

most brilliant, and the conduct of the men beyond 1793.
all praise ; while Lake's swift decision to escape from Aug. 18.
a most dangerous situation by an immediate attack
stamps him as a ready commander. But it is a grave
reflection upon the Duke of York that he should so
thoughtlessly have exposed some of his best troops
to needless danger, leaving them isolated and unsupported for several hours. It is still less to his credit
that, when he finally relieved them by a detachment
of Hessians, he actually left these also isolated and
unsupported within striking distance of a superior
enemy during the whole night, for no better purpose
than to rase some paltry French earthworks which
a few hours would suffice to throw up again. Because
the Prince of Orange was guilty of one act of signal
foolishness, there was no occasion to outdo him by
another.

At Menin the army was parted into two divisions.
The first, consisting of the Hanoverians, ten British
squadrons and foreign troops, or about fourteen thousand five hundred men, under the Hanoverian Marshal
Freytag, was to form the covering army ; the other,
of nearly twenty-two thousand men, including the
rest of the British troops, under the Duke in person,
was appointed to besiege Dunkirk. On the 19th, Aug. 19.
Freytag marched from Menin by Ypres upon Poperinghe, which he occupied with his main body on the
20th, at the same time pushing his advanced guard Aug. 20.
further north-west to Rousbrugge on the Yser. On
the following day a detachment of Hessians, with Aug. 21.
great skill and at small cost to themselves, drove the
French from Oost Capel and Rexpoede into the
fortress of Bergues, with the loss of eleven guns and
some four hundred men ; and Freytag then took up
his line of posts to cover the besieging army. His

1793. left was stationed at Poperinghe, covered by the fortress of Ypres; and from thence the chain ran north-west to Proven on the Yser, and westward up that stream by Bambecque to Wylder, where it turned north, and passing midway between Bergues and Rexpoede rested its right on a point called the White House, hard by the canal that runs from Bergues Aug. 23, 24. to Furnes. On the 23rd and 24th Freytag drove the French from Wormhoudt and Esquelbecque with the loss of nineteen guns, and surrounded Bergues by detachments at Warhem to east, Coudekerque to north, Sainte Quaedypre to south, and Steene to west. From this last an outer chain of posts was extended southward to Esquelbecque, and thence east by Wormhoudt and Herzeele to the Upper Yser at Houtkerque. The whole circuit thus embraced measured about twenty-one miles; from which it will be concluded that Freytag was a believer in the cordon-system.

Aug. 20. Meanwhile the Duke of York marched on the 20th Aug. 22. to Furnes; and on the 22nd, moving thence parallel with the strand, he drove in the enemy's advanced posts upon the entrenched camp of Ghyvelde, which Aug. 24. the French abandoned in the night. On the 24th, after several hours of sharp fighting, which cost the Allies nearly four hundred men,[1] the French were forced back from the suburb of Rosendahl into the town; whereupon the Duke entrenched himself in his chosen position, with his right resting on the sea and his left at Tetteghem, facing full upon the eastern side of the town and about two miles distant from the walls.

[1] The British engaged were the flank companies of the Guards and Line, and Royal Artillery. Casualties, seventy-eight killed and wounded.

The field of operations for the Duke's army may 1793. be described roughly as a quadrilateral, of which the sea forms the northern side, the canal from Dunkirk to Bergues the west, the canal from Bergues to Furnes the south, and a line drawn from Furnes to the sea the east. From east to west the ground thus enclosed was divided roughly into two parallel strips ; the northern half consisting of the sandhills known as the Dunes, together with a narrow plain of level sandy ground within them ; and the southern half of a huge morass called the Great Moor, which consisted partly of standing water, partly of swamp, but was all open to inundation by admitting the tidal water from the sluices of Dunkirk. Tetteghem, which formed the left of the Duke's position, rested upon this swamp, and commanded the only road that led across it to the White House, and so to Freytag's army. The position itself was in many respects disadvantageous. It was much broken up by innumerable little ditches, hedges, and patches of brushwood, all of which the troops had to clear away with their side-arms for want of better tools ; it was wholly destitute of drinking water, that in the canals being brackish, and that found in the wells unpalatable ; and, finally, it lay open to the minutest inspection from the tower of Dunkirk Cathedral. But this was not the worst. The Duke had looked for a fleet to cover his right flank, which had suffered from the enemy's gunboats during the march upon Ghyvelde, and for transports bringing heavy artillery and other materials for the siege ; and so far there was not a sign of them. " The principal object is to have what is wanted and to have it in time," Murray had written to Dundas in July ; and Dundas had replied that he was preparing artillery for Dun-

1793. kirk, but was in great want of gunners.[1] At last,
Aug. 27. on the 27th, the transports came with gunners, but
Aug. 29. without guns ; on the 29th a frigate, the *Brilliant*,
and a few armed cutters appeared off the coast ; and
Aug. 30. on the 30th Admiral Macbride arrived to concert
operations, but without his fleet.

By an arrangement, which was repeated at least
once more during the war, Macbride's squadron,
being intended to act with the Army, had been removed from the control of the Admiralty and placed
under the orders of Dundas, so that he alone was
responsible for this miscarriage.[2] " Why did you
not earlier suggest to me naval co-operation at Dunkirk ? " he wrote angrily to Murray on the 29th.
" I had always a conceit in my own mind as to its
usefulness, but I had no authority to quote for it."
This is an instructive example of Dundas's methods
as a War Minister. The project of besieging Dunkirk
emanated from himself and his colleagues in the
Cabinet, and from them alone. No military man approved it, though the Duke of York, out of loyalty to
his masters, dutifully upheld it ; and Dundas never
quoted any authority but his own for undertaking
it, nor for his constant interference with the conduct
of the operations that preceded it. He had indeed
a good many conceits in his own mind, the most fatal
of which was that he understood how to conduct a
campaign ; and he had privately made vague inquiries
of Murray, as to the need for naval co-operation,
so far back as in April.[3] But the point was not one
to be decided off-hand by a General, for the question
was not whether a fleet would be useful, but whether

---

[1] Murray to Dundas, 16th July ; Dundas to Murray, 19th July
1793.
[2] *Dropmore Papers*, ii. 444. Dundas to Grenville, 12th October
1793.   [3] Dundas to Murray, 16th April 1793.

it would be able to act in all weathers; and this 1793
purely naval matter appears never to have been considered at all. On the 15th of August, when the army
was not yet committed to the siege, General Ainslie,
the commandant at Ostend, warned Dundas that
he had not realised the difficulties which might be
raised by adverse weather at Dunkirk; and, as a
matter of fact, the *Brilliant* and her little flotilla had
not been on the coast three days before they were
blown away from their station. It was doubtless
owing to the uncertainty of naval assistance that
Murray gave the apparently astounding opinion, that
he regarded a squadron as useful though not very
material to the siege. But, apart from this, Dundas
had so often pressed the Duke of York to spare his
eight thousand Hessians, which formed almost one-
third of the force under his command, for another
service, that it was impossible for the Duke to divine
whether Ministers really intended to pursue their
design against Dunkirk or not. If they did, he had
a right to look to them for a siege-train and for the
necessary naval assistance, neither of which were
forthcoming, partly because Dundas did not know
his own mind, partly because he had committed himself to a multiplicity of operations beyond the power,
after ten years of steady neglect,[1] of either Army or
Navy to execute. However, as a substitute for the
much-needed ships and guns, he sent to Murray a
plan for the siege of Dunkirk, drawn up by no less
skilled a hand than that of Lord Chancellor Lough-
borough, possibly with some hope that the deficiencies
of Downing Street might be made good by the wisdom
of the woolsack. There are times when the conceit
of British politicians becomes touchingly ridiculous.

[1] Calvert, vi. 118; Murray to Dundas, 3rd September.

1793.   Very different was the change that had come over
military administration in France during the same
month of August. Upon the re-election of the Committee of Public Safety, which took place on the
Aug. 10. 10th, Barrère, who was a member, approached Prieur
of the Côte d'Or with the words, " We none of us
understand military matters. You are an officer
of Engineers ; will you join us ? " " There is only
one man in the Convention for the place," answered
Prieur, " and that is Carnot ; and I will be his second."
Aug. 14. Accordingly, on the 14th of August two new members
were added to the Committee, namely, Carnot, who
assumed control of the formation, training, and movements of the armies, and Prieur, who took charge of
arms, ammunition, and hospitals. These, together
with Robert Lindet, formed the most remarkable
group in one of the most remarkable administrative
bodies which has ever existed. Three of the members,
Barrère, Billaud Varennes, and Collot d'Herbois, were
known as the Revolutionaries, their business being
to guide and inspire political emotions ; three more,
Robespierre, Couthon, and Saint Just, were con-
cerned with legislative proposals, police, and the revolutionary tribunal, and bore the ominous name of
the High Hands ; but the last three, Carnot, Prieur,
and Lindet, were known simply as the Workers, a
title which no men have ever more worthily earned.
     Carnot's advent showed itself in prompt and ener-
Aug. 16. getic action. On the 16th of August a decree was
passed for a levy *en masse*, which, it was estimated,
would add four hundred and fifty thousand men to
the army ; and, since all exemptions and substitutes
were disallowed, the cream of the nation began for
the first time to flow into the ranks. Moreover, on
Aug. 29. the 29th of August, the old white coats of the Mon-

archy were abolished and the blue coat of the National 1793.
Guard made uniform for the entire host, a significant
hint that henceforth there were to be no further dis-
tinctions between regular troops and volunteers, but
a single National Army. Prieur, on his side, set up
manufactories of arms and gunpowder in Paris, and
stimulated the search for saltpetre in all directions.
The result of these measures lay hid in the future ; but
immediate and important movements were made on
the northern frontier. Carnot, with true insight,
had divined that England was in reality the most
dangerous member of the Coalition, and that to foil
her before Dunkirk would, from its political results,
be the most telling of all military operations.[1] Withdrawing therefore several thousand troops from
Coburg's front and from the army of the Moselle, he
massed them to westward, until, on the 24th of August, Aug. 24.
there were, apart from the eight thousand men in
Dunkirk itself, some twenty-three thousand in the
entrenched camp at Cassel, four thousand about
Lille, and twelve to fifteen thousand more from the
Moselle within a few days' march. Kilmain had been
recalled after the retreat from Cæsar's camp, and
replaced by General Houchard in supreme command.
Among Houchard's subordinate generals was Jourdan.
Dunkirk itself had for commandant General Souham,
an energetic officer whose fame was soon to spread
wide ; and one of Souham's battalions was commanded by Lazare Hoche.

Thus new men and a new principle of war, which
were to crush the cordon-system out of existence,
hung like an angry cloud to the south of Dunkirk ;
but the Generals of the Allies took no heed. Murray,
indeed, had heard with anxiety of the increase of the

[1] *Vie de Carnot*, i. 394.

1793. French force in his front, and had begged Coburg for reinforcements, which, however, could not be spared.[1] On the east Coburg was busy besieging Quesnoy, with corps of observation thrown out to east and west. He had called up eight thousand men under General Beaulieu from Namur to strengthen his weak cordon about Bouvines and Orchies; but to west of Beaulieu the space from Lannoy to Menin was guarded by some thirteen thousand Dutch— spiritless, disaffected troops, whose leader, the Prince of Orange, was half inclined to give up the contest because he could obtain no assurance as to his indemnity. West of the Dutch was the gossamer line of Freytag, and behind it lay the Duke of York, conscious, first, that Souham had opened the sluices, and that the steady rise of the inundation would shortly sever his communication with Freytag; secondly, that his right flank was under perpetual menace from the French gunboats; and thirdly, that his rear was insecure, since there was nothing to hinder the French from moving troops by sea. In this situation he was trying to take a fortress, which he was not strong enough to invest and which the enemy could consequently reinforce at any moment, by attacking it upon one side only without heavy artillery. He endeavoured to protect his flanks by throwing up entrenchments in the Dunes, but found that they filled with water at the depth of two feet; and he was fain to disarm a frigate at Nieuport and bring up her heavy guns to the front, in order to arm batteries, not only against the town, but towards the sea, to drive away the French gunboats. Thus at the beginning of September he was able to open fire; but meanwhile Houchard had not been idle, for on

[1] Murray to Dundas, 28th and 31st August 1793.

the 27th he fell in force upon the posts of Beaulieu 1793. and the Prince of Orange at Cysoing and Tourcoing. Aug. 27. He was beaten back by Beaulieu with the loss of four guns ; but the Dutch abandoned Tourcoing with suspicious alacrity, and would have retired to Tournai and Courtrai had not Murray sent a detachment to support them. " There is ill-will and disinclination to favour our present operations," wrote Murray ; and indeed the fact is hardly surprising.[1] The marvel is that he and the Duke of York should have remained in so dangerous a position, when a successful attack by the enemy upon the Dutch and a bold push forward would have carried the French to Furnes, and cut off the whole of the army about Dunkirk beyond rescue. Indeed, though they knew it not, this operation had actually been projected at the French headquarters.[2]

With the arrival of his last reinforcements from the Moselle, Houchard resolved to attack the scattered posts of Freytag, the nearest of which lay little more than five miles from Cassel. Assembling thirty thousand men, he led them forward early in the morning of the 6th of September in five columns, under Generals Sept. 6. Vandamme, Hédouville, Colland, Jourdan, and himself, the three first against Poperinghe, Proven, and Rousbrugge, the two last against Wormhoudt, Herzeele, and Houtkerke. Though outnumbered by ten to one, the Hanoverians and Hessians fought most obstinately, and the troops opposed to Houchard and Jourdan would have held their own behind the Yser at Bambecque, had not the French already penetrated to Rexpoede in their rear. The fighting lasted all day, the garrison of Dunkirk at the same time keeping the besieging army employed by a sortie ;

---

[1] Murray to Dundas, 31st August 1793.
[2] Sybel. ii. 417.

and at night Freytag retired upon Hondschoote, ordering General Walmoden, who commanded the posts about Bergues, to withdraw all his troops to the same place. Taking the road by Rexpoede, in ignorance that it was actually occupied by the French, Freytag blundered into the midst of a French picquet, and was, with the young Prince Adolphus (afterwards Duke of Cambridge), wounded and taken. The Prince was rescued, but the Field-Marshal was secured, and would have remained a prisoner, had not General Walmoden, guessing that his chief might have fallen into a trap, marched at once upon Rexpoede, stormed it then and there, and delivered him. Walmoden then assumed command, and, resuming the retreat, took up a convex position before Hondschoote, with his right leaning on the Bergues canal, his centre just in advance of Hondschoote itself, and his left resting on the village of Leysele. The whole of his front was covered by a maze of small ditches and hedges, through which the only access was a single dyke leading into Hondschoote; but this broken ground, however valuable for defence, deprived the Allies of the use of their cavalry, which was the arm in which above all they overmatched the French. From thence Walmoden sent urgent messages to the Duke of York for reinforcements; and it is significant that, owing to the inundation, no troops could reach him except by way of Bergues. There was therefore no reason why Freytag's corps should not have been concentrated about Hondschoote, where it would have covered the besiegers quite as efficiently and with infinitely less risk. The British Commander-in-Chief cannot be acquitted of neglect herein, though Freytag must bear part of the blame for extreme dispersion of his force.

DUNKIRK AND ENVIRONS
showing
THE POSITION OF THE ALLIES
from 24 Aug to 6 Sept. 1793.

English Miles
0 1 2 3 4 5

Allies ......
French ......
Advance of French —→

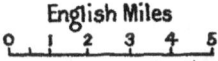

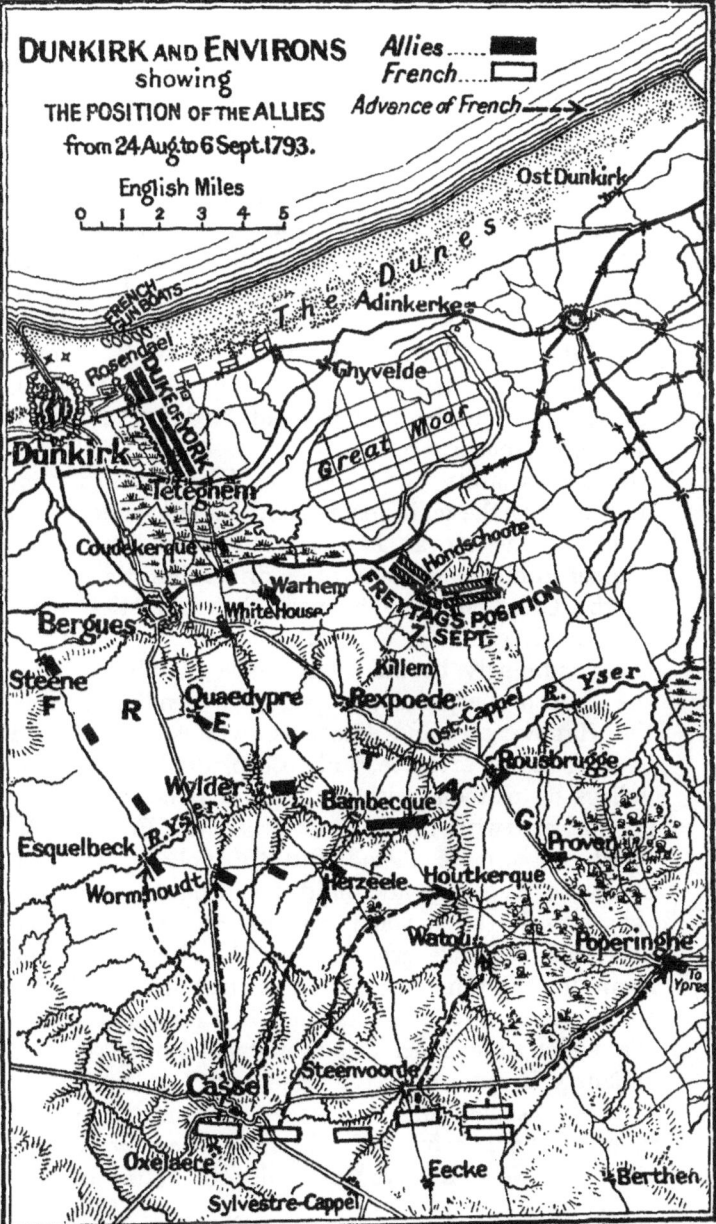

Ost Dunkirk

The Dunes

Adinkerke

FRENCH GUN BOATS

Rosendael

Ghyvelde

DUNKIRK WORK

Dunkirk

Great Moor

Teteghem

Coudekerque

Hondschoote

Warhem

FREYTAGS POSITION
7 SEPT

WhiteHouse

Bergues

Killem

Steene

Rexpoede

F

Quaedypre

Oost-Cappel

R. Yser

R

E

Y

Wylder

T

Rousbrugge

Esquelbeck

R. Yser

Bambecque

4

Provon

G

Wormhoudt

Herzeele

Houtkerque

Watou

Poperinghe

To Ypres

Cassel

Steenvoorde

Oxelaere

Eecke

Berthen

Sylvestre-Cappel

Stanford's Geog. Establ. London.

Houchard tried to follow up his success on the following day by a renewed attack, but his soldiers would not follow him; and Walmoden, though he took the precaution to send his heavy baggage to Furnes, repulsed him without difficulty. On the Sept. 8. 8th, however, Houchard advanced with fresh troops to the assault, himself leading twenty battalions, covered by several guns, to the principal attack by the dyke; while a second column on his left, under General Leclerc, tried to force its way along the canal, and a third, under Colland and Hédouville, moved up from Rousbrugge against Leysele. The plan of attack was faulty, for by holding Walmoden in front and pushing the main force round his left flank, which stood in the air at Leysele, Houchard must have compelled him to retire or to be driven into the swamp of the Great Moor. The new French tactics, however, made good the General's shortcomings. Taking cover cunningly behind every hedge, ditch, or bush, the French sharp-shooters poured a deadly fire into the Hanoverians and Hessians, who stood exposed in their array of three ranks deep, discharging their volleys by platoons with perfect discipline, and pressing forward with the bayonet when the French ventured too near to them. But the volleys did little injury to dispersed and hidden skirmishers, and the charge with the bayonet was hardly more effective over such intricate ground; for the French did not await it, but ran back to the nearest hedge and resumed their fire from behind it. For four hours Walmoden's brave men held their own with the greatest gallantry in spite of heavy losses, until at noon their last reserves of ammunition were exhausted, when, their left flank being seriously threatened by Hédouville, the General gave the order to retire in two

columns upon Furnes. A battalion of Hessians covered
the retreat with splendid tenacity; and the wreck
of the force took up a position between the two canals
just to the south of Furnes. The infantry had lost
at least a third of its numbers, perhaps even more;
and the Hanoverians, by the confession of their own
officers, were no longer to be depended upon.[1] It
was no reproach to them that this should have been
so, for no troops in the world can endure heavy punishment during consecutive days of unsuccessful fighting,
and remain unshaken. Their losses had been very
great, and their behaviour, by the admission both of
friend and foe, most admirable.

On this same day the garrison of Dunkirk made a
sally against the besiegers in the village of Rosendahl,
but was repulsed, though not without loss to the
Allies; and in the afternoon came the news of Walmoden's defeat. At four o'clock orders were given
for the heavy baggage to be sent back to Furnes, and
at eight a Council of War was held. The Duke of
York hoped to carry off his siege-guns, but the French,
having control of the sluices, had shut off the water
from the canal, so that it was no longer of use for
transport; and it was represented that delay might
mean the overpowering of Walmoden's army and the
cutting off of the Duke's retreat by Furnes. At
midnight therefore the besieging army retired in two
columns, with a confusion which shows the ineffi-
ciency of the Duke's staff. Transport being scarce,
the waggons were so much overloaded that the animals
could hardly drag them, and the troops were constantly checked by fallen horses and overturned
vehicles. Further, no orders for the retreat were
sent to the two battalions in Tetteghem, and the

[1] Murray to Dundas (private), 9th September 1793.

1793. whole of one column was delayed until they could join it. It was thus ten o'clock on the morning of Sept. 9. the 9th before the entire force reached the camp at Furnes, fortunately without the least molestation from the enemy.[1] There the Duke effected his junction with Walmoden, but took the precaution to send his heavy baggage to Ostend. He had been fortunate in escaping from a most dangerous position with no greater loss than that of his thirty-two heavy guns; but incessant fighting, a swampy encampment, bad drinking-water and fever had grievously thinned the ranks of his army. It was reported at the time that the siege of Dunkirk had cost the Allies from one cause and another nearly ten thousand men;[2] and I am disposed to think that this estimate is not exaggerated. "Our whole enterprise is defeated and our situation embarrassing in the extreme," wrote Murray. "It is uncertain whether we can maintain ourselves behind Furnes; at all events I think we shall hold good behind the canal at Nieuport." This Sept. 11. letter reached Downing Street on the 11th; and on that same day Macbride's fleet appeared before Nieuport, three weeks too late.

[1] *Narrative of an Officer*, pp. 91-92; Ditfurth, i. 127-128.
[2] *Ibid.* pp. 91-93, and see Ditfurth, i. 126.

VOL. IV. BOOK XII. CHAPTER VI

DURING August and the first week of September the results of the Government's incoherent enterprises began to crowd one upon another with rapidity enough to bewilder a clearer head than that of Dundas. The forces that he had set in motion in the Colonies seemed at first to promise great results at small cost. On the 12th of April General Cuyler, obedient to his instructions, embarked a force of about five hundred men [1] at Barbados, and sailed under convoy of Vice-admiral Sir John Laforey's squadron to Tobago. The enemy was prepared for his coming, for, as was usual with Dundas's secret expeditions, the whole island of Barbados was apprised of the project as early as the General ; [2] but none the less Cuyler landed on the 14th at Courland Bay, stormed on the same night the French fort that crowns the hill above Scarborough, and captured the island with trifling loss. The news of this success reached London on the 1st of June, and was followed a month later by that of the bloodless capture of St. Pierre and Miquelon by a small force sent from Halifax ; but the next intelligence from the west was less satisfactory. Though by no means over-trustful of the representations of the refugees from Martinique, whom Dundas had recommended to him, and who

April 12.

April 14.

May 14.

---

[1] Flank companies 9th, nine companies 4/60th, 50 artillery.
[2] Cuyler to Dundas, 22nd March 1793.

1793. assured him that eight hundred men would suffice to take the island, General Bruce embarked about June 10. eleven hundred troops at Barbados on the 10th of June,[1] and sailed for the island with Admiral Gardner's squadron. After concerting operations with the French June 16. Royalists, he landed his troops on the 16th at Case Navire, for an attack on St. Pierre ; but a panic, which set in among the Royalist levies on the morning fixed for the action, convinced him that it would be hopeless to trust them, and he accordingly re-embarked June 21. on the 21st for Barbados, carrying his pusillanimous allies away with him. Here, therefore, was an initial failure on the part of the monarchical party, which had promised such easy possession of the French West Indies ; and Bruce did not hesitate to add that, since the Republicans had admitted all black men to rights of government in Martinique, any further attack would be hopeless unless undertaken by a considerable force.

The news of this abortive expedition reached Aug. 13. London on the 13th of August ; and shortly afterwards came a letter from a gentleman in Tobago, warning the Government that French emissaries were busy all over the West Indies, and that there was great danger of a general rising of the negroes for the expulsion of the white proprietors from all the islands.[2] Here was information important enough to make Pitt think twice before he pursued his policy of cutting off the financial resources of the Revolution by ruining French West Indian trade, to say nothing of the fact that the said trade was already practically ruined by civil war in the French islands. There were other weak points

---

[1] Battalion companies of the 21st ; flank companies (apparently) of the 9th, 15th, 21st, 45th, 48th, 3/60th, 4/60th, 67th. Bruce speaks of eighteen flank companies, perhaps including details of the 25th and 29th, which were serving on the fleet as marines.
[2] Mr. Balfour to Dundas, 20th July 1793.

in the French armour besides the West Indies, so many 1793. indeed that Ministers might be excused for finding it difficult to determine which of them they should assail. The only method of overcoming that difficulty was that they should clearly define to themselves their Aug. 29. object in making war.

First then, there was the counter-revolution in the south of France ; where Lyons still defied the forces of the Convention, and where it was hoped that Sardinia, in return for the two hundred thousand pounds given her by the recent treaty, would intervene effectively, with Austria at her side. Next,[1] from this same quarter there came the very important but unexpected news that commissioners from Toulon, after some parley with Lord Hood, had agreed to declare for the Monarchy and the Constitution of 1791, and to give up to him the shipping, forts and arsenal, to be held in trust for King Lewis the Seventeenth until the end of the war. In return for this, however, they made the natural but very significant request that troops should be landed for their protection. Here, therefore, was the Government committed, though by no act of its own, to serious operations by land on the side of the Mediterranean. The responsibility assumed by Hood was very grave ; and for a time he hesitated to incur it. " At present," he wrote, two days after issuing his public reply to the offers of the commissioners, " I have not troops sufficient to defend the works. Had I five or six thousand good troops I should soon end the war." [2] He therefore anchored at Hyères and, mindful of the British alliances with the Mediterranean powers, wrote to the British Am-

[1] The official despatch reached the Government on 13th September, but the fact was known to Pitt on the 7th. *Dropmore Papers*, i. 422.

[2] Hood to Dundas, 25th August 1793.

1793. bassador at Naples for such forces as could be spared, at the same time asking help of the Spanish Admiral, Don Juan de Langara, who was lying with his squadron off the coast of Roussillon. Before, however, these reinforcements could arrive, he was so far satisfied by Aug. 28. the assurances of the French that he sailed into Toulon harbour and, landing fifteen hundred marines and soldiers who were acting as such, occupied the principal forts that defended the outer harbour. While thus engaged he was joined by Langara with the greater part of his squadron, who announced that he had one thousand troops ready to disembark at once, and had left four ships behind to bring three thousand more from the army in Roussillon. Full of gratitude, Hood gave Langara effusive thanks, and appointed Admiral Gravina, the Spanish officer next senior to Langara, to be commandant of Toulon.

All this was known to the Government by the 15th of September, by which time, as shall presently be told, more reassuring news had arrived from Flanders, to the effect that the French had been checked, and that Coburg's army had been liberated for action by the surrender of Quesnoy. It therefore behoved Ministers seriously to reconsider their military policy, and to make up their minds definitely whether their object in the war was to be, as they professed, resistance to unprovoked aggression and the overthrow of the Convention, or simple annexation of French possessions. In Flanders their great enterprise, undertaken with no military knowledge and for no military purpose, had failed ; they were as much as ever in the dark as to the ultimate designs of Austria, and they could not but be sensible that remarkably little had been accomplished by the Allies on the Rhine. As a matter of fact Frederick William, having discovered a glaring instance of Thugut's duplicity in the matter of the 1793. Bavarian exchange, had at the end of August practically decided to withdraw from the Coalition. This was as yet unknown to the British Ministers, for their ambassador at Vienna, Sir Morton Eden, was completely duped by Thugut; but they were conscious of an increasing coolness on the part of Prussia towards the war against the Revolution. In such circumstances, although the northern frontier of France was, from its proximity, the most convenient sphere of operations for a British army, they might well consider the advisability of removing all their forces from that quarter in order to concentrate them at Toulon, which Lord Hood's negotiations had already engaged them to protect. French successes in the north could be only temporary and unprofitable if the Allies, by assisting the counter-revolution in the south, should deprive the Convention of the richest provinces of France. A French force at Antwerp itself would signify little, if the Allies could rally the party of order from Bordeaux to Marseilles to put down the tyranny at Paris.

On the other hand, it was no light task to hold Toulon against all the host that the Convention might turn upon it. Sir Charles Grey, when consulted by Pitt as to the force that would be required, declared that fifty thousand good soldiers would be no more than adequate; upon which Pitt dismissed him with the remark that he hoped that a smaller body would suffice.[1] Probably he rested his opinion on Lord Hood's phrase about ending the war with six thousand men, which was of course nonsense, and nonsense of a kind which naval officers at that period were far too ready to talk and Ministers to hear. Mallet du Pan,

[1] Brenton's *Naval History*, i. 101.

1793. the clearest head in Europe, was urgent for making the counter-revolution in the south the centre of attack upon the Convention; but American experience had shown that the support of a disloyal faction is the most unstable of all foundations upon which to build the conduct of a war. Men of the same nation will fight each other like devils, but, when foreigners are called into the contest, all parties tend to combine against them. Moreover, the southern provinces were by no means unfavourable to the Revolution at large. On the contrary, they had enthusiastically acclaimed and supported it, until threatened with the massacre and pillage which had disgraced Paris in September 1792. It was therefore essential that the Allies should enter France in such strength as to be independent of all help from French forces in the field. It was certain that the worthless brothers of King Lewis the Sixteenth and their parasites would claim to place themselves at the head of any counter-revolution; and their presence alone might suffice first to paralyse and then to subvert it.

Again, it was doubtful whether any efficient force of the Allies, other than British, could be collected in the south. Sardinia was perfectly ready to advance at once to the rescue of Lyons if Austria would join her; and the Austrian General De Vins, being of the school of Loudoun, was anxious to show his superiority to his rivals Coburg and Clerfaye of the school of Lacy. But here again the mischievous rapacity of Thugut neutralised all action, for he would allow no Austrian troops to move from Italy unless Sardinia consented to concede the Novarese to Austria, indemnifying herself at the expense of France. The British Ministers were aware of this dispute about the Novarese, for Mulgrave had reported it,[1] and they had sufficient

---

[1] Mulgrave to Dundas, 1st September 1793.

experience of the Imperial Court to divine that it 1793. would not quickly be settled. Apart from Austria and Sardinia, troops could be obtained from Naples and from Spain ; but the assistance of two courts so effete and so corrupt was not likely to be efficient. In any case, it was certain that, if any real advantage was to be gained from the possession of Toulon, every British soldier must be withdrawn from other operations, and that the whole of England's military force must be assembled at that point. If this were impossible, it were best to instruct Hood to make sure of the French fleet, destroy the arsenal, and carry away the inhabitants who had yielded the place into his hands.

Then, besides Flanders and Toulon, there was La Vendée, where the contemptible ruffians whom the Jacobins had appointed to be generals were suffering defeat upon defeat. If by the help of the insurgents Nantes could be seized as a base, it was no very long march from Angers or Tours or Orléans to Paris ; but here again it was not a small force that was required, but every British battalion that could be spared.

Lastly, if the Ministers wanted to secure indemnities only, the West Indies lay open to them. No doubt it would be of advantage to possess the famous harbour of St. Lucia, to deliver Dominica from the menace of Martinique, her neighbour to windward, and to master Guadeloupe, with the nest of privateers which preyed upon all British commerce in those seas. Above all, the capture of Haiti would ensure at once the security of Jamaica, the possession of a country whose wealth, though more than half destroyed, was still appreciable, and the transfer to a British garrison of St. Nicholas Mole, which, being the gate of the Windward Passage and the Gibraltar of the West Indies, would give safe

1793. transit for the trade of the archipelago to England. Such an enterprise, however, would equally demand the entire land-force of the British Isles. It would be necessary not only to take the islands but to hold them, and to hold them not only, as heretofore, against the climate and against the fleet and armies of France, but against the entire negro population, which the Revolution had summoned to its aid. There was, as there still is, abundance of records of former attacks upon all those islands, showing that at the best of times each British battalion in the West Indies required to be renewed in its entirety every two years, and at the worst of times might be completely extinguished by a single hot season. Of all plans, therefore, this would be the most difficult, the most perilous, the most costly in execution and maintenance, and the least damaging to France ; not to mention the fact that the overthrow of the Convention, which had authorised the equality of the black man with the white, was really essential to its permanent success. Thus it should at least have been obvious to the Government that out of the four spheres of operations it could hope to act with effect in one alone ; and then only by throwing into the chosen sphere every trained soldier that it could muster.

Blind to all such considerations, Ministers decided not to select one, or at most two, of these spheres, but to fritter away their handful of forces between all four. Indeed, Dundas's orders between the 11th and 18th of September form a notable specimen of his

Sept. 11. ideas of carrying on war. The news of the failure at Dunkirk had at first completely unnerved him ; but, on realising how critical was the position of affairs in that quarter, he directed eight battalions [1] to embark

[1] 3rd, 19th, 27th, 28th, 42nd, 54th, 57th, 59th.

for Ostend, as a temporary measure. Then he warned 1793. the Duke of York that five thousand of his Hessians must be held ready to sail to Toulon as soon as this reinforcement reached him, and that the eight battalions themselves would be required elsewhere at the beginning of October. On the same day he wrote to Lord Hood that everything must give way to the importance of holding Toulon ; that he had appealed to Austria for troops ; and that he would send Hood the five thousand Hessians aforesaid, as well as two battalions out of the five stationed at Gibraltar. Four days later he warned General Bruce to be ready to receive at Barbados fifteen battalions, which were under orders for active service in the West Indies. Lastly, at the same time or very little later, he framed a design for a descent upon St. Malo and for the occupation of the Isle D'Yeu, off the coast of La Vendée.[1] It is now time to return to Flanders, and to follow in detail the reaction of Dundas's genius upon the operations in that quarter.

In the first peril of the retreat from Dunkirk the British commanders seem to have entertained serious thoughts of re-embarkation ;[2] but were reassured when Houchard did not follow up his stroke upon the force of Walmoden. For this the French general has been much blamed ; and indeed his failure to destroy the Duke of York's army was made the excuse for bringing him shortly afterwards to the guillotine. But in truth Houchard had lost his true opportunity through the unskilfulness of his attack upon Walmoden, wherein his troops, already half starved and less than

---

[1] Dundas to Murray, 11th, 14th September ; to Hood, 14th September ; to Bruce, 18th September 1793 ; Pitt to Grenville, *Dropmore Papers*, ii. 43 (the conjectural date of September attached to this last is wrong, and should be changed to October).

[2] *Narrative of an Officer*, i. 92.

1793. half disciplined, had been seriously shaken by their losses. He therefore reinforced the garrisons of Bergues and Dunkirk, and, in the hope of relieving Quesnoy, fell with thirty thousand men upon the flank of the Dutch cordon from Poperinghe and upon its front from Lille. His success was at first encouraging,

Sept. 12, 13. for he defeated his opponents completely with the loss of forty guns and three thousand men, and captured Menin. General Beaulieu, who had been despatched with over four thousand Austrians to the assistance of the Dutch, for some reason refused to act with them, but checked the advance of the French beyond Menin, and occupied Courtrai. The Dutch fled in disorder to Bruges and Ghent; and for the moment it seemed as though communication between the Duke of York and Coburg was hopelessly severed.

Sept. 12. The Duke, after leaving a detachment under Abercromby at Furnes, had withdrawn to the rear of the canal between Nieuport and Dixmuyde, in order to secure his retreat to Ostend; but he now ordered

Sept. 14. Abercromby back to Nieuport, and marched with the bulk of his force eastward to Thorout, where he was joined by two battalions[1] from England. From

Sept. 15. thence on the 15th he moved southward to Roulers; and on that day the situation underwent a total change.

Beaulieu, being attacked by Houchard before Courtrai, waited only for a reinforcement which the Duke had hurried forward to him, when, taking the offensive, he utterly routed the French, who fled in the wildest confusion, and, pursuing them to Menin, recaptured the town. The Duke entered Menin on

Sept. 16. the following day, where he received letters from Coburg who was already at Cysoing, not more than eighteen miles to the south, reporting that since the

1 19th, 57th, three companies of the 42nd.

fall of Quesnoy he had gained a brilliant victory over 1793. one of Houchard's divisions at Avesnes-le-Sec. This Sept. 12. action, which, though almost unknown to Englishmen, still remains one of the greatest achievements in the history of cavalry, was not only most glorious to the Austrians in itself, but was important as showing that the new tactics of the undisciplined French army were inapplicable to any but a strongly enclosed country. Nine Austrian squadrons, counting some two thousand men, without a single gun, had utterly dispersed seven thousand French, chiefly infantry, cut down two thousand of them, captured two thousand more, and taken twenty guns, all with a loss to themselves of sixty-nine men. These successes effectually checked the advance of the French. Houchard, after the defeat at Menin, had already given the order to retreat ; and the French retired to their former positions before Cassel, Lille, and Maubeuge.

Then arose the question what should be done next. The season was advancing, but events had marched rapidly in Paris since the revolt of Toulon. Following hard upon the news of Houchard's reverse came tidings that the Duke of Brunswick had defeated the French with a loss of four thousand men at Pirmasens, on the northern frontier of Alsace ; and this succession of disasters stirred the Jacobins to the ferocity of panic. On the 17th two savage laws were passed, which practically Sept. 17. placed all lives and all property at the arbitrary disposal of the reigning faction ; and then the demagogues turned with fury upon the generals. Loudest among them was Robespierre, who, profoundly jealous of any man who could do what he could not, was suspicious above all of soldiers. Thanks to his denunciations, Houchard and his staff were recalled under accusation Sept. 21. of treason ; and thereby another blow was added to

1793. the many already struck at the army.   The troops
were greatly demoralised by the continual change of
commanders,[1] whom the Commissioners of the Convention promoted or deposed at their arbitrary pleasure ;
and the commanders themselves were not less demoralised by the certain prospect of death if they failed to
achieve the impossible with troops that were neither
fed, nor clothed, nor paid, nor disciplined.   The Allies,
therefore, could still reasonably look for success from
a concentration of their whole army and a vigorous
offensive.

Dundas, since the failure at Dunkirk, had become
suddenly an advocate for keeping the whole of the
forces together, and for making an attack upon the
enemy before undertaking any further enterprise ; [2] but
with what precise object a general action was to be
fought he did not say, for the very sufficient reason that
he did not know.   The British Ministers, so far as they
favoured any operations at all in Flanders, would have
preferred a second attempt upon Dunkirk ; but they
gave, or professed to give, a free hand to the commanders, flattering themselves that, if the attempt
were abandoned, the British troops would be the sooner
released for service at Toulon and, above all, in the
West Indies.   Coburg, on the other hand, had already
put forward what was at any rate a definite plan, though
upon the old lines.   He wished to besiege Maubeuge,
which was certainly an important point, since it formed
the chief link in the communications between the French
armies of the north about Lille, and of the Ardennes
about Givet and Philippeville, while its entrenched
camp made it a point for a formidable concentration
of the French forces at large.   Moreover, it obstructed

[1] Poisson, ii. 525-526.
[2] Dundas to Murray, 13th September 1793.

the passage of the Austrian troops from east to west, 1793.
compelling all reinforcements from Luxemburg to
fetch a compass by Namur and Charleroi before they
could join the army of Flanders. The Dutch agreed
to come forward again to further the operations ; and
before the British Government, upon Murray's repre-
sentation, could finally make up its mind to co-operate
with the Austrians, Coburg had crossed the Sambre
with forty thousand men and invested Maubeuge.[1]

Thereupon there followed the usual distribution of
troops into a cordon. The besieging force numbered
fourteen thousand, the covering army, including twelve
thousand Dutch, twenty-six thousand men ; and to the
Duke of York was entrusted the task of protecting
Flanders along a front of some forty-five miles, from
Cysoing to Nieuport. For this purpose Coburg gave
him about sixteen thousand Austrian troops in addition
to those in the pay of Britain ; but, owing to the
vagaries of the British Minister for War, the corps was
exposed to the most dangerous risk. Hardly had the
eight reinforcing battalions from England joined the
army in Flanders, before Dundas ordered four of them
to return at once, and the remainder as soon as possible.
Further, not content even with this, he gave Murray
to understand that the embarkation of the Hessian
corps from Flanders was only deferred, and hinted that
a part of his artillerymen might also be spared for
Toulon. Now Dundas knew perfectly well that the
troops had passed through a very severe campaign,
had fought several actions and had suffered heavy
losses ; he knew perfectly well that no adequate steps
had been taken for filling up the gaps in the ranks ;
he could hardly have been ignorant that winter was

[1] Dundas to Murray, 13th, 14th, and 28th September ; 14th
October. Murray to Dundas, 14th and 15th October 1793.

1793. approaching; and Murray had twice warned him that the French were rapidly increasing their forces between Lille and the sea. Yet the Minister, though he had given the generals nominally a free hand, calmly withdrew battalion after battalion, until at last Murray told him plainly of the danger of the situation. The state of the army was most distressing : the force in British pay was reduced to twelve thousand fighting men, or less than half of its original numbers ; the sick and wounded of the whole army under the Duke's command numbered at least nine thousand, or more than one-fourth ; the troops were dangerously dispersed along a very wide front ; and, though Murray did not mention this, the Austrian Government had deprecated all field-fortification, on account of the damage that might ensue to meadows and the banks of canals.[1] Finally, he gave warning that, if the enemy made an attack, the Duke would be obliged to abandon Ostend. Dundas's reply to this was very characteristic. Without a word to Murray he ordered the Commandant at Ostend to retain the second batch of four battalions which, by his own order, had been sent there for re-embarkation to England ; and he wrote an angry letter to Abercromby, a subordinate officer, first expressing horror at the idea of abandoning Ostend, and then regretting that attempts had been made to keep those same four battalions in Flanders. " It would be impossible," he wrote, " to restrain the just indignation of the country, if, for the sake of feeding an army under a Prince of the blood, so substantial an interest to this country as that of the French West Indies had been sacrificed." [2]

[1] Ditfurth, i. 147.
[2] Murray to Dundas, 6th October. Dundas to Ainslie, 12th October ; to Abercromby, 13th October 1793.

Apart from the fact that such language, especially 1793. when addressed to a subordinate concerning his chief, was utterly unbecoming a Minister and a gentleman, it was not obvious why an army should be starved, whether in the matter of empty ranks or of empty stomachs, simply because it happened to be commanded by a Prince of the blood. If its presence in Flanders were an embarrassment to the Government, the simple remedy was to withdraw it altogether, rather than leave it so weak as to be in peril of destruction ; for there was no lack of employment for the troops elsewhere. This amazing outburst is no solitary instance of Dundas's bad taste, much less an unique example of his incapacity.

Meanwhile Murray's apprehensions increased ; and events soon came to justify them. Jourdan, on Carnot's recommendation, had succeeded Houchard in command of the army of the north ; and, with Carnot himself at his back, he now concentrated forty-five thousand men at Guise for the relief of Maubeuge, Oct. 7. leaving the remainder of his troops, some sixty thousand men, extended in a long line to the sea. Coburg sent pressing entreaties for reinforcements to the Duke of York, who at once moved about nine thousand men to Cysoing, and leaving half of them there, proceeded Oct. 10. with the rest—chiefly the wreck of the British troops— to join hands with the Austrian advanced corps a little to the south of Quesnoy at Englefontaine. It was, however, to no purpose, for Jourdan, having increased his force to sixty thousand men, attacked Coburg furiously on the 15th and 16th at Wattignies, and, Oct. 15, 16. despite very heavy loss to himself both in men and in guns, compelled him to raise the siege of Maubeuge. The Dutch, who had not behaved well in the action, retired to Mons ; but Coburg moved his headquarters

1793. to no greater distance than Bavai. He was there meditating further attacks upon the French, when the Committee of Public Safety, intoxicated with the
Oct. 18. success at Wattignies, ordered Jourdan peremptorily to take the offensive and to drive the hordes of the tyrant into the Sambre, which river, it may be observed, at that moment flowed between the opposing armies.
Oct. 22. A second and still more ludicrous order bade him keep his force together, menace several remote points simultaneously, operate in two divisions against Mons and Tournai, and withal act with prudence. Jourdan, however, not daring to attempt the passage of the Sambre, sent on the 20th one division to assail Marchiennes, and another under Souham against all the Allied posts from Cysoing to Werwicq, which last was held by six thousand men under Count Erbach. Both attacks were successful, though Marchiennes was re-
Oct. 22. taken on the 24th ; and on the 22nd Erbach was forced to fall back to Tournai and Courtrai, abandoning even Menin. On the 22nd likewise a division from Cassel attacked Ypres, while another from Dunkirk under Vandamme captured Furnes, and, pressing northward
Oct. 24. with twelve thousand men, opened on the 24th the bombardment of Nieuport. The town had been but hastily fortified, and the garrison consisted of only two weak Hessian battalions, a few dragoons, and the British Fifty-third Regiment, in all fewer than thirteen hundred men. For the moment it seemed certain that the British would be cut off from their base.

Murray, foreseeing this, had ordered all stores, beyond what was necessary for the moment, to be removed from Ostend. The Commandant disembarked some of the four battalions which, pursuant to Dundas's order, were about to sail to England ; and Dundas, on hearing of the situation, at once sent Major-general Grey, the appointed Commander of the West Indian expedition, 1793. with four more battalions [1] to take charge of the troops at Ostend, giving him full liberty to defend it or to bring away the whole of the eight battalions, as he might think best, without reference to the Duke of York. Meanwhile he clamoured for reports as to the intentions of Coburg, and for explanation of the reasons for the possible abandonment of Ostend; for it had not yet occurred to him that the French, by attacking in overwhelming force, might compel the Commander of the Allies to conform to their plan of operations instead of pursuing his own.[2]

However, matters soon righted themselves. The French were driven back with heavy loss from Cysoing Oct. 24. and Orchies. The garrison of Nieuport held its own gallantly, being reinforced on the 27th by another battalion of Hessians and by a few gunners from Ostend; and meanwhile the Duke of York was hastening back from Englefontaine and Tournai, while Coburg followed him westward with half of his army as far as Solesmes, midway between Cambrai and Landrecies. On the evening of the 28th Grey arrived at Ostend, Oct. 28. and at once sent the Forty-second and four companies of Light Infantry to the help of Nieuport. On the same evening the Duke of York having reached Camphin, a few miles east of Cysoing, detached Abercromby with four battalions and two squadrons [3] northward against the French post at Lannoy. The place was captured with little loss, and the British Light Dragoons

---

[1] 3rd, 28th, 54th, 59th. They had already made one voyage to Ostend and back.

[2] Murray to Dundas, 18th October; Ainslie to Dundas, 23rd October; Dundas to Grey, 26th October; to Murray, 27th October 1793.

[3] Two Austrian battalions, 3rd Guards, flank battalion of Guards, one squadron 7th L.D., and one squadron 15th L.D.

S

1793. did terrible execution in the pursuit of the flying enemy.
Oct. 29. On the following night another division, under the
Austrian General Kray, made a brilliant attack upon
the post of Marchiennes, driving out the French with
a loss of nearly two thousand men and twelve guns,
at a cost to itself of fewer than one hundred casualties.
Meanwhile the French, on hearing of the Duke of York's
advance upon their flank, had retired from Menin and
Oct. 30. Ypres ; and early on the next morning Vandamme,
fearing to be cut off, retreated from before Nieuport,
leaving four guns and a quantity of ammunition behind
him.   So easy was it to change the whole face of affairs
by concentrating a compact force against one point
and rolling up a cordon from end to end.   It is almost
comical to observe how at first both sides used the
cordon-system ; how the French, after abandoning it
with success, relapsed into it once more ; and finally
how the Allies, also abandoning it under British
direction, in their turn gained the upper hand.

Throughout this anxious period the interference of
Dundas with the operations had been incessant, and his
tone by no means the most courteous. The incoher-
ence and folly of his orders may best be judged from a
summary of the reply which Murray at length found
time to write on the 20th of October. " Let me point
out to you," he wrote, in effect, " that the same
messenger brought to me from you, first, advice to
besiege St. Quentin ; secondly, orders to keep a body of
troops at Ostend ; and, thirdly, strong exhortations
against division or detachment of our force. As to
Ostend, if Nieuport holds out, it is safe for the winter ;
and I see no reason why Nieuport should not hold out.
As to St. Quentin, this means taking a train of artillery
there in the month of November. It means also that
twenty thousand out of Coburg's twenty-five thousand

men must be detached, while the remaining five 1793. thousand remain quietly between three fortified towns and a forest, from which fifty thousand men may attack them from all sides at any time. Further, the detached force must draw its subsistence from a distance of forty miles across the whole French army without any other protection than that of those five thousand men." "I beg pardon," he continued, "for taking up your time with this kind of argument, which it was not your intention to enter into, but I think it is right to show that, perhaps, people in England are not more infallible in their judgments than those upon the Continent." Irony so keen sped home even through the dense armour of Dundas's conceit. "You have not sufficiently weighed the feeling of this country," he answered, taking refuge in bluster, "if you think that any successes could have counterbalanced the loss of Ostend." Murray hastened to soothe him by pointing out that the Duke of York, though against his own military judgment, had strictly obeyed the Cabinet's instructions as to the protection of Ostend, and that it was not Grey who had saved it but the Duke himself, who, before he knew of Grey's arrival, had forced Vandamme to retire by threatening his communications.[1]

This sharp passage of arms silenced Dundas for the time, though, as will be seen, it taught him little wisdom for the future. Meanwhile, after a few small affairs of outposts, the campaign came to an end. The Emperor of Austria sent orders to Coburg to fight a general action, for no particular object; and the Committee of Public Safety gave the like instructions to Jourdan, in the hope that he might be able to advance to Namur and so to threaten the Austrian line of communication.

[1] Murray to Dundas, 30th October and 12th November; Dundas to Murray, 8th November 1793.

1793. But neither was in a position to obey. The campaign had been most arduous, as a war of posts must always be, not only from the innumerable minor actions, but from the strain imposed on the troops by constant vigilance and by endless marching to and fro to reinforce the threatened points of the cordon. The losses on the side of the Allies had been great : those of the French had been enormous, not only in men but in material, for the Allies had taken from them over two hundred guns. In brief, both armies were thoroughly exhausted ; and yet the Allies had accomplished comparatively little, owing partly to the false plan imposed by England, partly to the false tactics of the Austrian commanders, still more to the misunderstandings and jealousy that make coherent action so difficult in an army composed of many nations. On the Rhine likewise little had been effected. Soon after the victory of Pirmasens the King of Prussia left his army for Posen ; Oct. 13. and, though the Austrian General Wurmser drove the French in utter confusion from the lines of Weissenburg, yet, in consequence of faulty dispositions and of the half-hearted co-operation of the Prussian troops, an advantage which might have been decisive was turned to little account. Prussia, in truth, was not anxious to aid Austria in gaining Alsace ; while the Polish question, as always, kept the two powers in an attitude of mutual suspicion and mistrust. There was nothing, therefore, left to the Allies but to take up cantonments for the winter, which they accordingly did, while Grey and the whole of the eight battalions with him returned to England. The Allies had missed their chance in Flanders ; and the chance was gone for ever.

VOL. IV. BOOK XII. CHAPTER IX

It is now necessary to sum up the relative conditions 1793. of France and the Allies at the close of 1793. The British enterprises against the French at Dunkirk, in La Vendée, and at Toulon had one and all failed ; but the tale of disaster was even then not fully told. Upon arrogating to itself the appointment of Generals in the field, the Committee of Public Safety had appointed Pichegru and Hoche to command respectively the Oct.-Nov. armies of the Rhine and Moselle. Pichegru had been a non-commissioned officer of artillery before the Revolution, had since obtained command of a battalion of volunteers, and, by assiduous courting of the Jacobin leaders, had become a Lieutenant-general without seeing a shot fired. Hoche, as we have seen, had risen from the ranks of the French Guards, had distinguished himself in high command at Dunkirk, and, above all, had attracted Carnot's attention by a memorandum condemning the dispersion of troops after the Austrian manner, and advocating everywhere concentration and a vigorous offensive. " This young fellow will go far," said Carnot, as he handed the document to Robespierre. " A very dangerous man ! " objected the other, who dreaded the success of any man except himself. The task prescribed to Hoche was to relieve Landau, then blockaded by the Prussians ; but he found his army in such ill condition that he hesitated to attempt any-

1793. thing until strengthened by Pichegru, when he made a general attack upon the Prussians under the Duke of Brunswick at Kaiserslautern, and was beaten back with Nov. 28-30. heavy loss. Thanks to Carnot's influence, however, his failure was forgiven to him ; and his new project, that he should reinforce Pichegru with two-thirds of his troops and fall upon the Austrians under General Wurmser at Hagenau, was approved. Wurmser perceived the gathering storm, and appealed to Brunswick for help ; but King Frederick William had expressly forbidden the Duke to engage himself in any important operations, and the Prussians did not move until too Dec. 23. late. On the 23rd of December Hoche opened his attack with great skill and success, and would have annihilated Wurmser, had not Brunswick interfered Dec. 26. at the last moment to check the pursuit of the French. The Austrian commander, furious because Brunswick had not supported him from the first, then returned to the eastern bank of the Rhine, thus uncovering the Prussian left, and obliging them likewise to abandon the greater part of the Palatinate, and to content themselves with protecting the neighbourhood of Mainz. Landau, therefore, was recaptured by the French ; the eastern frontier of France was purged of the enemy ; and, above all, the ill-feeling between Austria and Prussia was more than ever embittered. Broadly speaking, the French by the close of the year had contended successfully alike with the Coalition and with internal foes, having lost ground only in the Eastern Pyrenees to Spain, the enemy from which it could be most easily recovered.

Nevertheless the authority of the Committee of Public Safety was by no means yet fully assured. The Commune of Paris, representing the most infamous of the population, had been jealous of it from the first ;

and the useful service of the little band of Workers 1793. had been accomplished only with great difficulty and by constant concessions to the party of violence. Representatives of the people vested with arbitrary powers still accompanied the armies, interfering with the operations, punishing by summary execution the slightest fault or failure, whether realised or merely suspected, levying barbarous and oppressive requisitions, and thus driving officers, men, and civil population alike to despair. In no army was this policy of terror more ruthlessly pursued than in that of the Rhine, where unlimited powers were exercised by the representatives Lebas and St. Just, of whom the latter, a young man of twenty-six, gave himself the airs of omnipotent Jove, with a guillotine for thunderbolt. A campaign, however, cannot be won solely by decapitation of one's own troops ; and in the winter of 1793–1794 this fact began to impress itself, in respect not only of the army but of France at large, upon some of the ruling men in Paris. But it was no easy matter to convince the unspeakable rogues of the Commune of Paris that terror, which had brought to them personally enormous profit, was, as a national policy, a failure. Early in December 1793 the Committee of Public Safety took several measures to abridge the powers of the Commune ; and some of the men who had in earlier days been most violent favoured the reaction towards a milder rule ; but none the less Collot d'Herbois, who had been the author of most atrocious cruelties at Lyons since the recapture of the city, continued to obtain official approval of his conduct. Dread of summary restoration of order by some victorious General continually haunted the minds of many of the leaders, and notably of Robespierre ; and, since the only idea of this last was to support whichever

1793.
Dec. 25. party was at the moment the stronger, he upheld Collot, and sought popularity by proposing the execution of another batch of Generals. Thus the opening of the new year witnessed a complete revival of the system of terror.

Immediate mischief was the inevitable result. Carnot had wished after the victory of Savenay to institute a policy of conciliation in La Vendée ; but, on the contrary, a ruffianly soldier named Turreau was let loose upon the district with his " infernal columns," as if to exterminate a herd of wild beasts. The country was laid waste, the villages were burned, and such victims as could not escape the soldiery were swept into Nantes, to be murdered after such manner as might please the still greater ruffian, Carrier. Thereupon the people at once took up arms again. A smuggler bearing the nickname of Chouan [1] organised a band of his fellows for revenge, and was soon imitated by others. Charette and Stofflet again came forward as leaders ; and there began a desultory guerilla war, fraught with constant disaster to the Republican troops, which gnawed deeply into the heart of France. At the same time, as if to increase the difficulties of its capable commanders in the field, the Convention lent a ready ear to all complaints against them. The Representatives attached to the armies, with the true instinct of politicians of all times and nations, were careful to take to themselves the credit for every victory, and to impute to the military the blame for every reverse ; and a savage decree was passed that any General condemned to death should be executed in front of his own troops. Successful commanders ran as great a risk as unsuccessful. Kléber, Marceau, Lapoype, and Bonaparte were one and all denounced

1794.
Jan. 1.

[1] *Chat huant.*

in the spring of 1794 by the civilians who had aspired 1794.
to direct them in the field ; and it was only by much
labour and cunning that Carnot was able to save their
lives.

Nevertheless, despite all drawbacks, there was progress towards improvement in the French army.
True, there was still shameful rascality on the part of
contractors,[1] which was countenanced by Bouchotte
under the protection of Robespierre, and which caused
much suffering and desertion. The levy *en masse*
again had proved a failure ; but, on the other hand,
compulsion to personal service, without exemption
of any kind, had forced a better class of recruit into 1793.
the ranks ; and it was wisely determined to incorporate Nov. 22.
these new levies with the battalions at the front, which
possessed officers and non-commissioned officers of
experience to train them. Finally, the reorganisation
of the army into demi-brigades, consisting each of
two battalions of volunteers and one battalion of
regulars, was, after long delay, decreed and gradually 1794.
brought about. Innumerable useless corps were swept Jan. 8.
away ; the establishments of existing corps were increased ; and the law as to election of officers was
practically, though tacitly, ignored.[2] At the same
time a succession of decrees forbade the attendance of
deputations from regiments upon the Convention,
strove to check abuses and waste in the matter of
requisitions, and made a new regulation that no soldier Feb. 12.
should rise to any grade of command—from corporal
to general—who could not read and write. All this Feb. 15.
wrought for discipline and efficiency, for many of the
Colonels and Generals appointed by the Jacobins,
being unable to read a map or even a letter, had brought

---

[1] Poisson, iii. 139 *seq.*
[2] *Ibid.* 239-248 ; Rousset, pp. 293, 299.

1794. about great confusion at the War Office and frequent disaster in the field.[1] At the same time, strenuous efforts were made to improve the cavalry, which had hitherto been absolutely useless ; and its establishment was fixed at twenty-nine regiments of heavy and fifty-four of light cavalry, or ninety-six thousand men in all. The horse-artillery also, after but a single year of existence, was augmented to eight thousand men, and the field-artillery, including detachments for battalion guns, to twenty-six thousand men. The whole force of France at the beginning of 1794 reached six hundred thousand effective men, or about half of the figure which, from motives of policy or conceit, was invariably assigned to it by the orators of Paris.

Moreover, to turn military improvements to the best advantage, events conspired to throw power more and more into the hands of the Committee of Public Safety. By a clever decree, the Committee contrived to disarm the hired ruffians who supported the Com-
1793. mune, and to make over their weapons to the army ;
Dec. 22. and this blow was followed three months later by the accusation and execution of the leaders of the Commune itself, including Hébert, the supreme ruffian,
1794. and Ronsin and Vincent, two of the greatest scoundrels
March 29. in the War Office. The next attack was directed against Danton and others, who had recognised the failure of the policy of terror, and wished to end it ; and accordingly he and his followers went to the
April 5. guillotine on the 5th of April. This was the work of Robespierre, who at one time had been the firm ally of both of these factions, but was now seeking supreme power in order to carry out certain ideas of his own for the social regeneration of France. Being an absolutely mediocre man, of the type which small

---

[1] Rousset, 123-124, 236, 249 ; also generally, pp. 78-148.

provincial journals delight to honour with the title of 1794. " our talented townsman," he was wholly lacking in the ability and experience required for the business of administration ; and he seems to have agreed, without knowing what he did, to the abolition of Ministers for departments and the substitution of boards, responsible to the Committee of Public Safety, in their place. Hereby the little knot of Workers, who had real capacity as well as boundless industry, gained an affluence of power, and the military service an increase of efficiency ; for their labours were too high for the control of a petty lawyer who possessed no gift but that of composing bad essays, and knew no resource but that of cutting off heads. Nor was the activity of the Workers confined to France alone. Revolutionary agents had been busy all over Europe with persuasive tongues and still more persuasive purses. They had bribed high officials to second Carnot's military projects by conspiracies at Turin, Naples, Florence, and Genoa ; they had met with much encouragement in Holland, and counted on further success in Switzerland ; they had made some impression upon Denmark, had half gained Sweden, and had spared no expense to rouse the Turk against Austria. The cost of these negotiations was enormous, but the Government of France was playing for high stakes, knowing well that without victory in all quarters in the coming campaign, bankruptcy and starvation must inevitably bring down the Revolution with a crash.

On the military side Carnot had decided to strike at important points only, and elsewhere to stand on the defensive. In the south he designed to invade Italy, hoping that treachery at Turin would make the work easy ; but the principal struggle, as he knew, must be fought out in Belgium. He did not, however,

1794. confine his schemes of aggression to that quarter only. He recognised with true insight that Britain was France's most formidable enemy ; and he had actually projected and prepared for an invasion of England, with the help of the Brest fleet, and for a march upon London. The plan was bold, indeed wild in its extravagance, being founded on a false idea that disaffection in England was as deeply seated and as widely spread in action as it was noisy and inflated in speech. None the less the bare menace of invasion served a useful purpose—to scare and disconcert the British Government.[1]

Jan. 21. In truth it must have been with no very pleasant feelings that Ministers met Parliament in January 1794, having no better news to lay before the Houses than a tale of failure in all quarters. Pitt had, at least, the consolation that a section of the Whigs, headed by the Duke of Portland, in the same month announced to him their intention of separating themselves from Fox, and of giving the Ministry an independent support. It was, however, felt that such an arrangement could neither be satisfactory nor of long continuance, since, as Sir Gilbert Elliot put it, Portland's party would be no more than " a detached auxiliary force, to act on one occasion, to retire on another, and to be a perpetual object of anxiety to those whom they meant to serve, of hope to the enemy and of speculation to the rest of the world."[2] Moreover, there were members of it, most notably William Windham, who were extremely dissatisfied with the military policy, or want of policy, initiated by Dundas.[3] Negotiations were,

---

[1] Sybel, iii. 26-27 ; *Vie de Carnot*, i. 470 ; *Dropmore Papers*, ii. 501.   [2] *Life of Lord Minto*, ii. 383.

[3] " I think, if you see Dundas, it may not be amiss to urge the danger of running after distant objects while the great object lies still—of hunting the sheep till you have killed the dog. The most

therefore, set on foot for the inclusion of Portland and 1794. some of his friends in the Cabinet ; and, after six full months spent in bargaining, it was finally arranged, on the 11th of July 1794, that Portland should become Second Secretary of State, Lord Fitzwilliam Lord President, and Lord Spencer Lord Privy Seal, while Windham displaced the incompetent and corrupt Sir George Yonge as Secretary at War. It may be well to add at once that in December Lord Spencer exchanged the Privy Seal for the Admiralty with the capable but indolent Lord Chatham, while Lord Mansfield took over the Presidency of the Council, and Lord Fitzwilliam accepted the Lord-Lieutenancy of Ireland.

But these changes were accompanied by a reform of the greatest importance in the history of our military administration. Pitt was resolute in refusing to permit the War Department to lie in the Duke of Portland's hands ; wherein he was probably right, for the Duke, though he carried with him votes in the House of Commons, brought nothing to the Council Board beyond a certain ponderous irresolution. Pitt thereupon arranged, though with some difficulty, that Portland should administer the Home Department, including the Colonies, but should have no authority over naval and military business, for control of which he created a third and new Secretariat of State for War. In itself this measure was valuable and sound, but it was absolutely vitiated by the selection of Henry Dundas to fill the new post. In the face of the shameful blunders of the past eighteen months this appointment was almost criminal ; but

---

fatal error will be, I apprehend, the seeking to preserve the popularity of the war by feeding the avarice of the nation with conquests." —Windham to Mr. Elliot, December 1793. *Life of Lord Minto,* ii. 196.

1794. Pitt's ignorance of war was unfortunately surpassed only by his infatuated trust in his friend. Thus Henry Dundas became the First Secretary of State for War, the very worst man that could possibly have been chosen to found the traditions of such an office. His methods have found faithful imitation by all too many of his successors.[1]

So much may be said by anticipation of events which, though not actually accomplished, were practically assured at the opening of the session of 1794. But the secession of Portland's following by no means left the Opposition without keen critics of the conduct of military affairs. Tarleton the guerilla-leader of the American war, though a vain and shallow man, knew enough to hit the many weak points of Henry Dundas's enterprises, and he was backed by one abler and more solid than himself, Major Thomas Maitland, of the Sixty-second Foot, a brother of the extreme radical, Lord Lauderdale. We shall see more of Maitland, who is still remembered at Malta as " King Tom," in the years before us. Fox also, though as usual guilty of opposition which was purely factious, rightly pressed home upon the Government the duty of defining to themselves what was their true object. If, he argued, the purpose of the war were to substitute some form of government for the present tyranny in France, then Toulon was worth more than the West Indies; if on the other hand it was to obtain permanent possessions, then the West Indies were worth more than Toulon. To this the Government answered by the mouth of Jenkinson, that their end was to destroy the existing government in France; but both he and Pitt added that Toulon was not to

---

[1] Pitt to Grenville, 5th and 7th July 1794. *Dropmore Papers*, ii. 595, 597.

be considered of such importance as to justify a sacri- 1794. fice of the opportunity for acquiring the French West Indies. Plainer evidence could not have been given of the utter unfitness of both to direct a formidable war.[1]

But the Government's measures for the augmentation of the regular Army at the close of 1793, though not yet criticised in Parliament, were still more questionable than its military policy. In the first place, from blind assurance of an easy triumph, no sufficient provision had been made in time for raising additional men ; and the result was that in October 1793 it was a matter of the greatest difficulty to furnish a draft of one hundred men to stop the gaps in Abercromby's brigade in Flanders.[2] In August, however, Alan Cameron of Erracht after much importunity had received permission to raise a regiment of Highlanders without levy-money, and with a special stipulation that the men should not be drafted ; and thus was created the Seventy-ninth or Cameron Highlanders. In September 1793, new regiments began to follow each other more rapidly. First came a battalion formed by Lord Paget, whom we shall know better as a leader of cavalry under the successive titles of Lord Uxbridge and Marquis of Anglesey. The commission which he received to command it was the first that he ever held in the Army ; and the regiment took, and still keeps, the number of the Eightieth. Then came in succession Colonel John Doyle's regiment, now the Eighty-seventh ; Colonel Albemarle Bertie's, now the Eighty-first ; Colonel Thomas De Burgh's, recruited chiefly in Connaught

[1] *Parliamentary History*, vol. xxxi. ; Debates of 21st January, 3rd February, 10th April 1794.
[2] Adj.-gen. to the Duke of York, *C.C.L.B.* 31st October 1793.

1794. and still known as the Eighty-eighth Connaught Rangers; Major-general Leigh's, now the Eighty-second; and finally three Scottish battalions raised by Colonels Ferrier, Halkett, and Cunninghame, who had left the Scots Brigade of Holland during the American War and now tried to make a new brigade for their own land. Thus after a separation of over a century the old comrades of the Buffs rejoined them in Great Britain. In November other regiments were added, namely, General Bernard's, now the Eighty-fourth; General Cuyler's, now the Eighty-sixth; Colonel Nugent's, recruited by Lord Buckingham among his tenants at Stowe, now the Eighty-fifth; Colonel Fitch's, formed chiefly of recruits from Dublin, now the Eighty-third; and Colonel Crosbie's, now the Eighty-ninth.[1] From January to October 1794, there was a deluge of new battalions, of which it must suffice to mention here a second battalion of the Seventy-eighth, and three which began life in February, namely, that raised by Mr. Thomas Graham, the volunteer of Toulon, which was and still is the Ninetieth, and two Highland corps formed by Colonel Duncan Campbell and Lord Huntly, which though originally distinguished by other numbers [2] are known to us as the Ninety-first and Ninety-second Highlanders. Five regiments of Light Dragoons raised in February and March must also be mentioned, since we shall meet with them not unfrequently, namely, Beaumont's, Fielding's, Fullarton's, Loftus's, and Gwyn's, which were raised without expense to the Government, and bore the numbers Twenty-one to Twenty-five. Lastly, attention must be called to

---

[1] These regiments are arranged according to the dates of their letters of service.

[2] Campbell's was originally numbered 98th; Huntly's 100th.

a notable new departure in the formation of a Corps 1794.
of Waggoners in five companies, with a total strength March 7.
of six hundred non-commissioned officers and men,
one-tenth of them artificers. This was the first
attempt at a military organisation of the transport-
service.

It was reckoned that, in one way and another, at
least thirty thousand men were enlisted for the regular
Army between November 1793 and March 1794,[1]
and the number was the more astonishing since Fencibles and substitutes for the Militia had absorbed a
large number of recruits. It would, however, be a
fallacy to suppose that Ministers had yet thought out
any regular plan for continual filling of the ranks;
on the contrary, they had resorted to a variety of
hasty expedients founded upon no fixed principle,
and therefore unfitted to meet more than a temporary
emergency. Such procedure is invariably wasteful
and extravagant in the highest degree; but Yonge
and Dundas honestly believed themselves to have
found true economy in a clever and specious scheme
put forward by one of the Generals in Ireland, for
defraying the cost of new levies by the sale of commissions.[2] The experiment was tried on a grand

---

[1] Adj.-gen. to Prince Edward, *C.C.L.B.* 17th March 1794.
[2] *C.C.L.B.*, Adj.-gen. to Lieut.-gen. Cunninghame, 8th October
1793.
Here is an example of the scheme as used for raising a regiment
of 10 companies each of 60 men.

Proceeds of sale of 1 Lieut.-colonelcy, 1 Majority,
    1 Company, 1 Lieutenancy, 1 Ensigncy,
    amount to £9250
Cost of 600 men at £15 9000
                            Balance . . £250

Another scheme for augmenting battalions of infantry. As soon

T

1794. scale and with high hopes, not unmingled with mis-
giving, on the part of officers ; and indeed the prospect
of raising a large number of men without charge to
the country was sufficiently alluring. None the less
the scheme failed completely,[1] as is the common fate
of all projects which aspire to obtain a costly article
at a trifling outlay.

Beyond this experiment the Government could
think of no better plan for augmenting the Army than
to encourage young men of means to raise men for
rank, or in other words to offer them rank in the Army
in proportion to the number of recruits that they
could produce. This was an old system which hitherto
had been confined chiefly to the raising of independent companies, and had therefore led to no higher
rank than that of Captain. Even then it had been
vicious and had been repeatedly condemned ; and it
was no good sign that in 1793 a Lieutenant had
advertised in the London papers, offering two thousand guineas to any one who could raise him one
hundred recruits in six weeks, and get them passed

---

as 450 approved recruits have been raised, there shall be added to
it a Lieutenant-colonel, and a Major.

The Major will pay for his Lieut.-colonelcy . .	£600
The senior Captain will pay for his senior Majority	700
Another Captain ,, ,, junior Majority	550
Two Companies thus vacated will sell for . .	2800
Levy-money of £5 granted by Government for 450 men	2250

Total . .	£6900
Cost of 450 men at £15 (£10 bounty and £5 levy-money) would be	6750
Balance . .	£150

Thus the country is saved all expense but £5 a man levy-money.
S.C.L.B. 15th April, 1st and 12th November 1793 ; 20th January
1794.   [1] *S.C.L.B.* 9th July 1794.

at Chatham.[1]   But it was now extended to the raising 1794.
of a multitude of battalions, which, for the most part,
were no sooner formed than they were disbanded,
and drafted into other corps.   Thereby of course the
men were easily absorbed, but not so the officers, to
whom the Government had pledged itself to give
half-pay ; and thus it was possible for a young man
to obtain a pension for life from his country on investing a sufficient sum to raise a few score of recruits.[2]
But this was the least of the evils of the system.
There was instantly a rush to obtain letters of service ;
and commissions became a drug in the market.   It
was said that over one hundred commissions were
signed in a single day,[3] while the Gazette could not
keep pace with the incessant promotions.   The Army-
brokers, who in the days of purchase negotiated for
officers the sale of commissions, exchanges, and the
like, carried on openly a most scandalous traffic.
" In a few weeks," to use the indignant language of
an officer of the Guards, " they would dance any
beardless youth, who would come up to their price,
from one newly raised corps to another, and for a
greater douceur, by an exchange into an old regiment,
would procure him a permanent situation in the
standing Army."   The evils that flowed from this
system were incredible.   Officers who had been driven
to sell out of the Army by their debts or their misconduct, were able after a lucky turn at play to purchase reinstatement for themselves with the rank
of Lieutenant-colonel.   Undesirable characters, such
as keepers of gambling-houses, contrived to buy for

---

[1] *Star*, 13th April 1793.

[2] One Lieutenant drew half-pay for 80 years after the drafting
of the 104th (Royal Manchester Volunteers), which was one of
these ephemeral corps. *Records and Badges of the British Army*,
p. 833.   [3] *St. James's Chronicle*, 26th April 1794.

1794. their sons the command of regiments ; and mere children were exalted in the course of a few weeks to the dignity of field-officers. One proud parent, indeed, requested leave of absence for one of these infant Lieutenant-colonels, on the ground that he was not yet fit to be taken from school. It must be noted, too, that, thanks to the Army-brokers, these evils were not confined to the new regiments, but were spread, by means of exchange, all over the Army ; and, since the great majority of the regiments were abroad on active service, the old officers, who were daily facing danger and death, suddenly found themselves inferior in rank to men undistinguished by birth or intellect, and without the smallest pretension to military ability.

Little less dangerous was the enormous encouragement given to crimping by the sudden demand from all quarters for recruits. The Navy, as has been seen, was unable to find its complement of men for the fleet, despite the fact that the Common Council of London in January 1793 had offered an additional bounty of two pounds to seamen ; [1] and now there was thrown into competition with the press-gang a race of greedy, unscrupulous scoundrels, some of them holding and disgracing the King's commission, who made profit out of every boy or man that they could lay hold of by fair means or foul. Thus the ranks were filled, as Tarleton phrased it, with infancy and dotage ; recruiting became a mere matter of gambling ; and the price of men rose to thirty pounds a head.[2] So large a sum set a premium on every description of rascality in the trepanning of recruits by violence or by guile ; and the ordinary Englishman does not lightly bear with oppression of this kind. At length,

[1] *Public Advertiser*, 2nd February 1793.
[2] *St. James's Chronicle*, 19th July 1794.

on one day in August, an unfortunate lunatic, who 1794. had been enlisted by a sergeant and locked up in a brothel—the synonym for a recruiting-house—in London, hurled himself out of a window in the third story, into the street. Instantly a mob assembled, which delivered a succession of riotous attacks upon all houses of this description, and was only suppressed, after several days of disorder, by the calling out of the Guards and six regiments of cavalry.[1] Pitt defended the system on the ground that the Navy as well as the Army would be manned, by the turning over of soldiers to reinforce the marines; but this is only another instance of Pitt's callous ignorance and self-deception. The truth is that while doing nothing, and probably worse than nothing, for the Navy, it destroyed the efficiency of the Army for a time, and but for the timely interposition of a capable soldier would have destroyed it permanently. Who was responsible for the introduction of the system it is not easy to say, for there were so many disgraceful circumstances attending it that the whole subject was hushed up, and is now extremely obscure; but assuredly it was not Lord Amherst, nor is it credible that it can have been any soldier. It is safe to assert that it was the work of civilians; and if we seek among the civilians at the War Office for the two men of tried conceit, unwisdom, and incapacity, we can find them at once in Sir George Yonge and Henry Dundas.[2]

[1] *Ibid.* 19th August 1794.

[2] *Narrative of an Officer of the Guards*, ii. 76-79; Bunbury, *Great War with France*, Introd. p. xx.; *St. James's Chronicle*, 27th January 1795 (debate on Army Estimates of 21st January); *Journal of Sir Henry Calvert*, pp. 360, 384-85. The letters of Lady Sarah Lennox (the mother of the Napiers) throw a curious light on the scramble for promotion through the enlistment of recruits at this period. " Think of my bad luck about recruits. If I had seen an officer

Meanwhile new levies, even when raised under these false conditions, were not to be produced in a moment ; and thirty thousand recruits were not to be reckoned, even by the most sanguine of Ministers, as equivalent to the same number of old soldiers. The Government, therefore, renewed its contract for the hire of Hanoverians and Hessians on a greater scale, raising the total number of them to close upon thirty-four thousand men. To these were added five foreign corps, which were intended to supplement the dearth of light troops from which the British contingent had suffered so much during the campaign of 1793. As early as in May of that year, one Captain George Ramsay had offered to raise a small body of foreign riflemen, and had after some delay been permitted to enlist also a corps of Uhlans. Thus originated three corps which, in honour of the Commander-in-Chief in Flanders, were called by the name of York Chasseurs, York Rangers, and York Hussars. The formation of the remaining two, the Prince of Salm's Hussars and Hompesch's Hussars, was only authorised in February 1794, and consequently they were not ready for service at the opening of the campaign. No effort had been made to provide British soldiers for the work of light infantry, except by raising eight additional light companies for the Brigade of Guards, the men of which were distinguished by round hats with large green feathers, trousers instead of breeches and gaiters, and fusils instead of muskets. But with these details of dress

---

one fortnight sooner who is here, he would have sold me 20 at 11 guineas per man. Is not that unfortunate ; but they are now gone. My Dublin stock too, which was 40, has been reduced to 26," ii. 109, *and see also* ii. 101. " Is there any chance of recruiting men of five feet four inches for 10 guineas, and as much under as possible, in your neighbourhood." Evidently the wives of poor officers plunged into speculation to help their husbands with recruits.

their qualifications as light troops were exhausted ; 1794. for they received no sufficient instruction in their peculiar duty.[1]

The Light Dragoons likewise continued to belie their name, being trained in reality simply as cavalry of the line of battle ; but for this, probably, the civil rather than the military authorities of the Army were responsible, for at this period it was literally impossible to obtain officers for the mounted troops. It will be remembered that before the outbreak of the war the Adjutant-general had constantly, but in vain, endeavoured to obtain an increase of the wholly inadequate pittance of pay meted out to subalterns of dragoons. Even in peace the burdens laid upon them were too heavy to be borne, and to these were now added inadequate compensation for losses in the field, only eighteen pounds being granted to replace a charger which had cost thirty-five. The consequences became immediately apparent. The Duke of York was obliged to beg that the cornetcies of regiments serving in the Low Countries might be given away, since purchasers for them could not be found.[2] Thus the Light Dragoons were untaught, because there were no officers to teach them ; patrols and advanced detachments lacked the daring and adventurous leading of youth ; and one of the highest schools for the training of subalterns was wholly neglected. It is hardly possible to estimate the evil consequences of Pitt's misdirected parsimony, in devoting to the hire of mercenaries the money which should have been spent in the improvement of the British Army.

So much must be said of the regular forces ; but the year 1794 was not less remarkable for an enormous

[1] S.C.L.B. 15th April 1793. *Daily Chronicle*, 16th April 1793.
[2] York to Dundas, January 1794.

1794. increase in the number of the Fencible regiments, Militia and Volunteers, all due to Carnot's menace of invasion. The estimate for the Fencible Cavalry provided in March 1794 for forty troops; by May this figure had already risen to ninety-two troops, and was still rising. Next, the number of the embodied Militia for England was augmented to thirty-six thousand; while by an Act of the Irish Parliament, passed in 1793, sixteen thousand additional Militia were levied in Ireland. This latter was an entirely new departure; and it need hardly be said that the first ballots drawn on the west of St. George's Channel led to serious rioting.[1] Provision was also made in the estimates, and a Bill was introduced for the raising of six thousand Militia in Scotland; but this measure was for the moment deferred, in order that familiarity might ultimately facilitate its passing. The formation of the Scottish Militia, however, appears to have been begun in anticipation,[2] and men were enlisted who, later in Oct. 15– the year, were formed into over twenty battalions of Nov. 20. Fencible infantry. The extension of the ballot throughout the three kingdoms, though not actually completed until the passing of the Scottish Militia Act in 1797, must be regarded as the most important military step taken since the passing of the Militia Act of 1757 by the elder Pitt; and due credit should be allowed to the Government for it.

Meanwhile, to augment the English Militia to the prescribed figure, an Act was passed, after the model of that of 1778, empowering the Lord-Lieutenants to enrol volunteers, to be added to the Militia, and to be entitled to the same bounty, subsistence, and clothing. Finally, in April, was passed an Act, limited to the

---

[1] *Chronicle*, June 1793.
[2] *St. James's Chronicle*, 24th and 26th July 1793.

duration of the war, authorising the formation of district 1794.
corps or companies of Volunteers, to be entitled to pay
and subject to military discipline if called out for invasion or in aid of the civil power. This was the first
attempt to summon the manhood of the kingdom to
arms; for though Shelburne in the peril of 1782 had
sent a circular to all the Mayors and Lord-Lieutenants
in England with the object of forming a levy *en masse*,
yet the hastening of the peace, by Rodney's victory
of the Saints and by the relief of Gibraltar, had rendered
any elaboration of the plan unnecessary. Now, however, there sprang up an infinity of Volunteer corps,
infantry, artillery, and light horse or Yeomanry Cavalry,
first in single companies and troops, but very soon in
battalions and regiments. The first of the Volunteer
corps appears to have been the five Associated Companies of St. George's, Hanover Square, which was
formed in anticipation of the Act;[1] the first of the
Yeomanry was Lord Winchelsea's three troops of
" Gentlemen and Yeomanry," raised by the County
of Rutland.[2] The rapidity with which these Volunteers
were raised would be flattering to the national vanity
were it not susceptible of a commonplace explanation.
By a certain clause in the Act Volunteers were exempted
from service in the Militia, upon producing a certificate
that they had attended exercise punctually during six
weeks previously to the hearing of appeals against the
Militia list. This dissociation of the Volunteers from
the Militia was a great and disastrous blunder, which
has never yet been thoroughly repaired. It is, however,
sufficient to note for the present that the Government
had deliberately set up three different descriptions of
auxiliary forces, Militia, Fencibles, and Volunteers, all
competing with each other and with the regular Army.

[1] *S.C.L.B.* 26th March 1794.   [2] *Ibid.* 29th April 1794.

1794. The number of regular troops provided for in the estimates of 1794 (reckoning the Irish establishment at fourteen thousand) was one hundred and seventy-five thousand men, besides thirty-four thousand foreign troops, four thousand Fencibles, and fifty-two thousand Militia ; or, say, two hundred and sixty-five thousand men in all.

Simultaneously with these efforts at home, Pitt worked strenuously to restore unity and vigour to the Coalition. The relations of the coalesced powers at the close of 1793 were in the highest degree unsatisfactory. The Empress Catherine, still insatiable, despite the deterioration of her forces and the exhaustion of her treasury, had resumed her old designs upon Turkey, and had set a large force in motion towards Constantinople. The Emperor Francis, still under the guidance of Thugut and full of vague plans for increasing his territory, was drawing closer to the Empress in the hope of obtaining her countenance to the annexation of Venice by Austria, if indemnity in France should fail, and of sharing with her the ultimate partition of Turkey. Both were bitterly incensed against Prussia : Catherine because King Frederick William had diverted his troops from the invasion of France to the strengthening of his position in Poland ; Francis from jealousy that his rival should have enlarged his boundaries, when he himself had not. Frederick William, as has been seen, had practically withdrawn his forces from active operations on the Rhine ; and accordingly in December 1793 Pitt had sent Lord Malmesbury to Berlin to ascertain (if, indeed, anything could be ascertained in such a centre of intrigue and falsehood) what might be Prussia's motive for retiring from the struggle. In reply to Malmesbury, Frederick William, having obtained his desire in Poland, declared himself eager

to continue the contest against the Jacobins, but 1794.
absolutely prevented by lack of money. Thereupon
Pitt proposed to give Prussia a subsidy of two millions Feb. 5.
sterling, of which England should pay three-fifths, and
Holland and Austria each one-fifth. This was a liberal
offer ; and, since it was certain that Holland would
raise no objection, it lay practically with Austria to
give effect to it. It was well known that Austria was
in financial straits, that Hungary was full of unrest and
the Belgic Provinces much cooled in their loyalty, and
that, apart from these troubles at home, the Emperor
had contrived to quarrel with Sardinia abroad. Hence
it was beyond question that Austria could not carry on
the war without Prussia's assistance ; and, forasmuch
as Francis had already despatched emissaries to Berlin
to discuss the operations to be undertaken in the spring,
the natural presumption was that he would gladly close
with Pitt's proposal.

The British Government thereupon bestirred itself
to frame its projects for the coming campaign. The
Duke of York left Belgium for London on the 6th of
February ; and a few days later Mack, now advanced Feb. 12.
to the rank of Major-general, arrived there likewise
to concert plans with the Ministers. The Austrian
genius had shortly before submitted [1] a scheme calculated for a force of three hundred and forty thousand
men, which had been received with great satisfaction
by the British Cabinet and the Duke of York ; but,
since there was no earthly possibility that the Coalition
could put that number of men into the field, the whole
of this elaborate creation was valueless. Both Mack
and Coburg, however, pressed for a concentration of
forces and a march on Paris, though neither of them
could conceive the feasibility of taking the offensive

[1] York to Dundas, 2nd February 1794 (with enclosures).

1794. without leaving one hundred and twenty thousand men behind them to guard the frontier from the Meuse to the sea. The prime question, therefore, was one of men, and Pitt on his side promised his utmost endeavour to increase the British contingent to a figure which should ensure a genuine total of forty thousand fighting soldiers. As to the means whereby this force should be produced, Pitt was remarkably vague, being clear only that he could not spare the few thousand men under Lord Moira's command, since he wished to hold them ready to sail to any part of the British coast which might be threatened by a French invasion. Moira, therefore, though one of the ablest officers in the Army and adored by the men, was kept inactive, while his troops sickened and died of gaol-fever in overcrowded transports at Jersey.[1] However, Pitt made up his forty thousand men to his own satisfaction by naming various reinforcements, which he hoped to pour into Flanders during the summer and autumn ; for it was one of the delusions of this gifted man, as also of his friend Dundas, that an army of twenty thousand men, supplemented by monthly driblets of two thousand men during ten months, is the same thing as an army of forty thousand men ready for the field at the opening of the campaign.

The next requisite was that the Austrian, Prussian, and British contingents should each of them possess a siege-train, since, according to Mack, it was essential for the Allies to master every fortress on the French frontier from the Meuse to the sea. Pitt promised this also, on behalf of the British ; and then arose the question of commanders. Though well aware that the King's assent would be wrung from him only by extreme

[1] Dr. Hayes to Lord Cathcart, 1st February 1794 ; Monthly returns, 1st February to 1st May ; Ditfurth, ii. 32.

pressure, the Ministers were for recalling the Duke of 1794. York and appointing Lord Cornwallis, who had just returned from India, in his place. Herein they were undoubtedly right, for, after all allowance made for the extreme difficulty of his position, the Duke did not shine in the field. The Ministers, however, blamed him especially for the failure before Dunkirk, wherein they themselves were chiefly in fault ; and Mack, prompted apparently by the King, found little difficulty in making excuses for the Duke, who from the first had condemned the idea of attacking Dunkirk at all. It was finally arranged that he should retain command of the British contingent, but that he should be kept always in the neighbourhood of the principal army, with a few thousand Austrians attached to his own corps, so as to subordinate him the more completely to the Austrian Commander-in-Chief. This compromise bears so clearly the mark of the British politician that its origin cannot be doubtful. It is of a kind that may serve for the construction of a Cabinet, but it is not suitable for war, and was particularly ill-fitted to the projected campaign. For the rest, Pitt declared himself satisfied that the command should remain with Coburg, who was deservedly most popular among the Austrian troops ; and Mack rejoiced the heart of the British Cabinet by announcing that the Emperor would direct the operations as Generalissimo in person. Altogether the results of the conference were considered to be so satisfactory that the King presented Mack with a jewelled sword as a reward for his good service.[1]

The British Government's satisfaction was soon proved to be premature. The discussion of future operations with the Court of Berlin was, in fact, only a trick of Thugut to keep as many Prussian troops as

[1] Witzleben, iii. 64 *seq.*

1794. possible on the French frontier ; and the whole intent
of the Emperor's taking personal command was that
Coburg and other honest men in his army, who profoundly distrusted his chief adviser, should be kept
under proper restraint. Thugut now declared, in
answer to Pitt's proposals, that Austria would not
advance a penny towards the subsidies for the Prussian
army, being well able to dispense with every part of
it beyond the twenty thousand men which formed its
contribution towards the forces of the Empire. In
fact, he was so madly jealous and fearful of Prussia at
this time that he secretly proposed to Russia a scheme
March 11. for a joint attack upon her. On learning the Emperor's
decision, King Frederick William ordered Marshal
Möllendorf to begin the withdrawal of his troops from
the Rhine. Coburg was in consternation, for he knew
that, without Prussian help, the execution of the
approved plan of campaign would be impossible. He
therefore asked the Duke of York to join him in re-
questing Möllendorf to delay his retirement, and
despatched letter after letter to Vienna, adjuring the
Emperor in terms of touching devotion and patriotism
to send every man that he could raise to Flanders, and
to work loyally with Prussia to crush the terrible power
of the Revolution while there was yet time. Möllendorf courteously acceded to his desire ; but the Prince's
protests fell on deaf ears in the Imperial capital. There
were over sixty thousand men ready for service at
Vienna, but from his insane dread of Prussian aggression,
Thugut would not part with one of them ; and Coburg's
only reward for his faithful and disinterested counsel
was rude and ungracious rebuke. Just at the critical
moment, however, Lord Malmesbury checked the
further withdrawal of the Prussian troops, by threatening to break off all negotiation for a subsidy unless they

remained on the Rhine until he could receive further 1794.
instructions from London. This brought the impecunious King to reason, for without English money
he was lost. Shortly afterwards the parley was, with
Pitt's sanction, resumed ; and there was much haggling
over the sphere wherein the Prussian troops should be
employed, Frederick William declaring that for operations on the Rhine he would furnish eighty thousand
men, but for Belgium not more than fifty thousand.
Finally, Malmesbury succeeded in compromising
matters ; and a treaty was signed at the Hague on
the 19th of April, whereby Prussia, in consideration April 19.
of a lump sum of £300,000 and a subsidy of £50,000
a month, engaged herself to provide sixty-two thousand
men, to be employed wherever Great Britain and
Holland, their paymasters, should think fit. Ten days
later Fox in the House of Commons predicted that this April 30.
would be a useless waste of money ; and it will be seen
that he was a true prophet.[1]

Meanwhile Coburg was doing his utmost to prepare
his army for the heavy work that lay before it ; but
the Austrian forces had not improved since the previous
year. Heavy losses had brought many young soldiers
into the ranks ; and, owing to the extreme extension
of his line of cantonments, the troops had gained little
rest during the winter. The French delivered as many
as forty-five petty attacks between the 6th of January
and the 26th of March, each one of which meant the
setting of many detachments in motion for long and
harassing matches. Moreover, owing to the decay of
the Emperor's popularity in Belgium, the people would
do little or nothing for the troops ; and, Coburg being
unwilling to take from the inhabitants what they re-

[1] Sybel, iii. 49-65 ; York to Dundas, 22nd March, 3rd April
1794 ; Witzleben, iii. 70-84.

1794. fused to give, the men suffered greatly from want of food, fuel, and shelter. Money would, of course, have overcome all difficulties, but, though the Prince begged piteously for it, he could obtain none from Vienna ; and the consequences were most cruel. " Some regiments," he wrote in February, " have been without bread for several days, and two contractors have been driven to suicide." On the other hand, taking a true measure of his enemy, Coburg had issued instructions that the French must be attacked at all times and in all circumstances, and that, even in the defence of a position, at least a third of the men should be kept ready for a counter-attack. But there was one clause in his orders which seems to give the key to many an Austrian defeat. " Men defending entrenchments will sit in the banquette, arms in hand, until the enemy comes within three hundred paces, or even somewhat nearer, and then open a heavy fire." British troops were accustomed to hold their fire until the enemy was within thirty paces ; and hence it was that the French Army of Italy, when they met them in Egypt, found the red coats tougher adversaries than the white.[1]

Among the rest of the Allies matters were little better than with the Austrians. The Hessians in Flanders were far below their proper strength, sickness and constant skirmishes having swallowed up the additional recruits furnished during the winter ; while the brigade which had been attached to Moira's force left one hundred dead and two hundred and fifty invalided in the Isle of Wight, over and above five hundred sick men whom they carried with them to Ostend.[2] As to the British, everything was, as usual, behindhand, though the Duke of York had now a more energetic

[1] Witzleben, iii. 91, 62, 29 ; Ditfurth, ii. 10 sqq., 28.
[2] Ditfurth, ii. 30, 31.

Chief of Staff than Murray in Colonel James Craig, 1794. whom we saw last at Wilmington in 1781. Recognising from his American experience how serious was the Duke's deficiency in light troops, Craig tried to hire some from Prussia, but without success. There was a difficulty about the British siege-train, for it was discovered, some weeks after the Duke had made requisition for it, that the application had been mislaid at the Office of Ordnance. Though Dundas made profuse promises of British drafts and reinforcements, to the number of five thousand men, not one thousand of these had arrived by the middle of March, and Abercromby's brigade was quite unfit to take the field. The remount-horses were discovered to be very bad. Artillery-drivers, moreover, the dearth of which had been represented by the Duke for quite six months, were found to be so scarce in England that the Master-General was fain to seek them, though without success, in Hanover. A fresh disappointment arose in the matter of foreign troops, for it proved impossible to obtain three thousand Brunswickers, whom Dundas had counted upon taking over from the Dutch into the British service. Rapidly the forty thousand soldiers promised by Pitt dwindled away ; and Craig resigned himself to the inevitable fact that the deficiency would amount to at least ten thousand men. But this was not, to his thinking, the most formidable danger. With a boldness which must have shocked Pitt and Dundas, he wrote to the War Office a very strong and damaging criticism of the cordon-system, and predicted that nothing but misfortune could attend Generals who upon principle preferred dispersion to concentration.[1]

[1] Craig to Nepean, 7th, 22nd, 31st March, 11th April ; to York, 7th, 15th, 16th March ; York to Dundas, 9th, 22nd, 26th March, 1794.

U

1794.   So the month of March passed away, the unhappy Coburg waiting in anxious suspense to know first, when the troops that composed his heterogeneous army would be ready ; secondly, what their numbers might be when they were ready ; and thirdly, what the Emperor would expect him to do with them when it should please him to honour headquarters with his presence. Meanwhile Coburg had even in February given orders for the contraction of his cantonments ; and at the beginning of April, after much shifting, his force occupied the following positions.

The Right or western Wing of the Allied Army, covering maritime Flanders, was entrusted to Clerfaye with a force of Austrians, Hessians, and Hanoverians, who thus occupied the ground formerly entrusted to the British and Dutch. His headquarters were at Tournai, where an entrenched camp had been thrown up. In his front also Orchies and Marchiennes had been strengthened by field-works ; and on his right efforts had been made to restore the defences of Menin, Ypres, and Nieuport, though, except in the case of Ypres, with little result. The effective strength of Clerfaye's army in the field, after deduction of garrisons for the strong places, was about twenty-four thousand men.

On Clerfaye's left, and connected with it by a detachment of five thousand men under General Wurmb at Denain on the Scheldt, stood the Centre or principal army, consisting of about twenty-two thousand men under the Duke of York, about forty-three thousand men under Coburg himself, and of about nineteen thousand Dutch under the Prince of Orange. The Duke occupied the right with headquarters at St. Amand, Coburg the centre with headquarters at Valenciennes, and the Prince of Orange the left with headquarters at Bavai. It was reckoned that, after providing for garrisons, Coburg could spare sixty-five 1794. thousand men for active operations.

The Left Wing consisted of twenty-seven thousand Dutch and Austrians under Count Kaunitz, which were stretched over the space from Bettignies, a little to the north of Maubeuge, to Dinant on the Meuse.

To these must be added fifteen thousand more Austrians under General Beaulieu, cantoned between Namur and Tréves, bringing the grand total of the Allied force to something over one hundred and sixty thousand men, of which at the very most one hundred and twenty thousand were free for work in the field.[1]

It will be noticed that the corps of Clerfaye and of the Duke of York had exchanged the places which they had occupied during the previous year, pursuant to the design of the British Ministers that the Duke of York should be kept under the immediate eye of Coburg. The first result of this interference was to spoil Clerfaye's temper for the whole campaign ; for he judged his force too weak for its task of defending the maritime provinces ; and indeed it was only by the positive orders of Coburg that he consented to hold the command.[2] The whole arrangement, in fact, was calculated to cause confusion. It was bad enough that the lines of retreat for the British and Austrians should be in exactly opposite directions ; and the obvious course, upon the change of the Duke of York's station, would have been to have shifted his base to Antwerp. But far from this, not only was his base continued at Ostend, but, to make matters worse, a brigade of British was placed under Clerfaye's command, and a respectable number of Austrians under the Duke of York's ; so that in case

[1] Ditfurth (ii. 43) reckons the field force at from 120,000 to 130,000, but he includes British troops which were not on the spot, and reckons the strength of those present at too high a rate.

[2] Witzleben, iii. 94.

1794. of mishap, not only must the lines of retreat for the right and right centre intersect each other, but neither corps could retire upon its base without leading several of its regiments in the wrong direction.

Meanwhile on the French side Carnot had girded himself for a supreme effort. " We must finish matters this year," he wrote to Pichegru on the 11th of February ; " unless we make rapid progress and annihilate the enemy to the last man within three months, all is lost. To begin again next year would mean for us to perish of hunger and exhaustion." He therefore decided to combine the armies of the North, of the Ardennes and of the Moselle, and to mass two hundred and fifty thousand men along the line from Dunkirk to the Meuse. Of these about one hundred thousand were to move upon Ypres, march thence upon Ghent, master maritime Flanders, and then wheel eastward upon Brussels ; while at the same time another hundred thousand were to advance upon Namur and Liège, and sever communication with Luxemburg. In other words, he designed to turn and envelop both flanks of the Allied Army, leaving about fifty thousand men to stand on the defensive in the intermediate space between Bouchain and Maubeuge.

Of the many eminent critics who have passed judgment upon this plan, there is not one who has failed to point out and condemn its defects ; and indeed it is obvious that if the Allies, neglecting small detachments, should fall with their full strength upon either wing of the enemy, they might annihilate it. An advance of the French in overwhelming strength upon the communications of the Allies about Namur would have been equally effective and far less hazardous. Yet Carnot prescribed the invasion of the maritime provinces as the first object, partly no doubt with a view to the ultimate invasion of England, but chiefly, as I conceive, 1794. with the political object of threatening the retreat of the British and thus overawing the most formidable power in the Coalition. It is worth while to recall that in 1815 Wellington looked for Napoleon to turn the western flank of the Allies and cut the British off from the sea, and that he dreaded such a movement so much that he made his dispositions at Waterloo with a view to prevent it. Wellington's action has been as sharply criticised as Carnot's; and yet, when two such men agree upon such a point, their opinion is at least worth serious consideration. In any case, the threatening of the lines of communication both east and west was quite sufficient to distract the councils of the Allies, to set them quarrelling as to which among themselves should be sacrificed to the others, and so perhaps to bring about political discord and the rupture of the Coalition.

At the end of March Pichegru gave the strength of the army of the North at two hundred and six thousand, and of the army of the Ardennes at thirty-seven thousand men, making a total of two hundred and forty-three thousand present under arms, of which one hundred and eighty-three thousand were free for service in the field. The army of the North at the beginning of April was thus distributed. The Left Wing, seventy-one thousand men, extended from Dunkirk by Cassel and Lille to Pont-à-Marque; the Centre, forty-seven thousand men, from Arleux (near Douai) by Cambrai, Bouchain, and Bohain to Étreux, a little to the north of Guise; the Right Wing, thirty-six thousand men, from Avesnes by Cerfontaine, St. Rémy, and St. Waast to Maubeuge. This made a total of one hundred and fifty-four thousand men ready for the field; one half of them, under such leaders as Moreau and Souham, standing on

1794. the frontier of maritime Flanders. As early as on the 11th of March Carnot ordered Pichegru to begin the advance on Ypres; but the General, though willing to train his troops by countless skirmishes, made no movement until the 29th of March, when he attacked the Austrian advanced posts at Le Cateau with thirty thousand men, and was beaten back with the loss of twelve hundred killed and wounded and four guns. " It is dangerous," he reported, " to match our young troops against the enemy so soon " ; and therewith his operations incontinently ceased.

Meanwhile Coburg, still awaiting his orders, made no attempt to overwhelm any one of the scattered French divisions. At last on the 2nd of April the Emperor quitted Vienna, reached Brussels in company with his brothers, the Archdukes Charles and Joseph on the 9th, and on the 14th joined Coburg at Valenciennes. The Prince then laid before him the danger of the Allied position, with both wings too weak to take the offensive against an enemy which was reported to be three hundred thousand strong ; and followed this up by recommending the advance of the centre to the siege of Landrecies, for which Mack had prepared one of his usual elaborate schemes. Thus the Austrians reverted once more to a war of petty sieges, which could produce no decisive result. Indeed the only thing to be said for operations in the selected quarter was that the country was open and well suited to cavalry, in which arm the Allies were far superior both in quantity and quality to the French. The Emperor approved the plan ; and the troops were set in motion forthwith, nominally for a great review to be held in the Emperor's honour near Le Cateau. Thus, despite all Carnot's efforts to take the initiative, it fell to the Allies to open the new campaign.

April 2.

April 14.

VOL. IV. BOOK XII. CHAPTER X

On the 16th of April, as had been arranged, the whole 1794. of the main army was inspected by the Emperor on April 16. the heights of Cateau. The British infantry was represented, as in the last campaign, by three battalions of Guards, with a fourth battalion formed out of their flank-companies, and by Abercromby's brigade of the Fourteenth, Thirty-seventh, and Fifty-third. These last had at length received their first instalment of recruits to make good their losses during 1793, in the shape of a draft which was described as " much resembling Falstaff's men, and as lightly clad as any Carmagnole battalion " [1] of the French Army. The cavalry numbered twenty-eight squadrons, drawn from fourteen regiments [2] and

[1] Calvert, p. 187.

[2] Three squadrons of the 1st Dragoon Guards, two squadrons each of the Blues, 2nd, 3rd, 5th, 6th Dragoon Guards, 1st Royals, 2nd Greys, 6th Inniskilling Dragoons, 7th, 11th, 15th, 16th Light Dragoons. The 8th and 14th Light Dragoons were embarked or embarking to join the army. It has been a matter of much difficulty to discover how these regiments were brigaded.

Harcourt's Brigade. (?) 1st, 5th, 6th D.G. = 7 squadrons.

Mansel's Brigade. (?) Blues, 3rd D.G., Royals = 6 squadrons.

Laurie's Brigade. (certainly), Bays, Greys, Inniskillings = 6 squadrons.

Ralph Dundas's Brigade. 7th, 11th, 15th, 16th Light Dragoons, 1st squadron of the Carbineers = 9 squadrons.

After the death of Mansel on the 26th of April, Dundas took over his brigade, and Colonel Vyse took Dundas's. But the regiments seem to have been much shifted from one brigade to another.

Calvert, pp. 197, 204. *Cannon's Records*, Royal Horse Guards, p. 102.

1794. organised into four brigades, three of heavy and one of light dragoons, the last being supplemented by a picked squadron of the Carbineers under the command of Captain Stapleton Cotton, a lad of twenty, who in later years was to earn the title of Viscount Combermere. The review over, the Emperor took up his quarters in Le Cateau, whither the commanders forthwith repaired to him for orders.

April 17. The French troops under Pichegru in the immediate front of the Emperor consisted of three divisions, with an average strength of twelve thousand men each, extended along an entrenched position some eighteen miles long, on the wooded heights of Bohain and Nouvion. Of these Fromentin's division held Catillon on the Sambre, a village rather over four miles east and south of Le Cateau ; westward of Fromentin, Ballaud's division lay astride the road from Le Cateau to Guise, at Arbre de Guise and Ribeauville ; and, still further to west and south, Goguet's division held the ground about Vaux, Prémont, and Bohain. The nearest French troops beyond these to westward were fifteen thousand men under Chappuis about Cambrai ; while to eastward three divisions of the French right wing, numbering some thirty thousand men, lined the Sambre from St. Waast to Maubeuge.

There was therefore an opportunity of overwhelming one or other of these isolated bodies ; but the Austrians clung religiously to their old methods. The force was divided into eight columns, three of which were directed to move north-westward toward Cambrai, so as to check any movement from that side. These need trouble us no more. Of the remaining five, two on the left were ordered to drive the enemy out of Catillon, cross the Sambre, and after clearing

the forest of Nouvion to push forward their light ^{1794.}
troops. One column in the centre, under Coburg's ^{April 17.}
personal command, was designed to move by Ribeau-
ville upon Wassigny to master the heights further
to southward ; while two more on the right, under
the Duke of York and Sir William Erskine, were to
advance, the former upon Vaux, the latter upon
Prémont, to drive the enemy from their entrenched
positions there and at Bohain, and to press their
light troops forward upon Le Catelet. All commanders were expressly ordered to halt the main
portion of their troops on the captured ground, so
that there was no intention of pursuing the enemy in
the event of success.

It would be tedious to describe so feeble an operation. The scene of the engagement is a country much
broken by ravines and hollow roads, so that the heavy
artillery of some of the columns was with difficulty
brought forward ; but the French, being in a manner
surprised, were manœuvred out of their positions
with little trouble or loss. The Duke of York's and
Erskine's columns alone encountered resistance worth
mentioning, but they found little difficulty in turning
the French entrenchments, while the Austrian Hussars
and a squadron of the Sixteenth Light Dragoons
succeeded in cutting down great numbers of the retreating enemy. Altogether the Allies lost fewer
than seven hundred killed and wounded, while the
action was reckoned to have cost the French over
two thousand men, besides from twenty to thirty
guns, of which eleven were captured by the British
columns. Beyond this the French were little molested
in their retreat to Guise, and the trifling success of the
day was marred by disgraceful plundering and burning
on the part of the Allied troops after the engagement.

1794. The British had already shown tendencies in this direction, but had been checked by the Duke of York, who had hanged two offenders, caught red-handed, on the spot, without even the form of a drumhead court-martial. Now, however, the Austrians led the way in misconduct, either led astray by some of their savage auxiliaries, or in aimless revenge for their starvation during the winter ; and the British were only too ready to follow the example.[1]

April 18.   On the following day the army halted between Nouvion and Prémont, pushing its outposts further to southward, while detachments of Austrians were posted also at Prisches, a few miles north of Nouvion, and at La Capelle, Fontenelle, and Garmouset to eastward, so as to cover the left flank and rear of the army. Thereupon the Prince of Orange, whose troops had been advanced towards Cambrai on the 17th, countermarched to Le Cateau, and assembling his force at Forest, about three miles to the north

April 20. of it, on the 20th fell upon the enemy's posts over against Landrecies on the left bank of the Sambre. After a hard struggle, which cost him one thousand men and the French twice as many, he carried the French position, and at once opened the trenches

April 21. before the town. On the following day Pichegru delivered feeble and incoherent assaults upon the positions of Prisches and Nouvion, and upon the heights to the south of Wassigny, all of which were beaten off with the loss to him of many men and four guns. Further desultory fighting at the advanced

April 22. posts on the next day was equally unfavourable to Pichegru, as indeed he deserved for his folly in not concentrating the thirty thousand men, who lay ready to his hand at Maubeuge, for an overwhelming attack.

[1] Ditfurth, ii. 54. Craig to Nepean, 18th April 1794.

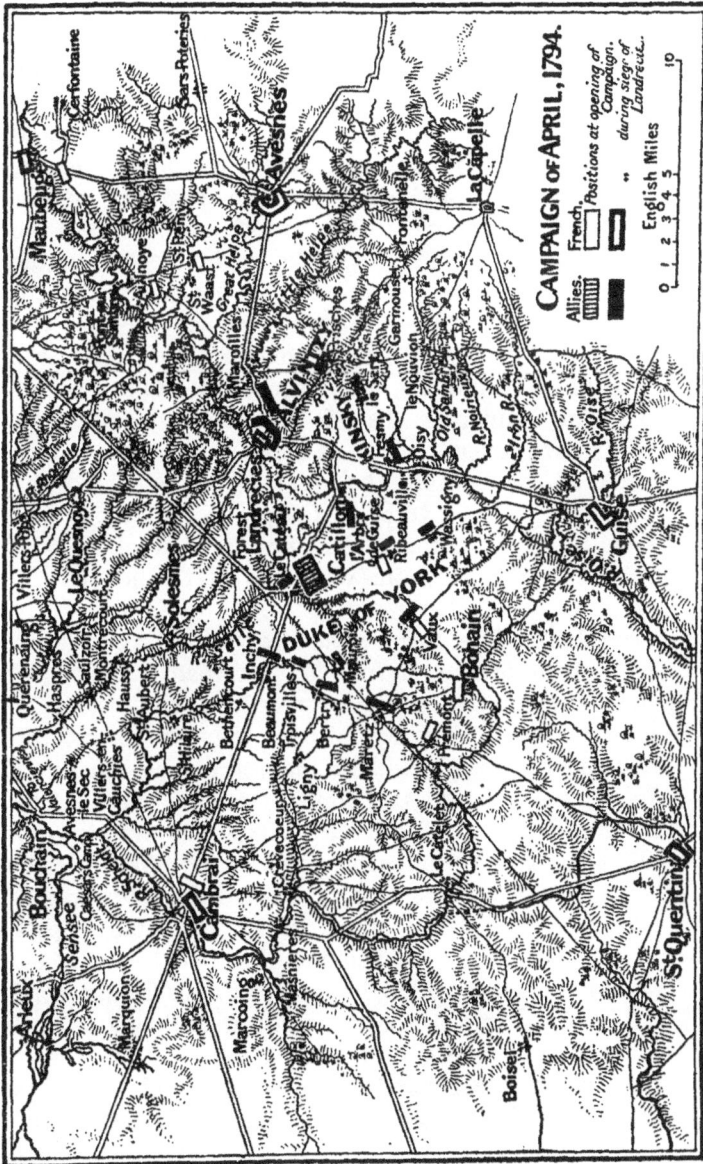

CAMPAIGN of APRIL, 1794.

French. Positions at opening of Campaign.

Allies. " " during siege of Landrecies.

English Miles

0 1 2 3 4 5   10

Stanford's Geog.l Estab.t, London.

1794. Coburg then judged it safe to proceed with the siege in earnest, and, withdrawing the covering army to the north, formed it in a huge semicircle around the besieging force. His left wing curved round from the heights that lie to eastward of Landrecies, and between it and the village of Maroilles, southward to Prisches, thence south-east across the Rivierette to Le Sart, and thence by Fesmy to the Sambre, the whole line being strongly entrenched, with several bridges thrown over the Rivierette. The force allotted for the defence of this tract was thirty-two battalions, fifty squadrons, and twenty-six light companies, the left under General Alvintzy, the right under General Kinsky. On the western bank of the Sambre the right wing completed the semicircle, with a total of twenty-six battalions and seventy-six squadrons. The first section of the defences on this side ran westward of Catillon to the Selle, from which stream the Duke of York's army carried the line north-westward to the road from Le Cateau to Cambrai. This, a broad paved way, runs straight as an arrow over the long waves of rolling ground that lie between the two towns, the undulations rising to their highest at the village of Inchy, upon which the Duke rested his right. The position thus occupied by the Allies was over twenty miles in extent, following a chain of hills of easy slope but seamed to east of Catillon by deep watercourses and hollows, and broken by small copses and enclosures in the neighbourhood of the villages. Westward from Catillon, however, towards Cambrai the hills subside into a broad plain, not unlike Salisbury Plain, except that the undulations are far longer and the acclivities therefore less severe. Covered with crops but unenclosed, its gentle slopes and unseen folds present an ideal field for the action and manœuvres 1794. of cavalry.

On the 23rd intelligence reached the Allies that April 23. fifteen thousand of the enemy had moved out from Cambrai in three columns towards the north-east, were driving in the outposts along the lower Selle, and had even crossed that river, apparently with the object of intercepting the Emperor Francis, who was returning from a visit to Brussels, to rejoin the head-quarters of the army. The Austrian General Otto, receiving information of these movements from Major-general Sentheresky at St. Hilaire, between four and five miles north-west of Inchy, at once joined him there ; and reconnoitring further north he found the enemy, apparently about ten thousand strong, near the village of Villers-en-Cauchies. Having with him only two squadrons of the Fifteenth Light Dragoons and as many of the Austrian Leopold Hussars, making together little more than three hundred sabres, Otto fell back to St. Hilaire, and sent a message to the Duke of York for reinforcements. Late at night he was joined by the Eleventh Light Dragoons, two squadrons of the Austrian Zeschwitz Cuirassiers, and Mansel's brigade of the Blues, Royals, and Third Dragoon Guards the whole numbering ten squadrons.

Early on the following morning he again moved April 24. northward down the valley of the Selle, keeping the Fifteenth and Leopold Hussars in advance and the remainder in support ; and at about seven o'clock the four advanced squadrons came upon a force of French light cavalry of twice or thrice their strength in a long belt of dwarf coppice, near the village of Montrecourt, and about two miles east of Villers-en-Cauchies. Being attacked on their left flank the French horsemen at once retreated with precipitation

1794. for a quarter of a mile, when they rallied, and then
April 24. retired steadily westward, covered by a cloud of
skirmishers. Finally they re-formed between Villers-
en-Cauchies and Avesnes-le-Sec, fronting to eastward,
and masking a force of unknown strength in their
rear. Otto appears to have followed up this cavalry
with great speed, for, on looking round for his sup-
ports, he could nowhere discover them. He halted
the advanced squadrons, but, perceiving that he had
already committed them too deeply, he assembled
the officers and told them briefly that there was
nothing for it but to attack. The English and Austrian
officers then crossed swords in pledge that they would
charge home ; and it was agreed that the British
should attack in front, and the Austrians on the
enemy's left flank towards Avesnes-le-Sec, which was
already a name of good omen in the annals of the
Austrian cavalry.

The Fifteenth led by Captain Aylett now advanced
at a rapid trot, breaking into a gallop at one hundred
and fifty yards from the French cavalry. These did
not await the shock but wheeled outwards, right and
left, and retired at speed, unmasking a line of French
skirmishers and guns, which opened fire before their
front was clear and killed several of their own soldiers.
In rear of the artillery six French battalions, or about
three thousand men, were massed together in quadrate
formation of oblong shape,[1] with the front rank kneel-
ing. A volley from the eastern face of this square,
together with a discharge of grape from the guns,
checked the attack for a moment ; but, cheered on
by their officers, the Fifteenth swept through the

---

[1] So say the records of the 15th Hussars. I suspect that there
were two squares with the guns between them, as at Avesnes-le-Sec
on 12th September 1793. Two squares side by side would give an
appearance of oblong shape to the formation.

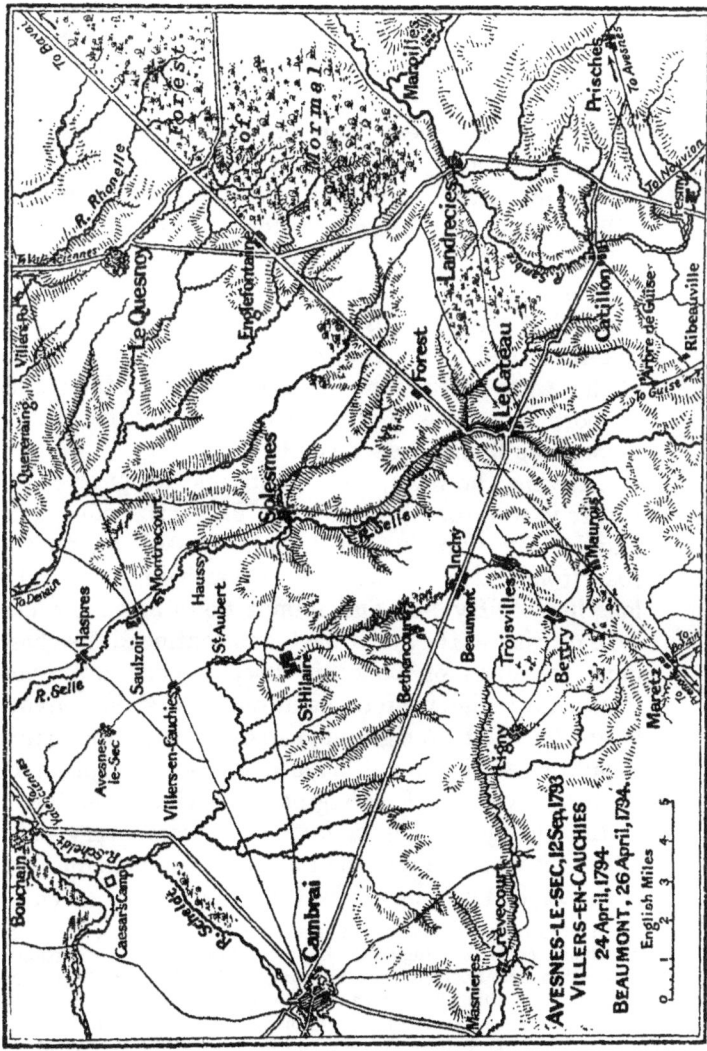

AVESNES-LE-SEC, 12 Sep. 1793
VILLERS-EN-CAUCHIES
24 April, 1794.
BEAUMONT, 26 April, 1794.

English Miles
0 1 2 3 4 5

Stanford's Geog. Establ London.

1794.
April 24.

battery and dashed straight upon the bayonets. The French infantry seems to have stood till the last moment, for Aylett fell with a deep thrust through the body, and four other officers had their horses wounded under them ; but the onset of the Dragoons was irresistible. One half of the square was dispersed instantly ; and the other half, after firing a volley, broke up likewise before the charge of the Fifteenth, and fled in wild disorder. In rear of the square were more French squadrons, upon which those that retired from the front had been re-formed ; but these had given way before the impetuous attack of the Austrian Hussars, and for half a mile the sabres of both Austrians and British dealt terrible havoc among the flying Frenchmen.[1]

Leaving, however, the Austrians to pursue the infantry towards Cambrai, the Fifteenth, now commanded by Captain Pocklington, passed on to the road from Villers-en-Cauchies to Bouchain, dispersed a long line of fifty guns and ammunition-waggons, which were retiring to the north-west, and continued the chase until the guns of Bouchain itself opened fire upon them, and a relieving force came out to save the convoy. Meanwhile not a sign appeared of the supporting squadrons which might have ensured the capture of the artillery ; and Pocklington, observing other forces of the enemy closing in upon him from every side, rallied his men and retired at a trot. The blue uniform of the Light Dragoons, however, caused the French to

[1] The records of the 15th Hussars for some reason seek to excuse the slaughter of the fugitives, by mentioning that the National Convention had decreed that no quarter should be given to the English ; and this mistake has been copied by Sir Evelyn Wood in his excellent account of the action in *Achievements of Cavalry*. As a matter of fact the decree was not made until the 26th of May ; and three hundred men need no excuse for taking no prisoners when attacking five thousand.

mistake them for friends ; and it was not until they 1794.
were close to Villers-en-Cauchies that Pocklington April 24.
perceived that he was cut off. The enemy was, in
fact, established in his front, blocking the road with
infantry and artillery at a point where a causeway
carried it across a valley, though to the south of the
village there were visible the scarlet coats of Mansel's
brigade. Wheeling about, therefore, for a short time,
Pocklington checked the pursuers that were following
him from Bouchain, and then, wheeling once more to
his proper front, he galloped through the French amid
a heavy fire of grape and musketry with little loss, and
safely rejoined his comrades.

Things, however, had not gone well with Mansel and
his brigade. Whether it was by Otto's fault or by his
own that he had gone astray, and whether he attempted
and failed in an attack upon the French who were
obstructing Pocklington's retreat, is a mystery. We
know only that Craig reported, with great regret, that
the brigade had behaved ill ; that he attributed the
fault mainly to Mansel, whom after the action of the
17th he had already reported as an incompetent officer ;
but that the troops also were to blame, though the
Royals had immediately recovered themselves and
protected the retreat of the other two regiments.
More curious still, the list of casualties shows that the
Third Dragoon Guards suffered the very heavy loss of
thirty-eight men and forty-six horses killed, besides
nine more men wounded and missing, though the
casualties of the Royals and the Blues were trifling.[1]
From this I infer that Mansel led his brigade to the
sound of the guns, and, being ordered to attack the

---

[1] In *Cannon's Records* of the 3rd Dragoon Guards these casualties
are ascribed to the action of the 26th of April. Whether the mistake
be due to accident or to design, it is to be regretted.

X

fresh division of the enemy that had come upon the
ground, contrived by irresolution and mismanagement
to bring the Third Dragoon Guards under enfilading
fire of the French cannon, and to throw the whole of
the six squadrons into confusion. In any case it is
certain that the brilliant attack of the Fifteenth was
insufficiently supported, and that Mansel and his
brigade, justly or unjustly, lay under reproach, until
two days later they redeemed their good name beyond
all chance of cavil. The casualties of the French in
this action were eight hundred men killed and four
hundred wounded, besides three guns taken ; while
the Fifteenth escaped with a loss of thirty-one men
and thirty-seven horses killed and wounded, and the
Leopold Hussars with a loss of ten men and eleven
horses killed and wounded and the same number
missing. The Emperor of Austria conferred on the
officers of the Fifteenth a gold medal and the much-
coveted order of Maria Theresa ; and the regiment
still bears on its appointments the name of Villers-en-
Cauchies. With a little more luck, or, it may be, a
little better management, Otto would have achieved
one of the greatest successes ever recorded of cavalry
against infantry, and annihilated the whole of the
force that had moved out from Cambrai.

As matters stood, however, the reverse to the French
produced little effect on Pichegru. Successive reinforcements had more than made good his losses ; and
on the 24th of April the combined strength of the
armies of the North and of the Ardennes, not counting
fifty thousand men employed as garrisons, was little
short of two hundred thousand men free for service
in the field, or nearly two to one of Coburg's force.
Relying upon this numerical superiority the French
General started for Lille, in order from thence to direct

operations against Clerfaye. At the same time, how- 1794.
ever, he set his troops in motion to raise the siege of
Landrecies, directing General Charbonnier with thirty
thousand men of the army of the Ardennes to attack
Kaunitz on the extreme left wing of the Allies, while
at the same time General Ferrand with forty-five
thousand from Guise should fall on the covering army
on the east and south, and General Chappuis with
thirty thousand men from Cambrai should assail the
Duke of York on the west.

Accordingly, early in the morning of the 26th the April 26.
French engaged the covering army simultaneously at all
points. On the east General Fromentin with twenty-
two thousand men assailed Maroilles and Prisches, and
after a long and severe struggle captured the latter
position, severing for the time communications between
Alvintzy and Kinsky. Alvintzy himself was disabled
by two wounds, and the situation was for a time most
critical until the Archduke Charles, who had succeeded
to the command of Alvintzy's troops, by a final and
skilful effort recovered the lost ground and drove the
French over the Little Helpe. This enabled him to
reinforce the centre under General Bellegarde, who
with some difficulty was defending the line from Oisy
to Nouvion against twenty-three thousand men.
Thereupon Bellegarde instantly took the offensive,
completely defeated the French, and captured from
them nine guns.

But far more brilliant was the success of the Allies
on the west, where Chappuis led one column along the
high-road from Cambrai to Le Cateau, while a second
column of four thousand men advanced upon the same
point by a parallel course through the villages of Ligny
and Bertry, a little farther to the south. Favoured by
a dense fog the two columns succeeded in driving the

advanced posts of the Allies from the villages of Inchy and Beaumont on the high-road, and of Troisvilles, Bertry, and Maurois immediately to south of them ; which done, they proceeded to form behind the ridge on which these villages stand, for the main attack. Before the formation was complete the fog cleared ; and the Duke, observing that Chappuis's left flank was in the air, made a great demonstration with his artillery against the French front, sent a few light troops to engage their right, and calling all his cavalry to his own right, formed them unseen in a fold in the ground between Inchy and Bethencourt, a village a little to westward of it.[1] The squadrons were drawn up in three lines, the six squadrons of the Austrian Cuirassiers of Zeschwitz forming the first line under Colonel Prince Schwarzenberg, Mansel's brigade the second line, and the First and Fifth Dragoon Guards and Sixteenth Light Dragoons the third, the whole of the nineteen squadrons being under command of General Otto.[2]

In this order they moved off, Otto advancing with great caution, and skilfully taking advantage of every dip and hollow to conceal his movements. A body of French cavalry was first encountered and immedi-

---

[1] Going over the ground, my companion and myself fixed upon a hollow about half a mile to west of Inchy, and on the north side of the road, as the spot where Otto concentrated his squadrons out of sight of the French. The left flank of the French infantry, upon which the attack was opened, we reckoned to have stood in a hollow about half a mile south-east of Inchy. After very careful study of the ground, I put forward these conjectures with some confidence.

[2] The establishment of an Austrian Cuirassier Regiment was six squadrons ; the British regiments, as originally organised in 1793, should have made thirteen squadrons ; but I imagine that losses had reduced one or other of them to a single squadron, for both Witzleben (iii. 132) and Ditfurth (ii. 57) give the number as six Austrian and twelve British squadrons.

ately overthrown, General Chappuis, who was with
them, being taken prisoner. Then the last ridge was
passed and the squadrons saw their prey before them—
over twenty thousand French infantry drawn up with
their guns in order of battle, serenely facing eastward
without thought of the storm that was bursting on
them from the north. There was no hesitation, for
Schwarzenberg was an impetuous leader, and the
Cuirassiers had been disappointed of distinction at
Villers - en - Cauchies ; the Blues, Royals, and Third
Dragoon Guards had a stain to wipe away ; the King's
and Fifth Dragoon Guards were eager for opportunity to
show their mettle ; and the Sixteenth Light Dragoons,
being the only Light Dragoons present, were anxious
to prove that they could do as well as the Fifteenth.
The trumpets rang out, and with wild cheering white
coats, red coats, and blue coats whirled down upon the
left flank and rear of the French. The French guns,
hastily wheeled round, opened a furious fire of grape,
while the infantry began as furious a fire of musketry ;
but the charging squadrons took no heed. Mansel,
stung by the imputation of cowardice, which had been
thrown out to account for his mishap on the 24th, had
vowed that he would not come back alive, and dashing
far ahead of his men into the thick of the enemy went
down at once ; but Colonel Vyse, of the King's Dragoon
Guards, taking command of both brigades, led them as
straight as Mansel. In a very few minutes the whole
mass of the French was broken up and flying southward
in wild disorder, with the sabres hewing mercilessly
among them.

The misfortunes of the enemy did not end here, for
one of their detachments, which had been pushed forward to Troisvilles, was driven back by a couple of
British guns under Colonel Congreve, and joined the

rest in flight. Meanwhile Chappuis's second column had advanced a little beyond Maurois with its guns, when the appearance of the fugitives warned them to retire ; but in this quarter, too, there was a vigilant Austrian officer, Major Stepheicz, with two squadrons of the Archduke Ferdinand's Hussars and four of the Seventh and Eleventh British Light Dragoons. Following up the French column he drove its rearguard in upon the main body a little to westward of Maretz, and a few miles further on fell upon the main body also, dispersed it utterly, and captured ten guns. Twelve hundred Frenchmen were killed in this part of the field alone, so terrible was the Austrian hussar in pursuit ; two thousand more had fallen under the sabres of Otto's division, which likewise captured twenty-two guns and three hundred and fifty prisoners. The shattered fragments of the French infantry fled by a wide detour to Cambrai ; and Pichegru's attack on this side was not merely beaten off, but his troops were literally hunted from the field.

So ended the greatest day in the annals of the British horse, perhaps the greater since the glory of it was shared with the most renowned cavalry in Europe. The loss of the Austrians was nine officers, two hundred and twenty-eight men, and two hundred and eight horses ; that of the British, six officers, one hundred and fifty-six men, and two hundred and eighty-nine horses, killed, wounded, and missing. The British regiments that suffered most heavily were the Blues and the Third Dragoon Guards, each of which had sixteen men and twenty-five horses killed outright ; and the determination of the Third to prove that the harsh criticism of their comrades on the 24th was unjust, is shown by the fact that five out of the six officers injured in the charge belonged to them. Mansel, the

Brigadier, who was also their Colonel, died as has been 1794.
told. Of the Captains one, his own son, was overpowered and taken in a desperate effort to extricate his
father, and another was wounded. Of the Lieutenants
one was killed and another, if not two more, wounded.
The Major in command, however, had the good fortune
not only to escape unhurt but to receive the sword of
General Chappuis. The total loss of the covering army
was just under fifteen hundred men ; that of the French
was reckoned, probably with less exaggeration than
usual, at seven thousand, while the guns taken from
them numbered forty-one.

On the following day the Emperor ordered his army April 27.
to devote itself to singing a *Te Deum* and to solemn
thanksgiving, which was very right and proper, but
might well have been deferred for forty-eight hours
until the full fruits of the victory had been gathered.
For although there were four fortresses, Avesnes, Guise,
Cambrai, and Maubeuge, within easy distance as a
refuge for fugitives, another day's pursuit would
assuredly have swept up many hundred stragglers,
while the mere sight of the Allied troops would probably
have sufficed to set the French levies running once
more. There was, however, better excuse than usual
for inaction, for among General Chappuis's papers had
been found evidence that a most formidable stroke
was about to fall, if it had not already fallen, upon
Flanders. It is now necessary to narrate the course of
events in that quarter, namely, on the right or western
wing of the Allies.

On the 23rd of April a force from Cambrai, acting April 23.
in concert with that which was beaten on the 24th
at Villers-en-Cauchies, had moved northward against
Wurmb's corps of communication at Denain, and, but
for the arrival of Clerfaye with some eight thousand

1794. men from Tournai, would have driven it across the Scheldt. On the 24th, 26th, and 27th the harassing of the advanced posts of the Allies about Denain continued, and meanwhile the true attack was developed, pursuant to Carnot's plans, on the extreme left of the April 24. French line. On the 24th Michaud's division of twelve thousand men marched from Dunkirk, part of it towards Nieuport on the north, the rest upon Ypres to south-east, sweeping back the feeble posts between the two places. Simultaneously Moreau's division of twenty-one thousand men moved eastward from Cassel upon Ypres, and drove all the outlying detachments on that side to take shelter under the ramparts. Then, leaving some of Michaud's division at Messines to watch April 25-27. the fortress from the south, Moreau pursued his way eastward against Menin, and surrounded that fortress upon all sides. At the same time Souham's division of thirty thousand men, under the personal direction of Pichegru, advanced from Lille north-eastward upon Mouscron, drove back upon Dottignies the weak detachment that defended it, and captured Courtrai, which April 26. was practically without a garrison. General Oynhausen, however, restored matters somewhat by collecting troops from Tournai at Dottignies and retaking the April 28. position of Mouscron, where reinforcements arrived in the nick of time to strengthen him.

The papers found upon Chappuis gave Coburg the key to all these movements; and on the evening of the 26th he sent twelve battalions and ten squadrons under General Erskine from his own army to St. Amand, bidding Clerfaye to recall at once to their proper stations the reinforcements which he had imprudently hurried to Denain. Clerfaye accordingly hastened by forced marches through Tournai to Mouscron, which he reached on the 28th, raising the garri-

son of that place to ten thousand men, exclusive of 1794.
about two thousand more in the detached posts of
Coyghem and Dottignies. The relief of Menin was
his first and most urgent object, and he had fully
resolved to attempt it on the 30th; but Pichegru
was too quick for him. On the 29th the two columns April 29.
under Generals Souham and Bertin fell, the one upon
Clerfaye's front, the other upon his left flank and
rear, with a superiority of three to one, and after a
hard struggle forced him from his position. The
Austrian General seems to have begun his retreat in
good order, but the movement speedily degenerated
into a flight; and when he rallied his beaten troops
at Dottignies he was the weaker by two thousand
men killed and wounded and twenty-three guns.
Happily six of the battalions sent from the army
before Landrecies had by that time reached Dottignies,
and, with these to hearten his demoralised force, he
retired eastward to Espierres, on the western bank of
the Scheldt.

This defeat decided the fate of Menin. The garrison consisted of rather more than two thousand men,
chiefly Hanoverians, but in part French Emigrants,
which latter if captured could expect nothing but the
guillotine. The commandant, Count Hammerstein,
therefore decided to cut his way out through the
besiegers, and with the fortune that favours the brave,
succeeded during the night of the 30th in forcing his April 30.
passage northward to Thourout and thence to Bruges.
Thus Menin and Courtrai, the two gates of the Lys,
were lost, and a gap was broken in the long cordon
of the Allies. Along the whole of the right wing
there was something like a panic, and the roads were
choked with long trains of supplies and stores flying
northward to Brussels and Ghent. At Ostend there

1794. had lately arrived the Eighth Light Dragoons and the Thirty-eighth and Fifty-fifth Foot, sadly belated, since the infantry, with Dundas's usual wisdom, had been embarked at Bristol; but General Stewart, the commandant at Ostend, did not think it prudent after Clerfaye's defeat to send them down country.[1] Happily Pichegru did not pursue his advantage as

May 3. he ought. He did indeed push a detachment northward from Menin upon Roulers, which was attacked and defeated with a loss of two hundred men and three guns by three squadrons of the Allied cavalry;[2] but there his activity ceased; and he solemnly sat himself down about Moorseele on the left bank of the Lys, with one flank resting on Menin and the other on Courtrai, as if to allow time for Coburg's army to come up in his front.[3]

Coburg meanwhile had passed through no enviable

April 28. days. On the 28th news reached him that Kaunitz on his left wing had been forced back by overwhelming numbers to the Sambre, while on his right wing Pichegru had made his way to Courtrai; but, however serious the outlook, he was still tied for the present to the miserable and useless fortress of Landrecies. By a strange irony Mack on that very day submitted a plan of future operations, whereby Bouchain, Cambrai, Avesnes, and Maubeuge were in succession to be besieged;[4] but circumstances on

[1] Stewart to Dundas, 30th April; Craig to Nepean, 25th April; Adjutant-general to Duke of York, 22nd April, 1794. These two unfortunate battalions spent three weeks on the passage.
[2] York to Dundas, 6th May 1794.
[3] It is curious to note that Jomini's account makes the French force front to the south, whereas Craig conceived of it as facing to the north; so that evidently it was prepared to face either way.
[4] Witzleben, ii. 167. Memorandum of the 28th of April in *W.O. Corres.*

the occasion were too strong for pedantry. Land- 1794.
recies fortunately fell on the 30th, and Coburg on the April 30.
same day ordered the Duke of York to lead the rest
of his force with all speed to Clerfaye's assistance,
and to drive the French from Flanders.

Heavy rain, however, delayed the Duke's progress ;
and it was not until the 3rd of May that he reached May 3.
Tournai, where he reunited Erskine's force with his
own and pushed forward a strong detachment three
miles westward to Marquain and Lamain, releasing
five thousand men, which had hitherto held those
points, to join Clerfaye. The front thus occupied
by the Allies, from Tournai in the south to Espierres
in the north, was from seven to eight miles long and
faced due west, their objective being the right flank
and communications of the French left wing. The
British brigade at Ostend, namely the Twelfth, Thirty-
eighth, and Fifty-fifth under Major-general Whyte,
and the Eighth Light Dragoons, were by this time
on their way to Clerfaye's army ; and the united
force of Clerfaye and the Duke of York was now
reckoned at about forty thousand men.[1] Pichegru,
on the other hand, had from forty to fifty thousand
between Menin and Courtrai, and twenty thousand
more under General Bonnaud (who had succeeded
Chappuis) at Sainghin, about five miles south-east
of Lille, to act as a reserve. At Clerfaye's proposal
it was agreed that on the 5th of May he himself should
cross the Lys a little below Courtrai and fall upon that
place from the north, while simultaneously the Duke

[1] Clerfaye (including the reinforcements from Ostend), nineteen
thousand ; Walmoden at Warcoing, six thousand ; Duke of York
at Tournai, eighteen thousand (Craig to Dundas, 6th May 1794).
Witzleben, however, reckons the united force at thirty thousand
men only (iii. 143), and Ditfurth gives but four thousand men to
Walmoden.

1794. of York should move eastward to cut it off from Lille. After all, however, Clerfaye, whether from diffidence or mere frowardness, would not venture on the attempt. Appeal was made to the Emperor Francis to give him positive orders to attack, but meanwhile Bonnaud concentrated over twenty-five

May 8-9. thousand men between Bouvines and Anstaing, a little to the west of Marquain, as if to threaten the Duke's left. When the Emperor's orders at last reached Clerfaye, he first wasted four days in reconnoitring, and at last made but a feeble attack on the 10th, contenting himself with the capture of the outermost fringe of Courtrai.

Pichegru seems to have had good information of Clerfaye's movements and possibly even of his intentions, for he left Moreau's division alone to deal with him ; and, having moved Souham's division to the

May 10. east bank of the Lys, himself on the same day attacked the line of the Allies in force. Souham advanced against the Hanoverians on the Allied right, but, though he forced the posts of Dottignies and Coyghem, was repulsed from Espierres. On the left of the Allies thirty thousand French moved out in two columns against the Duke of York's entrenched position between Lamain and Hertain ; the stronger column of the two, which included five thousand cavalry, following the main road from Lille to Tournai, the other turning south-east from Bouvines by Cysoing upon Bachy, as if to turn the Duke's left flank. This latter column was checked by a couple of battalions and three squadrons under command of an Austrian officer at Bachy, and was unable to penetrate further. The other and more formidable body carried the advanced posts of Baisieux upon the main road, and of Camphin about a mile to south of it, and forming on the plain between these two villages opened a 1794. furious cannonade from howitzers and heavy guns. May 10. Thereupon the Duke, perceiving a gap in the enemy's line, whereby the right of their main body was uncovered, ordered sixteen squadrons of British Dragoons and two of Austrian Hussars to advance into the plain of Cysoing by the low ground that lies south of the heights of Lamain, and from thence to attack.

The cavalry obeyed with alacrity ; but the ground on the plain, though perfectly level and unenclosed, was much broken by patches of cole-seed, grown in trenches after the manner of celery, which checked the progress of the heavy dragoons. Moreover the French infantry, for the first time since the Revolution, threw themselves into squares and faced the galloping horsemen with admirable firmness. Nine regiments of cavalry in succession charged up to the bayonets, but with insufficient speed, and fell back baffled.[1] Nevertheless they followed the French up the plain from south to north, until, a little to westward of Camphin, their left came under the fire of some French heavy batteries, established on the gently rising ground before the village of Gruson. The Duke then ordered a brigade of British infantry to move forward between that village and Baisieux, at the same time sending down four battalions along the track which the cavalry had taken, to support their attack. The French infantry thereupon retreated from Camphin in a northerly direction towards the village of Willems, their cavalry covering the movement ; while the British cavalry, now reinforced by six more squadrons, hovered about them watching for their opportunity to attack. At length they fell

[1] *Life of Lord Combermere*, i. 38.

upon the French horsemen on both flanks, and utterly
overthrew them, after which they renewed their
attempt upon the infantry, but again without success.
At last, however, a little to the south of Willems,
the battalion-guns of the British infantry came up
and opened fire, when the French, after receiving a
few shots, began to waver. The squadrons again
charged, and an officer of the Greys, galloping straight
at the largest of the squares, knocked down three men
as he rode into it, wheeled his horse round and overthrew six more, and thus made a gap for the entry of
his men. The sight of one square broken and dispersed demoralised the remainder of the French. Two
more squares were ridden down, and for the third
time the British sabres had free play among the French
infantry. Over four hundred prisoners were taken,
thirteen guns were captured, and it was reckoned that
from one to two thousand men were cut down. The
loss of the British was thirty men killed, six officers
and seventy-seven men wounded, ninety horses killed
and one hundred and forty wounded and missing,
the Sixth Dragoon Guards being the regiment that
suffered most heavily. It is hardly necessary to call
attention to the arm which was lacking on this day,
or to point out that a single battery of horse-artillery
would have enabled the cavalry to break the squares
at the first onset, would greatly have increased the
enemy's losses, and would have made the day's operations more decisive. Not for eighteen years was the
British cavalry destined again to ride over French
battalions as they rode on this day ; and then Stapleton Cotton was fated once more to be present, leading
not a squadron of Carbineers, but a whole division of
horse to the charge at Salamanca. But the 10th of
May 1794 is chiefly memorable as marking the date

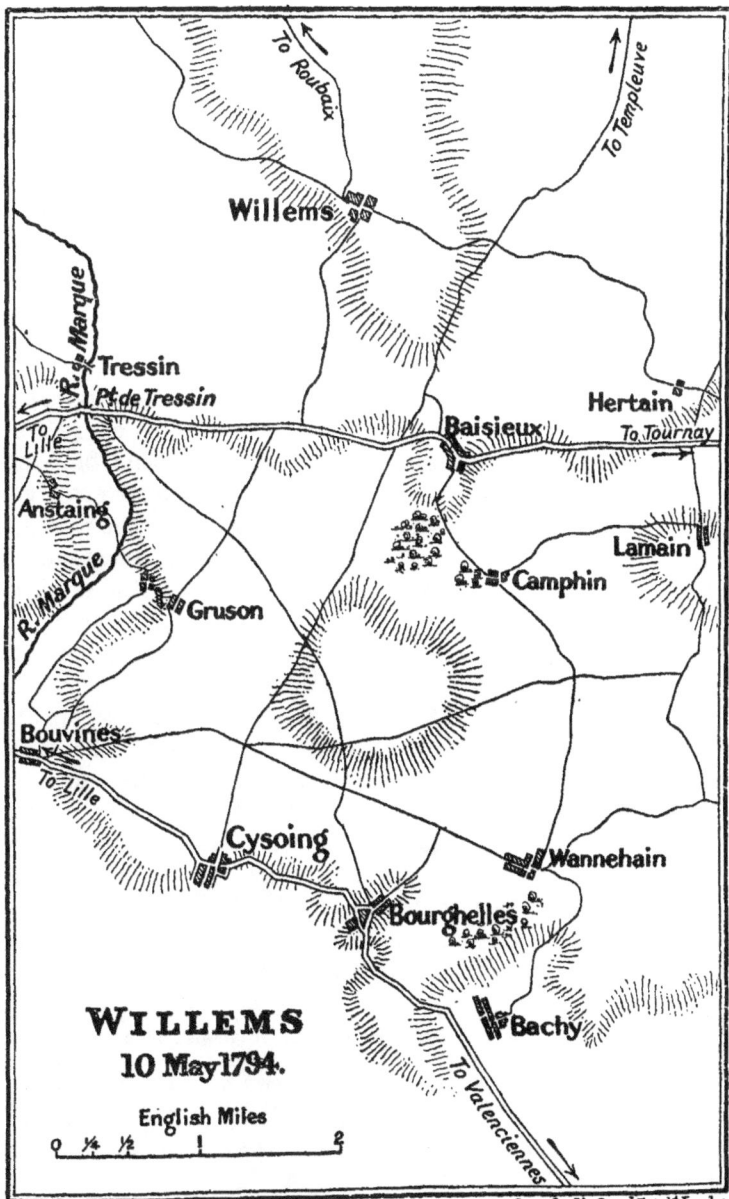

To Roubaix

To Templeuve

Willems

R. de Marque

Tressin

R. de Marque

Pt de Tressin

Baisieux

Hertain

To Tournay

To Lille

Anstaing

Lamain

Camphin

R. Marque

Gruson

Bouvines

To Lille

Cysoing

Wannehain

Bourghelles

Bachy

To Valenciennes

WILLEMS
10 May 1794.

English Miles

0   ¼   ½   1   2

Stanford's Geog.¹ Estab.ᵗ London.

1794. on which the new French infantry showed itself not
unworthy of the old.[1]

After the action the French main body retired
once more across the Lys to its old camp between
May 11. Menin and Courtrai; but on the 11th Souham attacked Clerfaye in his position at Lendelede, about
May 12. four miles north of Courtrai, and after an obstinate
engagement forced him to retire still further northward to Thielt, with the loss of fifteen hundred men
and two guns. Meanwhile the Duke of York, in
spite of his success on the 10th, became anxious as
to his position in presence of numbers so overwhelm-
ingly superior, and pressed Coburg to send him reinforcements. At the Emperor's headquarters, however, there was some hesitation whether the principal
army should move eastward to the assistance of
Kaunitz on the Sambre, or westward for the salvation
of Flanders. The first idea was to make a demonstration towards Cambrai with a part of the force; the
next to make a rapid march and invest Avesnes, also
with only a part of the force, in order to take pressure
off Kaunitz. The idea of moving with the whole
army to any given point seems to have occurred to
none of the Austrian Generals. Then came the Duke
May 11. of York's application for help, whereupon General
Kinsky was ordered with some six thousand horse
and foot to Denain, to enable Wurmb's detachment
at that place to join the Duke of York at Tournai.
May 12. One day later arrived news from Kaunitz that he had

[1] The regiments engaged were the Blues, Second, Third, Sixth
Dragoon Guards; First, Second, Sixth Dragoons; Seventh, Eleventh,
Fifteenth, Sixteenth Light Dragoons. Which were engaged throughout and which came up as reinforcements, I have been unable to
discover. The account of the action is drawn chiefly from Calvert,
Journal, pp. 203-205. *Narrative of an Officer*, ii. 41. Ditfurth,
ii. 75. *Life of Lord Combermere*, i. 38-39. The first is the most
important.

been compelled to fall back still further northward 1794. from the Sambre, and was attacked on all sides ; the fact being that Carnot on the 30th of April had directed fifteen thousand men from the army of the Rhine to join the army of the Ardennes, so as to ensure decisive superiority on the Sambre. Upon this, Coburg determined that the subdivision of the army into fragments must cease, and called upon the Emperor to choose between the Sambre and Flanders, as the sphere of action for the entire force. Intelligence of a successful engagement fought by Kaunitz and of Clerfaye's retreat to Thielt inclined the Emperor to Flanders ; and though, even then, Austrian pedantry insisted that some eight thousand men under the Prince of Orange must remain in the vicinity of Landrecies, yet the bulk of the army on the 14th commenced May 14. its march westward.

This movement, however, was by no means to the taste of some of the Emperor's advisers ; and it becomes necessary at this point to turn for a moment from the western to the eastern centre of European disturbance, and to glance at the influence which events in Poland had exerted upon the Imperial Cabinet. It has already been said that Thugut's only object in persuading the Emperor to take personal command in the field, was that the operations might subserve his own policy. With this view the Minister prepared to remove to Valenciennes, which was to be the political headquarters of the Empire during the Emperor's stay in the Netherlands ; but before he could leave Vienna he was startled by the news of a general rising in Poland. This insurrection under the leadership of Kosciusko broke out on the 25th of March, and spread with a rapidity and success March 25. which left the Russians absolutely helpless. Catherine,

Y

1794. greedy for the partition of Turkey, had already moved
the best of her troops southwards ; and the only force
of any kind upon the spot was that of Prussia, which
fact in itself was enough to kindle Thugut's jealousy.
April 20. On the 20th of April Kosciusko, after two days' fight-
April 25. ing, captured Warsaw ; and five days later Catherine,
while asking the Emperor for the troops due to her
by treaty, mentioned also how greatly she needed
the help of the Prussians, from whom likewise she
had claimed assistance. Meanwhile King Frederick
William, growing nervous lest the rebellion should
infect also his own Polish provinces, after some hesitation decided to throw the Treaty of the Hague to the
winds; wherefore, withdrawing twenty thousand of his
troops from the Rhine, he left Berlin on the 14th of
May to take personal command of his army in Poland.

All this was gall and wormwood to Thugut, and
the more so because Kosciusko had expressed a wish
to place Austrian troops in occupation of Poland
rather than yield it to the Prussians. He became
more and more anxious to have done with France, if
possible by a separate peace with the Republic, and
to devote all Austria's energies to the thwarting of
Prussia in the East. The embitterment of his hostility
towards Prussia brought him more than ever in conflict with Coburg and Mack, who desired above all
things a good understanding with the second great
power of Germany ; but, unfortunately, he found
two officers of like sentiments with himself in the
Prince of Waldeck, who held a high position on the
Staff, and General Rollin, who of all men possessed
greatest influence with the Emperor. It was therefore with profound dissatisfaction that Thugut's
ignoble clique saw the mass of the Austrian troops
drawn nearer to France and further from Poland ;

and though outwardly they swallowed their ill-humour, 1794.
yet they had every intention of compassing their own
ends, even by means the most infamous.[1]

On the 15th of May the Emperor joined the Duke May 15.
of York at Tournai, and the Archduke Charles brought
the Austrian army from Landrecies to St. Amand,
eleven miles to south of it. The field, on which the
decisive action was to be fought, was one that had
drunk deep of human blood. It may be described as
the parallelogram enclosed by a line drawn south-
eastward from Courtrai to Tournai, thence south-
westward to Pont-à-Marque, thence north-westward
through Lille to Wervicq, and thence north-eastward
back to Courtrai. To east it is bounded by the Scheldt,
to north by the Lys ; and through the midst of it,
flowing first from south to north past Pont-à-Marque
and Cysoing to Lannoy, and thence westward into the
Deule and so to the Lys, runs the Marque, a stream
impassable except by bridges, owing to soft bottom and
swampy banks. The principal bridges were those of
Pont-à-Marque on the great road to Paris, and Pont-à-
Tressin on the road from Tournai to Lille ; but there
were others on by-roads at Louyil, Bouvines, Gruson,
Tressin, L'Hempenpont, Pont-à-Breug and Marque,
most of them fortified and strongly held by the French.
Two smaller streams of the same character as the
Marque, but running from west to east, form also
important obstacles within this arena, namely, the
Espierres brook, which has its source close to Roubaix
and flows into the Scheldt at Espierres, and the Baisieux
brook, which rising near Hertain joins the Scheldt at
Pont-à-Chin. The ground is mostly level, with the
exception of the undulating heights that rise from the
Lys, the low ridge upon which stood the villages of

[1] Sybel, iii. 118-120. Witzleben, iii. 157-167.

1794. Roubaix and Lannoy, and the group of hills about
Tournai itself ; but it was thickly studded with villages,
linked together by chains of innumerable cottages and
farm-houses, which were all of them enclosed by hedges.
The fields were cut up by swampy brooks and by a
ramification of wide drains, which, with other enclosures,
practically forbade the movements of troops except by
road. The roads, however, even then were many ;
and the principal highways were nearly broad enough
to permit an advance in column of half-companies ; [1]
but all of them, as well as the waterways, were lined
with trees, making it extremely difficult to see the
movements of troops from a distance. Thus it was
and is a country unfit for cavalry, and far better adapted
in that day to the tactics of the French than of the
Allied infantry.[2]

Within the parallelogram the French were somewhat
widely scattered. Osten's division of ten thousand
men lay at Pont-à-Marque. To the left or northward
of it the bulk of Bonnaud's division of twenty thousand
men was encamped at Sainghin, with detachments
occupying also Pont-à-Tressin and Lannoy, further
north upon the Marque. Souham's division of twenty-
eight thousand, and Moreau's of twenty-two thousand
men lay on the south bank of the Lys between Courtrai
and Aelbeke, a village nearly four miles south of it,
with Thierry's brigade at Mouscron, and Compère's
brigade at Tourcoing to preserve communication with
Bonnaud. In all, the French army numbered eighty-
two thousand men.

---

[1] Ditfurth, ii. 90. He says actually that there was nearly room
for the full width of a company, of course in triple rank.

[2] Great part of the battle-field is now built over. Lille alone
covers a vast extent of it, and Roubaix and Lannoy are to all intent
part and parcel of Lille. But the general character of the ground,
and in particular its blindness, remains unchanged.

Against this force Coburg could pit sixty-two 1794. thousand, twelve thousand of them cavalry. Of the Allied army, fourteen thousand under the Archduke Charles were at St. Amand ; seventeen thousand under the Duke of York at Tournai ; nine thousand under Kinsky at Marquain ; four thousand Hanoverians under General von dem Bussche at Warcoing, on the Scheldt ; and, lastly, sixteen thousand men under Clerfaye were at Oyghem, about five miles north and east of Courtrai on the north bank of the Lys. The whole of these troops, excepting Clerfaye's corps, could easily be concentrated within twelve hours at Tournai, from which a swift and resolute attack upon the southern flank of Souham and Moreau, by Roubaix, Mouveaux and Bondues, might have cut them off from Lille, driven them into the arms of Clerfaye and overwhelmed them. The Austrians, however, were not to be weaned from their own methods, and accordingly on the 16th Mack prepared an elaborate plan, which he designed, and even declared, to be a plan of annihilation.

The army was as usual to be divided. The first May 16. column, of four thousand Hanoverians under Bussche, was to march by Dottignies upon Mouscron, detaching a third of its strength northward on the high road from Tournai to Courtrai, and, having captured Mouscron, was to open communication with the second column. The second column, of twelve battalions and ten squadrons, or about ten thousand men, under Field-Marshal Otto, was to advance by Leers and Wattrelos upon Tourcoing. The third column, of twelve battalions and ten squadrons under the Duke of York, was to move by Lannoy against Mouveaux, sixteen British squadrons being held in reserve at Hertain under General Erskine. The fourth column, of ten battalions

1794. and sixteen squadrons under Count Kinsky, was to be employed partly in covering the Duke's left flank; but the bulk of it was to advance on Bouvines and there force the passage of the Marque. The fifth column, of seventeen battalions and thirty-two squadrons under the Archduke Charles, was to march to Pont-à-Marque, sending a small detachment northward by Templeuve to preserve communication with the fourth column. Having gained the passage of the Marque the Archduke was to attack the enemy on the western side of the river, and, after leaving detachments to guard the bridges, to wheel northward, unite forces with Kinsky and move up with him to join the Duke of York at Mouveaux. Finally the sixth column under Clerfaye was to march from Oyghem on the left bank of the Lys, force the passage of the river above Menin on the morning of the 17th, and manœuvre in rear of the enemy about Mouscron and Tourcoing. Thus the design was to attack the enemy's front with half the army, turn both their flanks with the remainder, and destroy the French irremediably; but whether the surest way of attaining this object was to disperse the troops in isolated columns over a front of twenty miles in a blind and strongly enclosed country—this was a question over which Craig, at any rate, shook his head.

May 17. Miscarriages of the great plan began early. Clerfaye did not receive his orders for the movement towards Menin until late on the morning of the 16th, and did not march until the evening. His progress was much delayed by the heavy sandy roads, and, consequently, it was the afternoon of the 17th before his corps reached Wervicq, and attempted to cross the Lys by the bridge. The French, however, had covered it by entrenchments which blocked his passage; and, when the pontoons were asked for, it was found that by some mistake they had been left behind. Several hours were wasted 1794. while they were coming up, and the pontoon-bridge May 17. was consequently not laid until late at night, when a few battalions only crossed the river, the remainder of the force bivouacking on the left bank. The general result was that Clerfaye's corps, one-fourth of the whole army, counted for nothing in the first day's operations.[1]

The march of the remaining columns was begun in a thick fog which rendered concerted movements difficult, and the Austrian Staff seems to have made no allowance for the varying distances to be covered by the columns ; Kinsky having little more than seven miles to traverse from Froidmont to Bouvines, whereas the Archduke Charles had fully fifteen miles from St. Amand to Pont-à-Marque. Bussche concentrated at St. Leger, a little to west of Warcoing, in the night, advanced upon Mouscron, and captured it, but was driven out again with very heavy loss, and forced back to Dottignies. For this misfortune Mack was chiefly responsible, by directing the detachment of so large a proportion of this column on a perfectly aimless errand towards Courtrai. Otto, on Bussche's left, fared better, driving Compère's troops from Leers, Wattrelos, and Tourcoing; but, unfortunately, with no further result than to join them to Thierry's brigade behind Mouscron, to the greater discomfiture of the unfortunate Hanoverians.

To the left and south of Otto the Duke of York with about ten thousand men[2] advanced by Templeuve upon Lannoy which, after a sharp cannonade, he attacked with the brigade of Guards in front while

---

[1] Witzleben (iii. 197-198) considers the slowness both of Clerfaye and the Archduke Charles on this day to have been inexcusable.

[2] Brigade of Guards (4 battalions) ; 14th, 37th, 53rd Foot; 2 Hessian and 5 Austrian battalions ; 7th, 15th, 16th Light Dragoons (6 squadrons) ; 4 squadrons of Austrian Hussars.

1794.
May 17.
the Light Dragoons turned it by the left; but the enemy beat so hasty a retreat that they escaped with little loss. Leaving two Hessian battalions in Lannoy, the Duke pushed on to Roubaix, where the enemy stood, with greater force both of infantry and artillery, in an entrenched position; but, in spite of a very obstinate resistance, the Guards carried this post also with the bayonet. Having no intelligence of the columns on his right and left, the Duke rightly decided to leave his advanced guard at Roubaix, and to fall back with his main body to Lannoy; when to his dismay he received a positive command from the Emperor himself, who with the Headquarters Staff had accompanied the rear of his column, to push on to the attack of Mouveaux. This order was sheer folly, unless indeed it were dictated by wanton and deliberate wickedness;[1] but it was reiterated in spite of all protests, and though the evening was falling and the troops were weary with a long and harassing day's work under a burning sun, the Duke reluctantly obeyed. The French position at Mouveaux was enclosed by palisades and entrenchments and flanked by redoubts; but for the third time the brigade of Guards drove the enemy out brilliantly with the bayonet. The Seventh and Fifteenth Light Dragoons under Abercromby's personal direction at once pressed forward in pursuit, and galloping round the village, which had been kindled by the

[1] Hamilton (*History of the Grenadier Guards*, ii. 304) says, I know not on what authority, that the pretext for this order was that Clerfaye required assistance. It is certain that the Austrian Headquarters had heard nothing and knew nothing of Clerfaye's situation at this time, so that, if General Hamilton's story be more than mere gossip, the order was probably urged by Waldeck or some other of Mack's enemies, with the object of bringing his elaborate combinations into contempt. The fact that the British would be the chief sufferers in case of mishap, would rather have encouraged this faction in the Austrian Staff to the measure.

flying French, overtook the fugitives, and cut down three hundred of them. Three guns were captured ; and one small party of the Fifteenth actually rode into the French camp at Bondues,[1] nearly two miles to west of Mouveaux, and set the troops there running in every direction. The main body of the Duke's column then bivouacked astride of the road between Mouveaux and Roubaix.

With the two columns south of the Duke, however, affairs had gone but indifferently. Kinsky's advance from Froidmont was delayed by a message from the Archduke Charles, to the effect that his force could not possibly reach the Marque at the appointed hour of six in the morning ; but in due time Kinsky moved forward to Bouvines, and drove the French from their entrenchments. The enemy, however, broke down the bridge over the Marque as they retired, and, until the advance of the Archduke began to make itself felt, Kinsky was unable to repair it, since the passage was commanded by a battery of heavy guns. The Archduke's column had meanwhile left St. Amand at ten o'clock on the evening of the 16th, and after driving back the French advanced posts at Templeuve [2] and Cappelle, a little to east of Pont-à-Marque, finally succeeded in forcing the passage of the river at that point. But it was not till two o'clock in the afternoon, instead of six in the morning of the 17th, that his army had passed to the west bank of the Marque ; and his soldiers were too much exhausted to move further than Lesquin, a little east of the road between Pont-à-Marque and Lille. There

---

[1] The *Gazette* prints this place as Bouderes ; and the mistake has been copied into many regimental histories. It is only one among innumerable instances of the slovenliness of the clerks of the War Office at that time.

[2] Not to be confounded with the village of the same name further north, on the road from Tournai to Lannoy.

he bivouacked on the heights between Lesquin and
Peronne, a village about three miles to south-east of it ;
his men having been on foot for twenty-two hours,
marched more than twenty miles over bad roads, and
fought a sharp action for the passage of the river. His
advance, however, had forced the enemy to evacuate
Sainghin, and thus enabled Kinsky to repair the bridge
at Bouvines ; but none the less Kinsky, with excess of
caution, would not cross the river, and encamped for
the night on the right bank, which was for him the
wrong bank, of the Marque.

At the beginning of this day the French commanders
had no information of any movements of the Allies
beyond the march of Clerfaye ; and, accordingly, the
divisions of Souham and Moreau, together with Vandamme's brigade, had crossed to the left bank of the
Lys. The advance of the Allies from the east and the
combats about Tourcoing, however, soon undeceived
them. Pichegru being, as Soult said, fortunately
absent, Generals Souham, Moreau, Macdonald, and
Reynier met in council at Menin ; and on the evening
of the 17th they decided to make new dispositions and
to set their troops at once in motion. Vandamme's
brigade alone was left on the north bank of the Lys to
watch Clerfaye, and the remainder of the troops on that
site crossed the river to take up their appointed stations.
Malbrancq's brigade was posted between Roncq and
Blancfour, villages lying from three to four miles due
south from Menin on the road to Lille ; to the left of
Malbrancq, Macdonald's brigade crowned the heights
of Mount Halluin ; the rest of Souham's division,
under Generals Daendels and Jardon, lay some three
miles away to the east of Macdonald, occupying a line
between Aelbeke and Belleghem, a village lying a
little to the south of Courtrai ; and the gap between

Macdonald and these troops was filled by the brigades 1794.
of Compère and Thierry about Mouscron. Thus the
formation of the French left wing was that of a double
echelon ; the three divisions being arranged at the
three angles of an isosceles triangle, with the van at the
apex, Mouscron, and the rear before Menin and Courtrai.
The right wing, consisting of Bonnaud's and Osten's
divisions, some thirty thousand strong, was assembled
about Flers, two miles and a half to the east of Lille ;
where orders arrived on the evening of the 17th from
Souham that a general attack was designed for the
morrow, in which the duty of Bonnaud's division would
be to march upon Lannoy and Roubaix.

It was not without anxiety that the reports from
the various columns of the Allies were awaited on
the evening of the 17th at the Austrian headquarters
at Templeuve. The failures of Bussche to capture
Mouscron, and of the Archduke Charles to reach the
point assigned to him, had sufficed to mar Mack's
plans ; and of Clerfaye there was no news whatever.
Orders were therefore sent at three o'clock next morn- May 17-18.
ing to the Archduke Charles to march at once with his
own and Kinsky's corps upon Lannoy ; while the Duke
of York and Otto were directed to attack Mouscron
at noon, in the hope that before that time something
would have been heard of Clerfaye. But it seems to
have occurred to none of the Austrian Staff that the
disposition of the Allied army, as prescribed by Mack,
positively invited the French to take the offensive.
On this night Bussche lay at Dottignies and Coyghem
with his weakened corps of Hanoverians. On his left
the main body of Otto's column, seven and a half
battalions and three squadrons, was at Tourcoing, with
detachments of two battalions at Wattrelos, and of
three battalions and three squadrons at Leers, on the

1794.
May 17-18. line of his retreat. Thus his force was distributed in isolated patches along a length of five miles, with its right flank not only unprotected, but actually threatened by a superior force of the enemy, lying within three miles both of Tourcoing and Wattrelos.

On Otto's left the Duke of York's column was as dangerously dispersed. The Guards, with the Seventh and Fifteenth Light Dragoons, under Abercromby, were at Mouveaux; four Austrian battalions and the Sixteenth Light Dragoons were at Roubaix; the Fourteenth, Thirty-seventh, and Fifty-third were on the road between Roubaix and Lille, in order to repel any attack from the garrison of the latter place; two Hessian battalions lay at Lannoy, and four squadrons of Austrian hussars were engaged in patrolling. The Duke's right was indeed covered, but his left was exposed to attack not only by the garrison of Lille but by Bonnaud's superior force about Flers; and thus both his column and Otto's practically passed the night pent in on three sides by forces of thrice their strength. To the left, or southward, there was a gap of four miles between the Duke's troops and the nearest of Kinsky's detachments, which lay at Pont-à-Tressin and Chereng, with the main body still further south at Bouvines; while the Archduke Charles, with nearly one-fourth of the whole army, lay over against him at Sainghin on the other side of the Marque, with advanced detachments pushed far to the south-west at Seclin. Finally, Clerfaye, with rather more than a fourth of the entire Allied force, was still on the western side of the Lys at Wervicq. Certainly the dispositions lent themselves to a plan of annihilation.

May 18. At three o'clock on the morning of the 18th, while Coburg was signing the orders for his troops, the

French army began its march to the attack. On 1794. the south Osten's division was left about Flers and May 18. Lezennes, to watch the Archduke Charles and Kinsky; while Bonnaud, dividing his eighteen thousand men into two columns, directed them northward, the one by L'Hempenpont upon Lannoy, the other by Pont-à-Breug upon Roubaix. Simultaneously Malbrancq's brigade marched south from Roncq upon Mouveaux; Macdonald's from Mount Halluin upon the western front of Turcoing; Compère's from Mouscron upon the northern front; Thierry's, also from Mouscron, together with Daendel's from Aelbeke, upon Wattrelos; while Jardon's brigade moved from Belleghem towards Dottignies to hold the Hanoverians in check. Excluding this last brigade, sixty thousand men in all were thus turned upon the six posts in which the eighteen thousand men under Otto and the Duke of York were dispersed.

Otto's force, being nearer to the enemy, was the first to feel the weight of the attack. General Montfrault, who commanded at Tourcoing, perceiving the overwhelming strength of the enemy, begged reinforcements from the Duke of York, who sent him two Austrian battalions from Roubaix, but with strict orders that they should return in the event of their arriving too late to save the town. As a matter of fact they did arrive too late, for the garrison had already been driven from Tourcoing; but none the less they attached themselves, as was perhaps natural, to Montfrault, who stood fast on the eastern skirts of the town and held back the enemy for a time, until a French battery unlimbering on ground to the north of him, forced him to retire. Seeing himself threatened by large bodies of cavalry, Montfrault formed his troops into a large square, with four battalions and light artillery in front, one battalion on each flank, and the cavalry in the rear. In this order he fell back, his heavy artillery and waggons being enclosed in the centre of the square, and his light troops skirmishing on all four sides. It was about half-past eight when he began his retrograde movement; but already Wattrelos, the first post on his rear, was in possession of the enemy. The garrison, two Hessian battalions, had manfully resisted an attack of six times their number until eight o'clock, when, finding themselves in danger of being surrounded, they retired, and, with the help of two companies sent forward by General Otto, withdrew successfully to Leers. Montfrault thereupon found himself compelled to leave the main road for a by-way, which ran between Wattrelos and Roubaix, in order to continue his retreat.

Between six and seven o'clock, rather later than the opening of the attack on Tourcoing and Wattrelos, Bonnaud's two columns came up from the south upon Lannoy and Roubaix; and shortly afterwards Malbrancq's brigade from the north fell upon Mouveaux, while a part of the French force that had captured Tourcoing appeared also on the north of Roubaix. The Duke of York despatched urgent messages to recall the two Austrian battalions which he had sent to Otto, but of course in vain; and meanwhile he made such head as he could with his handful of troops against overwhelming odds. The troops at Mouveaux were disposed in two sides of a square, the left showing a front towards the east at Mouveaux, the guns stationed in the angle at the northern end of the village, and the right thrown back to the hamlet of Le Fresnoy. To the south, the British brigade of the Line under Major-general Fox, near Croix, sought

to bar the way against part of Bonnaud's division
from Lille ; but to defend the rest of the ground there
were but three Austrian battalions. Of these half a
battalion was stationed in Roubaix itself, and the
remainder echeloned to the right rear of Fox's brigade
behind the sources of the Espierres brook, which ran
along the southern skirts of the village. These
Austrian battalions seem to have been the first to
give way, and one of them, by Craig's account, did
not behave as it ought ; but they were pressed hard
both in front and on their right flank, which, owing
to the absence of the two battalions sent to Otto, was
wholly uncovered. One brigade of Bonnaud's division
therefore succeeded in forcing its way between Mouveaux and Roubaix to Le Fresnoy ; and the Duke
thus saw Abercromby and the brigade of Guards
absolutely cut off from him. Moreover, though he
knew it not, the victorious French of Thierry's and
Daendels's brigades were coming down from Wattrelos
upon his rear. Seldom has a General found himself,
through no fault of his own, in a more extraordinary
position. He had been assured that the Archduke
Charles would join him from the south, and he had
therefore ordered Abercromby to defend Mouveaux
to the last extremity ; but not a sign of an Austrian
was to be seen whether to south or north. His first
instinct was to ride to the Guards at Mouveaux ;
but this was seen to be out of the question. He then
tried to make his way to Fox's brigade, but found
that the French were in possession of the suburbs of
Roubaix, and that he was cut off from this brigade
also. Realising then that, his Austrian battalions
being dispersed, he had not a man left to him except
two squadrons of the Sixteenth Light Dragoons, he
took a small escort from them and rode to Wattrelos,

1794. hoping to obtain from Otto the means for extricating
May 18. the Guards.   Meanwhile he sent orders to Abercromby
to retire to the heights on the east side of Roubaix.

Montfrault, however, had fared ill in his attempt
to withdraw.   Until he reached the ground between
Wattrelos and Roubaix, his square preserved good
order ; but being attacked at that point by overpowering numbers from the south as well as from
north and west, it was broken up, and fled in disorder towards Leers.   Meanwhile General Fox, finding
himself absolutely isolated, at length gave the order
for his brigade, which so far had held its own, to retire.
The retreat began in perfect order, and the brigade,
having successfully fought its way to the road at
Lannoy, followed it for some distance, under incessant
fire from all sides, until checked by a battery covered
by an abatis, which the French had thrown up on
the road.   The first shots from this battery struck
down several men, and Fox for the moment feared
that surrender would be inevitable ; but fortunately
in the ranks of the Fourteenth was a French emigrant
who knew the district well, and undertook to lead
the brigade across country.   It pursued its retreat
therefore under constant fire of artillery and musketry.
in front and on both flanks, and with cavalry constantly threatening its rear ; but it kept its assailants
at bay, and at one moment made so sharp a counter-
attack as to take temporary possession of some French
guns.   Thus partly by good luck, partly by good
conduct, partly by the misconduct and mismanagement of the enemy, the three battalions contrived to
reach Leers, with the loss of all their battalion-guns
excepting one, and of nine officers and five hundred
and twenty-five men out of eleven hundred and twenty.
The greatest credit was given to General Fox for the

coolness, skill, and patience with which he extricated 1794. his brigade. May 18.

Abercromby appears to have begun his retreat from Mouveaux at about nine o'clock, but of necessity very slowly, having with him a considerable number of guns. The retirement was conducted in perfect order as far as Roubaix, the Seventh and Fifteenth Light Dragoons covering the rear with great gallantry. At Roubaix the French, though in occupation of the suburbs, were not in possession of the little walled town, which was still held by a dismounted squadron of the Sixteenth Light Dragoons. The place consisted of a single long street, the direct continuation of which led to Wattrelos, while, just outside the eastern gate, the road to Lannoy turned sharply to the right, being bordered on one side by a deep ditch and on the other by the Espierres brook. To defile through the town took necessarily much time, but the guns emerged safely and the Guards also. Next to the Guards were the Austrian Hussars, still in the street; then in rear of them a party of the Fifteenth; next to this party were the Sixteenth, who were formed up in the market-place; and in rear of all were the remainder of the Fifteenth, holding the pursuing French in check. All was still in order when a French gun posted on the Wattrelos branch of the street suddenly opened fire from the edge of the town, sending shot after shot among the Austrian Hussars. The ordeal would have been a severe one for any troops, and presently the Hussars dismounted and tried to find a way out among the houses, but in vain. The trial became unendurable as the French pressed on and opened fire on all sides upon the horsemen thus pent in for slaughter; and at last the whole body remounted, galloped wildly

Z

1794.
May 18.
down the road, swung round the corner, where the
French infantry thrust vainly at them with their
bayonets, and raced onward for three or four hundred
yards, when the foremost troopers suddenly found
the way blocked by horseless guns. The French
had brought a second gun to enfilade the road to
Lannoy, and the drivers of the British cannon had
fled. The shock of this mass of galloping horsemen
suddenly checked was appalling. In an instant the
ground was strewn with men and horses, kicking and
struggling in frantic confusion, while a number of
bât-horses dashed into the ranks of the Guards, plung-
ing and lashing out, with their loads hanging under
their bellies. For a short time the disorder appears
to have been beyond remedy, for a belt of wood surrounding the town gave excellent shelter to the French
sharpshooters, who had a very easy target in the mass
of struggling men and animals. Very soon, however,
the Guards recovered themselves, and cleared a way
for the cavalry to pass on beyond the wood to open
ground. There the Light Dragoons rallied, the rear-
guard was re-formed, and the retreat, always under
heavy fire, was resumed towards Lannoy.

That village, which was enclosed by a low earthen
rampart and a shallow ditch, had likewise been
attacked early by one of Bonnaud's brigades from
Lille, but had been defended with the greatest gallantry
by two battalions of Hessians, who were apparently
still in possession when the British troops approached
it, though surrounded on the west side, and indeed
nearly on all sides, by the French.[1] The British

[1] The evidence upon this point is very conflicting. All the
English accounts state that, when the British reached Lannoy on
their retreat, the place was in possession of the French. Ditfurth,
on the other hand (ii. 133, 137 *seq*.), is very positive that it was
held by the Hessians until 1 p.m., which, in his opinion, was long

officers, however, could see no sign of a friendly garri- 1794.
son, and Colonel Congreve was actually wheeling his May 18.
cannon round to open fire on the place, when there
galloped up to them some blue-coated horsemen,
who, being mistaken for Hessians, were allowed to
approach without molestation, and succeeded in
cutting the traces of some of the guns before they
were discovered. The Guards then perceiving their
retreat to be cut off, faced about against their pursuers, and, leaving the high road, made their way
across country as best they could south-eastward to
Marquain. The Hessians in Lannoy, either before
or shortly after this, were forced to evacuate the
village, and, finding the road to Leers blocked by the
enemy, were likewise obliged to make their way across
country in disorder, losing out of nine hundred officers
and men some three hundred and thirty, of whom two
hundred were cut off and captured in Lannoy itself.

Meanwhile the Duke of York, conspicuous by

---

after the British would have reached it ; and the evidence which
he adduces is very strong. Against this, it is certain that the
British would have been only too thankful to rally at Lannoy if
they could, and that they were greatly disappointed to find themselves cut off from it. It is also to be noted that Ditfurth rakes up
everything that he can to the discredit of the English, but was not
at the pains to read a single English account of the action, except
the Duke of York's letter as published in the *Gazette*, and that his
account of their movements is consequently full of errors. I incline
to the opinion that the Hessians were still in Lannoy, but that the
French around them were so numerous as to cut the British off
from it—in fact, that the French practically held it invested, with
a covering force powerful enough to keep the British at a distance.
The same was the case at Roubaix, which the Sixteenth Light
Dragoons contrived to hold. till Abercromby retreated, though the
Austrians, the Duke of York, and Abercromby himself all believed
it to be in the hands of the French. It still remains to be explained
why the Hessians made no sign of their presence when Abercromby's
column approached, for the British artillerymen actually began to
lay their guns upon it in the assurance that it was in the enemy's
hands.

the star on his breast, had been hunted all over the country by the enemy's dragoons, and had escaped, as he frankly owned, only by the speed of his horse. On reaching Wattrelos he found it in the hands of the French, but passing beyond it under constant fire he came upon a gallant little party of Hessians still holding the bridge of the Espierres brook. These by a final attack with the bayonet gained a little respite for him, but were presently swept away from the bridge, and escaped only by fording the brook neck-deep. The Duke, thinking apparently that the bridge was lost, or not knowing of its existence, spurred his horse into the brook ; but the animal rearing up and refusing to enter the water, he dismounted, scrambled over on foot, and taking a horse from one of his aide-de-camps, at last succeeded in finding Otto. About Leers and Nechin the fragments of Otto's force, together with some of the Duke of York's men, rallied upon the few battalions that held these places. The French did not press their advantage, and at half-past four the action came to an end. The loss of the Allies was about three thousand men killed, wounded, and missing, which was relatively slight, for, with proper management and conduct on the part of the French, not a man of the Duke's and Otto's columns would have escaped alive. The Brigade of Guards lost one hundred and ninety-six officers and men killed, wounded, and missing, the flank-companies being the heaviest sufferers ; while the Seventh, Fifteenth, and Sixteenth Light Dragoons, who by general admission behaved admirably, lost fifty-two men and ninety-two horses. The total loss of the British of all ranks was nine hundred and thirty, besides which nineteen out of their twenty-eight guns were captured.

It may be asked what the rest of the army was doing 1794. on this day, while these two columns, together less than May 18. one-third of the whole, were in process of annihilation. The answer is that, for some reason, it observed a con- spiracy of inaction. Bussche sat still at Dottignies exchanging occasional shots with Jardon's brigade. Clerfaye crossed the Lys near Wervicq at seven o'clock in the morning, and turning eastward advanced between Bousbecque and Linselles, where he was met by Van- damme's brigade, which numbered eight thousand men against his sixteen thousand. He engaged the French, overthrew their right wing, took eight guns, and then remained stationary; until, being informed of the approach of more French troops about Bondues, he withdrew to the Lys, which he recrossed on the next day, and thence retreated northward. The behaviour of Kinsky and of the Archduke Charles was still more extraordinary. Kinsky, on being asked by one of his officers for orders at six o'clock in the morning, replied that he was sick and no longer in command. The Archduke Charles received at five in the morning the order to move at once upon Lannoy, a distance of six miles, so that his troops might well have come upon the scene of action between eight and nine. He did not march till noon, though within sound of the guns, nor did he strike the road from Tournai to Lille until three, when he received orders to return to Tournai. The military renown justly earned later by the Arch- duke forbids us to believe that this delay was due to ignorance ; and the fact that, though the Duke of York had early informed the Emperor of his danger, not a word was sent to hasten the Archduke or Kinsky, shows clearly that their torpidity was not unexpected nor disapproved at headquarters. Jealousy of the Duke of York and of Mack are among the reasons assigned

1794. to account for the general paralysis of the Austrian commanders ; but possibly the true reason was that Thugut was sick of the war in Belgium, and wished the English to sicken of it also.   Why he should have chosen the slaughter of several hundred British and Austrians as the best means of forwarding his purpose, and how he persuaded Austrian officers to second him therein, are matters which only an Austrian can determine. For us it must suffice that the decisive battle of the campaign was lost by the deliberate design of the Imperial Generals.   Before long they were to learn that those who court defeat for dishonest ends may, when they least desire it, find defeat thrust upon them.[1]

[1] There are few actions which I have found so difficult to describe as this of the 18th of May. I have drawn my account from Witzleben, iii. 201-230 ; Ditfurth, ii. 130-157 ; Jomini ; *Narrative of an Officer*, ii. 47-51 ; Cannon's *Records of the Seventh and Fifteenth Hussars and Sixteenth Lancers* ; Calvert's *Journal* ; and Craig's letters to Nepean of 19th May 1794 (Record Office).

VOL. IV. BOOK XII. CHAPTER XI

THE entire army of the Allies, with the exception of 1794.
Clerfaye's corps, was gathered into camp about Tournai
in the course of the 19th, the Emperor being received May 19.
in silence when he rode into the town, while the Duke
of York was loudly cheered by the inhabitants.[1] The
condition of the army was very far from satisfactory.
The troops themselves, or at any rate the British, were
not seriously shaken by the rout of the previous day ;
but the Emperor and the Austrian commanders were
much discouraged, and the animosity of the various
nations towards each other was dangerously embittered.   The British, above all, were furious against
the Austrians for leaving them to be overwhelmed
without so much as an attempt to assist them.   " It
is impossible," wrote Craig to the War Office, " to
bring the Austrians to act except in small corps.   I
lament that we should be destined as victims of their
folly and ignorance.   Do not be surprised at the word
ignorance : I am every day more and more convinced
that they have not an officer among them."   These
were hard words, but they were true and just, though
the Archduke Charles in later days redeemed himself
from this reproach.   However, for the moment the May 20.
commanders laid aside their differences and agreed
that the attack should be renewed, this time with united

[1] Calvert, p. 269.

343

1794. forces, upon Mouscron ; and meanwhile Coburg dispersed the whole army in a semicircle around Tournai ; the advanced posts running from Camphin on the south by Baisieux, Willems, Nechin, Leers, Estaimpuis, and St. Legers to Espierres, while the inner circle of entrenchments ran from the Scheldt on the north by Froyennes, Marquain, and Lamain to the suburb of St. Martin and the citadel of Tournai itself.

The French Generals, as already narrated, made no effort to follow up their victory of the 18th, but awaited the return of Pichegru, who, on the news of the victory, hastened from the Sambre to turn it to account. On the 22nd, after a consultation with his officers, Pichegru decided to make a general attack upon Coburg's position, and directed that Souham with four brigades,[1] numbering from thirty to forty thousand men, should assail it on the right or northern half of its front from Espierres to Leers, while Bonnaud's division should fall upon its left about Templeuve, and Osten's division should make a demonstration still further to the south May 23. about Baisieux. On the following day between six and seven o'clock in the morning the action began ; and after long and hard fighting the Allies were finally driven from three important points, namely, Blandain and the hill of La Croisette immediately adjacent to it, a little to the west of Tournai, and Pont-à-Chin upon the Scheldt, a little below the city. To abandon to the enemy these posts, particularly Pont-à-Chin, which lay on the direct road from Courtrai to Tournai and commanded the navigation of the Scheldt, was impossible ; and Coburg decided that they must be recovered at any cost. Throughout this long day's fighting the troops that had borne the brunt of the

---

[1] The French brigades at this period were of the strength of divisions.

work on the 18th had been held in reserve ; but at about six o'clock in the evening Fox's brigade of the British Line was called out to recover Pont-à-Chin, which had already been taken and retaken three or four times. The brigade went into this action with fewer than six hundred men, having lost half of its numbers just four days before ; but the three gallant regiments, though unsupported, carried the village unhesitatingly with the bayonet, pressed on to the low heights to south of it, swept everything before them, so far as their front extended, and captured seven cannon. The day ended, after a severe struggle of fifteen hours, in the retreat of the French, with the loss of some six thousand men and seven guns ; the fire, both of musketry and artillery, having been the heaviest ever remembered by the oldest soldiers present. Both sides, however, fought for the most part in dispersed formation, and inflicted, comparatively speaking, little damage upon each other. The one exception was Fox's brigade. " Had their order of attack," wrote Calvert, " been adopted by the Allies in general, the day would probably have ended in the ruin of the French." But the losses of the brigade amounted to one hundred and twenty killed, wounded, and missing ; and there are few troops that can be trusted, after losing half their numbers on Sunday, to storm a position held by a superior force and lose one-fifth of their remnant on Thursday. Some indeed claim that but for this handful of British soldiers the day would have been lost to the Allies ; [1] but whether this be true or not, the 22nd of May should be a great anniversary for the Fourteenth, Thirty-Seventh, and Fifty-Third.

It was directly after this action that the course of

1794.

May 22.

[1] Jones, *Campaign of 1794.* The author was a captain in the Fourteenth.

1794. events in Poland began to tell upon the councils of the
May 23. Imperial Headquarters at Tournai. On the 23rd, Mack,
disgusted by the failure of his elaborate plans, resigned
his post as Chief of the Staff, and, having first expressed
his opinion that the reconquest of Belgium was hopeless,
retired for the time into private life. His successor,
Waldeck, being a fellow-conspirator with Thugut, was
still more eager for the evacuation of the Netherlands ;
and the Emperor was easily tempted to share their
May 24. views. On the 24th a Council of War was held for
form's sake, wherein the Emperor set forth the situation in such a light as to gain a ready vote from his
Generals that further efforts in the Netherlands were
useless. The Duke of York alone pleaded earnestly
for a renewal of the attack upon Flanders ; and, as
fate ordained it, his representations were seconded by
unexpected successes of the Allies on the Sambre and
in the Palatinate. On the 24th Marshal Möllendorf
and the Prussians surprised the French about Kaiserslautern and drove them back with a loss of three thousand men and twenty guns ; and on the same day
Count Kaunitz gained a still more important victory
on the Sambre. The fact was that serious differences
had arisen at Paris between Carnot on the one side and
Robespierre and St. Just on the other, because Carnot
insisted on keeping the direction of the military operations in his own hands. Robespierre, to whom the
art of war was as incomprehensible as a Chinese manu-
script, was furious with jealousy and rage. " At the
first reverse, Carnot's head shall fall," cried the despicable creature, galled by the cold contempt with which
his inflexible colleague rebuffed his attempts at interference ; and to re-establish civil influence at the seat
of war, St. Just, Lebas, and five more Commissioners
set out on the 2nd of May for the army of the Sambre.

There they introduced the rule of terror in its worst 1794.
form, and with it, of course, confusion unspeakable.
They fought with the Generals, they fought among
themselves ; and in the midst of this chaos St. Just
took upon himself the supreme direction of the operations whereby the Austrians were to be crushed. Four May 18, 20,
several times he ordered the army to pass the Sambre, 22, 24.
wasting the lives of his troops with obstinate imbecility.
Finally he gave Kaunitz the opportunity for a counter- May 24.
attack, in which, with inconsiderable loss to themselves,
the Austrians routed the French completely, killing
and wounding two thousand men, and capturing three
thousand more, besides fifty pieces of cannon.

This heavy blow to the French right wing offered
a fair occasion for the Allies to renew the offensive in
Western Flanders ; and the Duke of York urged this
step upon his colleagues with all his might. The
British Government too, reckoning that the troops,
promised by Prussia in return for a British subsidy,
must be nearly ready, decided to send out Lord Cornwallis to concert operations with Möllendorf, and
directed him also to consult the Emperor and the Duke
of York on his way to the Prussian Headquarters.
But, as has already been told, King Frederick William
was occupied rather with Poland than France at the
moment ; and he had also been much irritated by
certain dispositions which had been proposed for his
army by Mack in the middle of May. " I am astonished at the fashion in which Mack thinks to make
use of my troops," wrote the King. " Does Mack
imagine that we can live on air ? " echoed Möllendorf ; [1]
both of them being secretly delighted with so good an
excuse for remaining inactive. Then suddenly, on the
29th of May, the Allied Camp at Tournai was thrown May 29.

[1] Witzleben, iii. 168-169.

1794. into consternation by the announcement that the Emperor was about to return to Vienna. Aided by the defeat of the 18th, Thugut had succeeded in persuading his imperial master to abandon the Austrian Netherlands ; and even Mack, the unpopular Quartermaster-general, had supported him by recommending not only the evacuation of the country but the conclusion of peace with France.

The truth was that jealousy of Prussia had prevailed over all other considerations, and that the Emperor had decided to offer help to the Empress Catherine in quelling the Polish insurrection. He hoped, however, at the same time to delude Prussia into keeping thirty thousand men upon the Rhine, and England into furnishing a subsidy for the ostensible prosecution of the war with France ; and it was therefore imperative upon him to conceal his intentions. He accordingly gave out that the object of his departure was to hasten the recruiting of his forces ; and in his final letter to Coburg, who very unwillingly retained the command, he gave him only vague instructions to adapt his action to the exigencies of the campaign and to save his troops as much as possible. But this duplicity deceived no one, and the less because Waldeck, before he had succeeded Mack as Chief of the Staff, had openly declared that the war in Belgium must be ended. The Austrian troops were profoundly discouraged, and two-thirds of the officers asked permission to retire. They can hardly be blamed, for the succession of murderous actions fought by the Allies against the French on the northern frontier of France, between the 17th of April and the 22nd of May 1794, has few parallels in the history of war. For a month Austrians, British, and Germans had contended almost unceasingly against superior numbers, slaying or taking, not with-

out heavy loss to themselves, French soldiers by the 1794.
ten thousand, and capturing French cannon by the
score.   Yet all had been to no purpose, partly because
the leaders had deliberately chosen a foolish plan of
operations, partly because they had steadily refused
to follow up their successes, partly because on the 18th
of May they had held two-thirds of the army inactive
within sound of the guns which were overwhelming
their comrades.   The bravest men will not fight upon
such terms.   They will not be butchered to serve the
intrigues of politicians whose dishonesty would disgrace a sergeant, and of potentates whose incapacity
would disqualify a corporal.   In days to come Austria
was to pay dearly in Italy for the 29th of May 1794.[1]   May 29.

Immediately before the Emperor's departure came
news from Kaunitz that the French had again crossed
the Sambre in force ; which compelled Coburg to send
him large reinforcements, and thus to weaken the right
and centre of the Allies in order to strengthen their
left.   At the same time, for the sake of keeping the
Dutch in good humour, Coburg was obliged to give
the supreme command in that quarter to the Crown
Prince of Orange, to the natural disgust of Kaunitz,
who had shown much ability and achieved great successes.   The great safeguard, however, to eastward
was that St. Just insisted upon controlling the French
operations ; and it need not be said that against such
an adversary even the Prince of Orange was victorious.
But far more serious were the movements of the French
on the western flank.   Apprised of Coburg's detachment of troops to the Sambre, hoping still to further
Carnot's projects for invasion of England, and above
all conscious of the advantage offered to French tactics

[1] Sybel, iii. 120-125. York to Dundas, 26th May 1794 (with
enclosures).

1794. by the enclosed country of Western Flanders, Pichegru determined to prosecute his operations on that side. Accordingly, leaving between thirty and forty thousand men in positions about Mouscron and Menin to hold Coburg in check, he marched with about the same number on Ypres. On the 1st of June about fifteen thousand men surrounded the fortress on the west and south, and opened their first parallel ; while some twenty thousand more under Souham took post about Passchendaele, about six miles to the north-east, to cover the siege from Clerfaye, who was lying at Thielt. On that same day, by a curious irony, Lord Howe defeated the Brest fleet, taking eight French ships and sinking two more. This action, in which the regiments on the fleet, and particularly the Sixty-Ninth,[1] played no inconspicuous part, closed for the present all Carnot's projects of an invasion.

June 1.

The event, however, in no way disturbed the plans of Pichegru. On the 4th of June Clerfaye contrived to pass two battalions into Ypres to strengthen the garrison ; but he declared himself unable, with the fifteen thousand men that remained to him, to relieve the place unless he were reinforced. By express command of the Emperor, who had lingered at Brussels on his homeward journey, Coburg sent him some ten thousand men in two detachments, reckoning that, after the recent victory on the Sambre, he could safely draw a few troops from that quarter. Clerfaye, however, continued to display the sluggishness which had characterised his conduct from the beginning of the campaign. On the 6th, before his reinforcements had reached him, he made a feeble advance against Souham in four columns, and was of course unsuccessful ; and on the 10th, when his force had

June 4.

June 6.

June 10.

[1] Captain William Parker to the Admiralty, 3rd June 1794.

been raised to over twenty thousand men, he was 1794.
assailed and defeated with loss by Souham before he
could make up his mind to act. On that same day
Coburg had designed to make a diversion in Clerfaye's
favour, by an attack on Mouscron, upon a plan calculated so exactly to expose the Duke of York's column
to destruction, as on the 18th of May, that the Duke
refused to accept it until it was altered. This, however, was of small importance, for the French, having
perfect information of the intended movements,
appeared in every direction in such force that the
enterprise was abandoned. The state of things at the
Austrian headquarters was indeed almost beyond
belief. Insensible to all ideas of duty and discipline,
the young staff-officers, described by Craig as " in
general the most contemptible of puppies," had talked
openly of the projected movement in the coffee-
houses at noon, though the Duke of York received
no information of it until ten hours later, nor any
orders until four o'clock on the next morning.
" Mack used to keep these gentry in order," wrote
Craig, " and, had he been here, the prison would have
been full of them next day ; but indeed it would never
have happened." Meanwhile Clerfaye remained so
incurably supine that the Duke of York more than June 12.
once entreated Coburg to entrust the relief of Ypres
to himself, but in vain. Roused by repeated orders June 13.
to attack, Clerfaye at last moved against Souham in
five columns, gained some advantage at first, captured ten guns, and then as usual sat still until Souham
had gathered troops sufficient for a counter attack,
when he immediately retired to his old position at
Thielt.

This sealed the fate of Ypres, the key of maritime
Flanders, the chief support of the right flank of the

1794. Allies, the bulwark which protected the British communications with Ostend. The Duke of York pleaded
hard for a last effort to save it, by a march of the
whole army to join Clerfaye ; but without success.
" The truth is," wrote Craig, " that the Austrian
army is incapable of further action. The men are
disheartened and the officers disgusted and disunited."
It was finally decided that, to cover Ostend and the
Dutch frontier, Clerfaye should take up a position
between the Lys and the Scheldt about Deynse, some
ten miles to the south-west of Ghent ; keeping half
of his force between Bruges and Ostend, and sending
the Eighth Light Dragoons, Thirty-eighth and Fifty-
fifth, which had formed part of his force, to Ostend.
" We are too weak by ten thousand men to hold this
defensive position," wrote Craig ; " if the French
see their chance and push Clerfaye, they will force
us to abandon this position about Tournai and will
pass the Scheldt in spite of us ; and then ten to one
we shall find ourselves separated from him and beaten
in detail. . . . Sooner than hold the defensive position
I would concentrate the whole army, eighty thousand men, march to the Sambre, attack them at any
risk and march back again. . . . You may expect to
hear from us soon in Holland." Clearly there was
one among the despised British officers who could have
taught the Austrians a lesson.[1]

The situation was indeed a desperate one. The
Austrians, having taken no pains to restore the fortifications of Tournai, had thrown up an entrenched
camp for its protection on the western side. These
lines extended from the city southward along the
Scheldt to Maulde, and required so many men for

[1] Duke of York to Dundas, 10th, 13th, 14th June 1794. Craig
to Nepean, 10th, 13th, 14th June 1794. Calvert, pp. 238-253.

their defence that few could be spared for active 1794. operations. Some seven thousand Frenchmen at Mons-en-Pévèle kept the left of the Allies in continual alarm for the safety of Orchies, which was the key of Maulde and of the passage of the Scheldt at Mortagne ; for if that passage were forced, the communication between Coburg and the army of the Sambre would be endangered. A little to the north of Mons-en-Pévèle was the entire garrison of Lille, and still further to the north, between Lille and Menin, stood from twenty to thirty thousand more French troops. Behind this screen to westward, from fifty thousand to sixty thousand of the enemy were engaged as the besieging and covering armies at Ypres ; and far beyond them to the north lay the right wing of the Allies under Clerfaye, stretched in a weak attenuated line from Ostend to the Lys, and only maintaining communication with Tournai by the circuitous route of the Scheldt. On the eastern flank the French had now some seventy-five thousand men on the Sambre, with a capable leader in Jourdan, albeit one still hampered by the interference of St. Just ; and this was the only quarter in which recent events had gone favourably for the Allies. Such a situation could not last long, and the strain upon Coburg must have been cruelly severe. On the 16th, June 16. however, there came a gleam of hope. The French on that day again passed the Sambre, but for the fifth time were driven back with heavy loss ; and Coburg, having summoned four battalions from that quarter, determined on the 18th to march and join June 18. with Clerfaye in a final attempt to relieve Ypres. The troops were already in motion, when in the evening the news came that the French had crossed the Sambre for the sixth time, and successfully invested

2 A

1794. Charleroi. Thereupon the enterprise was abandoned.
June 19. On the following day Ypres surrendered, and thus Carnot's original plan of turning both flanks of the Allies began, after two months of murderous fighting, to accomplish itself.

Enabled by the fall of Ypres to turn the whole of his attention to eastward, Coburg at once proposed that he should march with all the Austrian troops to Charleroi, and leave the Duke of York to guard the line of the Scheldt from Tournai to Condé. The Duke answered that his instructions were to keep the whole of the troops in British pay together, but that, if ordered, he would gladly lead the whole of them with Coburg to the Sambre. Since, however, his force was absolutely inadequate to guard the line of the Scheldt, he insisted that, if it were left behind, an Austrian garrison should remain at Tournai, and that he himself should take up a position on the eastern bank of the Scheldt between that city and Oudenarde, so as to ensure his retreat in case of mishap.

The offer to march to the Sambre was fair, and it is difficult to understand why Coburg did not embrace it ; for, if the battle on the Sambre were lost, it would obviously be impossible for the Duke's troops to remain isolated in Flanders. Coburg did, however, reject it, though he consented to station about five thousand Austrians under General Kray between Denain and Orchies, promising that, if he succeeded in forcing back the enemy on the Sambre, he would return without delay, but that, in the event of his failure, he should not expect the Duke of York to maintain his position on the Scheldt. He also took the significant step of transferring the Austrian hospitals and stores at Valenciennes, as well as the magazines about Tournai, to Brussels and Antwerp ; the removal

of the stores at Brussels having begun some time 1794.
before.[1] Finally, on the 21st, he marched away; June 21.
and the Duke, since the corps in British pay had now
shrunk to seven thousand men, contracted his quarters,
and took up a new position closer to Tournai.

But meanwhile the news that Ostend was in danger
had, as usual, stirred Dundas to unwonted exertion
in England. He still made a fetish of the place, and
his original intention seems to have been to defend
it, without any particular reference to the Duke of
York's operations. On the 17th of June, therefore,
he ordered Lord Moira's force in the Isle of Wight
and the Channel Islands to sail for Ostend at once,
together with drafts of recruits and three fresh regiments from Ireland, making in all a reinforcement
of about ten thousand men. On the 20th Moira's
troops embarked, and on the 21st the Eighth, the
Forty-Fourth, and the recruits arrived at Ostend.
The drafts, it must be remarked, arrived without arms
or military appointments of any kind; and it was
only a fog at sea that prevented a whole regiment,
the Ninetieth, from being also landed there without
either arms or clothing, Dundas having ordered it to
embark without enquiry as to these details.[2] But
Pichegru meanwhile did not remain idle, and leaving
Ypres on the 20th marched upon Clerfaye's position
at Deynse. The Austrian General, after a short
defence of his entrenchments, retired, with the loss June 23.
of not a few men and three guns, first to Ghent, and
then beyond it, finally taking up a position on the
north side of the canal that runs from Ghent to Sluys,
where he was presently joined by his detachments June 24.
from Bruges. On the 25th of June there arrived at June 25.

---

[1] Duke of York to Dundas, 28th June 1794. Ditfurth, ii.
171-172.   [2] Calvert, 277. *Life of Lord Lynedoch*, 91.

1794. Ostend, after a voyage of nineteen days from Cork, one squadron of the Fourteenth Light Dragoons and the Thirty-third regiment, the latter under the command of an officer whose name it still bears, but who was then an impecunious younger son of five-and-twenty, possessed indeed of some skill in playing the violin, but still distinguished by no higher title than June 26. that of Colonel Arthur Wellesley. On the morrow Moira with the last of the reinforcements[1] also reached Ostend, where he found an advanced guard of the French within four miles of the town, a large force of several thousand men close behind it, and the Commandant very wisely embarking his garrison with a view to retreat. The whole district was in a state of panic ; but Moira promptly landed the whole of his men, and having observed the difficulties of defending Ostend, and the military worthlessness of the place, quietly selected his fighting ground outside it. " I am not at all satisfied with my position," he wrote calmly to Dundas, " but since you appear to attach importance to the town I will do my best to maintain it." " The defences are so detestable," he added cheerfully to Nepean, " that I shall go into the open field if we must come to blows. If you are to lose everything it does not signify if you are beaten into the bargain."[2] It is dangerous for a General, be he even so able as Moira, to address an English Minister of War in this strain ; for, in the event of mishap, the words may be brought up as evidence against him in Parliament to prove that he was reckless, careless, neglectful, or despondent.

During these days the Duke of York remained in

[1] 3rd, 19th, 27th, 28th, 40th, 42nd, 54th, 57th, 59th, 63rd, 87th, 89th.
[2] Moira to Dundas and to Nepean, 26th June 1794.

painful suspense at Tournai, until the news of Clerfaye's 1794.
defeat on the 23rd warned him to move northward
without delay. As Craig had perceived, the French
by crossing the Scheldt at Oudenarde could prevent
the Duke of York from joining Clerfaye, crush both
armies in detail, and then, passing eastward, could
annihilate Coburg. The Duke therefore called in
Kray's Austrians for the defence of Tournai, and June 24.
marched north-eastward on the right bank of the
Scheldt to Renaix, where he learned that on the same
day a French corps had summoned Oudenarde. On June 25.
the morrow Pichegru crossed the Lys at Deynse with
the main body of his army, and striking south from
thence encamped on the 27th at Huysse, between four June 27.
and five miles north of Oudenarde. On that same
night came a message from Coburg to the Duke of
York that on the previous day he had made his attack June 26.
on the French about Charleroi and had failed. This
was the battle of Fleurus, which had been suddenly
broken off by the Austrian commander before decisive
advantage had been gained by either side ; and it is
still a question whether Coburg's action was dictated
by the requirements of Thugut's policy or by his own
military judgment. However that may be, he retreated in good order upon Brussels, halting on the
27th in a position running from Soignies on the west June 27.
through Braine L'Alleud to Gembloux on the east.
This movement uncovered the Duke of York's left
rear, and placed him in a most dangerous position.
He had with him barely ten thousand men, nearly
half of them cavalry, which in so close a country were
of little service ; and from the church-tower at Oudenarde he could see thirty thousand of the enemy in his
front. The French, by passing the Scheldt, could
at any time cut off his retreat to the north, in which

1794. case his only line of safety lay eastward towards Grammont ; and this in its turn would be closed if Coburg should continue his retrograde movement towards Namur, which was his first stage on the road to Vienna.

June 28. On the morning of the 28th the enemy appeared in force before Oudenarde, showing every sign of making the dreaded movement across the river ; and the Duke despatched orders to Moira to join Clerfaye immediately. For two days Pichegru continued his menaces on the Scheldt, and then suddenly on the June 30. evening of the 30th he retired, having received orders from Paris to occupy Nieuport, Ostend, and the island of Walcheren in force, with a view to the invasion of England. Ostend, which, together with Nieuport, Henry Dundas had kept under his own orders, was evacuated in good time, while directions to that purport were still on their way from England. Moira's instructions extended no further than to the defence of Ostend, but, in the critical circumstances of the case, he proposed to join his force to Clerfaye, and to act with him against the French left. Clerfaye at first welcomed the offer, but, on hearing of the misfortune of Fleurus, declared that he could make no engagement with the British whatever. This was unpleasant for Moira, who had counted on the help of the Austrians in protecting the transport of his camp-equipage on the canal from Bruges to Ghent. The situation was dangerous, for the French were in force at three different places within two hours' march of the canal, bent upon preventing his junction with Clerfaye. Without a moment's hesitation Moira sent his baggage northward to Sluys, and by a rapid march made his way to Ghent, just in time to anticipate a movement made by the French to intercept him. Thus a valuable reinforcement was secured to 1794. the Allies; and three more perilous days were passed without mishap, thanks rather to the Committee of Safety at Paris than to the Austrian commanders in the field.[1]

On the evening of the 30th the Duke of York rode June 30. over from Renaix to Braine L'Alleud to consult Coburg; and it was then agreed that Clerfaye's force should change places with the Duke's, so as to bring the Austrian corps nearer to its own main army, and the British contingent nearer to the sea. At the actual conference both Coburg and the Archduke Charles declared that, having no orders from the Emperor to evacuate the Austrian Netherlands, they felt bound in honour to defend them. Waldeck indeed opposed even a withdrawal from the line of the Scheldt. All this, however, was mere trifling, for two days later Coburg July 2. wrote that his right wing had been driven back from Soignies, and that the Duke would do well to retire to a position appointed him between Brussels and Antwerp. The fall of Mons on the 1st of July having also laid bare the Duke's left flank and rear, he took the hint, and while protesting against the desertion of the country, gave his orders for retreat in the morning by way of Grammont and thence upon Alost. Tournai, through the courtesy of the French, was peaceably evacuated by the Austrians, though Condé, Valenciennes, Landrecies, and Quesnoy were held. The line of the Scheldt was abandoned, and the Duke of York's troops were withdrawn from every garrison except Nieuport. As to this last the Duke, as in duty July 2. bound, asked for Dundas's orders, saying that, if the

[1] Duke of York to Dundas, 28th June, 2nd July; Craig to Nepean, 27th June; Moira to Dundas, 28th and 29th June, 1st July 1794.

1794. Government wished to reconquer Flanders, the place should be kept ; otherwise the garrison, which included five hundred French emigrants, should not for pity's sake be exposed to the risk of capture.

Then followed a miserable tragedy. Dundas, apparently before the receipt of this letter, wrote on the 3rd of July to General Diepenbrock, the Commandant at Nieuport, promising to send transports for the embarkation of the garrison, if necessary, but adding that the Government attached great importance to the retention of the place. Within two days the French had broken ground before the miserable little port, where the water was so shallow that ships could not July 16. come near the shore ; and less than a fortnight later the unfortunate garrison, which included a few British troops, was compelled to surrender. Forthwith the French massed the emigrants in the ditch of the fort and played upon them with grape-shot until the whole of them were destroyed. It was well known that this would inevitably be the fate of those unhappy men if they fell into the hands of the Republicans ; and German authors have not hesitated to censure the Duke of York because, according to the current, though unjust, opinion, he neglected to order the evacuation of Nieuport while there was yet time. It were, indeed, devoutly to be wished that the Duke had respected Dundas less, and had withdrawn the garrison without consulting him, though it is manifest that he would thereby have drawn upon himself the censure of the Government. The blame, therefore, for this shameful business must remain with Dundas ; and it was a very great misfortune for England that he was not called to account for it.[1]

[1] York to Dundas, 2nd and 3rd July ; Dundas to Diepenbrock, 3rd and 7th July ; Diepenbrock to Dundas, 5th July 1794.

Meanwhile the Duke continued his retreat north- 1794. ward down the river Dendre, reaching Lombeek Ste. Catherine, about eight miles west of Brussels, on the 4th of July. On the morrow the leaders of the coalesced July 5. armies again met in conference at Waterloo, when it was decided that Clerfaye's force should pass eastwards towards Brussels, and that the army of the Allies should ultimately occupy a line from Antwerp, by Louvain, Wavre, and Gembloux, to Namur, but that until the 7th, at any rate, the line in advance of Brussels, extending from Alost by Braine-le-Comte and Nivelles to Sombref, should be maintained. Ghent had already been evacuated ; and accordingly on the next day Clerfaye's force began its march to join Coburg, while Moira moved to Alost and brought his troops for the first time under the Duke's personal command. But Jourdan meanwhile was not inactive. On the 6th he July 6. attacked the whole line of the Austrians from Braine-le-Comte to Gembloux ; and, though repulsed after hard fighting on the east, where a concentrated attack might have given him possession of the Austrian line of communications, he succeeded in pushing Coburg's right wing back from Braine-le-Comte and Nivelles to Waterloo. Thereupon Coburg warned the Duke of York that he must retire eastward and cancel the agreement made on the 5th. The Duke answered with cold sarcasm that it was a new thing for the Austrians to retire before thirty thousand Frenchmen, and appealed to the Archduke Charles to keep Coburg to his engagements ; but received from him only a sad reply that orders must be obeyed. On the 7th and 8th Jourdan renewed his attacks, directing the best of his strength against the Austrian left, which he forced back to the battlefield of Ramillies. He then immediately invested Namur ; upon which Coburg, fearing to be cut off from

1794.
July 7. the Meuse, ordered the whole of his army to retire upon Tirlemont.

The Duke meanwhile, since his left was uncovered by the retreat of the Austrians, withdrew, at Coburg's request, very slowly northward to Assche, and thence struck north-eastward to the Dyle, which he crossed at Malines, fixing his headquarters at Contich, some eight miles north of that city. A new line of defence was then taken up, which sufficiently showed the divided counsels of the Allies. On the right the British contingent, now numbering some thirty thousand men, was posted on the Dyle from Antwerp to Malines. On its left the Prince of Orange with the Dutch troops and from two to three thousand Austrians covered the line from Malines to Louvain ; and from Louvain the rest of the Austrian army, between forty-five and fifty thousand men, was extended in a south-easterly direction by Tirlemont, Landen, and Waremme to the Meuse, with a detachment of four thousand more on the eastern bank of that river, and between it and the Ourthe. Thus the British and Dutch, who desired to defend Holland, could be deserted at any moment which the Emperor should select for the pursuit of his own particular object, namely, to carry his army away to share the plunder of Poland. Craig, for his part, felt no doubt whatever that the British and Dutch would very soon be left to their own resources.[1]

The reader may have felt surprised that, with a force of nearly one hundred and fifty thousand men, the French should not have pressed the Allies harder, and made an end of them long before. The fact was that the Committee of Public Safety had interfered with the Generals on the 4th of July, by an order that the

[1] Coburg to York, 7th and 8th July ; York to Coburg, 7th July ; to Dundas, 7th and 10th July ; Craig to Nepean, 11th July 1794.

recapture of Valenciennes, Condé, Landrecies, and 1794.
Quesnoy should take precedence of any further operations ; and accordingly the army in Belgium had been
weakened to provide for this service. This was the
work of Robespierre, who at the time was inclined
towards peace ; and indeed peace appears to have been
a common topic of conversation between the French
and Austrian outposts from the beginning of July.[1]
Thirty thousand French soldiers were accordingly withdrawn to Valenciennes, as many more were wasted in
occupying ports of embarkation for England, and the
remainder were ordered to push the Allies completely
out of Belgium, and then to occupy a cordon from
Antwerp to Namur. Pichegru, therefore, took command in person of the left wing, and on the 12th moved July 12.
with eighteen thousand men against Malines, while
Jourdan on the right simultaneously advanced against
Louvain, Jodoigne, and Huy on the Meuse. On the
evening of the 12th Pichegru drove the Duke of York's
advanced posts into Malines, where they were promptly
reinforced ; but the fortifications of the town were in
ruins, and, on renewing the attack on the 15th, the July 15.
French captured the place with little difficulty. The
troops charged with the defence were Hessians and
Dutch ; and it appears certain that the conduct of one
or the other of them was not irreproachable, though
there are indications also that the Duke himself was
partly responsible for the mishap.

The Duke then threw his left back along the line
of the Nethe from Lierre to Duffel ; but meanwhile
Jourdan had on the same day mastered Louvain, and July 15.
in the course of the two following days Jodoigne and
Namur also. The Dutch troops about Louvain, upon
the loss of that town, fell back northward across the

[1] Sybel, iii. 150-152, 171. Craig to Nepean, 4th July 1794.

1794. Demer, while the Austrians retired eastward ; and thus the line of the Allies was fairly broken owing to their own divergent plans.   The Duke of York had already in these days concerted operations with the Prince of
July 18. Orange for the recapture of Malines on the 18th,[1] when he received a letter from Coburg saying that, owing to the loss of that place and of Louvain, he had ordered the troops formerly stationed at the latter city to fall back to Diest, and was himself withdrawing from Tirlemont to Landen.   The Duke begged him before doing so to essay a general forward movement, but received only a vague and unsatisfactory reply ; and
July 20. on the morning of the 20th a staff-officer, while inspecting the left of the Dutch position, discovered that the Austrians at Diest were already retreating south-eastward on Hasselt, Coburg having given them orders to this effect without saying a word of his intentions to the
July 22. Duke of York.   With his left flank thus again laid bare,
July 24. the Duke was obliged to evacuate Antwerp and retire due north from it across the Dutch frontier to Rozendahl. Coburg likewise fell back to eastward, crossed the Meuse at Maastricht, and took up a position about seven miles south and east of that fortress at Fouron le Comte. Thus the British and Austrians were finally parted.

It cannot be said that either of them was sorry to take leave of the other.   Even in 1793 their relations had not been too cordial, for the Austrians, in their jealousy, would never allow foreign troops to pass through their fortified towns, even during a forced march ; and thus the British were frequently condemned to make long and fatiguing detours.[2]   But the betrayal of the Duke of York's column on the 18th of May, and the subsequent operations, deliberately con-

---

[1] York to Dundas, 15th, 19th, 20th, 23rd July 1794.
[2] *Narrative of an Officer of the Guards*, ii. 35.

trived to hasten the evacuation of the Netherlands, 1794. converted the dislike of the British for the Austrians into the bitterest hatred and contempt. At headquarters, again, the presence of a soldier such as Craig, with ideas far more enlightened than those of the Austrians, and with some means of insisting upon them through the medium of the Duke of York, can hardly have contributed to harmony. It may be added that the Austrian troops were as severe in their criticism of their chiefs, and particularly of Waldeck, as were any of the British, proclaiming loudly that the abandonment of Belgium was due to French gold.[1] In fact the Austrian army, between heavy losses and deep distrust of its leaders, was utterly demoralised ; nor is it surprising that this should have been so. It is indeed more than probable that, if Coburg had wished to make a stand after the action of Fleurus, his men would not have supported him. Of course Coburg had to bear the responsibility for all this, and to digest as best he might some very bitter reproaches from the Duke of York ; yet it seems that in truth he was the person the least to blame. Though as a commander in the field he was slow, unenterprising, enamoured of vicious methods, and possessed of no military quality except that of looking carefully to the wants of his troops, yet he did not lack insight, sound sense, imperturbable calm, and the instinct of honesty and straightforwardness. His name is forgotten in England, though his portrait is still occasionally to be found in English print-shops, showing that at one time he had gained a certain fame, which was destined speedily to perish. It can only be said of him that he was beloved by his men, that he bore the sins of others without complaining, and that he was a loyal servant to an unfaithful master.

[1] Craig to Nepean, 11th July 1794.

VOL. IV. BOOK XII. CHAPTER XII

1794. WHILE the Allies in the Netherlands were thus giving way on all sides during the months of June and July, the British Government naturally bethought itself of the sixty thousand men which it had agreed to hire from Prussia for operations in that quarter. The Ministers had reckoned that these troops would be ready by the end of May; and accordingly, as has been told, Lord Cornwallis was sent from England to arrange with Marshal Möllendorf as to the part to be taken by the Prussians in the campaign. Visiting the Duke of York on the way, Cornwallis agreed with him that the protection of West Flanders, and, if possible, the siege of Lille, were the matters of most urgent importance ; and he formulated his request to Möllen-

June 20. dorf accordingly. He soon discovered that he had been sent upon a fool's errand. Möllendorf, instead of sixty thousand, had but forty thousand men, deficient in stores and supplies and absolutely wanting in transport, which he declared himself unable to furnish without ready money from England. The ' real difficulty was that the Allies were all at variance as to the use that should be made of the Prussian troops. England wanted them to aid in recovering West Flanders. Holland would at first have preferred them to remain upon the Rhine, but presently yielded to the demands of England. The Emperor of Austria

366

not only raised strong objections to the march of 1794. Prussian troops to Belgium, but claimed thirty thousand of the sixty thousand men for the protection of the Empire, declaring that their removal from the Rhine would expose all Germany to the ravages of the French. Between these conflicting claims Möllendorf found little difficulty in sitting still and doing nothing, which was precisely what the advisers of King Frederick William most desired. By the 18th of June Cornwallis had made up his mind that scanty help was to be expected from Prussia, at any rate during the present campaign; and neither he nor Lord Malmesbury was slow to express very decided opinions as to the ill-faith of the Prussian Court.[1]

This was the situation when the failure of the Austrian attack at Fleurus determined the Emperor to evacuate the Low Countries. That potentate thereupon reversed his language as to the Prussian contingent, and urged that Möllendorf should advance into Belgium; nor did he hesitate, on the 15th of July, to order Coburg still to defend the Austrian Netherlands, though he said nothing about sending reinforcements to enable him to do so. This despicable lying and trickery had, of course, but one object, that of drawing more money from England under false pretences. The English Government, however, though it had learned that no reliance was to be placed on Thugut's statements or promises, decided in the middle of July to send Lord Spencer and Thomas July 19. Grenville to Vienna, to urge once more the renewal of the offensive in Belgium. So far, therefore, the Emperor seemed likely to gain his point; and since

[1] Cornwallis to Dundas, 8th and 18th June 1794, and see *Cornwallis Correspondence*, ii. 239-255; *Malmesbury Correspondence*; *Dropmore Papers*, ii. 564-566, 577, 592, 594.

1794. the King of Prussia had shown remarkable weakness in dealing with the insurrection in Poland, Francis had every reason to hope that decisive action in that country would be delayed, until his own and the Russian armies could appear there in sufficient force to dictate the final settlement according to their own desires. The Prussian Ministers, on the other hand, when they learned of the despatch of Spencer and Grenville to Vienna, became nervous lest England should transfer the promised subsidy from her to Austria ; and they began to turn their thoughts to the negotiations of a separate peace with France.[1]

Meanwhile, through the energy of Carnot, reinforcements had been found for the French army of July 2-13. the Rhine, which, after a fortnight's hard fighting on the heights about Kaiserslautern, forced Möllendorf to retire under the cannon of Mainz with a loss of two thousand men and sixteen guns. The Austrian troops on the Rhine thereupon withdrew from the left bank of the river ; and the miscarriage of a plan, concerted a fortnight later for recovery of the lost ground, set the Generals of the two nations quarrelling July 28. more bitterly than ever. The end of July brought yet another stroke of good luck to France in the overthrow of Robespierre and the execution of himself, St. Just, and other of his principal colleagues. Robespierre's latest achievement as a military administrator had been to decree that no quarter should be shown to British or Hanoverians in the field, an order which was disobeyed by the French troops and laughed at by the British. The supreme imbecility, apart from all other faults, of his rule had brought France to the last stage of exhaustion ; and, indeed, if the Allies had succeeded in keeping the French armies out of

[1] Sybel, iii. 240-243.

Belgium, the latter must have perished of starvation.[1] 1794.
Robespierre's death marked the close of the Terror July.
and the beginning of a return to common sense in
the matter of administration. The man, however, had
lived long enough to waste the energies of the armies
of the North in the recovery of the four captured
fortresses in the frontier, when they should have
been scattering the Allies to the four winds ; and
thus it came about that the Duke of York enjoyed
a few weeks' respite for the formation of new plans.

It was fortunate for him that it was so, for he now
found himself in serious trouble with his army. This
was the result of the insane system, allowed by Dundas,
of raising men for rank. The regiments despatched
to Holland contained only a very few old soldiers
mixed with great numbers of recruits, who were utterly
without training and discipline. "Many of them
do not know one end of a fire-lock from the other,"
wrote Craig, "and will never know it." Six of the
battalions had been deprived of their flank-companies,
that is to say, of their best men, to make up General
Grey's force in the West Indies ; and no sooner did
the new levies find themselves released from the
crimping-house and the gaol for active service, than
they fell to plundering in all directions. The Duke
was obliged to issue a very severe order on the 27th
of July [2] to call the army to its senses ; but, with
such officers as had been obtained under Dundas's
scheme, it was impossible to expect the slightest
obedience. In the first place the army was lament-
ably deficient in Brigadiers and Generals of division.
Moira had only accepted the command of his force
on the condition that he should not serve in Flanders ;
and though, in view of the perilous condition of the

[1] Poisson, iv. 262.   [2] Ditfurth, iii. 217.

2 B

1794. Allies when he landed, he had waived his objections
July. for the time, yet there was another obstacle not so
easily to be overcome. Albeit enjoying an independent command of eight thousand men, Moira was
almost the junior Major-general of the army. Major-
general Crosbie, who was with him, also held a more
important command than his seniors, such as Ralph
Abercromby and David Dundas, the latter of whom
joined the Duke of York at the end of July. Both
Moira and Crosbie, therefore, went home, from delicacy
towards the feelings of their superiors ; and the loss
of Moira was bitterly regretted as that of a very able
officer who was idolised by his men.

The British troops now consisted of four brigades
of cavalry and seven of infantry,[1] making altogether

[1] CAVALRY—
    David Dundas's Brigade—2nd, 6th D.G. ; 2nd, 6th D.
    Ralph Dundas's Brigade—Blues ; 3rd, 5th D.G. ; 1st D.
    Laurie's Brigade—7th, 11th, 15th, 16th L.D.
    Vyse's Brigade—1st D.G. ; 8th, 14th L.D.
    Foreign Troops—
        Uhlans Britanniques, Irving's Hussars, Choiseul's Hussars.

INFANTRY—
First Brigade—3rd, 88th, 63rd. | *Fifth Brigade*—19th, 54th, 42nd.
Second Brigade—8th,[1] 44th,[1] 33rd.[1] | *Sixth Brigade*—27th, 89th, 28th.
Third Brigade—12th,[1] 55th,[1] 38th. | *Seventh Brigade* — 40th,[1] 57th,
Fourth Brigade—14th, 53rd, 37th. | 59th, 87th.
    Foreign Troops—
        Loyal Emigrants, York Rangers, Rohan's Regiment.

	officers		N.C.O.'s and men	
British Cavalry,	165	officers,	4,350	N.C.O.'s and men.
Hanoverians and Hessians	168	,,	2,939	,,
Total Cavalry	333	,,	7,289	,,
British Infantry,	583	,,	21,170	,,
Hanoverians and Hessians	322	,,	8,722	,,
Total .	1,238	,,	37,181	,,

Total of all arms, including artillery, etc., say, 1300 officers,
40,000 N.C.O.'s and men.

[1] The flank companies of these battalions were in the West Indies.

some twenty-five thousand men ; but for all these 1794.
there were, after the departure of Moira and Crosbie, July.
only four Generals—David Dundas, Stewart, Abercromby, and Fox, the last of whom was fully employed
as Quartermaster-general. This was the more serious
because the commanders of the new battalions, who
had been juggled into seniority by the Government
and the army-brokers, were not fit to command a
company, much less a brigade. Some of them were
boys of twenty-one who knew nothing of their simplest
duties. Though they went cheerfully into action,
they looked upon the whole campaign as an elaborate
picnic, for which they did not fail to provide themselves with abundance of comforts ; and thus the
baggage-columns were filled with private waggons
under the charge of insubordinate drivers. The
junior officers, who were so scarce that few regiments
had as many subalterns as companies, appear in many
cases to have been worse than the senior, as is always
to be expected when commissions are to be obtained
for the asking ; nor with bad examples before them
were they likely to improve. Thrust into the Army
to satisfy the claims of dependents, constituents,
importunate creditors, and discarded concubines,
many of these young men were at once a disgrace
and an encumbrance to the force. Hard drinking,
which was the fashion then in all classes from highest
to lowest, was, of course, sedulously cultivated by
these aspirants to the rank of gentleman ; and it was
no uncommon thing for regiments to start on the
march under charge of the Adjutant and Sergeant-
major only, while the officers stayed behind, to come
galloping up several hours later, full of wine, careless
where they rode, careless of the confusion into which
they threw the columns, careless of everything but

1794.
July.

the place appointed for the end of the march, if by chance they were sober enough to have remembered it.   These evils, too, were extremely difficult to check, for in 1794, as in 1744, political interest rather than meritorious service was the road to promotion.   While the shameful traffic of the army-brokers and the raising of endless new regiments continued, every officer who could command money or interest was sure of obtaining advancement at home without the knowledge of his chief in the field, and had, therefore, not only no encouragement to do his duty, but an actual reason for avoiding it.   Thus the men were very imperfectly disciplined ; there were no efficient company-officers to look after them ; no efficient Colonels to look after the company-officers ; no Generals to look after the Colonels.   Craig sought a remedy in begging for more Generals.   " We cannot get on," he wrote, on the 5th of August, " without a good supply and a supply of good.   The evil to the discipline of the army increases every day, and is likely to become very serious." [1]

But the Duke's difficulties did not end with the defects of his officers and men.   It had lately become the practice in time of peace to issue to each regiment the materials for its clothing, to be made up by the regiment itself, a system which had probably been designed to obtain for the Colonels the largest possible profit.   Nor must the Colonels be blamed herein, for they were expected to make that profit, which in those days was practically the only emolument open to general officers.   It was, of course, impossible for troops in the field to spend three or four months in

[1] Craig to Nepean, 5th August 1794 ; Ditfurth, ii. 213 *seq.* ; Memorandum of the Duke of York, 23rd December 1794 ; Calvert, pp. 385-386 ; see vol. ii. of this *History*, p. 88.

making up their clothes; and the result was that 1794. the Duke's army was left almost naked. Moreover, July. in the hurry of raising innumerable new corps, the responsibility for such details as clothing, accounts, musters, and so forth had been overlooked; the new officers knew nothing of the extremely complex methods of military finance;[1] and the sudden vast increase of business thrown upon agents and officials was greater than they could immediately bear. Finally, quite apart from these failings in respect of the raiment of entire battalions, no effort whatever was made to clothe the recruits who were sent out to fill up the gaps in the various corps. These unfortunate men, on being drafted into the depots in England, received what was called slop-clothing, which signified a linen jacket and trousers; and it is an actual fact that many of them were sent on active service in this dress, without waistcoat, drawers, or stockings. The result was that the Duke of York's corps was in a worse state in respect of clothing than had been hitherto recorded of any British army.[2]

Another great difficulty, of which Craig had complained again and again, was the want of drivers for the artillery. Lord Moira had brought with him guns but no drivers; and there were but two captains (not enough, as Craig said, to do a fortieth part of the work) at disposal for the superintendence of a huge mass of horses. Thus a new train of artillery, which had been sent out to replace the cannon lost at Tourcoing, became a positive embarrassment. The Com-

---

[1] No officer could hope to master these mysteries without the help of two fat little duodecimo volumes called *The Regimental Companion*, and a third and slighter volume entitled *Military Finance*.

[2] Craig to Nepean, 31st August; Craig's Memorandum of 23rd December 1794.

missariat also, as used so often to happen with British armies, was in a very bad state. The men of the new corps of Royal Waggoners had been recruited in London, and were the worst refuse of the population. They were known, in fact, as the " Newgate Blues." " A greater set of scoundrels never disgraced an army," wrote Craig, in his usual pithy style. " I believe it to be true that half of them, if not taken from the hulks, have at times visited them. . . . They have committed every species of villainy, and treat their horses badly." But the very worst department of all was that of the hospitals, wherein the abuses were so terrible that men hardly liked to speak of them. In December 1793 the inhabitants of one of the English ports had been stupefied by the arrival of one hundred invalid soldiers from Ostend in indescribable distress. They had been on board ship for a week in the bitter wintry weather, without so much as straw to lie upon. Some of them were dead ; others died on being carried ashore. No provision had been made for their comfort on landing, and, but for the compassion of the gentry who subscribed money for their relief, the poor fellows might well have perished.[1] Nothing was done to amend this state of things. Dundas's idea of putting an army in the field was to land raw men on a foreign shore, and to expect discipline, arms, ammunition, clothing, victuals, medical stores, and medical treatment to descend on them from Heaven. Some kind of a medical staff was improvised out of drunken apothecaries, broken-down practitioners, and rogues of every description, who were provided under some cheap contract ; the charges of respectable members of the medical profession being deemed exorbitant. " The dreadful

[1] *Sunday Reformer*, 29th December 1793.

mismanagement of the hospital is beyond descrip- 1794.
tion," wrote Craig, " and the remedy beyond my July.
power. Every branch and every fibre of every branch
draws a contrary way. I really doubt if there will
be any way to get any good from this department
but by tying them all together and sending them to
you to be changed for a new set." [1]

Such was the composition of the force with which
the Duke of York now undertook, in concert with
the Dutch, to protect Holland, or, in other words,
to conduct that most delicate and trying of operations—manœuvring with inferior numbers over a
wide front to hold a superior force in check. The
first difficulty arose with the Dutch, for the Prince
of Orange, apparently enamoured of the Austrian
methods, was eager to scatter the troops over a multitude of different points ; but this the Duke, with
Craig at his back, steadily refused to do. The Prince
then urged that the Dutch fortresses should be garrisoned by British troops ; but the said fortresses
were all in bad condition, and were repairing only
with that incredible slowness which was peculiar to
the Dutch Government. The Duke, therefore, refused this also ; feeling tolerably sure that, if he consented, his battalions would be sacrificed piecemeal
for the defence of Holland, while the Dutch looked
on without raising a man to help them. The two
gates of Holland on the south were Bergen-op-Zoom
and Breda, and on the east Grave and Nimeguen,
with the fortress of Bois-le-Duc midway between
Breda and Nimeguen. The two eastern gates were
safe so long as the Austrians retained Maastricht and

[1] Craig to Nepean, 12th and 31st August, 5th and 8th
September 1794. The class of medical officer obtained by Government is described in *Autobiography of Sir J. M'Grigor*, pp. 93, 94.

1794. their position on the Meuse ; but the Austrians were
July. not to be trusted. Accordingly, the Duke resolved
to garrison Breda, Bergen-op-Zoom, and, if possible,
Bois-le-Duc with Dutch troops ; himself taking up
a position on the north bank of the river Aa, with
his right resting on Bois-le-Duc and his left on the
great morass called the Peel. From this central point
he judged that he could move to the help of any of
the Dutch fortresses to southward, cover the province of Gelderland, and keep Grave and Nimeguen
within reach in case of mishap on that side.

He was about to march thither from Rozendahl when
the news came that Moreau, who was advancing northward along the coast after the capture of Nieuport, had
driven back the Dutch posts and had besieged Sluys.
The Prince of Orange thereupon besought the Duke
to stand fast, producing a letter from Coburg which
contained not only an assurance of his ability to hold
the passage of the Meuse, but even a hint of possible
offensive movements. After some hesitation the Duke
consented to a compromise by moving to Osterhout, a
little to the north-east of Breda, so as to give some
countenance both to Breda and Bergen-op-Zoom. He
July 31. marched, accordingly, on the 31st of July, unmolested
by the enemy, who were in force around Antwerp ; and
the Prince of Orange then came to the wise but rather
belated decision to evacuate all the Dutch fortresses
to the south of the Scheldt. The Duke, therefore,
Aug. 8. lent him a strong detachment of his men to hold the
communications between Breda and Bergen-op-Zoom,
so as to release Dutch troops to cover the retreat of
these garrisons and to relieve Sluys.[1]

Just at this moment Henry Dundas, hearing of

[1] York to Dundas, 25th, 27th, 30th July, 1st and 6th August ;
Craig to Nepean, 25th July 1794.

Moreau's advance, and having by chance a few troops unemployed, decided to send a naval armament to Flushing, together with five battalions under Lord Mulgrave, for the defence of the Dutch territories in that quarter. As was his rule in such cases, Dundas kept Mulgrave under his own immediate command, but withal instructed him not to go against any order of the Duke of York,—an arrangement admirably calculated to paralyse the force and to raise discord between the commanders. Mulgrave, who had started apart from his troops, reached Flushing on the 17th, and finding that none of them had arrived, occupied himself in examining the situation. He was soon satisfied that the French had no further designs for the campaign than to take Sluys and Flushing, as ports from which to ship the harvest of the Austrian Netherlands to France. Meanwhile, the Dutch no sooner heard of his coming than they suspended their operations for the relief of Sluys, in the hope that Mulgrave would do the work for them ; and the French, having also full intelligence of everything, increased their force at Sluys to twenty-five thousand men, which made the relief practically impossible. Dundas, meanwhile, wrote with the greatest confidence of the success of that operation, which his own interference had condemned to failure ; announcing also that Mulgrave's force, which had not yet even arrived at Flushing, would be required elsewhere in a month. At length the five battalions sailed into Flushing on the 26th, nominally thirty-two hundred strong, and actually with the following qualifications for immediate service in the field. The Thirty-first [1] was composed chiefly of recruits, of whom two hundred and forty were un-

---

[1] Its flank companies, and those of the 34th, were detained for the West Indies.

1794. armed.   The Seventy-ninth had but one officer to each company, and but eight rounds of ball-ammunition a man.   The Eighty-fourth had twenty rounds a man, but, the regiment having never ceased marching from quarter to quarter ever since it had been raised, the men were wholly untrained.   The Eighty-fifth had thirty rounds a man, but half of the soldiers had never had arms in their hands.   The Thirty-fourth alone appears to have been fit and ready for work.   Fortunately there was no work for them to do, for Sluys surrendered on the very day of their arrival ; and Mulgrave, after landing them at Flushing to learn the elements of their business, suggested that at least two of the battalions had better remain there and be made into soldiers, instead of sailing to certain annihilation in the West Indies.   To this Dundas agreed, for he purposed to take from the Duke of York ten of Moira's battalions, and was well content to leave him inferior troops in their place.   Meanwhile, as a specimen of utter imbecility, this despatch of Mulgrave's detachment has few equals even in English military annals. The mere promise of help was sufficient to relax the exertions of the Dutch.   The troops were embarked so late as to miss the object of the expedition, and, even if they had been embarked in time, they were of quality too poor to have accomplished it.   In brief, the whole enterprise bears the unmistakable mark of Henry Dundas.[1]

Meanwhile Spencer and Grenville had throughout August pursued their negotiations at Vienna with very indifferent success.   One point Thugut was ready to concede, namely, the recall of Coburg, who indeed re-

[1] Dundas to Mulgrave, 7th and 13th August ; Mulgrave to Dundas, 17th, 19th, 26th, 30th August, 3rd September ; Dundas to York, 22nd August 1794.

signed on the 9th of August, being worn down in body 1794.
and mind, and thoroughly disgusted with his command.
But Thugut absolutely refused to order troops from
the Rhine to Belgium, and demanded the guarantee
of a loan of three millions for the present campaign
besides a new subsidy for the next. It was necessary
to refer these pretensions to the Cabinet in London ;
and long before the reference had even been made, the
Austrian Council of War ordered Clerfaye, who was Aug. 12,
to succeed Coburg, to devote all his efforts to the
defence not of Belgium but of Luxemburg, Mainz, and
Mannheim. But though the Allies were idle, the
French were not ; and, thanks in part to a threat of the
Committee of Public Safety to massacre the garrisons
unless the fortresses were delivered, they had recovered
both Quesnoy and Landrecies by the 15th of August.
The fall of Sluys, and the recall of the troops detached
to Walcheren also enabled Pichegru to begin a forward
movement, and on the 27th he advanced from Antwerp Aug. 27.
north-eastward to Hoogstraeten, driving in all the
Dutch posts, and seeming to threaten the turning of
the Duke of York's left. The Duke, thereupon, on
the advice of a Council of War, retired on the 30th to Aug. 30.
his chosen position between Bois-le-Duc and the Peel,
while Pichegru sent a strong detachment eastward to
occupy Einhoven in force.[1]

Meanwhile a message had reached the Duke of York
from Clerfaye, suggesting a general forward movement
to save the beleaguered cities of Valenciennes and

---

[1] On the 29th of August the Duke reorganised his force as
follows :

    First Brigade—Maj.-gen. Stewart, 3rd, 40th, 55th, 59th, 89th.
    Second Brigade—   8th, 27th, 28th, 57th.
    Third Brigade—   12th, 33rd, 42nd, 44th.
    Fourth Brigade—Maj.-gen. Fox, 14th, 37th, 38th, 63rd.
    Fifth Brigade—   19th, 53rd, 54th, 88th.

1794. Condé ; and on the 1st of September a conference was
Sept. 1. held between the Allied commanders at Bois-le-Duc
to consider the proposal. It was not yet known to
them, apparently, that Valenciennes had already
surrendered to the French on the 29th of August, and
that Condé was at the last gasp ; and there was some
talk among them of an advance of the British to recapture Antwerp, while the Austrians on the Meuse
protected their rear. The news that both fortresses
had fallen, and that the French forces thus liberated
for the field were hastening to the front, naturally
deranged this plan ; and though the Duke was anxious
still to make the attempt, Craig perceived little hope
of success, chiefly because he could not trust the
Austrians to give hearty co-operation. In truth, the
Allies had let slip the favourable moment through
their own dissensions, and the opportunity was not
Sept. 4. to recur again. On the 4th of September Pichegru
marched northward from Hoogstraeten to Meerle, as
if to threaten Breda, but on the 10th turned eastward,
after leaving a detachment before that place, and on
the 12th reached Oosterwyk. On the following day
Sept. 13 he attacked the Duke's advanced posts at Bokstel,
and on the 14th captured them, making two battalions
of Darmstadt-Hessians prisoners. This was an unpleasant mishap, for these troops had hitherto always
behaved admirably ; but, though they complained of
the Duke for not supporting them, the Duke in his
secret report declared them to have been panic-stricken.
Alive, however, to the importance of regaining this
post and the line of the Dommel, the Duke ordered
Sept. 15. Abercromby forward next day with ten battalions and
as many squadrons of British, to recover the lost
ground. The movement was very nearly disastrous,
for Abercromby only just missed falling into the midst

of Pichegru's main army, which was on march to the 1794. eastward ; but quickly apprehending the situation, he withdrew his troops in excellent order with the loss of about ninety men, two-thirds of them prisoners. This skirmish is notable both because it brought Colonel Arthur Wellesley of the Thirty-third under fire for the first time, and because it led to the trial of four officers, three of them belonging to a most distinguished regiment, for cowardice. This was a healthy sign, for it showed that the older officers were bent on ridding the Army at the earliest possible moment of the worthless comrades imposed on them by Dundas.[1]

On the same day the Duke received information that this demonstration against Bokstel was but a feint, the main force of the enemy, reported to be eighty thousand strong, being in motion to turn his left. His intelligence seems to have been extremely vague and imperfect at this time ; but being dissatisfied with his position, to which, owing to dry weather, neither the Peel nor the Aa afforded adequate protection, he decided that the retention of it was not worth the risk of being cut off from his retreat to the Maas. He therefore retired on the next day to that river, crossed it at Grave and Sept. 16. took up a position on the north bank, with his headquarters at Wychen, a few miles to the north of Grave. It then remained for him to make his dispositions to defend the line of the river, the unprotected portion of which extended for some seventy-five miles from Fort Loevestein, at the western end of the Bommeler Waert [2] on to the west, to Venloo on the east. Any effective

[1] Craig to Dundas, 19th September 1794.
[2] The Bommeler Waert is the triangular tongue of land enclosed between the Waal and the Meuse immediately to the east of Gorkum. It is very nearly an island, the entrance to it from the east being very narrow and defended by a fort, then, as now, called Fort St. Andries.

1794. defence with the forces at his disposal was impossible, and the Duke therefore arranged that all troops in British pay should be sent to him from West Flanders, and that the Dutch, who were sitting inactive behind their fortresses, should send men to repair and to defend Crevecoeur and Bommel.

The Duke's next effort was to concert offensive operations with Clerfaye, who lay on his left ; and he had the greater hopes of a favourable issue, since the new Secretary at War, William Windham, was already on his way to that officer on a mission from London. But the Austrian Commander also had been unfor-

Sept. 17-18. tunate. On the 17th and 18th General Latour's corps of seven thousand men, which guarded his left on the Ourthe, was driven back by a greatly superior force of Jourdan's right wing under General Schérer ; whereupon Clerfaye, who had watched the whole process without moving one soldier of his forty thousand to save Latour, immediately retired behind the Roer, leaving eight thousand men as a garrison for Maastricht. The Austrian General therefore rejected all idea of the offensive as impossible, but consented to maintain communication with the Duke if he would extend his left to Venloo, which, like all the Dutch fortresses, was in miserable repair and without a sufficient garrison. The Duke agreed, and so the matter was arranged ; Clerfaye, however, giving the Duke clearly to understand that if his right were turned he should cross the Rhine.[1]

The Duke thereupon made his plans for protecting a line of from seventy-five to ninety-five miles of river with a force of thirty thousand soldiers of all ranks, the sick list having by this time claimed close upon

[1] York to Dundas, 19th, 21st, 22nd September (enclosing correspondence with Clerfaye) ; Craig to Dundas, 19th September 1794

seven thousand men of his army. His right from the 1794.
Bommeler Waert to Grave was held by about five
thousand Hessians, their main body being stationed
at Alfen, a little to the east of the island ; Grave was
held by two Dutch battalions ; east of Grave four
brigades of infantry and two of cavalry lay about
Mook ; Abercromby, with two more brigades of infantry and one of cavalry, stood higher up the river at
Gennep ; and six thousand Hanoverians under Walmoden prolonged the line from Gennep to Venloo, with
their main body at Well. Craig, however, did not
deceive himself as to the inevitable issue, being firmly
convinced that there was an understanding between
the Austrians and French ; wherein he appears to have
been correct.[1] " We shall have to fall back behind
the Waal," he wrote ; " depend on it, this will happen
in a few days . . . and in a fortnight the Austrians
will be behind the Rhine." Jourdan followed up the
Austrians, leaving Kléber to invest Maastricht ; whereupon Clerfaye, who had sixty thousand men behind
the Roer, forthwith called loudly on the Duke of York
to relieve that fortress. Grenville at the Foreign Office,
anticipating something of the kind, had already despatched urgent representations to Vienna requiring
the concurrence of the Austrians in this operation, but
of course to no purpose. The Duke, by advice of
Abercromby and Walmoden, sent Craig to stir up
Clerfaye, and, that the Austrians might have no pretext
for complaint, moved sixteen thousand men at great
risk towards Venloo. But all was perfectly useless, for
Clerfaye declined to budge. An attack of the French
on his position on the 2nd of October gave him the Oct. 2.

[1] Craig to Nepean, 20th September 1794. Sybel, iii. 432 *note*.
From this it appears that all documentary evidence of the agreement
has been carefully destroyed, but that there is a hint of secret
negotiations actually proceeding on the 18th of September 1794.

1794. excuse that he wanted ; and he immediately retreated across the Rhine.[1]

Sept. 22.   Pichegru meanwhile, on the 22nd of September, had completely invested Bois-le-Duc, and sent two divisions forward to line the Maas over against the Duke of York's position. The French were now in the greatest distress from want of provisions, which had to be brought from Antwerp in waggons, and that by long detours in order to circumvent the Dutch fortresses. It was therefore imperative for Pichegru to possess Bois-le-Duc as an advanced base ; and the place was the more difficult for him to master since he had no siege-artillery. Unfortunately the cowardice of the Dutch delivered to him all that he wanted. On the

Sept. 24. 24th he opened a feeble bombardment with his field-pieces upon Fort Crevecoeur, which guarded the passage into the Isle of Bommel from the south ; and

Sept. 28. on the 28th, the place, though amply provisioned and in a good state of defence, was yielded up by the Dutch Commandant. Thereby Pichegru gained not only forty-two heavy guns, but the command of the sluices whereby the inundation of Bois-le-Duc could be let flow or drawn off. The loss of Crevecoeur did not improve the good feeling of the British towards the Dutch, who, from the first entry of the Duke of York into their country, had showed the bitterest animosity

Sept. 30. against his men. Intelligence now reached the Duke that a general insurrection of the French party in the

Oct. 3. United Provinces was imminent ; and three days later the retreat of Clerfaye compelled him to retire north-ward across the Waal, over which he had already thrown a bridge of boats. The movement was con-

[1] York to Dundas, 25th and 29th September, 1st and 3rd October; Craig to Nepean, 1st October ; Grenville to York, 25th September 1794.

ducted with some confusion owing to the mismanage- 1794.
ment of the Duke's Staff; but Pichegru suffered the
Allies to shuffle themselves without the slightest
molestation into their appointed positions. The
Hessians held the Bommeler Waert on the south bank
of the Waal, and the line of the Linge over against it
on the north bank. At the village of Geldermalsen
on the Linge the right of the British joined the left
of the Hessians, extending from thence eastward along
the Waal to the road from Nimeguen to Arnheim;
where the Hanoverians carried the line to its end at the
parting of the Waal and the Leck, maintaining communication with Clerfaye's Austrians at Emmerick.
Nimeguen, though ill fortified and provided for, was
also held on the southern bank of the Waal.

By this time even the long-suffering Cabinet in
England was growing weary of paying subsidies to
Austria and Prussia for service which they never
rendered. On the 4th of October Dundas advised Oct. 4.
the Duke of York that the Government had resolved
to give them no more money, and ordered him to cut
off the allowance hitherto paid to Clerfaye unless he
agreed to active concert of operations. Thugut, however, had in many respects gained his point. The
British Government, thinking that a bad ally was
better than none, had consented on the 14th of September to guarantee to Austria a loan of three millions
in consideration of her services during the first campaign; at the same time renouncing a project which
had been put forward for placing Clerfaye's force,
together with the Duke of York's, under the supreme
command of Cornwallis. Thugut was jubilant; for
everything was going as he wished. In Poland,
Suvorof was rapidly putting down the insurrection,
in stemming which the Prussian Generals had shown

1794. the greatest feebleness ; Belgium was already abandoned, as he had desired ; and the Cabinet of London
had rewarded Austria for her treachery by financial
assistance. In the circumstances he could not do less
than give promises of effectual help in the defence of
Holland, though of course without the slightest intention to fulfil them.

Meanwhile the behaviour of the Dutch grew more
and more suspicious. Bois-le-Duc was disgracefully
Oct. 10. surrendered on the 10th of October by the Commandant ; and a regiment of French emigrants, which
formed part of the garrison, having been denied permission to cut its way through the besiegers, was
massacred in cold blood. On the same day, by a
curious coincidence, the British Government warned
the Dutch that, unless they exerted themselves, the
British army should be withdrawn ; at the same time
proposing to put the Duke of Brunswick in command
of the British and Dutch forces in order to keep them
Oct. 18. together. Then a week later, as if to bribe the Stadtholder to compliance, Dundas authorised the payment of one hundred thousand pounds to the Dutch,
which was simply so much money wasted ; for the
Prince of Orange would do nothing for the defence
of the country, and wished to employ the British
for the repression of his own rebellious subjects.
How, in the face of the Duke of York's letters, the
British Ministers in London hesitated to order the
immediate withdrawal of the army is incomprehensible, except on the supposition that they still trusted
to the proved ill-faith of the Emperor Francis.[1]

The French, meanwhile, continued to follow up
their advantages. Jourdan, on the east, after leaving

---

[1] Dundas to York, 10th, 12th, 16th, 18th October ; York to
Dundas, 16th, 18th, 23rd October 1794.

detachments to besiege Venloo and Maastricht, had 1794.
occupied Cologne on the 6th of October, and drawn Oct. 6.
up his army in face of Clerfaye's main body, which
was extended along the Rhine from Duisburg to Bonn
and beyond. Moreau, who had taken over the command owing to Pichegru's illness, also pushed forward
seven thousand men in front of Grave, posted thirty
thousand between Ravestein (a little to west of Grave)
and Bois-le-Duc, and ten thousand men opposite the
Bommeler Waert. On the 18th he began to lay a Oct. 18.
bridge of boats over the Meuse at Alfen, and, being
allowed by scandalous carelessness on the part of the
Allies to complete it, passed a considerable force
over the river. On the 19th he attacked the posts Oct. 19.
at Apeltern and Druten, to east and north-east of
Alfen, carried them after a very obstinate resistance
from the Thirty-seventh and Rohan's Emigrants,
and succeeded in capturing the greater number of
the Thirty-seventh,[1] who had mistaken a party of
French Hussars for the Emigrant cavalry in the
British service. At the same time intelligence came
that a strong French detachment had passed the
Meuse between Roermond and Venloo, and was head-
ing for Cleve, thus threatening to turn the Duke's
left. Accordingly, in his public despatch, the Duke
announced that he was about to draw the whole army
to the north of the Waal ; but privately he reported
that he could not do so, since the Dutch, in spite of
many promises, had made no effort to put Nimeguen
in a state of defence. On the 20th the French threw Oct. 20.
a permanent bridge across the Meuse a little to the

---

[1] Craig explained that this was owing chiefly to the inexperience
of a young Colonel. Thus the army-brokers had contrived to lift
children to the command even of regiments that had been eighteen
months on active service.

1794. north-west of Ravestein at Batenburg, and two days later began a new series of attacks upon the advanced posts, at the same time making demonstrations about Oct. 27. St. Andries on the Bommeler Waert. By the 27th the troops round Nimeguen had been driven into the outskirts of the town, and the Duke, who had transferred his headquarters to Arnheim, called all of them except fourteen battalions to the north bank of the Waal. The French main body then took up a position between Grave and Nimeguen, threatening to seize the two eastern keys of Holland.

Oct. 28.   At this critical moment Clerfaye paid a visit to the Duke at Arnheim, and promised that by the 3rd of November a corps of some seven thousand Austrians under General Werneck should arrive to assist in an offensive movement from Nimeguen. At the same time some effort was made to persuade Möllendorf to move to the Rhine about Bonn, and to support Clerfaye's left. But the British Government had recently, though none too soon, cut off the subsidy to the Prussians ; and Möllendorf's answer was that his orders were to send twenty thousand of his men to South Prussia and fifteen thousand men to Westphalia, so that evidently nothing was to be expected from that Nov. 1. quarter. On the 1st of November the French broke ground before Nimeguen, and on the same day Werneck announced that his corps could not arrive before the 7th. Meanwhile the French erected batteries a little above Nimeguen at Ooi, which, though silenced for a time by the guns of the Allies on the opposite bank, so seriously damaged the bridge of boats that General Walmoden, who was in command, thought it prudent to withdraw the greater part of the garrison to the Nov. 4. northern bank. On the 4th, however, he made a sortie with the troops that remained, including six

British battalions, supported by seventeen squadrons 1794.
of British and Hanoverian cavalry.[1] The British, advancing under a very heavy fire, swept the enemy out
of their trenches without drawing a trigger, and the
cavalry pursuing the fugitives inflicted on them heavy
loss. The casualties of the Allies in this affair were
over three hundred killed and wounded ; but, though
the sortie checked the progress of the French for the
time, yet by the 7th they had not only repaired the
batteries destroyed by the Allies, but had erected
another which brought a cross fire to bear on the
bridge of boats. Moreover, a letter arrived from
Werneck that his arrival at Nimeguen, which he had
fixed for the 7th, would be impossible until the 16th
—a message which the Duke rightly interpreted to
signify that he would not come at all.

On the night of the 7th, therefore, the bridge was Nov. 7.
repaired sufficiently to enable the garrison to evacuate
the place ; and the troops filed across the river. Two
Dutch battalions were the last to leave the place under
the Dutch General Haak, who, most improperly, was
the first man of his nation to set foot on the bridge.
As he did so, a shot struck one of the pontoons with
some effect, whereupon he immediately ran across
the bridge crying out that all was lost, and reported
with shameless mendacity that all his troops had
passed over except the rear-guard. Upon this the
pontoon-bridge was immediately fired, since a flying
bridge had already been prepared for the passage of
the rear-guard. As luck would have it, however, a
shot from the French batteries cut the hawser ; the

[1] The troops engaged were the 15th Light Dragoons, 8th, 27th,
28th, 55th, 63rd, 78th. The last-named regiment, together with
the 80th, had arrived at Flushing at the end of September, when
Dundas intended to withdraw some of the older regiments for
service in the West Indies.

1794. flying bridge began to swing round ; and, to save it from running foul of the kindled boats, the sailors dropped the anchor and so brought it up. When the burning pontoons had floated away, some British seamen, who were employed on the bridge, were for cutting it adrift, but the Dutchmen would not allow them to do so, preferring certain capture to the risk of a few cannon-shot. Thus eleven hundred of them were taken, either through their own cowardice or through that of Haak—a lamentable occurrence in an army which in the past had approved itself to be of incomparable steadfastness and valour.[1]

The Duke, therefore, now held the line of the Waal including the Bommeler Waert, and might well hope to hold it, if the Dutch did their duty, until the army went into winter quarters. He had already put most of his cavalry into cantonments across the Yssel, but the Dutch threw every possible obstacle in the way of providing for the comfort of the troops. The weather too grew wintry, and the men, miserably clothed and housed in open barns, began to fall down very fast from cold and typhus fever. None of them had greatcoats except some of the Guards, Four-teenth, Thirty-seventh, and Fifty-third, who had received those which had been provided by public subscription in 1793, and which were now worn out. Flannel waistcoats had been supplied to the rest by their officers, who had subscribed over a thousand pounds for the purpose ; and it appears that, without exaggeration, they had little other clothing. Sheer nakedness, in fact, had been the cause of much, though not of all, of the plundering that had disgraced the army ; and this evil had been aggravated by the

[1] York to Dundas, 7th and 11th November ; Craig to Nepean, 10th November 1794.

bitter hostility of the inhabitants towards the British. 1794.
Not content with resenting real outrages, which were
far too abundant, they never ceased flying to the
Duke with frivolous and groundless complaints ; and
so disobliging were the authorities that Lord St.
Helens, Ambassador at the Hague, tried for two
months in vain to find places where the British might
be allowed to establish additional hospitals. On
the 27th of November the infantry in British pay Nov. 27.
numbered twenty-one thousand and the sick nearly
eleven thousand ; and when a man was ordered to
hospital his comrades would exclaim, " Ah, poor
fellow, we shall see thee no more, for thou art under
orders for the shambles." On one occasion five
hundred invalids were embarked from Arnheim in
barges under charge of a single surgeon's mate, without
sufficient provisions, without even sufficient straw,
and brought to Rhenen, where they were left on
board for want of sufficient space to admit them to
the hospital. A Dutch gentleman counted at one time
the bodies of forty-two men who had thus perished
of neglect in the barges and had been thrown out
dead on to the bank. Meanwhile the rascals who
bore the name of surgeon's mates charged forty thousand pounds for wine for the sick, and, not content
with robbing the State by themselves drinking what
was supplied, actually plundered the helpless patients
committed to their care. Such was the economy of
Dundas's military administration—to obtain recruits
by the offer of lavish bounties, to break down their
health by giving them insufficient clothing, and to
contract with scoundrels so to maltreat them, medically,
that they should not recover.[1]

[1] *Narrative of an Officer of the Guards*, ii. 89-91 ; York to Dundas,
27th November 1794 ; Harcourt to York, 15th December 1794.

1794.   Fortunately for himself the Duke of York was
summoned home on the 27th of November to hold
personal communication [1] with Ministers ; and indeed
it seemed as if the campaign were ended.   Upon
his departure he placed the British troops under
Lieutenant-general Harcourt, and the foreign troops
in British pay under Lieutenant-general Walmoden,
apparently dividing the supreme command between
the two.   This arrangement was evidently due to the
Duke's unwillingness to subject the British to the
Hanoverian Walmoden, who was senior to Harcourt ;
but, even so, it seems to be absolutely indefensible.
The French, being exhausted by the campaign, went
into temporary cantonments, Moreau's division on
the west bank of the Rhine over against the line
from Wesel to Emmerick, Souham's in and about
Nimeguen, Bonnaud's between the Meuse and the
Waal, and the remainder about Bois-le-Duc and
Grave.   The Allies were distributed along the north
bank of the Waal from Tiel eastward to the Pannarden
Canal, which connects the Waal with the Leck (as
the Rhine from Arnheim downward is called), the
Dutch taking charge of the Bommeler Waert.   Eastward from the Pannarden Canal to Wesel the Allied
left was to be covered by thirty thousand Austrians
under General Alvintzy, which Clerfaye, on the instance
of Henry Dundas, agreed to furnish for a payment
of one hundred thousand pounds a month.

   The Allies' line of defence seems to have been
wrongly chosen, for, owing to the Pannarden Canal,
the mass of the waters of the Waal was returned into
the Leck, from which cause the Leck was less liable

   [1] Ditfurth, who never loses an opportunity of abusing the
English, of course puts a discreditable construction upon the
Duke's departure, not knowing that he was sent for by Ministers
(ii. 313).

to be frozen. Harcourt had endeavoured to establish a second bridge over the Rhine besides that of the Arnheim, but the Dutch, from malice or negligence, obstructed the forwarding of the materials, as indeed they obstructed everything that might help the British. Altogether the situation was not a happy one, for, though rain had fallen continuously from the beginning of November, there was no saying when a frost might set in and turn the rivers into stable ice. Moreover, Moreau, roused by orders from Paris, became active again. On the 11th of December the French crossed the Waal in boats at several different points to the attack of the Allied posts, and, though beaten back, left behind them an unpleasant sense of insecurity.[1]

On the 16th Pichegru returned and resumed the command, and on the 18th the weather changed from rain to a severe frost. In a very few days the Maas and Waal were full of floating ice, which began to pack together, threatening to cover the whole breadth of their streams ; while on the Leck the rapidity of the current swept away the bridge of boats at Arnheim. Harcourt, foreseeing that before long the ice on the Waal would become passable by the enemy, prepared to retreat northward. Just at this most critical moment, moreover, there arrived orders from Dundas that seven British battalions of his army were required for service elsewhere ; that of these seven the Fortieth, Forty-fourth, and Sixty-third must march to Helvoetsluys at once ; and that Alvintzy, who so far had thrown every possible difficulty in the way of co-operation with the Allies, must find troops to take their place. Further, it was now

Dec. 11.

Dec. 18.

[1] York to Dundas, 27th and 29th November ; Harcourt to York, 11th and 15th December 1794. Ditfurth, ii. 310.

1794. ascertained that the Dutch had gone far in negotiation with the French, and there were strong rumours that an armistice had been concluded between them. Meanwhile the cold increased; sentries were frozen at their posts; and the ice on the Waal, in front of the Allies, became strong enough to give passage to the French, while that on the Leck in their rear, though thick enough to prevent the passage of boats, was too thin to bear cavalry or artillery. Harcourt's anxiety was extreme; and he begged Dundas urgently for some further instructions as to the duty expected of him, since the order to weaken the force by sending home seven battalions was not in itself of any great assistance.

Dec. 27. Affairs were in this condition when, on the 27th, the French crossed the Meuse on the ice to the Bommeler Waert, surprised the Dutch posts there, and pushed on by Bommel over the frozen Waal to Tuil. The Dutch at this place fled instantly without firing a shot, some of the fugitives running on even to Utrecht. At Meteren, a few miles north of Tuil, the French were checked by the Hessians; but, with their right flank exposed by the flight of the Dutch, it was doubtful whether these could maintain their position. Their commander, however, General Dalwig, decided to stand fast, and ascertained by reconnaissance next

Dec. 28. day that the French did not exceed two thousand men; whereupon Walmoden ordered ten battalions and six squadrons of British and Emigrants under David Dundas to Geldermalsen, a short distance north of Meteren, in the hope of annihilating this foolhardy French detachment. Accordingly, at one o'clock on

Dec. 30. the morning of the 30th, the force moved out from Meteren in three columns, two of them to move direct upon Tuil from the north and north-east, while the

third, under Lord Cathcart, fetched a compass to close 1794.
in upon the enemy from the west. Cathcart's column
unfortunately found the roads impassable and never
came into action ; but Dundas nevertheless attacked
without him, and drove the French, after a sharp fight,
from their entrenchments and across the Waal, with the
loss of four guns and many killed and wounded, while
his own casualties did not exceed fifty. This checked
the ardour of the enemy for the moment, and during
a few days there was peace upon the Waal.[1]

Walmoden now reinforced his right about Tuil, for
the news had reached him that the fortresses of Gertruydenburg and Heusden, on the extreme right of the 1795.
Allied line, were in serious danger ; and on the 3rd of Jan. 3.
January 1795 he shifted his quarters to Amerongen,
due north of Tiel, and on the north bank of the Leck.
Grave at this same time capitulated, and released a
large number of French troops for the field. Moreau's
division therefore took up cantonments over against
Alvintzy's corps from Xanten down the Rhine to the
Pannarden Canal. Souham's division, now transferred
to Macdonald, occupied the space between the Meuse
and Waal as far as the point opposite to Tiel ; two
more divisions were in the Bommeler Waert, and yet
two more about Gertruydenburg and Breda. On the
3rd of January the weather again became intensely
cold, and at noon on the 4th two French detachments Jan. 4.
from the Bommeler Waert marched over the ice, drove
in the posts before Tuil and at Hesselt, a little to the
east of it, after hard fighting, and thus gained a passage
by which they could move westward on the north

[1] Dundas to Harcourt, 13th and 24th December ; Harcourt to
Dundas, 23rd December ; to York, 25th and 29th December ;
Walmoden to York, 22nd, 25th, 29th December 1794, 1st January
1795. The regiments engaged in the action were the 19th, 33rd,
42nd, 78th, 80th.

1795. bank of the Waal. On the following day the French
Jan. 5. attacked Tuil itself, whereupon the Dutch gunners at
once fled from their batteries on the river ; but, advancing from thence against Geldermalsen, the enemy was
repulsed with some loss by the Thirty-third, Forty-
second, and Seventy-eighth, under the direction of
General David Dundas. It was, however, plain that
these posts could not be held against a strong attack
so long as frost practically neutralised their natural
defences ; and Walmoden recalled Dundas and all
the troops in that quarter to the north side of the Leck,
in order to take up a new line of cantonments extending
from Arnheim on the east by Wageningen, Reenen,
Amerongen, and Wyk-by-Duurstede to Honswyk.

Jan. 6.   A sudden thaw on the 6th offered hopes of re-
establishing the old position on the Waal, and orders
were issued on the 7th for a reconnaissance in force
of the whole line of the French posts on the following
Jan. 8. day ; but on the morning of the 8th the frost abruptly
set in again, though not before the troops were already
in motion beyond power of recall. On the right,
Dundas succeeded in driving the enemy from their
posts on the Linge to the Waal, and in recovering Buren
and Tiel. The brunt of the work fell upon the Fourteenth, Twenty-seventh, and Twenty-eighth under
Lord Cathcart ; and these drove the enemy in succession from the villages of Buurmalsen and Geldermalsen
and captured a gun, not, however, without a loss of one
hundred and thirty men to themselves. On the left
the orders seem to have miscarried, probably through
the confusion due to divided command. Before the
operation could be carried any further, Pichegru, finding that the ice on the Waal was stronger than ever,
Jan. 10. on the 10th fell upon the Allied line in great force at
three different points between the Pannarden Canal

and Tiel. The attack was repulsed upon the right, 1795. but the Austrians were forced back on the left flank, and Walmoden ordered the whole force to withdraw once more behind the Leck. This was effected with little loss ; Colonel Coote's brigade of the Fortieth, Fiftieth, and Seventy-ninth being the only British forces severely engaged. Walmoden had fully intended to continue the retreat eastward across the Yssel ; but Lord St. Helens, at the Hague, unfortunately protested against this, and another thaw enabled Walmoden to acquiesce. On the night of the 12th frost again set in more severely than ever, and on the 14th the French attacked along the whole line from Arnheim to Reenen. They were beaten back with heavy loss ; but Walmoden, feeling that he was unable to hold his ground, on the following morning gave the Jan. 15. order for a further retreat.

The days that followed are amongst the most tragical in the history of the Army. During November and December the discipline of the troops in Holland had greatly improved, but with the coming of the frost and the hardships that attended the constant alarms and marches on the Waal, it had once more broken down completely. Certain regiments of French emigrants, which had joined the army late in the year, were the worst offenders ; but it seems certain that some of the British were not far behind them. The country to the north of Arnheim is at the best of times an inhospitable waste, and there were few dwellings and few trees to give shelter or fuel after a dreary march through dense and chilling mist over snow twice thawed and refrozen. Marauders from the regiments of every nationality swarmed round the columns ; the drivers of the waggons freed themselves from all control, and the line of march was disorderly beyond description. When the day

1795. was ended, the troops of different nations fought for such scanty comforts as were to be found; and once there was a pitched battle between the Guards and the Hessians, who had been on bad terms with each other from the beginning of the campaign. Day after day the cold steadily increased; and those of the army that woke on the morning of the 17th of January saw about them such a sight as they never forgot. Far as the eye could reach over the whitened plain were scattered gun-limbers, waggons full of baggage, of stores, or of sick men, sutlers' carts and private carriages. Beside them lay the horses, dead; around them scores and hundreds of soldiers, dead; here a straggler who had staggered on to the bivouac and dropped to sleep in the arms of the frost; there a group of British and Germans round an empty rum-cask; here forty English Guardsmen huddled together about a plundered waggon; there a pack-horse with a woman lying alongside it, and a baby, swathed in rags, peeping out of the pack, with its mother's milk turned to ice upon its lips,—one and all stark, frozen, dead. Had the retreat lasted but three or four days longer, not a man would have escaped; and the catastrophe would have found a place in history side by side with the destruction of the host of Sennacherib and with the still more terrible disaster of the retreat from Moscow.[1]

Jan. 19. By the 19th the surviving fragments of the battalions reached their destination on the Yssel, where they were cantoned on the west side of the river from Zutphen to the sea. But there was no hope of long repose for them there. Harcourt perceived clearly that the re-embarkation of his force was now the only resource left

[1] Jones, *Campaign of 1794*, pp. 171-175; Ditfurth, ii. 362 *sq.*; *Narrative of an Officer of the Guards*, ii. 100-104.

to him, and that the place of embarkation must be on 1795.
the Weser, since the lack of supplies and the incapacity
of his commissariat - officers would inevitably forbid
him to remain long on the Ems. Within a week, want
of victuals and the hostility of the inhabitants compelled him to continue his retreat from the Yssel ; and
on the 27th the march eastward was resumed, the main Jan. 27-29.
body of the British retiring towards Osnabrück, the
Germans upon Münster. One detachment of British,[1]
however, was sent northward under Lord Cathcart's
command to fetch a compass through West Friesland
and along the borders of Groningen, in order to ascertain whether the people of these provinces were as ill-
affected as their fellows towards the House of Orange.
By whose orders this isolated force was despatched
upon such an errand is uncertain ; it is only known
that the column was followed up and incessantly
harassed by the enemy, and that it was not very
successful in discovering friendly sentiments among
the Dutch. Upon reaching the Ems, the army halted,
and on the 5th February took up cantonments on the
western bank of the river, Cathcart on the extreme
north guarding the passes of the Bourtanger Moor
from the Dollart southward, while Abercromby fixed
his headquarters further to south and west of the river
at Bentheim, and the Hanoverians retired to Münster.

The state of the troops by this time was worse than
ever, for thousands of sick had perforce been left
behind on the Yssel. " Your army is destroyed,"
wrote Walmoden to the Duke of York ; " the officers,
their carriages, and a large train are safe, but the men
are destroyed. The army has now no more than six
thousand fighting men, but it has all the drawbacks of
thirty-three battalions, and consumes a vast quantity

[1] 15th Light Dragoons ; 27th, 28th, 80th, and 84th Foot.

1795. of forage." A more terrible reproach was never yet
levelled against any force ; nevertheless it was rather
the politicians than the military commanders who had
made such a reproach possible, by flinging commissions
broadcast to any man or even child who could afford
to satisfy the crimps. Upon entering German territory
the men met with kindlier treatment from the inhabitants ; but the infamous conduct of the French
Emigrant Corps threatened to turn the Germans also
into enemies. It now became abundantly clear that
most of these regiments were simply frauds, imposed
upon the English Ministers by a band of unscrupulous
adventurers. But the English army, of course, had to
bear the burden of their sins ; and the Hanoverians
and Hessians, naturally espousing the cause of their
countrymen, turned upon the British with a bitterness
which destroyed all cohesion between the nations of the
Allies.[1]

Meanwhile the French, after leaving their opponents
to retreat unmolested from the Leck, resumed their
advance, and at the end of January occupied Kampen
and Zwolle on the Yssel. They made, however, no
attempt to hinder the further retirement of the Allies ;
and their movements for the next fortnight were of
the most leisurely description. Then arrived rumours
of a French understanding with Prussia, of the neutral-
isation of North Germany, and of a line of demarcation
to be drawn according to the actual territory occupied
by the opposing armies. The French at once woke
to the importance of gaining immediate possession of
Groningen and East Friesland, and General Macdonald's
corps was detached to invade Groningen, while those
of Moreau and Vandamme remained in observation

[1] Walmoden to York, 3rd February ; Harcourt to York (three
letters), 11th February 1795.

on the Yssel. On the 19th of February Macdonald 1795. occupied the town of Groningen, and thence turning eastward he, on the 27th, attacked Cathcart's fortified Feb. 27. posts at Winschoten. He was repulsed ; but two days later the attack was renewed with success by General Reynier, and Cathcart was forced to retreat, which he March 1. did with great dexterity, crossing the Ems upon the 3rd. The entire British force then fell back to the March 3. east bank of the Ems to hold the line from Emden to Rheine, headquarters being fixed at Osnabrück.

Five days later the British Cabinet at last decided to withdraw its troops from the Continent, and on the 11th Harcourt, to his infinite relief, received intimation March 11. that transports for twenty-three thousand men were on their way to him. The Hanoverians were in consternation over the danger to which Hanover was exposed by this measure, but there was no help for it. A few days later Prussian troops arrived to hold the line of March 16. the Ems, and on the 22nd the British began their march to Bremen for embarkation. The Prussians did their utmost by obstruction, discourtesy, and insolence to disoblige them on their passage through the country ; but this was natural, for they had always professed contempt for the British as a nation of traders, and a tradesman is never so despicable to a dishonest customer as when he refuses to grant him further credit. Finally, on the 14th of April, the in- April 14. fantry and part of the artillery took ship for England, leaving the remainder of the artillery and the whole of the cavalry behind them under Lord Cathcart and David Dundas. The number embarked was nearly fifteen thousand, some proportion of the sick having been recovered ; so that the losses after the retreat from the Leck must have amounted to about six thousand men, of which not a tithe were killed or

1795. wounded in action. Thus disgracefully ended the first
expedition of Pitt and Dundas to the Low Countries.

AUTHORITIES.—The British despatches relating to the
expeditions to Flanders will be found in *W.O. Orig. Corresp.*
46-48, and in Entry Book No. 11. The number of private
letters included in this collection makes it of unusual value.
For the campaigns at large the best accounts known to me are
in Ditfurth's *Die Hessen in den Feldzügen, 1793, 1794, und 1795*
(Kassel, 1839), and in Witzleben's *Prinz Friedrich Josias von
Coburg-Saalfeld* (Berlin, 1859), which is not a little built upon
Ditfurth, but contains much that is valuable of its own and a
superb atlas of maps. On the French side the short memoir
of David and the life of Pichegru are of little worth compared
with the narrative of Jomini. Marshal Macdonald's *Mémoires*
are disappointing at this period. Of English printed accounts
the most important is Jones's *Historical Journal of the British
Campaign in 1794*. The *Journal* of Corporal James Brown
of the Coldstream Guards supplies a few interesting details.
Sir H. Calvert's *Journal and Correspondence* is often of value ;
and there is a great deal of most useful information in the foot-
notes to the miserable doggerel called the *Narrative of an
Officer of the Guards*. Unfortunately the author, like Brown
and Calvert, was a Coldstreamer, for which reason all three
confine themselves chiefly to the doings of the brigade of
Guards. The regimental histories of the 14th Foot and 15th
Hussars have occasionally interesting material, but, taken
altogether, the regimental records are disappointing.

THE END

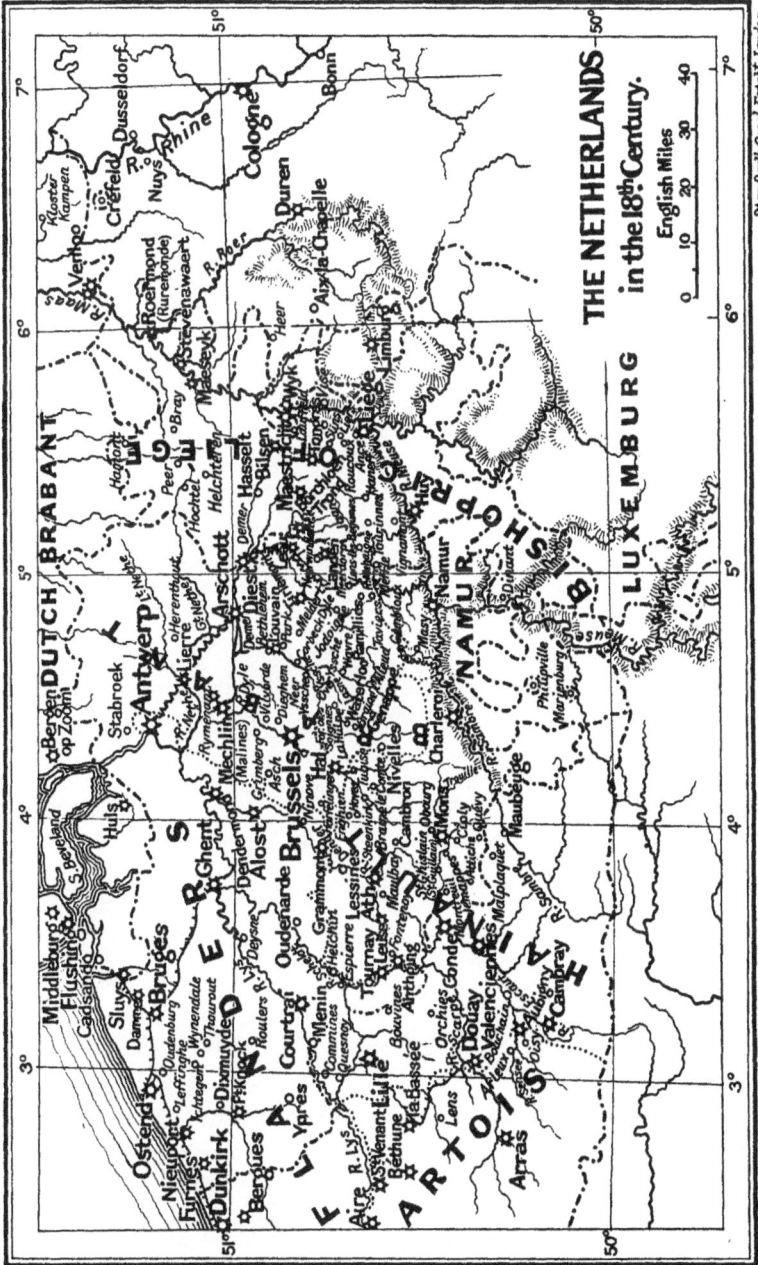

THE NETHERLANDS
in the 18th Century.

English Miles

0   10   20   30   40

Stanford's Geog¹ Estab.ᵗ London.

DUTCH BRABANT

ANTWERP

BISHOPRIC

LUXEMBURG

NAMUR

HAINAULT

ARTOIS

FLANDERS

Brussels

Ghent

Bruges

Ostend

Dunkirk

Middelburg

Flushing

Cologne

Düsseldorf

Crefeld

Bonn

Düren

Aix la Chapelle

Roermond (Ruremonde)

Stevensvaert

Maestricht

Liège

Hasselt

Diest

Louvain

Mechlin (Malines)

Lierre

Arschott

Alost

Oudenarde

Courtray

Ypres

Lille

Bergen op Zoom

Stabroek

Hulst

Sluys

Cadsand

Nieuport

Furnes

Bergues

Béthune

Aire

Arras

Lens

Douay

Valenciennes

Cambray

Condé

Maubeuge

Charleroi

Nivelles

Philippeville

Marienburg

Namur

www.ingramcontent.com/pod-product-compliance
Lightning Source LLC
Chambersburg PA
CBHW031938080426
42735CB00007B/180